PIT BOSS
WOOD PELLET SMOKER
& GRILL COOKBOOK

Become an Expert Barbecue Pitmaster with Your Grill.
Enjoy Family Meals and be the Perfect Dinner Host with
500+ Recipes for the Best-of Smoking & BBQ

BOB FRANKLIN

2 BOOK IN 1:

1) WOOD PELLET SMOKER AND GRILL COOKBOOK.

2) TRAEGER GRILL & SMOKER COOKBOOK

Summary

Chapter 1.   Introduction

Smokers work by cooking the meat over a wood fire, which gives the meat a very special taste. Barbequing has become very popular in the recent past, and a lot of people have purchased their own smoker grills for themselves. This is why choosing the best one is very important. Wood Pellet Smoker and Grill are the best because they are constructed with added features for high performance.

Wood pellet smoker grills are heating appliances that are made to cook meat or fish. Normally, the food is cooked slowly over low heat. Most of the grills have a capacity of two hundred and sixty-eight degrees Fahrenheit. This heat, when combined with the meat, allows the food to smoke and cook. However, some wood pellet smoker grills can have as high as four hundred degrees Fahrenheit. When cooking with one of these grills, it is possible to sear steaks or cook brisket and ribs.

When choosing the best smoker grill, the material should be considered. Normally, most of the grills are made of cast iron. This is because it is non-porous, strong, and does not rust. However, the material of choice for cast iron is the alloy, which is known as Enameled Steel, manufactured by the Thermold Corporation. This material will not rust.

Wood pellet smoker grills have several advantages:

1. No dirt disposal

When wood pellet smoker grills are in use, many parts are exposed to lots of dirt. This is why when the smoker is cleaned, a new layer of dirt may be formed. With smoke plated grills, this problem is solved. This is because the grills are placed in the smokers, and the smoke is circulated around the food and through the grills. This does not allow the dirt to build up, and the grills are kept clean. It also saves a lot of time since you will not have to clean them as often. For example, you will not have to clean the grills when smoking different foods like fish or chicken.

2. The ability to smoke and clean

After a little learning, most smokers and grills can be cleaned in the same process. The smoker has an open cover and the smoker bowl. When using the smoker, food is placed in the smoke, and everything is put together tightly. In this case, the smoker grills are well-insulated. This is mentioned in the manual of the smoker, and the smoker grills are built with tight covering. When grease is needed to cook, you will clean the grease tray and clean the smoker.

3. Large capacity

Most smokers have a large capacity. The size of the smoker does not dictate the size of the piece. You can use smoker grills for barbecuing many different foods. The grills have a large burning surface to ensure that your meat is cooked properly and effectively.

4. Long Lasting

The materials the grills are made of are very durable. Most smokers are made of cast iron. The material is non-porous, so it does not rust and does not stain.

5. Easy to use

In order to use a smoker, there is a small learning curve. Many parts of the smoker are exposed, even when it is used inside the house. The smoker is prohibited in the location where it has been used in the past. Then, when using the smoker, burning wood is not necessary. You do not need to cut wood, fuel, and other heating materials. This is why wood pellet smoker and grill is very easy to use. It is very convenient, especially for people who have limited space.

6. Reliable

Another advantage of using a smoker grill is its reliability. Since there are many parts exposed in the smoker, the temperature of the food is easily monitored. The temperature of the food is also known from the length of time you decide to cook it. It is, therefore, an effective way for people who are unable to tend to the food while cooking.

Wood pellet smoker grills are useful because they are convenient. This is because wood pellets provide the same smoking action as a real pit but with a lot less work. Besides that, they do not take up too much space. You can even store it inside a closet when it is not in use. You will only need to keep it in an open space in order to use the smoker grill.

Chapter 2. The Advantages Of Wood Pellet Smoker And Grill

Although pellets have existed for over 20 years, they were used mainly for heating and cooking with them is a relatively new phenomenon. This is why many people are not sure how easy, efficient or safe cooking with pellets is. In fact, it is far less complicated than most people think and if you use 100% natural wood pellets without fillers or additives, food prepared this way is not only tasty but healthy too.

However, to gain the most from food cooked on a wood pellet smoker grill, you have to follow certain rules. Barbecuing the healthy way is a slow cooking method where food is prepared over a fire as low as 200 degrees F. Long cooking over low heat breaks down the plant's lectin, resulting in tender food that melts in your mouth.

Smoking is also a type of slow cooking where food is cooked with indirect heat at a temperature below 200 degrees F which gives the food a unique flavor. If prepared properly, grilled food retains more nutrients than when cooked in water or fried. Veggies also retain more vitamins and minerals and you usually end up eating less fat. Therefore, learning how to grill and investing in a good wood pellet smoker grill is a wise choice.

8   reasons why you should start using wood pellet smoker grill:

1.   It's convenient

These grills are user friendly and although the electronic parts intimidate many people, it's very easy to learn how to use them. Grilling soon becomes a pleasure even if you've never done it before.

2.   It's economical

Pellet smoker grills are fuel-efficient. They usually burn about one pound of pellets per hour and in that time you can cook a lot of food.

3.   You will avoid flare-ups

The firepot is shielded from direct contact with the food by a heat deflector and grease drip tray. Besides, a fan circulates the air throughout the cooking process. The Set & Forget controls guarantee no flare-ups so you don't have to worry about your eyebrows or long hair.

4.   You will save time

In the busy world we live in, everything that helps you save time is greatly appreciated. When you use a pellet grill, all you have to do is press the power button, select the desired cooking temperature, and add the food.

Within as little as ten minutes, the fire will be ready and you can start roasting or baking. This means you can have grilled food even when you get back from work in the evening because cooking it won't take any longer than it would take to prepare a meal on a stove. Besides, food can be smoked in as little as half an hour, rather than a couple of days as used to be the case in the past. All you would have to do is prepare the food for smoking and get the right flavor of pellets.

5. Your meals will taste better

Not everyone enjoys the flavor of smoke but most people, who like barbecues, do. Wood smoke gives a very special flavor to foods, as well as to nuts, and vegetables. This is why all professional BBQ chefs use wood for grilling for smoking because it gives the food an unmistakable BBQ flavor. The flavor can even be varied with different kinds of wood or wood pellets. Once you become more experienced, you can mix and match to give your food a unique flavor it will be recognized by.

6. You can BBQ in any weather

You can use a wood pellet smoker and grill in any kind of weather as it does not affect the temperature – the temperature will remain within a ten-degree range of your set temperature.

7. The versatility

The biggest advantage of a wood pellet grill over a gas grill is that the precise control of cooking temperature between 180-500 degrees F makes it possible to use this grill to prepare many different types of meals. You can sear, smoke, roast or bake. You can even bake a cake in this grill.

8. Value for money

The wood pellet grills come in a range of $250 to over $1000. The best quality ones have stainless steel components and come with a 4-year guarantee. There are many options with grills and smokers. You can choose gas, charcoal, wood, wood pellet, or an electric one. However, the most expensive grills come with certain benefits not found in other cheaper models which usually last only one season. The wood pellet grill can last for decades if looked after properly.

Top Wood Pellet Smoker Brands

When choosing a wood pellet smoker, or anything else for that matter, you have to be clear about what you need it for, how often you are likely to use it, and what your budget is. The best wood pellet smokers currently available on the market include:

Traeger Grills TFB88PZBO Pro Series 34 Pellet Grill and Smoker

Amongst the best pellet smokers in the market. This Traeger model allows for grilling, baking, barbecue, smoking, and roasting. It is quite big and it is possible to cook six whole chickens at the same time. The digital controller guarantees consistent cooking. Its size is ideal for a small patio. Price: Unavailable.

REC TEC Grills RT-590 Bundle

This pellet grill weighs about 100 pounds and can hold about 30 pounds of pellets. However, despite its size, it is easy to pack in the car and take to a different location. It has great temperature control and can reach up to 500 plus degrees F. It is a great product and can be used for backyard cooking, camping, tailgating, etc. Price: Unavailable.

Green Mountain Grills Pellet Grill

This is possibly the best small pellet smoker because you can use it at home or take it with you when you are camping. The pellet grill is Wi-Fi-enabled. There is a mobile application that you can use with Android. The temperature can easily be adjusted. Price: Unavailable.

Pit Boss 700FB Pellet Grill

This is one of the best BBQ pellet smokers. It has a full digital control that enables you to choose a precise temperature. You can sear steaks and fish with the sliding plate. It is simple to assemble and loading the pellets into the grill is easy. Price: $428

Z Grills 8-in-one BBQ Smoker

This grill allows you to grill, bake, braise, smoke, roast, and barbecue. This smoker is a 7-in-1. You can use a variety of cooking methods so that your foods come out exactly as you want them. It also has a large hopper capacity and cooking space. Price: $340

Traeger Grills TFB57PZBO Pro Series 22 Pellet Grill and Smoker

This grill can be used to BBQ, roast, and smoke and comes with great temperature stability. There is plenty of room on the grill to cook for five people. It boasts porcelain-covered grates and auto-start ignition. It weighs 100 pounds but is relatively easy to move around. Price: Unavailable.

Camp Chef SmokePro DLX Pellet Grill

This is one of the best pellet smokers on the market today. Lots of cooking space and lots of different features. Temperature is regulated with the push of a button. You can use it to smoke, bake, grill or sear. There is a very large cooking area and temperatures range from 160-500 degrees F. Price: $549

Z Grills ZPG-7002 Wood Pellet Grill and Smoker

Easy for you to use to roast, bake, grill, or braise. It has an impressive large rack area which makes it ideal for everyday family meals or when you invite friends over for a BBQ. Price: $421

Traeger Grills TFB38TOD Renegade Pro Pellet Grill

Even newbies can cook like a pro with this grill. You simply set it, add some ingredients, and let it do the cooking. It can be used for grilling, smoking, roasting, and baking. Very easy to use. Price: $699

Camp Chef Smoker Vault 24

This is the best vertical pellet smoker that has a grease management system to ensure even cooking. It's easy to use and large enough to cook multiple foods at a time but small enough to use in a small outdoor space. Price: $250

Chapter 3.   Different Smoker Types

ELECTRIC SMOKERS

The electric smoker is the best ever for its ease of use. You start it, put the food in it, and finally leave the rest of the work to the smoker. There is no food that an electric smoker cannot grill: fish, poultry, meat, cheese, bread. It requires little attention, unlike other appliances that require filling the water tank, lighting wood or coal, and frequent fuel checks. The electric smoker requires only 2-4 ounces of wood chips, and in this way prepares perfect smoked foods. Furthermore, the machine maintains the temperature perfectly. On an aesthetic level, the elegant appearance and small size make it appropriate even in an apartment or condominium. With simple functions and trouble-free cooking, the electric smoker is an ideal choice even for novice cooks.

GAS SMOKERS

Gas or propane smokers are very similar to a gas grill that uses propane as a fuel. Therefore the cooking heat remains constant. Gas smokers are also easy to use, you set the temperature and you can let it go. However, it is important to check frequently that the fuel is not running out. On the other hand, one of the best aspects is that a gas smoker can be used when there is no electricity or when you need an oven. A gas smoker can raise the temperature up to 450 degrees, becoming even more useful for being used as an oven. Another great feature of the gas smoker is its portability which makes it usable anywhere. Just pack it up and carry it on your travels.

CHARCOAL SMOKERS

Nothing tastes better than the flavor that coal gives your food. Unfortunately, often, between setting the smoke, checking the fuel level, maintaining the temperature and checking the cooking, the whole operation can be very problematic, not to mention the risk of burning the food. These risks disappear with practice and experience. However, this type of smoker guarantees high levels of flavor.

PELLET SMOKERS

Pellet smokers are increasing due to their ability to maintain a constant temperature. An automated insertion system allows the cook to monitor the fuel level. The addition of the thermostat completes the ability to control temperature and grilling better. In addition, smoked food uses the heat of hard wood, giving it a delicious, rich and intense flavor. The only drawback of the pallet smoker is their high cost.

The Types of Wood for Smoking

Wood is a fundamental element for cooking an exquisite smoked dish. Depending on the type of wood chips, the foods will in fact receive different aromas. That's why you should know which wood is best suited to the type of food you choose to cook in the smoker. The various types of wood and the characteristics that make them suitable for various types of food are illustrated below.

1- Alder: A lighter smoker wood with natural sweetness.

Best to smoke: Any fish especially salmon, poultry and game birds.

2- Maple: This smoker wood has a mild and sweet flavor. In addition, its sweet smoke gives the food a dark appearance. For better flavor, use it as a combination with alder, apple or oak smoker woods.

Best to smoke: Vegetables, cheese, and poultry.

3- Apple: A mild fruity flavor smoker wood with natural sweetness. When mixed with oak smoker wood, it gives a great flavor to food. Let food smoke for several hours as the smoke takes a while to permeate the food with the flavors.

Best to smoke: Poultry, beef, pork, lamb, and seafood.

4- Cherry: This smoker wood is an all-purpose fruity flavor wood for any type of meat. Its smoke gives the food a rich, mahogany color. Try smoking by mixing it with alder, oak, pecan and hickory smoker wood.

Best to smoke: Chicken, turkey, ham, pork, and beef.

5- Oak: Oakwood gives a medium flavor to food which is stronger compared to apple wood and cherry wood and lighter compared to hickory. This versatile smoker wood works well blended with hickory, apple, and cherry woods.

Best to smoke: Sausages, brisket, and lamb.

6- Peach and Pear: Both smoker woods are similar to each other. They give food a subtle light and fruity flavor with the addition of natural sweetness.

Best to smoke: Poultry, pork and game birds.

7- Hickory: Hickory wood infuses a strong sweet and bacon flavor into the food, especially meat cuts. Don't over smoke with this wood as it can turn the taste of food bitter.

Best to smoke: Red meat, poultry, pork shoulder, ribs.

8- Pecan: This sweet smoker wood lends the food a rich and nutty flavor. Use it with Mesquite wood to balance its sweetness.

Best to smoke: Poultry, pork.

9- Walnut: This strong flavored smoker wood is often used as a mixing wood due to its slightly bitter flavor. Use walnut wood with lighter smoke woods like pecan wood or apple wood.

Best to smoke: Red meat and game birds.

10- Grape: Grape wood chips give a sweet berry flavor to food. It's best to use these wood chips with apple wood chips.

Best to smoke: Poultry

11- Mulberry: Mulberry wood chips is similar to apple wood chips. It adds natural sweetness and gives berry finish to the food.

Best to smoke: Ham and Chicken.

12- Mesquite: Mesquite wood chips flavor is earthy and slightly harsh and bitter. It burns fast and strongly hot. Therefore, don't use it for longer grilling.

Best to smoke: Red meat, dark meat.

The Difference between Barbecuing a Meat and Smoking It

There are mainly two extremely popular methods of cooking meat: grilling and smoking. These are different systems, which require different equipment, temperatures and cooking times. Here is a small diagram that compares these two methods.

BARBECUING MEAT:

Using the barbecue requires slow, indirect, low heat cooking between 200 and 250 degrees F; it is a cooking suitable for meats such as beef breast, whole pork, turkey or pork shoulder. They are tough-muscled animals that require slow cooking over low heat to enjoy moist, tender meat. The result will be incredible. You understand that the cooking is perfectly successful when the meat comes off the bone. When using the barbecue, fuel must be checked and refilled often, and this must be done quickly as lifting the lid exposes the meat to the air. This way the meat can dry or dry out.

Cooking on the barbecue requires that the grill must be heated in advance until it is hot to the right point. Then we light coals or briquettes in the quantity necessary to ensure that the fire goes out in time to allow perfect cooking. In the meantime it is necessary to season the meat; when the grill has reached temperature it is time to place the seasoned meat on it. It is essential that the grill reaches the perfect temperature.

Equipment: Fire pit, grill or a charcoal burner with lid.

Fueling: Lump wood charcoal, charcoal briquettes or wood chips combination like apple. Cherry and oak wood chips.

Best to smoke: A big cut of meats like Briskets, whole chicken, sausages, jerky, pork, and ribs.

Temperature: 190 to 300 degrees F

Timing: 2 hours to a day long.

SMOKING MEAT:

Smoking is a very ancient cooking technique, dating back to the inhabitants of caves. Excellent method of food preservation, over time its popularity has never waned. Smoking is the best way to bring out the rich and deep flavor of the meat, which tastes heavenly when smoked to the point where it can come loose from the bone.

During smoking the food is cooked slowly, at a temperature below 200 degrees F, so it takes a long time and a lot of patience. However, this procedure gives the meat a fabulous aromatic flavor, making it soft and silky. There are three ways to smoke food: cold smoke, hot smoke and the addition of liquid smoke. Liquid smoke is currently becoming the most common and widespread of these three types. The main advantage of this system is that the aroma of the smoke can be controlled in this way; in addition, the effect of liquid smoke on meat is practically immediate.

There is also another method, called water smoking. In this case, the best machine is the water smoker, a tool specifically designed to introduce water into the smoking process. Water helps to control the temperature of the smoker and this is a perfect system if you are cooking large meat for many hours.

Equipment: A closed container or high-tech smoker.

Fueling: The container will need an external source for a smoke. Wood chips are burn to add smoky flavor to the meat. However, the frequent check should be made to monitor and adjust temperature for smoking.

Best to smoke: A big cut of meats like Briskets, whole chicken, pork, and ribs.

Temperature: 68 to 176 degrees F

Timing: 1 hour to 2 weeks

The Difference between Cold and Hot Smoking

Instead now let's see the difference between the cold and hot smoking system: in cold smoking, the meat is cooked between 68 and 86 degrees F, to end up being not smoked but moist. This is a good way to smoke chicken breast, steak, beef, pork chops, salmon and cheese. Cold smoking rather than cooking gives it extra aroma and flavor. In fact, in this case, the meat must still be seasoned or cooked before smoking.

On the other hand, hot smoking cooks the meat completely, and while doing so it enhances its flavor to the maximum. The meat should cook until it reaches an internal temperature between 126 and 176 degrees F, and it shouldn't go up to 185 degrees F in any case, because if this happens the meat will harden, shrink and warp. Large cuts of meat such as brisket, ham, ribs and pulled pork achieve extraordinary taste when hot smoked.

The Most Important Elements of Smoking

We can describe six important elements in order to obtain a perfect smoking.

1- Wood chips: they are used as fuel, alone or together with charcoal. They add exceptional flavor to the meat. However, it is good to use them only if they are suitable for the meat being prepared.

2- Smoker: you can choose between four types. Options include: electric smoker, charcoal smoker, gas smoker and pellet smoker. Each type has pros and cons.

3- Smoking time: this is an essential element for an optimal result. In this regard it is necessary that the internal temperature reaches certain values, indicated above. It may take anywhere from two hours to more than two weeks.

4- Meat: in all these preparations the absolute protagonist is meat, which at the end of the smoking process must be softer, juicier and tastier than ever. The use of wood chips completes the work.

5- Rubbing: the meat should be rubbed with aromas, salt and spices, to give it greater sweetness, taste and warmth. The preparation of this mix must achieve an adequate balance of flavors.

6- Mop: Mop is the liquid that can be used for smoking meat. Gives flavor to helps maintain tenderness and moisture throughout the smoking process.

Chapter 4. Temperature Control

Now that we have a better grasp on achieving the best smoky results, and gauging how long we should be cooking for the best results, it's time to think about how we can control the temperature of our wood pellet grill.

Tricks for Better Temperature Control

In this section, we will look at the potential aspects that can lead to temperature swings in your wood pellet smoker and what steps you can take to control the temperate better and prevent significant fluctuations.

Think About the Weather

One of the most influential factors when it comes to temperature fluctuation on a wood pellet grill is something that is entirely out of our control: the weather. It is also a factor that we often don't consider as influential when it really is!

A strong wind, torrential rain, cold weather, hot weather, direct or indirect sunlight, or high humidity can all impact the temperature of your wood pellet smoker and create temperature fluctuations that are unusual.

Use an Insulated Grill Blanket

One way to take the weather factor out of the equation is to get you weather-protecting insulated grill blankets. These blankets offer a warm blocker and stop your smoker from being impacted by the elements, especially heavy rain or snow. The types of blankets are perfect for extremely cold weather and also make sure that your smoker is as efficient as possible, and you aren't wasting wood pellets.

Understand the Thermometer

While it is of great benefit that wood pellet smokers come with a thermostat to keep an eye on a temperature, they can also be misleading. While not directly causing any changes in temperature, a fluctuating thermometer can confuse grillers and lead to them making changes to the temperature when they don't need to.

The thermometers are there for a quick reference point and are not an exact science, especially on the less-expensive models. You should use them as a guide or a marker and not as a definite.

Use a Meat Probe

As we have touched on already, the temperature control panel on most wood pellet smokers is only good to offer a guestimate on the true temperature of the grill. A better way to know the cooking time required would be to check your meat with a meat probe. This way, you will be able to judge how quickly the meat is getting hotter and whether that ties into what you want the temperature you want it to be at.

Just make sure that the probe is clean before each check, as an unclean probe could lead to readings that are inaccurate.

Clean Your Smoker

Keeping your smoker clean is also another vital aspect of ensuring you are in control of the temperature.

If your grill is dirty, then it can lead to grease fires and flameouts, as well as other hazards that will impact the temperature of your smoker. Make sure you clean out your grill after every use, including removing all of the ash from your burn pot, removing any unused pellets, and cleaning the grill itself.

Use High-Quality Pellets

Using wood pellets that are of high quality will also help you stay in control of your temperature. Cheap pellets tend to split much easier and leave behind dust, which in turn burns quicker than normal. This then leads to large temperature fluctuations.

It is also vital that you store your pellets in a dry and cool place, ideally sealed off. If pellets become damp or gather moisture, then your pellet smoker will not work at its top performance level.

Keep the Lid Closed

Yet another reason not to open the lid! The outside air coming into contact with the grill will directly affect the temperature of your cook and may throw your timings off. Adhere to the famous BBQ saying; if you are looking, then it isn't cooking!

It's also worth checking that the chamber doesn't have any holes or signs of corrosion through wear and tear. If so, then it makes it much easier for heat to escape, which makes the temperature more likely to fluctuate.

Keep Your Grill in the Shade

Direct sunlight has been proven to impact the internal temperatures of wood pellet grills, as they are made from steel. It can also trick the thermostat, which in turn will mean your wood pellet smoker releases the wrong amount of pellets for the temperature you are aiming for.

Where possible, try to place your grill in a safe place that is out of direct sunlight, putting you back in control of your grill.

Chapter 5. Breakfast Recipes

1. Breakfast Sausage

Preparation Time: 5 minutes
Cooking Time: 30 minutes
Servings: 6-8
Ingredients:

- 12 Breakfast Links
- 1 tbsp. Mustard, Dijon - style
- ½ cup Apricot Jam

Directions:

1. Open the grill and start on Smoke. Once you have a fire close the lid and let it preheat to 350F.
2. In a saucepan warm the Apricot Jam mixed with the mustard.
3. Place the sausages on the grate and cook 15 minutes turning them 2 times. Use tongs and rill the sausages a few times in the sauce mixture and grill for 3 more minutes.
4. Serve with the sauce mixture and enjoy!

Nutrition:
Calories: 180 Cal
Fat: 20 g
Carbohydrates: 18 g
Protein: 15 g
Fiber: 1 g

2. Cinnamon Pancakes

Preparation Time: 20 minutes
Cooking Time: 10 minutes
Servings: 2-4
Ingredients:

- 1 Egg, beaten lightly
- 1 tbsp. oil
- 1 cup of Milk
- 1 cup Flour
- 2 tsp. of Baking powder
- 2 tbsp. Sugar
- ½ tsp. of Salt
- 1 tsp. of Vanilla
- 1 tsp. Vanilla
- 1 ¼ cups of Powdered Sugar
- 2 oz. of Cream cheese
- 4 tbsp. unsalted butter
- 1 tbsp. Cinnamon, ground
- ¾ cup Brown sugar, packed
- ½ cup melted Butter

Directions:

1. Make the filling: In a bowl combine the cinnamon, brown sugar and butter. Mix. Scoop into a zip lock bag. Set aside.
2. Make the batter: Whisk together the sugar, salt, baking powder, and flour. Whisk in the egg, milk, and vanilla until combined.
3. Prepare the glaze: In a bowl heat cream cheese and butter until melted. Whisk well until smooth. Add vanilla and powdered sugar. Whisk and set aside.
4. Heat a skillet on the grill and spray with a cooking spray. Scoop a ½ cup of the batter and pour on the skillet.
5. The grill should be ready before you start cooking. Open the lid and start the smoke and once there is a fire set to high temperature. Close the lid and let it preheat for 15 minutes.
6. Cut the zip lock bag's corner and squeeze out the filling on the pancake.
7. When bubbles start to appear flip and cook for about 2 minutes.
8. Serve with the glaze and enjoy.

Nutrition:
Calories: 550 Cal
Fat: 15 g
Carbohydrates: 80 g
Protein: 11 g
Fiber: 5 g

3. Zucchini with Red Potatoes

Preparation Time: 15 minutes
Cooking Time: 4 hours
Servings: 4
Ingredients:

- 2 zucchinis, sliced in 3/4-inch-thick disks
- 1 red pepper, cut into strips
- 2 yellow squash, sliced in 3/4-inch-thick disks
- 1 medium red onion, cut into wedges
- 6 small red potatoes cut into chunks
- Balsamic Vinaigrette:
- 1/3 cup extra virgin olive oil
- 1/4 teaspoon salt
- 1/4 cup balsamic vinegar
- 2 tsp. Dijon mustard
- 1/8 teaspoon pepper

Directions:

1. For Vinaigrette: Take a medium-sized bowl and blend together olive oil, Dijon mustard, salt, pepper, and balsamic vinegar.
2. Place all the veggies into a large bowl and pour the vinaigrette mixture over it and evenly toss.

3. Put the vegetable in a pan and then smoke for 4 hours at a temperature of 225°F.
4. Serve and enjoy the food.
Nutrition:
Calories: 381 Cal
Fat: 17.6 g
Carbohydrates: 49 g
Protein: 6.7 g
Fiber: 6.5 g

4. Cinnamon Pumpkin Seeds

Preparation Time: 5 minutes
Cooking Time: 20-25 minutes
Servings: 8
Ingredients:
- 8 cups pumpkin seeds
- 2 tablespoons melted butter
- 2 tablespoons sugar
- 1 teaspoon ground cinnamon
Directions:
1. Set your wood pellet grill to smoke.
2. Preheat it to 350 degrees F.
3. Toss the pumpkin seeds in the butter, sugar and cinnamon.
4. Spread in a baking pan.
5. Roast for 20 to 25 minutes.
Nutrition:
Calories: 285 Cal
Fat: 12 g
Carbohydrates: 34 g
Protein: 12 g
Fiber: 12 g

5. Smoked Crepes

Preparation Time: 10 minutes
Cooking Time: 2 hours
Servings: 6
Ingredients:

- 2-pound apples, sliced into wedges
- Apple butter seasoning
- 1/2 cup apple juice
- 2 teaspoon lemon juice
- 5 tablespoon butter
- 3/4 teaspoon cinnamon, ground
- 2 tablespoon brown sugar
- 3/4 teaspoon cornstarch
- 6 crepes
Directions:
1. Preheat your wood pellet grill to 225 degrees F. Season the apples with the apple butter seasoning. Add to the grill. Smoke for 1 hour. Let cool and slice thinly. Add to a baking pan. Stir in the rest of the ingredients except the crepes. Roast for 15 minutes. Add the apple mixture on top of the crepes. Roll and serve.
Nutrition:
Calories: 130 Cal
Fat: 5 g
Carbohydrates: 14 g
Protein: 7 g
Fiber: 1 g

6. Apple Veggie Burger

Preparation Time: 10 minutes
Cooking Time: 35 minutes
Servings: 6
Ingredients:
- 3 tbsp. ground flax or ground chia
- 1/3 cup of warm water
- 1/2 cups rolled oats
- 1 cup chickpeas, drained and rinsed
- 1 tsp. cumin
- 1/2 cup onion

- 1 tsp. dried basil
- 2 granny smith apples
- 1/3 cup parsley or cilantro, chopped
- 2 tbsp. soy sauce
- 2 tsp. liquid smoke
- 2 cloves garlic, minced
- 1 tsp. chili powder
- 1/4 tsp. black pepper
Directions:
1. Preheat the smoker to 225°F while adding wood chips and water to it.
2. In a separate bowl, add chickpeas and mash. Mix together the remaining ingredients along with the dipped flax seeds.
3. Form patties from this mixture.
4. Put the patties on the rack of the smoker and smoke them for 20 minutes on each side.
5. When brown, take them out, and serve.
Nutrition:
Calories: 241 Cal
Fat: 5 g
Carbohydrates: 40 g
Protein: 9 g
Fiber: 10.3 g

7. Coconut Bacon

Preparation Time: 10 minutes
Cooking Time: 30 minutes
Servings: 2
Ingredients:
- 3 1/2 cups flaked coconut
- 1 tbsp. pure maple syrup
- 1 tbsp. water
- 2 tbsp. liquid smoke
- 1 tbsp. soy sauce

- 1 tsp. smoked paprika (optional)

Directions:

1. Preheat the smoker at 325°F.
2. Take a large mixing bowl and combine liquid smoke, maple syrup, soy sauce, and water.
3. Pour flaked coconut over the mixture. Add it to a cooking sheet.
4. Place in the middle rack of the smoker.
5. Smoke it for 30 minutes and every 7-8 minutes, keep flipping the sides.
6. Serve and enjoy.

Nutrition:

Calories: 1244 Cal
Fat: 100 g
Carbohydrates: 70 g
Protein: 16 g
Fiber: 2 g

8. Roasted Green Beans with Bacon

Preparation Time: 15 minutes
Cooking Time: 20 minutes
Servings: 6
Ingredients:

- 1-pound green beans
- 4 strips bacon, cut into small pieces
- 4 tablespoons extra virgin olive oil
- 2 cloves garlic, minced
- 1 teaspoon salt

Directions:

1. Fire the Traeger Grill to 4000F. Use desired wood pellets when cooking. Keep lid unopened and let it preheat for at most 15 minutes

2. Toss all ingredients on a sheet tray and spread out evenly.
3. Place the tray on the grill grate and roast for 20 minutes.

Nutrition:

Calories: 65 Cal
Fat: 5.3 g
Carbohydrates: 3 g
Protein: 1.3 g
Fiber: 0 g

9. Garlic and Herb Smoke Potato

Preparation Time: 5 minutes
Cooking Time: 2 hours
Servings: 6
Ingredients:

- pounds bag of Gemstone Potatoes
- 1/4 cup Parmesan, fresh grated
- For the Marinade
- 2 tbsp. olive oil
- 6 garlic cloves, freshly chopped
- 1/2 tsp. dried oregano
- 1/2 tsp. dried basil
- 1/2 tsp. dried dill
- 1/2 tsp. salt
- 1/2 tsp. dried Italian seasoning
- 1/4 tsp. ground pepper

Directions:

2. Preheat the smoker to 225°F.
3. Wash the potatoes thoroughly and add them to a sealable plastic bag.
4. Add garlic cloves, basil, salt, Italian seasoning, dill, oregano, and olive oil to the zip lock bag. Shake.
5. Place in the fridge for 2 hours to marinate.

6. Next, take an Aluminum foil and put 2 tbsp. of water along with the coated potatoes. Fold the foil so that the potatoes are sealed in
7. Place in the preheated smoker.
8. Smoke for 2 hours
9. Remove the foil and pour the potatoes into a bowl.
10. Serve with grated Parmesan cheese.

Nutrition:

Calories: 146 Cal
Fat: 6 g
Carbohydrates: 19 g
Protein: 4 g
Fiber: 2.1 g

10. Fruits on Bread

Preparation Time: 30 minutes
Cooking Time: 1 hour and 30 minutes
Servings: 8
Ingredients:

- 1/2 cup milk
- 1 teaspoon sugar
- 1/4 cup warm water
- 2 1/2 teaspoon active yeast, instant
- 2 1/2 cups all-purpose flour
- 2 tablespoon melted butter
- 1 egg
- 1/2 teaspoon vanilla
- 1/2 teaspoon salt
- Vegetable oil
- 1 tablespoon ground cinnamon
- Chocolate spread
- Fruits, sliced

Directions:

1. Add the milk, sugar, water and yeast in a bowl. Let sit for 10 minutes.

2. In another bowl, add the flour.

3. Create a well in the center.

4. Add the sugar mixture, butter, egg, vanilla and salt.

5. Mix and knead.

6. Place in a bowl.

7. Cover with clean towel.

8. Let rise for 1 hour.

9. Start your wood pellet grill.

10. Set it to 450 degrees F.

11. Grease a cast iron skillet with the oil.

12. Create balls from the mixture.

13. Press and sprinkle with the cinnamon.

14. Fry for 1 minute per side.

15. Spread with chocolate and top with sliced fruits.

Nutrition:
Calories: 110 Cal
Fat: 2 g
Carbohydrates: 21 g
Protein: 5 g
Fiber: 2 g

11. Easy Smoked Vegetables

Preparation Time: 15 minutes
Cooking Time: 1 ½ hour
Servings: 6
Ingredients:

• 1 cup of pecan wood chips

• 1 ear fresh corn, silk strands removed, and husks, cut corn into 1-inch pieces

• 1 medium yellow squash, 1/2-inch slices

• 1 small red onion, thin wedges

• 1 small green bell pepper, 1-inch strips

• 1 small red bell pepper, 1-inch strips

• 1 small yellow bell pepper, 1-inch strips

• 1 cup mushrooms, halved

• 2 tbsp. vegetable oil

• Vegetable seasonings

Directions:

1. Take a large bowl and toss all the vegetables together in it. Sprinkle it with seasoning and coat all the vegetables well with it.

2. Place the wood chips and a bowl of water in the smoker.

3. Preheat the smoker at 100°F or ten minutes.

4. Put the vegetables in a pan and add to the middle rack of the electric smoker.

5. Smoke for thirty minutes until the vegetable becomes tender.

6. When done, serve, and enjoy.

Nutrition:
Calories: 97 Cal
Fat: 5 g
Carbohydrates: 11 g
Protein: 2 g
Fiber: 3 g

12. Smoked Cherry Tomatoes

Preparation Time: 20 minutes
Cooking Time: 1 ½ hours
Servings: 8-10
Ingredients:

• 2 pints of tomatoes

Directions:

1. Preheat the electric smoker to 225°F while adding wood chips and water to the smoker.

2. Clean the tomatoes with clean water and dry them off properly.

3. Place the tomatoes on the pan and place the pan in the smoker.

4. Smoke for 90 minutes while adding water and wood chips to the smoker.

Nutrition:
Calories: 16 Cal
Fat: 0 g
Carbohydrates: 3 g
Protein: 1 g
Fiber: 1 g

13. Smoked Salted Caramel Apple Pie

Preparation Time: 30 minutes
Cooking Time: 30 minutes
Servings: 4-6
Ingredients:
For the apple pie:

• 1 pastry (for double crust pie)

• 6 Apples

For the smoked, salted caramel:

• 1 cup brown sugar

• ¾ cup light corn syrup

• 6 tablespoons butter (unsalted, cut in pieces)

• 1 cup warm smoked cream

• 1 teaspoon sea salt

Directions:
Grill Prep:

1. Fill a container with water and ice

2. Grab a shallow, smaller pan, and then put in your cream. Take that smaller pan and place it in the large pan with ice and water.

3. Set this on your wood pellet smoker grill for 15 to 20 minutes.

4. For the caramel, mix your corn syrup and sugar in a saucepan, and then cook it all using medium heat. Be sure to stir every so often, until the back of your spoon is coated and begins to turn copper.

5. Next, add the butter, salt, and smoked cream, and then stir.

6. Get your pie crust, apples, and salted caramel. Put a pie crust on a pie plate, and then fill it with slices of apples.

7. Pour on the caramel next.

8. Put on the top crust over all of that, and then crimp both crusts together to keep them locked in.

9. Create a few slits in the top crust, so that the steam can be released as you bake.

10. Brush with some cream or egg, and then sprinkle with some sea salt and raw sugar.

On the Grill:

1. Set up your wood pellet smoker grill for indirect cooking.

2. Preheat your wood pellet smoker grill for 10 to 15 minutes at 375 degrees Fahrenheit; keeping the lid closed as soon as the fire gets started (should take 4 to 5 minutes, tops).

3. Set the pie on your grill, and then bake for 20 minutes.

4. At the 20-minute mark, lower the heat to 325 degrees Fahrenheit, and then let it cook for 35 minutes more. You want the crust to be a nice golden brown, and the filling should be bubbly when it's ready.

5. Take the pie off the grill and allow it to cool and rest.

6. Serve with some vanilla ice cream and enjoy!

Nutrition:
Calories: 149 Cal
Fat: 2 g
Carbohydrates: 30 g
Protein: 3 g
Fiber: 2 g

14. Cilantro and Lime Corn

Preparation Time: 15 minutes
Cooking Time: 15 minutes
Servings: 4
Ingredients:
- 4 corn cobs
- 1 tablespoon lime juice
- 2 tablespoons melted butter
- Smoked paprika
- 1 cup cilantro, chopped

Directions:
1. Preheat your wood pellet grill to 400 degrees F.
2. Grill for 15 minutes, rotating every 5 minutes.
3. Brush the corn cobs with a mixture of lime juice and butter.
4. Season with the paprika.

Nutrition:
Calories: 100 Cal
Fat: 2 g
Carbohydrates: 19 g
Protein: 3 g
Fiber: 2 g

15. Roasted Trail Mix

Preparation Time: 10 minutes
Cooking Time: 15 minutes
Servings: 6
Ingredients:
- 1 cup pretzels
- 1 cup crackers
- 1 cup mixed nuts and seeds
- 3 tablespoons butter
- 1 teaspoon smoked paprika

Directions:
1. Start your wood pellet grill.
2. Preheat it to 225 degrees F.
3. Toss all the ingredients in a roasting pan.
4. Smoke for 15 minutes.
5. Let cool and serve.

Nutrition:
Calories: 150 Cal
Fat: 11 g
Carbohydrates: 11 g
Protein: 5 g
Fiber: 2 g

16. Apple Crumble

Preparation Time: 30 minutes
Cooking Time: 1 hour and 30 minutes
Servings: 8
Ingredients:
- 2 cups and 2 tablespoons flour, divided
- 1/2 cup shortening
- Pinch salt
- 1/4 cup cold water
- 8 cups apples, sliced into cubes
- 3 teaspoons lemon juice
- 1/2 teaspoon ground nutmeg
- 1 teaspoon apple butter seasoning
- 1/8 teaspoon ground cloves
- 1 teaspoon cinnamon
- 1/4 cup butter

Directions:

1. Set your wood pellet grill to smoke.

2. Preheat it to 350 degrees F.

3. Mix 1 1/2 cups flour, shortening and salt in a bowl until crumbly.

4. Slowly add cold water. Mix gently.

5. Wrap the dough in plastic and refrigerate for 20 to 30 minutes.

6. Place the apples in a bowl.

7. Toss in lemon juice. Take the dough out.

8. Press into a pan.

9. In a bowl, combine the 2 tablespoons flour, nutmeg, apple butter seasoning, ground cloves and cinnamon.

10. Add this to the bowl with apples.

11. Add the butter and mix with a mixer until crumbly.

12. Spread this on top of the dough.

13. Bake for 1 hour.

Nutrition:

Calories: 283 Cal

Fat: 6 g

Carbohydrates: 55 g

Protein: 1 g

Fiber: 0 g

17. Mini Quiches

Preparation Time: 15 minutes

Cooking Time: 20 minutes

Servings: 8-12

Ingredients:

- ¼ cup Fresh Basil, chopped
- 4 oz. Mozzarella cheese, shredded
- 10 Eggs
- 3 cups of Baby Spinach
- ½ Onion, diced
- 1 tbsp. Olive oil
- Cooking Spray
- Black pepper and Salt to taste

Directions:

1. Spray a muffin tin (12) with a cooking spray.

2. Turn on medium heat and heat the oil in a skillet. Add onion. Cook 7 minutes and then add the spinach. Cook for 1 more minute.

3. Once done transfer the mixture to a board. Once cooled chop.

4. Preheat the grill to 350F with the lid closed.

5. In the meantime, break the eggs in a bowl and whisk them until frothy. Add the spinach, onion, basil, and cheese. Add pepper and salt to season

6. Pour the mixture into the muffin tin cups.

7. Place the tin on the preheated grill and bake for 20 minutes.

8. Serve right away or let them cool and refrigerate. They can last for 4 days in the fridge.

Nutrition:

Calories: 280 Cal

Fat: 6 g

Carbohydrates: 21 g

Protein: 11 g

Fiber: 1 g

Chapter 6. Mains Recipes

18. Italian Meatballs

Preparation Time: 1 hour
Cooking Time: 3 hours 20 minutes
Servings: 8 - 12
Ingredients:

- ½ cup of Breadcrumbs
- 1 tablespoon of Worcestershire Sauce
- 2 Eggs
- 1 lb. of Ground Beef
- 1 lb. of Italian Sausage, ground
- ½ cup grated Parmesan Cheese
- 1 teaspoon of Onion Powder
- Salt to taste
- Black pepper to taste
- 1 ½ teaspoon Parsley
- 1 teaspoon red pepper, crushed

Directions:

1. Combine all ingredients in a bowl and mix them with your hands. Mix until well combined.
2. Once mixed, shape 1 ½ inches balls and place them on a baking sheet lined with parchment paper. Make sure to leave some space between the meatballs.
3. Preheat the grill to 180F with the lid closed.
4. Now lay down the meatballs on the grate—smoke for about 20 minutes.
5. Turn the heat up to 350F and let them cook for 10 minutes more.
6. Serve with spaghetti and top with marinara sauce.

Nutrition:
Calories: 180
Proteins: 12g
Carbs: 6g
Fat: 22g

19. Roasted Beef with Herbs and Garlic

Preparation Time: 2 hours
Cooking Time: 3 hours 30 minutes
Servings: 8 - 12
Ingredients:

- 6 lb. (1 piece) Boneless Rib Roast (prime)
- ½ cup chopped fresh Parsley
- ½ vegetable oil
- 2 tablespoons Wine vinegar, red
- 1 tablespoon Rosemary needles, fresh
- 5 Garlic cloves, chopped
- 2 cups of Beef Broth
- Rib Rub Seasoning as needed
- Black pepper and salt to taste

Directions:

1. Take a butcher's string and tie the rib roast at about 2 inches interval.
2. In a food processor or a blender, combine the rosemary, parsley, wine vinegar, and garlic. Add 2 tablespoons Oil. Blend just to chop the herbs and garlic. Pour in the leftover oil and mix until blended.
3. Place the meat in a plastic bag. Pour the mixture in and coat well.
4. Let it marinate at room temperature for about 2 hours or in the fridge for 8 hours. Just make sure to let it rest 30 minutes at room temperature before cooking.
5. Remove the meat from the bag—season with rib rub seasoning.
6. Now place the rib roast with the fat side facing up in a pan for roasting. Pour the broth in the bottom.
7. Preheat the grill to high temperature with the lid closed.
8. Place the pan on the grate—roast for about 30 minutes.
9. Now lower the temperature to 250F and cook for 2 - 3 hours more.
10. Transfer on a board to rest. Cover it loosely with foil.
11. Make the sauce: Pour the drippings from the pan in a saucepan. Skim off the fat that will rise. Taste for seasoning and add more pepper and salt if needed.
12. Carve the rib roast into slices. Serve with the sauce and enjoy!

Nutrition: Calories: 700
Proteins: 37 Carbs: 0 Fat: 60

20. Asian Rib - Eye Steak

Preparation Time: 2 hours
Cooking Time: 10 minutes
Servings: 4
Ingredients:

- 4 Rib Eye Stakes 1 inch thick
- 2 tablespoons Water, warm
- 2 teaspoons Ground black pepper

- 2 teaspoons of Onion Powder
- 1 teaspoon of Garlic powder
- 10 minced anchovy fillets
- 1 tablespoon of Brown Sugar
- 1 tablespoon Mustard, dry

Directions:

1. In a large bowl, combine all ingredients (not the meat). Stir well to make a paste.
2. Now rub the steaks on all sides with the paste. Refrigerate for 2 hours.
3. Preheat the grill to high heat with a closed lid.
4. Cook the stakes for 5 minutes on each side until the internal temperature reaches 135F. Once done set aside to rest for 10 minutes.
5. Serve and enjoy!

Nutrition: Calories: 280 Proteins: 21g Carbs: 5g Fat: 22g

21. Smoked Beef Stew

Preparation Time: 30 minutes
Cooking Time: 4 hours
Servings: 6 - 8
Ingredients:

- 2 ½ lbs. Beef Roast, sliced into 1 -inch cubes
- 2 Potatoes for boiling, cut into pieces (peeled)
- 4 Carrots cut into pieces (peeled)
- 1 ½ teaspoon Thyme, dried
- 1 - 2 Bay leaves
- 2 teaspoons of Worcestershire sauce
- 1 tablespoon of Tomato paste

- 2 Garlic cloves, minced
- 1 onion sliced lengthwise
- 3 cups Beef broth, low sodium
- Optional: ½ cup of Red wine
- 2 tablespoons Oil
- Black pepper and Salt
- 2 tablespoons of Flour
- 2 - 3 tablespoons Potato flakes
- For Servings: Buttered noodles or Biscuits
- For Garnish: Parsley, chopped

Directions:

1. In a bag, add the flour, Salt, and black pepper to taste. Add the meat pieces. Toss and coat.
2. Heat the oil in a large pot until hot. Add the meat pieces. Cook until browned. Add the wine, broth, and scrape the brown bits using a wooden spoon. Add thyme, bay leaves, Worcestershire, tomato paste, garlic, and Onion. Cover the pot.
3. Preheat the grill to 300F with the lid closed.
4. Place the pot on the grate and cook for 2 hours. After 2 hours, add the potatoes and carrots. Cook until the veggies and meat are tender, 2 hours more.
5. If you need to thicken, the gravy add 2-3 tablespoons —potato flakes.
6. Serve garnished with parsley.

Nutrition:
Calories: 240
Proteins: 19g

Carbs: 17g
Fat: 11g

22. Corned Beef with Cabbage

Preparation Time: 20 minutes
Cooking Time: 5 hours
Servings: 6 - 8
Ingredients:

- 1 Cabbage head, chopped into wedges
- 1 lb. Potatoes
- 2 cups halved Carrots
- 2 tablespoons Dill, chopped
- ¼ teaspoon of Garlic salt
- ½ cup unsalted butter
- 1 can Beer (12 oz.)
- 4 cups Chicken Stock
- 3 - 5 lbs. (1 piece) Beef Brisket, corned

Directions:

1. Preheat the grill to reach 180F.
2. Rinse the meat and use paper towels to pat dry and place on the grate. Smoke 2 hours.
3. Increase the temperature, 325F with the lid closed.
4. Transfer the brisket to a pan for roasting. Sprinkle with seasoning. Pour the beer and stock in the pan.
5. Cover with foil tightly and let it cook for 2 ½ hours.
6. Remove the foil and add the potatoes and carrots. Season with garlic salt and add butter slices.
7. Cover with foil again. Cook 20 minutes. Add the cabbage recover and cook for an additional 20 minutes.

8. Serve garnished with chopped dill and enjoy.
Nutrition: Calories: 180 Proteins: 9g Carbs: 19g Fat: 8g

23. Peppercorn Steaks and Creamy Sauce

Preparation Time: 1 hour 20 minutes
Cooking Time: 1 hour 30 minutes
Servings: 4 - 6
Ingredients:
FOR THE STEAKS:
- 4 Beef Tenderloin Steaks
- Coarsely ground black pepper
- Coarsely ground green peppercorns
- Salt to taste
- 2 tablespoons Cold coffee (strong) or Bourbon
- 2 Garlic cloves, minced
- ½ cup of Dijon Mustard
- 1 tablespoon Worcestershire sauce

CREAMY SAUCE:
- ½ cup of Heavy cream
- ½ cup of Chicken Stock
- ½ cup Wine, white
- 1 Garlic clove, minced
- 16 0z. Mushrooms, thinly sliced (Crimini)
- 1 tablespoon Oil
Directions:
1. In a bowl, add the Worcestershire sauce, bourbon or coffee, garlic, and mustard. Whisk well to combine.
2. Lay the tenderloin steaks on a plastic wrap and spread the mixture over the meat. Wrap the tenderloin tightly. Let it sit for about 1 hour at room temperature.
3. Unwrap and season with green peppercorns, black pepper, and Salt. Pat the seasoning onto the steak. Preheat the grill to 180F with the lid closed.
4. Place the steaks on the grate. Smoke for 1 hour. Set aside.
5. Set the temperature of the grill to high. Close the grill once hot cook the steaks for 2 - 30 minutes or until the internal temperature is 130F.
6. Make the creamy sauce. Heat the oil in a pan. Add the onions. Sauté for a few minutes, and then add the garlic. Pour the stock and wine and add the mushrooms. Let it simmer for 7 minutes, or until the sauce is thickened. Season with black pepper and salt to taste. Set aside.
7. Transfer the steaks to a plate and let it rest for about 10 minutes (covered with foil). Carve into slices.
8. Serve the steaks topped with sauce and enjoy!
Nutrition: Calories: 250 Proteins: 38g Carbs: 4g Fat: 20g

24. Smoked Burger with Cheese Sauce

Preparation Time: 15 minutes
Cooking Time: 1 hour
Servings: 4
Ingredients:
FOR THE SAUCE:
- ¼ cup of Milk
- 1 teaspoon Red hot sauce
- 1 tablespoon of Butter
- 2 Garlic cloves, minced
- 16 oz. Cheese, Velveeta
BURGERS:
- 4 Burger Buns
- 3 teaspoon Beef Rub
- 2 lbs. Beef, ground
- 1 lb. Green chilies, grilled, pilled, and sliced into strips
- 2 Garlic cloves, minced
- ½ Onion, sliced
- 1 tablespoon unsalted Butter
Directions:
1. Preheat the grill to 180F.
2. Make the sauce in a pan that is safe oven heat the butter. Add the garlic. Sauté for 30 seconds, and then add the cheese. Stir and cook until melted. Add the hot sauce.
3. Transfer on the grill. Smoke for about 30 minutes. Set aside.
4. Make the chili - onions: In a pan, heat butter. Cook the onions until tender. Add garlic and chills. Cook until warmed. Set aside.
5. Increase the temperature to 500F (if you have 500F).
6. Now form 4 patties from the beef—season with the Beef Rub.
7. Cook the burgers for 10 minutes per side. Flip them after the first 5 minutes.
8. Cut the buns and grill them for 3 minutes.
9. Assemble the burgers. Place the patty first on the bun, pour the sauce and add the chili onion.

10. Serve and enjoy!
Nutrition: Calories: 620
Proteins: 30g Carbs: 55g Fat: 30g

25. BBQ Burgers

Preparation Time: 5 minutes
Cooking Time: 15 minutes
Servings: 6
Ingredients:
- 6 Buns for Hamburger
- 6 Hamburger Beef patties, Kobe
- Beef Rub Seasoning
- Toppings you like

Directions:
1. Preheat the grill with a closed lid on high.
2. Season the burgers with the rub. Place on the grill and cook 10 minutes on one side. Flip and cook for an additional 5 minutes.
3. The internal temperature needs to be 150F.
4. Toast the buns.
5. Assemble the hamburger. Place the patties on one half of the bun, add the topping you like and place the other half of the bun.
6. Serve and enjoy.

Nutrition:
Calories: 320
Proteins: 15g
Carbs: 30g
Fat: 11g

26. Cocoa Rub Steak

Preparation Time: 50 minutes
Cooking Time: 50 minutes
Servings: 2
Ingredients:
- 1/8 cup of Cocoa Powder
- ½ cup Coffee Rub
- 2 Rib - eye roast steaks, boneless (2 ½ inches cut)

Directions:
1. Trim the silver skin and excess fat from the roast.
2. Cut the roast into 2 ½ inches thick steaks. You can also ask your butcher to cut it.
3. Keep just 2 steaks and place the remaining in the freezer.
4. Combine the cocoa powder and coffee rub. Season the 2 steaks lightly with the seasoning mix.
5. Let it rest at room temperature for 45min.
6. Preheat the grill to 225F with the lid closed.
7. Grill the steaks for 20 min on one side and 20 minutes more on the other. The internal temperature should be 105 - 110F. Set aside.
8. Increase the temperature to 450F. Grill the steaks for 4 minutes per each side. The final temperature of the steaks should be 130 - 135F.
9. Let the steaks rest for about 5 - 10 min. before serving. Enjoy!
Nutrition: Calories: 280
Proteins: 22g Carbs: 0g Fat: 23g

27. Smoked Brisket Pie

Preparation Time: 15 minutes
Cooking Time: 45 minutes
Servings: 8
Ingredients:
- 1 cup Onions, peeled and blanched (pearl)
- ½ cup Peas, frozen
- 1 Garlic clove, minced
- 1 Onion, chopped (yellow)
- 2 Carrots, chopped (peeled)
- 2 tablespoons of Butter
- 2 cups chopped Leftover Brisket
- 1 Egg
- 1 Sheet Pastry dough, frozen
- 2 cups of Beef Stock

Directions:
1. In a pot add the butter. Place it over medium - high heat. Once the butter is melted sauté the carrots for 10 minutes.
2. Add the Onion. Cook 7 minutes and then add the garlic. Cook 30 seconds.
3. Add in the brisket, peas, and stock. Let it simmer until thick so that it coats the spoon. In case it doesn't thicken make slurry from cornstarch and add it. Season with black pepper and Salt to taste.
4. Pour the mixture in a baking dish and cover it with the dough. Make cuts on the top.
5. In a bowl whisk the egg and brush the pastry.
6. Preheat the grill to 350F with closed lid. Once heated place the baking dish on the grate and let it bake 45 minutes. Set aside.
7. Let it rest for 10 minutes and serve. Enjoy!
Nutrition: Calories: 320
Proteins: 12g Carbs: 22g Fat: 16g

28. Love Steak

Preparation Time: 5 minutes
Cooking Time: 12 minutes
Servings: 2
Ingredients:

- 20 oz. Rib steak or Strip Steak (boneless) Butterflied
- ½ tablespoon Oil
- 2 tablespoons chopped Chocolate, dark
- 2 teaspoons Pepper, Freshly Cracked
- Salt to taste

Directions:

1. Butterfly the steak into a heart shape.
2. Combine the remaining ingredients and place on the steak.
3. Preheat the grill with closed lid to 450F.
4. Grill for 7 minutes on each side. Let it rest for 5 min. and serve. Enjoy with your favorite side dish!

Nutrition: Calories: 620; Proteins: 60g; Carbs: 16g; Fat: 40g

29. Beer Beef

Preparation Time: 15 minutes
Cooking Time: 7 hours
Servings: 8 - 12
Ingredients:

- 1 Beef Brisket 9 - 12 lbs. the at outside trimmed
- 5 garlic cloves, smashed
- 1 Onion, sliced
- 5 tablespoons of Pickling Spice
- 1 tablespoon of curing Salt for each lb. of meat
- ½ cup of Brown sugar
- 1 ½ cups Salt
- 3x12 oz. Dark beer
- 3 quarts Water, cold
- Rib seasoning

Directions:

1. In a stockpot combine the curing Salt, brown sugar, Salt, beer, and water. Stir until well dissolved.
2. Add the garlic, Onion and pickling spice. Place in the fridge.
3. Add the meat in the brine but make sure that it is submerged completely. Brine for 2 - 4 days. Stir once every day.
4. Rinse the brisket under cold water. Sprinkle with rib seasoning.
5. Preheat the grill to 250F.
6. Cook the brisket for 4 to 5 hours. The inside temperature should be 160F.
7. Wrap the meat in a foil (double layer) and add water (1 ½ cup). Place it back on the grill and let it cook for 3 to 4 hours until it reaches 204F internal temperature.
8. Set aside and let it sit for 30 min. Crave into thin pieces and serve. Enjoy!

Nutrition: Calories: 320 Proteins: 38g Carbs: 14g Fat: 12g

30. Smoked Chili

Preparation Time: 20 minutes
Cooking Time: 1 hour
Servings: 6 - 8
Ingredients:

- 2 oz. Chocolate, dark
- 1 can (15 oz.) Diced Tomatoes
- 2 cans (15 oz.) Beans with Chili Sauce
- ½ cup Strong Coffee or Dark Beer
- 2 cups Chicken or Beef Bouillon
- 1 teaspoon Oregano, dried
- 1 tablespoon Cumin, ground
- 2 tablespoons of Chili powder
- 2 tablespoons of Tomato Paste
- 2 ½ lbs. of Ground Chunk
- Salt
- 3 Garlic cloves, minced
- 1 Bell pepper, diced (red)
- 1 Onion, diced
- 2 tablespoons oil

Directions:

1. Preheat the grill with a closed lid to 350F.
2. Place a Dutch oven on the grate in the heating process.
3. Once the temperature is 350F add oil, bell pepper, Onion, garlic, and Salt. Close the grill. Cook 12 minutes stirring occasionally.
4. Add the meat and break it apart. Cook with a covered lid until cooked, about 10 minutes.
5. Add the oregano, cumin, chili powder, and tomato paste. Cook 2 minutes and then add the chicken/beef bouillon and coffee/beer. Stir well.
6. Close it and let it simmer 10 minutes. Add the chocolate, diced tomatoes, and chili beans. Stir.
7. Let it cook 20 minutes with closed lid.
8. Taste and adjust seasoning if needed.
9. To add smokier flavor, you should reduce the heat so

that it reaches the smoking setting. Leave it for 1 hour.

10. Serve with tortilla chips, sour cream, green onions, grated cheese, and fresh cilantro. Enjoy!

Nutrition: Calories: 310 Proteins: 14g Carbs: 24g Fat: 16g

31. Hawaiian Burger

Preparation Time: 10 minutes
Cooking Time: 15 minutes
Servings: 2
Ingredients:
- 4 Cheese Slices (preferably Swiss)
- 4 buns
- 1 ½ lb. of Ground beef
- 4 slices of Spam
- 1 tablespoon of Sriracha
- 4 slices of Pineapple
- 4 tablespoon Mayo
- ½ tablespoon ground black pepper
- 1 teaspoon of Salt

Directions:
1. In a bowl combine the meat, black pepper, and Salt. Mix well with hands. Once combined form patties 1/3 lb. each.
2. Preheat the grill with the lid open to high.
3. Grill the patties for 6 minutes on each side. Top with cheese 1 minute before removing from the grill.
4. Grill the pineapple and span, flipping occasionally. Cook just until warmed. Place one more cheese on the spam and cook 1 minute until melted.
5. Toast the buns. Slice them open and first place the pineapple, the patty, top with spam and finish with the other half of the bun.
6. Serve right away and enjoy!

Nutrition: Calories: 1150 Proteins: 45g Carbs: 83g Fat: 90g

32. Brisket Tacos

Preparation Time: 15 minutes
Cooking Time: 45 minutes
Servings: 6 - 8
Ingredients:
- 4 - 5 lbs. Brisket (leftovers)
- 15 - 20 Flour Tortillas (6 inches)
- 4 Tomatoes, diced, seeded (Roma)
- 4 - 5 Avocados
- ½ cup of Beef broth
- 1 minced Jalapeno
- ½ Onion, minced
- 1 Lime, the juice
- ½ cup of Sour Cream
- Black pepper and Salt to taste

Directions:
1. Preheat the grill with a closed lid to 300F.
2. If the brisket is not sliced, slice it into ¼ inch slices. Now place them in a foil, double layer, and add broth. Seal well and grill about 50 minutes, just to warm it.
3. In the meantime, mash avocados and add black pepper, Salt, lime juice, sour cream, Onion, jalapeno, and tomatoes. Mix well and set aside.
4. With a foil wrap the 6 - inch tortillas and grill 15 minutes.
5. Remove the tortillas and brisket. Assemble the brisket tacos. Top with your homemade guacamole and even add more toppings. Enjoy!

Nutrition: Calories: 385 Proteins: 28g Carbs: 32g Fat: 18g

33. Pork Collar with Rosemary Marinade

Preparation Time: 15 minutes
Cooking Time: 30 minutes
Servings: 6
Ingredients:
- 1 Pork Collar (3 - 4lb.)
- 3 tablespoons Rosemary, fresh
- 3 minced Shallots
- 2 tablespoons chopped Garlic
- ½ cup of Bourbon
- 2 teaspoons Coriander, ground
- 1bottle of Apple Ale
- 1 teaspoon ground Black pepper
- 2 teaspoons Salt
- 3 tablespoons oil

Directions:
1. In a zip lock bag combine the black pepper, Salt, canola oil, apple ale, bourbon, coriander, garlic, shallots, and rosemary.
2. Cut the meat into slabs (2 inches) and marinade in the refrigerator overnight.
3. Preheat the grill to 450F with the lid closed. Grill the meat for 5 minutes and lower the temperature to 325F. Pour the marinade over the meat. Cook 25 minutes more.

4. Cook until the internal temperature of the meat is 160F.
5. Serve and enjoy!
Nutrition: Calories: 420 Proteins: 30g Carbs: 4g Fat: 26g

34. Simple Pork Tenderloin

Preparation Time: 15 minutes
Cooking Time: 20 minutes
Servings: 4 - 6
Ingredients:
- 2 Pork Tenderloins (12 - 15 oz. each)
- 6 tablespoons hot Sauce, Louisiana style
- 6 tablespoon smelted Butter
- Cajun seasoning as needed

Directions:
1. Trim the silver skin from the meat.
2. In a large bowl combine the hot sauce and melted butter. Roll the meat in this mixture. Season with Cajun seasoning.
3. Preheat the grill to 400F with the lid closed.
4. Grill the meat for 8 minutes on each side. The internal temperature should be 145F. If you want well - done cook until 160F.
5. Let it rest for a few minutes before cutting. Serve with your favorite side dish and enjoy!
Nutrition: Calories: 150; Proteins: 20g; Carbs: 0g; Fat: 3g

35. Bacon Mac' n Cheese

Preparation Time: 20 minutes
Cooking Time: 1 hour 30 minutes
Servings: 3
Ingredients:
- 3 tablespoons of Flour
- 2 tablespoons unsalted Butter
- ½ lbs. Macaroni, elbow
- 1 tablespoon Mustard, powder
- 3 cups of Milk
- 1 Egg
- ¼ teaspoon Chile powder
- ½ teaspoon of Smoked Paprika
- 1 small Bay leaf
- 8 oz. shredded Cheddar
- Black pepper to taste
- 1 teaspoon Salt
- 15 slices bacon, uncooked
- BBQ sauce or one you like

Directions:
1. In a pot add water and Salt. Once boiling, add the pasta until it's cooked.
2. In the meantime, in another pot add the butter. Turn on medium heat and let it melt. Once melted add the mustard and flour. Cook stirring constantly for 5 minutes.
3. Add the paprika, chili powder, bay, and milk. Let it simmer for about 10 minutes. Discard the leaf. Whisk the egg and temper into the milk whisking constantly. Season with black pepper and Salt and add the cheddar cheese. Stir.

4. Add the macaroni into the cheese mixture than stir. Transfer into a casserole dish. Refrigerate for 4h.
5. On a baking sheet dump, the elbow macaroni upside down. Place the bacon on top.
6. Preheat the grill to 350F. Close the lid.
7. Smoke the macaroni for 30 minutes and then cook for 1h.
8. Brush with sauce 10 minutes before setting aside.
9. Serve and enjoy!
Nutrition: Calories: 302 Proteins: 10g Carbs: 40g Fat: 18g

36. Pork Roast with Mustard and Apple Glaze

Preparation Time: 30 minutes
Cooking Time: 2 hours
Servings: 6 - 8
Ingredients:
- 4 - 5 lb. (1 piece) Pork loin, bone in
- 2 teaspoons of Molasses
- 1 tablespoon Apple - flavored liqueur like Applejack
- 1 tablespoon of Honey
- 1 tablespoon Mustard, Dijon - style
- 3 tablespoons ground Mustard
- 1 tablespoon chopped fresh Rosemary
- 2 cups of Apple juice or cider
- 2 - 3 bay leaves, crumbled
- 3 Garlic cloves smashed

- 1 quart of Apple juice or cider
- 1 quart Water
- ¾ cup of Brown sugar
- ¾ cup Salt

Directions:

1. The meat brined overnight so plan ahead.
2. In a bowl combine apple cider, water, brown sugar, and Salt. Stir until dissolved. Add the bay leaves and garlic.
3. Put the meat in a plastic bag (sealable) and pour in the brine. Seal, place in a bowl and refrigerate overnight or for 8 hours.
4. Pat dry the pork meat, discard the brine. Tie it between bones using kitchen twine. Season with black pepper.
5. Place the loin on a rack and in a roasting pan with the fat side facing up. Wrap the pork bones with foil.
6. Preheat the grill to 350F with the lid closed.
7. The glaze: in a pan add 2 cups of apple juice or cider bring to a boil. Add in the molasses, Applejack, honey, and mustard. Stir and keep warm.
8. Place the pan on the grill. Cook for about 1 hour. Brush the meat with the apple glaze. Roast for 45min- 1h more until the internal temperature is 145F.
9. Let it rest for about 20 minutes.
10. Discard the foil and remove the twine. Brush with the glaze. Slice into chops and serve.

Nutrition: Calories: 380 Proteins: 22g Carbs: 30g Fat: 15g

37. Roasted Ham

Preparation Time: 15 minutes
Cooking Time: 2 hours
Servings: 8 - 12
Ingredients:

- 8 - 10lb. Ham, whole bone in
- 2 tablespoons Mustard, Dijon
- ¼ cup Horseradish
- 1 bottle BBQ Apricot Sauce

Directions:

1. Preheat the grill to 325F with closed lid.
2. Lone a roasting pan with foil and place the ham. Place on the grill. Cook 1h and 30 minutes.
3. In a small pan combine the sauce, mustard, and horseradish. Turn on medium heat. Simmer for few minutes and set aside. Keep warm.
4. After 1h 30 minutes grilling the ham brush with the glaze. Cook for 30 minutes more. The internal temperature should be 135F.
5. Let it rest for about 20 minutes. Slice and serve. Enjoy!

Nutrition: Calories: 460
Proteins: 43g
Carbs: 10g
Fat: 20g

Chapter 7. Basic Recipes

38. Fish Stew

Preparation time: 20min
Cooking Time: 25min
Servings: 8
Ingredients:

* 1 jar (28oz.) Crushed Tomatoes
* 2 oz. of Tomato paste
* ¼ cup of White wine
* ¼ cup of Chicken Stock
* 2 tbsp. Butter
* 2 Garlic cloves, minced
* ¼ Onion, diced
* ½ lb. Shrimp divined and cleaned
* ½ lb. of Clams
* ½ lb. of Halibut
* Parsley
* Bread

Directions:
1. Preheat the grill to 300F with closed lid.
2. Place a Dutch oven over medium heat and melt the butter.
3. Sauté the onion for 4 - 7 minutes. Add the garlic. Cook 1 more minute.
4. Add the tomato paste. Cook until the color becomes rust red. Pour the stock and wine. Cook 10 minutes. Add the tomatoes, simmer.
5. Chop the halibut and together with the other seafood add in the Dutch oven. Place it on the grill and cover with a lid.
6. Let it cook for 20 minutes.
7. Season with black pepper and salt and set aside.
8. Top with chopped parsley and serve with bread.
9. Enjoy!

Nutrition:
Calories: 188
Protein: 25g
Carbohydrates: 7g
Fat: 12g

39. Smoked Crab Legs

Preparation time: 5 Minutes
Cooking time: 15 Minutes
Servings: 5
Ingredients:

* 1 Pinch of black pepper
* ¾ Stick of butter to the room temperature
* 2 Tablespoons of chopped chives
* 1 Minced garlic clove
* 1 Sliced lemon
* 3 Lobster, tail, about 7 ounces
* 1 Pinch of kosher salt

Directions:
1. Start your Wood Pellet Grill on smoke with the lid open for about 3 to 7 minutes
2. Preheat to about 350°F; then blend the butter, the chives, the minced garlic and the black pepper in a bowl
3. Cover with a plastic wrap and set aside
4. Blend the butter, the chives, the minced garlic, and the black pepper in a bowl; then cover with a plastic wrap and set it aside.
5. Butterfly the lobster tails into the middle of the soft part of the underside of the shell and don't cut completely through the center of the meat
6. Brush the tails with olive oil and season with 1 pinch of salt
7. Smoke Grill the lobsters with the cut side down for about 5 minutes
8. Flip the tails and top with 1 tablespoon of herbed butter; then grill for an additional 4 minutes
9. Remove from the smoker grill and serve with more quantity of herb butter
10. Top with lemon wedges; then serve and enjoy your dish!

Nutrition:
Calories: 90
Fat: 1g
Carbohydrates: 0g
Dietary Fiber: 1 g
Protein: 20g

40. Spicy Smoked Shrimp

Preparation time: 30 Minutes
Cooking time: 15 Minutes
Servings: 3
Ingredients:

* 2 lbs. of peeled and deveined shrimp
* 6 Oz of Thai chilies
* 6 Garlic cloves
* 2 Tablespoons of a chicken rub of your choice
* 1 and ½ teaspoons of sugar
* 1 and ½ tablespoons of white vinegar
* 3 Tablespoons of olive oil

Directions:
1. Place all your ingredients besides the shrimp

in a blender; then blend until you get a paste

2. Place the shrimp in a bowl; then add in the chili garlic mixture; then place in the refrigerator and let marinate for about 30 minutes

3. Remove from the fridge and thread the shrimp on metal or bamboo skewers for about 30 minutes

4. Start your Wood pellet smoker to about 225° F and preheat with the lid closed for about 10 to 15 minutes

5. Place the shrimp on a grill and cook for about 2 to 3 minutes per side or until the shrimp are pink

6. Serve and enjoy your dish!

Nutrition:
Calories: 20
Fat: 10g
Carbohydrates: 10g
Dietary Fiber: 0 g
 Protein: 16g

41. Grilled Shrimp with Pineapple and Coconut

Preparation Time: 30 minutes
Cooking time: 1 hr. 25 minutes
Servings: 4
Ingredients:

- ½ c. coconut milk
- 4 tsp. Red Tabasco Sauce
- 2 tsp. soy sauce
- ¼ c. fresh orange juice
- Juice of 2 limes
- 40 pieces large-sized shrimp
- ¾ lb. sliced pineapple
- Canola oil
- Chopped cilantro

Directions:
1. Combine the lime juice, orange juice, soy sauce, Tabasco sauce, soy sauce, and coconut milk in a medium bowl. Whisk together thoroughly.

2. Add the shrimp and coat by tossing and leave it to marinate in the fridge for 2 hours.

3. Preheat the grill to a medium temperature, take the shrimp out of the marinade, and thread them onto skewers.

4. Brush the grill lightly with canola oil and arrange the shrimp on the grill.

5. Grill for 3 minutes on both sides and then brush them with the marinade.

6. Grill for a further 2 minutes on both sides and brush with the marinade.

7. Take the shrimp off the grill, garnish with the cilantro and serve.

Nutrition:
Calories: 329,
Fat: 3 g,
Carbohydrates: 52 g
Protein: 22 g

42. Smoked Peppers

 Preparation time: 5 minutes
Cooking time: 20 Minutes
Servings: 4
Ingredients:

- 1 Bag of pearl onions, of about 14.4 oz.
- 1 Bag of 1 lb. of small sweet peppers
- Cooking sprays, like butter or olive oil
- 1 Pinch of Garlic salt
- 1 Pinch of Black pepper
- ¼ Teaspoon of steak seasoning

Directions:
1. Preheat your wood pellet smoker grill to a temperature of about 350° F

2. Spray the rack of your wood pellet smoker grill with cooking spray and cut the tops of the peppers into half; then remove the seeds

3. Spray the peppers with cooking spray and cover with the garlic salt, the black pepper, and the seasoning; then place on top of the rack

4. Smoke the peppers for about 15 to 20 minutes

5. Serve and enjoy!

Nutrition:
Calories: 62
Fat: 3.6g,
Carbohydrates: 0g
Dietary Fiber: 1.4g
Protein: 1g

43. Smoked Aubergines

Preparation time: 10 Minutes
Cooking time: 30 Minutes
 Servings: 3
Ingredients:

- 2 Medium whole aubergine
- 2 Medium spring onions
- 2 Teaspoons of toasted sesame seeds
- 4 Teaspoons of miso paste
- 2 Teaspoons of soy sauce
- 1 Teaspoon of sesame oil
- 1 Garlic clove
- 1 Inch of fresh ginger, cube

Directions:
1. Add the miso, the soy, and the sesame oil to a bowl; then crush a garlic clove
2. Grate the ginger and stir with the help of a teaspoon until you get a paste
3. Slice the aubergine into half; then score the flesh to create a pattern of diamond shape
4. Add the miso paste on top of the aubergine
5. Brush to add the miso concoction to the aubergine flesh
6. Through diagonal scoring of the aubergine
7. Let the paste to rest for about 30 minutes
8. Place the aubergine with the side up over indirect heat at a temperature of about 320°F
9. Smoke for about 30 minutes
10. Add a few cherry woods pellets to the coals for any extra flavor.
11. Turn the aubergine over onto direct heat and cook for about 60 seconds
12. Serve and enjoy your dish!
Nutrition:
Calories: 112
Fat: 6g
Carbohydrates: 8g
Dietary Fiber: 4 g
Protein: 5g

44. Smoked Mackerel
Preparation time: 15 Minutes
Cooking time: 30 Minutes
Servings: 9
Ingredients:

- ½ Teaspoon of Garam Masala
- 1 Pinch of dried red chili flakes
- 1 Tablespoon of softened butter
- 3 and ½oz of smoked mackerel fillets
- To prepare the raita
- 2 Tablespoons of Greek-style plain yogurt
- 1 Tablespoon of roughly chopped fresh mint
- Half a lime, only use the juice
- ½ Thinly sliced halved cucumber
- 6 Roughly chopped radishes
- 1 Pinch of salt

Directions:
1. Start by making the raita and to do that, combine the yogurt with the mint and 1 squeeze of lime juice in a medium bowl and season it with 1 pinch of salt
2. Add in the cucumber and the radishes; then cover and put in the refrigerator until you are ready to use it
3. Preheat the charcoal grill to a high heat and line a baking pan with a kitchen foil.
4. In a medium bowl, combine the Garam Masala with the chili and the butter; then spread the butter over the mackerel
5. Place the fillets over the baking tray and place it on the smoker and close the smoker with a lid
6. Smoke the mackerel for about 30 minutes
7. Remove the mackerel from the smoker; then set it aside for about 5 minutes
8. Serve and enjoy your mackerel with the raita!
Nutrition:
Calories: 283
Fat: 23.4 g
Carbohydrates: 2g
Protein: 20g
Dietary Fiber 0.1 g

45. Grilled Tilapia "Ceviche"
Preparation Time: 30 minutes
Cooking time: 10 minutes
Servings: 4
Ingredients:

- 1 lb. tilapia filets
- ¼ c. chopped parsley
- ¼ c. chopped fresh cilantro
- ¼ c. freshly squeezed lime juice
- 2 tbsps. olive oil
- ½ tsp. red chili flakes
- 5 minced green onions
- 2 diced tomatoes
- 2 sliced celery stalks
- ½ minced green bell pepper
- Salt
- Pepper

Directions:
1. Mix lime juice, olive oil, vegetables, and herbs in a large bowl.
2. Grilling:
3. Preheat the grill to 400F.
4. Sprinkle pepper and salt on both sides of the tilapia and place on the grid.
5. Close the dome and cook for 3 minutes.

6. Gently flip the fish and cook for another 2-3 minutes or until the fish is opaque. Set aside.

7. Flake apart the tilapia filets and gently stir into the vegetable mixture to combine.

8. Serve room temperature or chilled.

Nutrition:

Calories: 220,

Fat: 4 g,

Carbohydrates: 17 g,

Protein: 33 g

46. Grilled Sweet Potatoes

Preparation Time: 30 minutes

Cooking time: 30 minutes

Servings: 4

Ingredients:

Potato Ingredients:

- 2 lbs. chopped sweet potatoes
- 4 tbsps. extra virgin olive oil
- ½ tsp. salt

Dressing Ingredients:

- ¼ c. chopped cilantro
- 1 tsp. lime zest
- 2 tbsps. fresh lemon juice
- ¼ c. extra virgin olive oil
- 1 tsp. salt

Directions:

1. Preheat the grill to a high temperature.

2. Place potatoes in a medium bowl and pour the olive oil and salt over the top. Toss to coat.

3. To make the dressing, combine the ingredients into a medium-sized bowl and whisk together thoroughly.

4. Arrange the potatoes onto the grill and cook for 6 minutes on each side.

5. Remove potatoes from the grill and place them in the bowl with the dressing. Coat by tossing and serve.

Nutrition:

Calories: 160,

Fat: 11 g,

Carbohydrates: 16 g,

Protein: 1 g

47. Smoked Shrimp

Preparation time: 10 Minutes

Cooking time: 3 Hour

Servings: 10

Ingredients:

- 2 Pounds of jumbo shrimp
- ½ Cup of extra virgin olive oil
- 6 Finely chopped garlic cloves
- 2 Tablespoons of finely chopped parsley
- ½ Teaspoon of cayenne pepper
- ½ Teaspoon of black pepper
- ½ Teaspoon of salt
- 1 Bag of charcoal
- 1 Chimney starter
- 2 bags of wood chips

Directions:

1. Light a charcoal smoker for about 30 minutes before starting to cook

2. Wrap the wood chips into an aluminum foil pouch; then punch some holes into the foil and set aside to let the smoke escape

3. Season the shrimp with the garlic, the parsley, the cayenne pepper, the black pepper, and the salt.

4. Drizzle the virgin olive oil on top of the prepared shrimps; then skewer the shrimps on a prepared kabob and place the shrimp kabobs on the smoker when the temperature reaches about 225° F

5. Put the wood chip foil pouch on top of the charcoal or right into the inside of the metal smoker box

6. Smoke the shrimp for around 30 to 35 minutes

7. Serve and enjoy your smoked shrimps

Nutrition:

Calories: 283

Fat: 23.4 g

Carbohydrates: 2g

Protein: 20g

Dietary Fiber 0.1 g

48. Smoked Bacon Wrapped Scallops

Preparation time: 8 Minutes

Cooking time: 40 Minutes

Servings: 7

Ingredients:

- 10 to 12 jumbo scallops
- 8 to 10 slices of bacon
- ½ Cup of butter
- 1 Pinch of salt
- 1 Pinch of pepper
- Toothpicks
- Some aluminum foils

Directions:

1. Light a charcoal smoker for about 30 minutes

2. Wrap the wood chips into an aluminum foil pouch; then punch little holes into the foil to let the smoke escape

3. Take the strips of bacon; then wrap each slice around each of the jumbo scallops and use toothpicks to secure bacon slices around the scallops

4. Melt a small quantity of butter in a medium bowl with a basting brush; coat the bacon and the scallops

5. Place the bacon-wrapped scallops in a sheet of aluminum foil; then place the wood chip foil pouch over the charcoal

6. Smoke the scallops for about 30 minutes; then remove the scallops from the smoker and let rest for about 5 minutes

7. Serve and enjoy your dish!

Nutrition:
Calories: 283
Fat: 23.4 g
Carbohydrates: 2g
Protein: 20g
Dietary Fiber 0.1 g

49. Smoked Chicken Breasts with Dried Herbs

Preparation time: 15 minutes
Cooking time: 40 minutes
Servings: 4
Ingredients:
- 4 chicken breasts boneless
- 1/4 cup garlic-infused olive oil
- 2 clove garlic minced
- 1/4 tsp. of dried sage
- 1/4 tsp. of dried lavender
- 1/4 tsp. of dried thyme
- 1/4 tsp. of dried mint

- 1/2 Tbsp. dried crushed red pepper
- Kosher salt to taste

Directions:
1. Place the chicken breasts in a shallow plastic container.
2. In a bowl, combine all remaining ingredients, and pour the mixture over the chicken breast and refrigerate for one hour.
3. Remove the chicken breast from the sauce (reserve sauce) and pat dry on kitchen paper.
4. Start your pellet grill on SMOKE (hickory pellet) with the lid open until the fire is established). Set the temperature to 250℉ and preheat, lid closed, for 10 to 15 minutes.
5. Place chicken breasts on the smoker. Close pellet grill lid and cook for about 30 to 40 minutes or until chicken breasts reach 165℉.
6. Serve hot with reserved marinade.

Nutrition:
Calories: 391
Carbohydrates: 0.7g
Fat: 3.21g
Fiber: 0.12g
Protein: 20.25g

50. Grilled Potato Salad

Preparation Time: 30 minutes
Cooking time: 20 minutes
Servings: 4
Ingredients:
- 24 oz. Baby potatoes
- 4 garlic cloves
- 4 tbsps. Oil
- ¼ tsp. Salt

- ¼ tsp. Pepper
- 1 tbsp. Rice wine vinegar
- 1 tbsp. Chives
- 3 tbsps. Fresh Dill
- Dill cream
- 1 c. Sour cream – 1 cup
- 2 tbsps. Lemon juice – 2 tbsp.
- 1 tbsp. chopped onion
- Salt
- Pepper
- Sugar

Directions:
1. Preheat the grill to medium-high heat.
2. In a bowl, smash black garlic with 1 tbsp. oil and salt. Add the pepper, vinegar, and remaining oil.
3. Strain the potatoes and toss just enough vinaigrette, so they lightly coat.
4. Grill the potatoes until they are lightly charred.
5. Toss with fresh herbs and rest of the vinaigrette.
6. Serve with sour cream.
7. To make the cream, whisk all the ingredients in a bowl.

Nutrition:
Calories: 182,
Fat: 11 g,
Carbohydrates: 18 g,
Protein: 3 g

51. Grilled Shrimp Melody

Preparation Time: 30 minutes
Cooking time: 15 minutes
Servings: 4
Ingredients:
- 1 lb. potatoes
- 2 sliced ears of corn

- 6 tbsps. melted butter
- 8 oz. chicken breasts
- 1 lb. Shrimp
- 2 tbsps. fresh lemon juice
- 2 tsp. fresh thyme
- 2 minced garlic cloves
- 2 tsp. seafood seasoning
- 2 tbsps. chopped parsley

Directions:
1. Preheat the grill to a high temperature.
2. Arrange 8 pieces of aluminum foil.
3. Divide the potatoes, shrimp, chicken, and corn onto the sheets of foil.
4. Using a medium bowl, mix the minced garlic, melted butter, chopped thyme, and lemon juice. Whisk together thoroughly.
5. Pour the mixture over the shrimp mix and season with the seafood seasoning.
6. Wrap the foil around the shrimp mix and arrange on the grill, cook for 15 minutes.
7. Remove from the grill, garnish with the parsley and serve.

Nutrition:
Calories: 111,
Fat: 6 g,
Carbohydrates: 10 g,
Protein: 13 g

52. Grilled Yellow Squash

Preparation Time: 30 minutes
Cooking time: 20 minutes
Servings: 8
Ingredients:

- 4 medium Yellow squash
- ½ c. extra virgin olive oil
- 2 crushed garlic cloves
- Salt
- pepper

Directions:
1. Preheat the grill for medium heat.
2. Using a medium pan, heat olive oil and add garlic cloves.
3. Cook over medium heat until the garlic becomes fragrant and sizzle.
4. Brush the slices of squash with garlic oil. Then season with salt and pepper.
5. Grill squash slices until they reach the desired tenderness, about 5 to 10 minutes per side. Occasionally turn and brush with additional garlic oil.

Nutrition:
Calories: 87
 Fat: 7 g
Carbohydrates: 6 g
Protein: 2 g

53. Chicken Breast with Lemon

Preparation time: 15min
Cooking Time: 15min
Servings: 6
Ingredients:

- 6 Chicken breasts, skinless and boneless
- ½ cup Oil
- 1 - 2 Fresh thyme sprigs
- 1 tsp. ground black pepper
- 2 tsp. Salt
- 2 tsp. of Honey

- 1 Garlic clove, chopped
- 1 Lemon the juice and zest
- For service: Lemon wedges

Directions:
1. Make the marinade: In a bowl combine the thyme, black pepper, salt, honey, garlic, and lemon zest and juice. Stir until dissolved and combined. Add in the oil and whisk to combine.
2. Clean the breasts and pat dry. Place them in a plastic bag. Pour the pre-made marinade and massage to distribute evenly. Place in the fridge, 4 hours.
3. Preheat the grill to 400F with the lid closed.
4. Drain the chicken and grill until the internal temperature reaches 165F, about 15 minutes.
5. Serve with lemon wedges and a side dish of your choice.

Nutrition:
Calories: 230
Proteins: 38g
Carbohydrates: 1g
Fat: 7g

54. Pellet Smoked Chicken Burgers

Preparation time: 20 minutes
Cooking time: 1 hour and 10 minutes
Servings: 6
Ingredients:

- 2 lb. ground chicken breast
- 2/3 cup of finely chopped onions

- 1 Tbsp. of cilantro, finely chopped
- 2 Tbsp. fresh parsley, finely chopped
- 2 Tbsp. of olive oil
- 1/2 tsp. of ground cumin
- 2 Tbsp. of lemon juice freshly squeezed
- 3/4 tsp. of salt and red pepper to taste

Directions:
1. In a bowl add all ingredients; mix until combined well.
2. Form the mixture into 6 patties.
3. Start your pellet grill on SMOKE (oak or apple pellets) with the lid open until the fire is established. Set the temperature to 350℉ and preheat, lid closed, for 10 to 15 minutes.
4. Smoke the chicken burgers for 45 - 50 minutes or until cooked through, turning every 15 minutes.
5. Your burgers are ready when internal temperature reaches 165 ℉.
6. Serve hot.

Nutrition:
Calories: 221
Carbohydrates: 2.12g
Fat: 8.5g
Fiber: 0.4g
Protein: 32.5g

55. Perfect Smoked Chicken Patties

Preparation time: 20 minutes
Cooking time: 50 minutes
Servings: 6
Ingredients:
- 2 lb. ground chicken breast

- 2/3 cup minced onion
- 1 Tbsp. cilantro (chopped)
- 2 Tbsp. fresh parsley, finely chopped
- 2 Tbsp. olive oil
- 1/8 tsp. crushed red pepper flakes, or to taste
- 1/2 tsp. ground cumin
- 2 Tbsp. fresh lemon juice
- 3/4 tsp. kosher salt
- 2 tsp. paprika
- Hamburger buns for serving

Directions:
1. In a bowl combine all ingredients from the list.
2. Using your hands, mix well. Form mixture into 6 patties. Refrigerate until ready to grill (about 30 minutes).
3. Start your pellet grill on SMOKE with the lid open until the fire is established). Set the temperature to 350℉ and preheat, lid closed, for 10 to 15 minutes.
4. Arrange chicken patties on the grill rack and cook for 35 to 40 minutes turning once.
5. Serve hot with hamburger buns and your favorite condiments.

Nutrition:
Calories: 258
Carbohydrates: 2.5g
Fat: 9.4g
Fiber: 0.6g
Protein: 39g

56. Grilled Chicken with Pineapple

Preparation Time: 1 hour
Cooking time: 1 hr. 15 minutes
Servings: 6

Ingredients:
- 2 lbs. Chicken tenders
- 1 c. sweet chili sauce
- ¼ c. fresh pineapple juice
- ¼ c. honey

Directions:
1. Combine the honey, pineapple juice, and sweet chili sauce in a medium bowl. Whisk together thoroughly.
2. Put ¼ cup of the mixture to one side.
3. Coat the chicken in the sauce.
4. Place a lid over the bowl and leave it in the fridge for 30 minutes to marinate.
5. Heat the grill to high heat.
6. Separate the chicken from the marinade and grill for 5 minutes on each side.
7. Use the reserved sauce to brush over the chicken.
8. Continue to grill for a further 1 minute on each side.
9. Take the chicken off the grill and let it rest for 5 minutes before servings.

Nutrition:
Calories: 270
Fat: 2 g,
Carbohydrates: 25 g,
Protein: 33 g

Chapter 8.   Beef Recipes

57. Smoked and Pulled Beef

Preparation Time: 10 minutes
Cooking Time: 6 hours
Servings: 6
Ingredients:

- 4 lb. beef sirloin tip roast
- 1/2 cup BBQ rub
- 2 bottles of amber beer
- 1 bottle barbecues sauce

Directions:
1. Turn your wood pellet grill on smoke setting then trim excess fat from the steak.
2. Coat the steak with BBQ rub and let it smoke on the grill for 1 hour.
3. Continue cooking and flipping the steak for the next 3 hours. Transfer the steak to a braising vessel. Add the beers.
4. Braise the beef until tender then transfer to a platter reserving 2 cups of cooking liquid.
5. Use a pair of forks to shred the beef and return it to the pan. Add the reserved liquid and barbecue sauce. Stir well and keep warm before serving.
6. Enjoy.

Nutrition:
Calories 829,
Total fat 46g,
Saturated fat 18g,
 Total carbs 4g,
Net carbs 4g,
Protein 86g,
 Sugar 0g,
Fiber 0g,
Sodium: 181mg

58. Wood Pellet Smoked Beef Jerky

Preparation Time: 15 minutes
Cooking Time: 5 hours
Servings: 10
Ingredients:

- 3 lb. sirloin steaks, sliced into 1/4-inch thickness
- 2 cups soy sauce
- 1/2 cup brown sugar
- 1 cup pineapple juice
- 2 tbsp. sriracha
- 2 tbsp. red pepper flake
- 2 tbsp. hoisin
- 2 tbsp. onion powder
- 2 tbsp. rice wine vinegar
- 2 tbsp. garlic, minced

Directions:
1. Mix all the ingredients in a zip lock-bag. Seal the bag and mix until the beef is well coated. Ensure you get as much air as possible from the zip-lock bag.
2. Put the bag in the fridge overnight to let marinate. Remove the bag from the fridge 1 hour before cooking.
3. Start your wood pallet grill and set it to smoke. Layout the meat on the grill with half-inch space between them.
4. Let them cook for 5 hours while turning after every 2-1/2 hours.
5. Transfer from the grill and let cool for 30 minutes before serving.
6. Enjoy.

Nutrition:
Calories 80,
Total fat 1g,
Saturated fat 0g,
Total carbs 5g,
 Net carbs 5g,
Protein 14g,
Sugar 5g,
Fiber 0g,
Sodium: 650mg

59. Reverse Seared Flank Steak

Preparation Time: 10 minutes
Cooking Time: 10 minutes
Servings: 2
Ingredients:

- 1.5 lb. Flanks steak
- 1 tbsp. salt
- 1/2 onion powder
- 1/4 tbsp. garlic powder
- 1/2 black pepper, coarsely ground

Directions:
1. Preheat your wood pellet grill to 225f
2. In a mixing bowl, mix salt, onion powder, garlic powder, and pepper. Generously rub the steak with the mixture.
3. Place the steaks on the preheated grill, close the lid, and let the steak cook.
4. Crank up the grill to high then let it heat. The steak should be off the grill and tented with foil to keep it warm.
5. Once the grill is heated up to 450°F, place the steak back and grill for 3 minutes per side.
6. Remove from heat, pat with butter, and serve. Enjoy.

Nutrition:
Calories 112,
Total fat 5g,
Saturated fat 2g,
Total carbs 1g,
Net carbs 1g,
Protein 16g,
Sugar 0g,
 Fiber 0g,

Sodium: 737mg

60. Smoked Midnight Brisket

Preparation Time: 15 minutes
Cooking Time: 12 hours
Servings: 6
Ingredients:

- 1 tbsp. Worcestershire sauce
- 1 tbsp. beef Rub
- 1 tbsp. Chicken rub
- 1 tbsp. Blackened Saskatchewan rub
- 5 lb. flat cut brisket
- 1 cup beef broth

Directions:

1. Rub the sauce and rubs in a mixing bowl then rub the mixture on the meat.
2. Preheat your grill to 180°F with the lid closed for 15 minutes. You can use super smoke if you desire.
3. Place the meat on the grill and grill for 6 hours or until the internal temperature reaches 160°F.
4. Remove the meat from the grill and double wrap it with foil.
5. Add beef broth and return to grill with the temperature increased to 225°F. Cook for 4 hours or until the internal temperature reaches 204°F.
6. Remove from the grill and let rest for 30 minutes. Serve and enjoy with your favorite BBQ sauce.

Nutrition:
Calories 200,
Total fat 14g,
Saturated fat 6g,
Total carbs 3g,

Net carbs 3g,
Protein 14g,
Sugar 0g,
Fiber 0g,
Sodium: 680mg

61. Grilled Butter Basted Porterhouse Steak

Preparation Time: 10 minutes
Cooking Time: 40 minutes
Servings: 4
Ingredients:

- 4 tbsp. butter, melted
- 2 tbsp. Worcestershire sauce
- 2 tbsp. Dijon mustard
- Prime rib rub

Directions:

1. Set your wood pellet grill to 225°F with the lid closed for 15 minutes.
2. In a mixing bowl, mix butter, sauce, Dijon mustard until smooth. Brush the mixture on the meat then season with the rub.
3. Arrange the meat on the grill grate and cook for 30 minutes.
4. Use tongs to transfer the meat to a pattern then increase the heat to high.
5. Return the meat to the grill grate to grill until your desired doneness is achieved.
6. Baste with the butter mixture again if you desire and let rest for 3 minutes before serving. Enjoy.

Nutrition:
Calories 726,
Total fat 62g,
Saturated fat 37g,
Total carbs 5g,
Net carbs 4g,
Protein 36g,
Sugar 1g,

Fiber 1g,
Sodium: 97mg,
Potassium 608mg

62. Cocoa Crusted Grilled Flank steak

Preparation Time: 10 minutes
Cooking Time: 6 minutes
Servings: 6
Ingredients:

- 1 tbsp. cocoa powder
- 2 tbsp. chili powder
- 1 tbsp. chipotle chili powder
- 1/2 tbsp. garlic powder
- 1/2 tbsp. onion powder
- 1-1/2 tbsp. brown sugar
- 1 tbsp. cumin
- 1 tbsp. smoked paprika
- 1 tbsp. kosher salt
- 1/2 tbsp. black pepper
- Olive oil
- 4 lb. Flank steak

Directions:

1. Whisk together cocoa, chili powder, garlic powder, onion powder, sugar, cumin, paprika, salt, and pepper in a mixing bowl.
2. Drizzle the steak with oil then rub with the cocoa mixture on both sides.
3. Preheat your wood pellet grill for 15 minutes with the lid closed.
4. Cook the meat on the grill grate for 5 minutes or until the internal temperature reaches 135°F.
5. Remove the meat from the grill and let it cool for 15 minutes to allow the juices to redistribute.

6. Slice the meat against the grain and on a sharp diagonal.

7. Serve and enjoy.

Nutrition:
Calories 420,
Total fat 26g,
Saturated fat 8g,
Total carbs 21g,
Net carbs 13g,
 Protein 3g,
Sugar 7g,
 Fiber 8g,
Sodium: 2410mg

63. Wood Pellet Grill Prime Rib Roast

Preparation Time: 10 minutes
Cooking Time: 4 hours
Servings: 10
Ingredients:
• 7 lb. bone prime rib roast
• prime rib rub
Directions:
1. Coat the roast generously with the rub then wrap in a plastic wrap. Let sit in the fridge for 24 hours to marinate.

2. Set the temperatures to 500°F.to to preheat with the lid closed for 15 minutes.

3. Place the rib directly on the grill fat side up and cook for 30 minutes.

4. Reduce the temperature to 300°F and cook for 4 hours or until the internal temperature is 120°F-rare, 130°F-medium rare, 140°F-medium, and 150°F-well done.

5. Remove from the grill and let rest for 30 minutes then serve and enjoy.

Nutrition:
Calories 290,

Total fat 23g,
Saturated fat 9.3g,
Protein 19g,
Sodium: 54mg,
Potassium 275mg

64. Smoked Longhorn Cowboy Tri-Tip

Preparation Time: 10 minutes
Cooking Time: 4 hours
Servings: 7
Ingredients:
• 3 lb. tri-tip roast 1/8 cup coffee, ground
• 1/4 cup beef rub
Directions:
1. Preheat the grill to 180°F with the lid closed for 15 minutes. Meanwhile, rub the roast with coffee and beef rub. Place the roast on the grill grate and smoke for 3 hours. Remove the roast from the grill and double wrap it with foil. Increase the temperature to 275°F. Return the meat to the grill and let cook for 90 minutes or until the internal temperature reaches 135°F.

2. Remove from the grill, unwrap it and let rest for 10 minutes before serving.

Nutrition:
Calories 245,
 Total fat 14g,
Saturated fat 4g,
Protein 23g,
Sodium: 80mg

65. Wood Pellet Grill Teriyaki Beef Jerky

Preparation Time: 10 minutes
Cooking Time: 5 hours
Servings: 6
Ingredients:
• 3 cups soy sauce
• 2 cups brown sugar

• 3 garlic cloves
• 2-inch ginger knob, peeled and chopped
• 1 tbsp. sesame oil
• 4 lb. beef, skirt steak
Directions:
1. Place all the ingredients except the meat in a food processor. Pulse until well mixed.

2. Trim any excess fat from the meat and slice into 1/4-inch slices. Add the steak with the marinade into a zip lock bag and let marinate for 12-24 hours in a fridge.

3. Set the wood pellet grill to smoke and let preheat for 5 minutes.

4. Arrange the steaks on the grill leaving a space between each. Let smoke for 5 hours.

5. Remove the steak from the grill and serve when warm.

Nutrition:
Calories 80,
Total fat 1g,
Saturated fat 0g,
Total Carbs 7g,
Net Carbs 0g,
Protein 11g,
Sugar 6g,
Fiber 0g,
Sodium: 390mg

66. Grilled Butter Basted Rib-eye

Preparation Time: 20 minutes
Cooking Time: 25 minutes
Servings: 4
Ingredients:
• 2 rib-eye steaks, bone-in
• Salt to taste
• Pepper to taste
• 4 tbsp. butter, unsalted

Directions:
1. Mix steak, salt, and pepper in a zip-lock bag. Seal the bag and mix until the beef is well coated. Ensure you get as much air as possible from the zip-lock bag.
2. Set the wood pellet grill temperature to high with the lid closed for 15 minutes. Place a cast-iron into the grill.
3. Place the steaks on the hottest spot of the grill and cook for 5 minutes with the lid closed.
4. Open the lid and add butter to the skillet. When it's almost melted place the steak on the skillet with the grilled side up.
5. Cook for 5 minutes while busting the meat with butter. Close the lid and cook until the internal temperature is 130°F.
6. Remove the steak from the skillet and let rest for 10 minutes before enjoying with the reserved butter.
Nutrition:
Calories 745,
Total fat 65g,
Saturated fat 32g,
Total Carbs 5g,
Net Carbs 5g,
Protein 35g,

67. Wood Pellet Smoked Brisket
Preparation Time: 20 minutes
Cooking Time: 9 hours
Servings: 10
Ingredients:
- 2 tbsp. garlic powder
- 2 tbsp. onion powder
- 2 tbsp. paprika
- 2 tbsp. chili powder

- 1/3 cup salt
- 1/3 cup black pepper
- 12 lb. whole packer brisket, trimmed
- 1-1/2 cup beef broth
Directions:
1. Set your wood pellet temperature to 225°F. Let preheat for 15 minutes with the lid closed.
2. Meanwhile, mix garlic, onion, paprika, chili, salt, and pepper in a mixing bowl.
3. Season the brisket generously on all sides.
4. Place the meat on the grill with the fat side down and let it cool until the internal temperature reaches 160°F. Remove the meat from the grill and double wrap it with foil. Return it to the grill and cook until the internal temperature reaches 204°F.
5. Remove from the grill, unwrap the brisket, and let sit for 15 minutes.
6. Slice and serve.
Nutrition:
Calories 270,
Total fat 20g,
Saturated fat 8g,
Total Carbs 3g,
Net Carbs 3g,
Protein 20g,
Sugar 1g,
Fiber 0g,
Sodium: 1220mg

68. Beef Jerky
Preparation Time: 15 minutes
Cooking Time: 5 hours
Servings: 10
Ingredients:
- 3 lb. sirloin steaks
- 2 cups soy sauce

- 1 cup pineapple juice
- 1/2 cup brown sugar
- 2 tbsp. sriracha
- 2 tbsp. hoisin
- 2 tbsp. red pepper flake
- 2 tbsp. rice wine vinegar
- 2 tbsp. onion powder
Directions:
1. Mix the marinade in a zip lock bag and add the beef. Mix until well coated and remove as much air as possible.
2. Place the bag in a fridge and let marinate overnight or for 6 hours. Remove the bag from the fridge an hour before cooking 3) Startup the wood pellet and set it on the smoking settings or at 1900F.
3. Lay the meat on the grill leaving a half-inch space between the pieces. Let cool for 5 hours and turn after 2 hours.
4. Remove from the grill and let cool. Serve or refrigerate
Nutrition:
Calories 309,
Total fat 7g,
Saturated fat 3g,
Total carbs 20g,
Net carbs 19g
Protein 34g,
Sugars 15g,
Fiber 1g,
Sodium 2832mg

69. Smoked Beef Roast
Preparation Time: 10 minutes
Cooking Time: 6 hours
Servings: 6
Ingredients:
- 1-3/4 lb. beef sirloin tip roast
- 1/2 cup BBQ rub
- 2 bottles of amber beer

- 1 bottle BBQ sauce

Directions:

1. Turn the onto the smoke setting.
2. Transfer the beef to a pan and add the beer. The beef should be 1/2 way covered.
3. Braise the beef until fork tender. It will take 3 hours on the stovetop and 60 minutes on the instant pot.
4. Remove the beef from the ban and reserve 1 cup of the cooking liquid.
5. Use 2 forks to shred the beef into small pieces then return to the pan with the reserved braising liquid.
6. Add BBQ sauce and stir well then keep warm until serving. You can also reheat if it gets cold.

Nutrition:

Calories 829,
Total fat 46g,
Saturated fat 18g,
Total carbs 4g,
Net carbs 4g,
Protein 86g,
Sugars 0g,
Fiber 0g,
Sodium 181mmg

70. Beef Tenderloin

Preparation Time: 10 minutes
Cooking Time: 45 minutes
Servings: 6
Ingredients:

- 4 lb. beef tenderloin
- 3 tbsp. steak rub
- 1 tbsp. kosher salt

Directions:

1. Preheat to high heat. Meanwhile, trim excess fat from the beef and cut it into 3 pieces. Coat the steak with rub and kosher salt. Place it on the grill.

Close the lid and cook for 10 minutes. Open the lid, flip the beef and cook for 10 more minutes. Reduce the temperature of the grill to 2250F and smoke the beef until the internal temperature reaches 1300F.

2. Remove the beef from the grill and let rest for 15 minutes before slicing and serving.

Nutrition:

Calories 999,
Total fat 76g,
Saturated fat 30g,
Protein 74g,
Sodium 1234mmg

71. New York Strip

Preparation Time: 5 minutes
Cooking Time: 15 minutes
Servings: 6
Ingredients:

- 3 New York strips
- Salt and pepper

Directions:

1. If the steak is in the fridge, remove it 30 minutes before cooking.
2. Preheat the to 4500F.
3. Meanwhile, season the steak generously with salt and pepper. Place it on the grill and let it cook for 5 minutes per side or until the internal temperature reaches 1280F.
4. Remove the steak from the grill and let it rest for 10 minutes.

Nutrition:

Calories 198,
Total fat 14g,
Saturated fat 6g,
Protein 17g,
Sodium 115mg

72. Stuffed Peppers

Preparation Time: 20 minutes
Cooking Time: 5 minutes
Servings: 6
Ingredients:

- 3 bell peppers, sliced in halves
- 1 lb. ground beef, lean
- 1 onion, chopped
- 1/2 tbsp. red pepper flakes
- 1/2 tbsp. salt
- 1/4 tbsp. pepper
- 1/2 tbsp. garlic powder
- 1/2 tbsp. onion powder
- 1/2 cup white rice
- 15 oz. stewed tomatoes
- 8 oz. tomato sauce
- 6 cups cabbage, shredded
- 1-1/2 cup water
- 2 cups cheddar cheese

Directions:

1. Arrange the pepper halves on a baking tray and set aside.
2. Preheat your grill to 3250F.
3. Brown the meat in a large skillet. Add onions, pepper flakes, salt, pepper garlic, and onion and cook until the meat is well cooked.
4. Add rice, stewed tomatoes, tomato sauce, cabbage, and water.
5. Cover and simmer until the rice is well cooked, the cabbage is tender and there is no water in the rice.
6. Place the cooked beef mixture in the pepper halves and top with cheese.

7. Place in the grill and cook for 30 minutes.

8. Serve immediately and enjoy it.

Nutrition:

Calories 422,

Total fat 22g,

Saturated fat 11g,

Total carbs 24g,

Net carbs 19g

Protein 34g,

Sugars 11g,

Fiber 5g,

Sodium 855mg

73. Prime Rib Roast

Preparation Time: 10 minutes
Cooking Time: 2 hours
Servings: 8
Ingredients:

- 5 lb. rib roast, boneless
- 4 tbsp. salt
- 1 tbsp. black pepper
- 1-1/2 tbsp. onion powder
- 1 tbsp. granulated garlic
- 1 tbsp. rosemary
- 1 cup chopped onion
- 1/2 cup carrots, chopped
- 1/2 cup celery, chopped
- 2 cups beef broth

Directions:

1. Remove the beef from the fridge 1 hour before cooking.

2. Preheat the Wood Pellet to 2500F.

3. In a small mixing bowl, mix salt, pepper, onion, garlic, and rosemary to create your rub.

4. Generously coat the roast with the rub and set it aside.

5. Combine chopped onions, carrots, and celery in a cake pan then place the bee on top.

6. Place the cake pan in the middle of the and cook for 1 hour.

7. Pour the beef broth at the bottom of the cake pan and cook until the internal temperature reaches 1200F.

8. Remove the cake pan from the and let rest for 20 minutes before slicing the meat.

9. Pour the cooking juice through a strainer, and then skim off any fat at the top.

10. Serve the roast with the cooking juices.

Nutrition:

Calories 721,

Total fat 60g,

Saturated fat 18g,

Total carbs 3g,

Net carbs 2g

Protein 43g,

Sugars 1g,

Fiber 1g,

Sodium 2450mmg

74. Fine Indian Smoked T-Bone

Preparation Time: 20 minutes
Cooking Time: 45 minutes
Servings: 12
Ingredients:

- 1-pound beef tenderloin, cut into 1-inch cubes
- 2 pounds strip steak, cut into 1-inch cubes
- 1 large onion, cut into 1-inch cubes
- 1 bell pepper, cut into 1-inch cubes
- 1 zucchini, cut into 1-inch cubes
- 10 ounces cherry tomatoes
- ¼ cup olive oil
- ½ cup steak seasoning

Directions:

1. Take a large bowl and add tenderloin, strip steak, onion, zucchini, bell pepper, tomatoes and mix well with olive oil

2. Season with steak seasoning and stir until the meat has been coated well

3. Cover the meat and allow it to refrigerate for 4-8 hours

4. Preheat your smoker to 225 degrees Fahrenheit using your desired wood

5. Make the kebabs by skewering meat and veggies alternatively Make sure, to begin with, meat and end with meat Transfer the skewers to your smoker rack and smoke for 45 minutes

6. Remove once the internal temperature reaches 135 degrees Fahrenheit (for a RARE finish)

7. Serve and enjoy!

Nutrition:

Calories: 559

Fats: 5g

Carbs: 57g

Fiber: 1g

75. The South Barbacoa

Preparation Time: 15 minutes
Cooking Time: 3 hours
Servings: 10
Ingredients:

- 1 and ½ teaspoon pepper

- 1 tablespoon dried oregano
- 1 and ½ teaspoon cayenne pepper
- 1 and ½ teaspoon chili powder
- 1 and ½ teaspoon garlic powder
- 1 teaspoon ground cumin
- 1 teaspoon salt
- 3 pounds boneless beef chuck roast

Directions:

1. Add dampened hickory wood to your smoker and preheat to 200 degrees Fahrenheit
2. Take a small bowl and add oregano, cayenne pepper, black pepper, garlic powder, chili powder, cumin, salt, and seasoned salt
3. Mix well
4. Dip the chuck roast into your mixing bowl and rub the spice mix all over
5. Transfer the meat to your smoker and smoker for 1 and a ½ hours
6. Make sure to turn the meat after every 30 minutes, if you see less smoke formation, add more Pellets after every 30 minutes as well
7. Once the meat shows a dark red color with darkened edges, transfer the meat to a roasting pan and seal it tightly with an aluminum foil
8. Preheat your oven to 325 degrees Fahrenheit
9. Transfer the meat to your oven and bake for 1 and a ½ hours more
10. Shred the meat using two forks and serve!

Nutrition:
Calories: 559
Fats: 5g
Carbs: 57g
Fiber: 1g

Chapter 9.   Pork Recipes

76. Smoked Pork Ribs Black Pepper

Preparation time: 30 minutes
Cooking Time: 6 Hours
Servings: 1
Ingredients:
- Pork Baby Back Ribs (6-lbs., 2.7-kgs)
- Salt – ½ cup
- Black pepper – ¾ cup
- Sweet smoked paprika – 1 tablespoon
- Sugar – 3 tablespoons
- Mustard powder – 1 tablespoon

Directions:
1. Combine salt with black pepper, sweet smoked paprika, sugar, and mustard powder. Stir until mixed.
2. Rub the pork baby ribs with the salt mixture then place in disposable aluminum pan. Set aside.
3. Preheat the smoker to 225°F (107°C) with charcoal and peach wood chips then wait until it reaches the desired temperature.
4. Once the smoker is ready, place the disposable aluminum pan in the smoker.
5. Smoke the pork baby ribs for 6 hours or until the internal temperature has reached 205°F (96°C).
6. Remove the smoked pork ribs from the smoker then transfer to a serving dish.
7. Serve and enjoy.

Nutrition:
Carbohydrates: 4g
Protein: 86 g
Fat: 46 g
Sodium: 181 mg
Cholesterol: 295 mg

77. Smoked Brown Pork Butt with Apple Injection

Preparation time: 30 minutes
Cooking Time: 6 Hours
Servings: 10
Ingredients:
- Pork Butt (6-lbs., 2.7-kgs)
- The Liquid Injection
- Chicken stock – 1 ¼ cups
- Apple juice – 1 ½ cups
- Apple cider vinegar – 3 tablespoons
- Barbecue sauce – 3 tablespoons
- Worcestershire sauce – 1 ½ tablespoons
- The Rub
- Brown sugar – 3 tablespoons
- Salt – 3 tablespoons
- Smoked paprika – 2 tablespoons
- Onion powder – 2 ¼ tablespoons
- Garlic powder – 2 tablespoons
- Oregano – ¾ tablespoon
- Cumin – ¾ teaspoon
- Black pepper – ¾ teaspoon

Directions:
1. Pour chicken broth into a saucepan then add apple juice, apple cider vinegar, barbecue sauce, and Worcestershire sauce into the saucepan.
2. Bring to a simmer and stir until incorporated.
3. Remove from heat and let it cool for approximately 30 minutes. Set aside.
4. Combine the rub ingredients then mix well.
5. Preheat the smoker to 225°F (107°C) with charcoal and peach wood chips. Use the indirect heat.
6. While waiting for the smoker, inject the pork butt with the liquid injection then coat the pork butt with the rub mixture.
7. Once the smoker has reached the desired temperature, place the seasoned pork butt in the smoker.
8. Smoke the pork butt for 12 hours and check the smoke once every hour. Add more soaked peach wood chips if it is necessary.
9. When the pork butt is ready or the internal temperature has reached 205°F (96°C), remove the smoked pork butt from the smoker then transfer to a serving dish.
10. Let the smoked pork butt cool for a few minutes then chop or pull the pork.
11. Serve and enjoy.

Nutrition:
Carbohydrates: 4g
Protein: 86 g
Fat: 46 g
Sodium: 181 mg
Cholesterol: 295 mg

78. Refreshing Smoked Pork Tenderloin with Orange Glaze

Preparation time: 30 minutes
Cooking Time: 6 Hours

Servings: 10
Ingredients:
- Pork Tenderloin (6-lbs., 2.7-kgs)
- The Glaze
- Unsweetened orange juice – 1 ½ cups
- Sugar – 1 cup
- Olive oil – 1 ¼ cups

Directions:
1. Preheat the smoker to 225°F (107°C) with charcoal and peach wood chips. Use the indirect heat.
2. Pour orange juice into a saucepan then bring to boil.
3. Once it is boiled, stir in sugar and stir until the sugar is completely dissolved.
4. When the mixture is incorporated, remove from heat then let it cool for a few minutes.
5. After that, stir in olive oil then mix well.
6. Place the pork loin in a disposable aluminum pan then drizzle the orange juice mixture over the pork.
7. Once the smoker has reached the desired temperature, place the pan in the smoker.
8. Smoke the pork tenderloin for about 6 hours or until the internal temperature has reached 145°F (63°C).
9. When it is done, remove the pan from the smoker and transfer to a serving dish together with the liquid.
10. Cut the pork tenderloin into thick slices then serve.
11. Enjoy!

Nutrition:
Carbohydrates: 4g

Protein: 86 g
Fat: 46 g
Sodium: 181 mg
Cholesterol: 295 mg

79. Simple Smoked Garlic Pork Chop

Preparation time: 30 minutes
Cooking Time: 6 Hours
Servings: 10
Ingredients:
- Pork Chops (6-lbs., 2.7-kgs)
- Olive oil – ¼ cup
- The Rub
- Salt – ¼ cup
- Pepper – 2 tablespoons
- Garlic powder – 2 tablespoons
- Minced garlic – 2 tablespoons

Directions:
1. Preheat the smoker to 250°F (121°C) with charcoal and hickory wood chips. Use the indirect heat.
2. Rub the pork chops with salt, pepper, garlic powder, and minced garlic. Set aside.
3. Preheat a skillet over medium heat then pour olive oil into the skillet.
4. Once the olive oil is hot, stir in the seasoned pork chops then sauté until just wilted.
5. Transfer the sautéed pork chops to a disposable aluminum pan then place in the smoker.
6. Smoke the pork chops for 5 hours and check the smoke regularly. Add more soaked hickory wood chips if it is necessary.

7. Once the internal temperature has reached 145°F (63°C), take the smoked pork chops from the smoker.
8. Transfer the smoked pork chops to a serving dish and serve with any kinds of fruit and vegetable, as you desired.
9. Enjoy.

Nutrition:
Carbohydrates: 4g
Protein: 86 g
Fat: 46 g
Sodium: 181 mg
Cholesterol: 295 mg

80. Smoked Pork Shoulder with Herbs

Preparation time: 15 minutes
Cooking Time: 6 Hours
Servings: 1
Ingredients:
- Boneless Pork Shoulder (6-lbs., 2.7-kgs)
- The Rub
- Salt – 2 tablespoons
- Turmeric – 1 ½ tablespoons
- Cumin – ¾ tablespoon
- Coriander – ¾ tablespoon
- Sugar – ½ tablespoon
- Cardamom – 1 teaspoon

Directions:
- Preheat the smoker to 250°F (121°C) with charcoal and hickory wood chips. Use the indirect heat.
- Place salt, turmeric, cumin, coriander, sugar, and cardamom in a bowl then mix well.
- Rub the pork shoulder with the spice mixture then

place in a disposable aluminum pan.

• Place the pan in the smoker then smoke the pork shoulder for 6 hours. Add more charcoal and wood chips if it is needed.

• Check the smoked pork shoulder and when the internal temperature has reached 145°F (63°C), take the smoked pork chops from the smoker.

• Place the smoked pork shoulder on a flat surface then let it cool for a few minutes.

• Shred the smoked pork shoulder then transfer to a serving dish.

• Serve and enjoy.

Nutrition:
Carbohydrates: 4g
Protein: 46 g
Fat: 16 g
Sodium: 28 mg
Cholesterol: 95 mg

81. Sweet Smoked Rabbit Honey

Preparation time: 30 minutes
Cooking Time: 12 Hours
Servings: 10
Ingredients:

• Rabbits 2 (6-lbs., 2.7-kgs)
• The Rub
• Minced garlic – 3 tablespoons
• Garlic powder – 2 tablespoons
• Lemon juice – 3 tablespoons
• Salt – 2 tablespoons
• Pepper – 2 ½ tablespoons
• The Glaze

• Honey – ¼ cup
• Olive oil – 2 tablespoons

Directions:
1. Rub the rabbits with minced garlic; garlic powder, lemon juice, salt, and pepper then cover with plastic wrap.
2. Refrigerate the seasoned rabbits for about 8 hours until the spice is completely absorbed to the rabbits.
3. Preheat a smoker to 225°F (107°C) with charcoal and hickory wood chips.
4. When the smoker is ready, unwrap the rabbits then place in the smoker.
5. Smoke the rabbits for 3 hours and check once every hour. Add more charcoal and wood chips to keep the smoke.
6. After 3 hours, remove the rabbits from the smoker then brush with olive oil and honey mixture.
7. Place the glazed rabbits in a disposable aluminum pan then return back to the smoker.
8. Smoke the rabbits for another 3 hours then brush with remaining honey and olive oil mixture once every hour.
9. When the smoked rabbits are done, remove from the smoker and transfer to a serving dish.
10. Cut the rabbits into pieces then serve.
11. Enjoy!

Nutrition:
Carbohydrates: 4g
Protein: 46 g
Fat: 16 g
Sodium: 28 mg
Cholesterol: 95 mg

82. Smoked Rabbit with Dry Rub

Preparation time: 30 minutes
Cooking Time: 7 Hours
Servings: 5
Ingredients:

• Rabbits 2 (6-lbs., 2.7-kgs)
• The Rub
• Paprika – 1 cup
• Cayenne pepper – ¼ cup
• Black pepper – ½ cup
• Garlic powder – ¾ cup
• Onion powder – ¼ cup
• Salt – ½ cup
• Dried oregano – ¼ cup
• Thyme – ¼ cup

Directions:
1. Combine all of the dry rub ingredients then mix well.
2. Cut the rabbits into pieces then rub with the spice mixture.
3. Marinate the spiced rabbits for 3 hours—more time is good but 3 hours is enough.
4. Preheat a smoker to 225°F (107°C) then place the spiced rabbits in the smoker.
5. Smoke the rabbits for four hours and when the internal temperature has reached165°F (74°C), remove the smoked rabbits from the smoker.
6. Place the smoked rabbits on a serving dish then enjoy.

Nutrition:
Carbohydrates: 4g
Protein: 46 g
Fat: 16 g
Sodium: 28 mg
Cholesterol: 95 mg

83. The Beer Smoked Rabbit

Preparation time: 30 minutes
Cooking Time: 5 Hours
Servings: 10
Ingredients:

- Rabbits 2 (6-lbs., 2.7-kgs)
- The Rub
- Minced garlic – ¼ cup
- Salt – 2 ½ tablespoons
- The Glaze
- Beer – 3 cups

Directions:
1. Combine salt and minced garlic then rub the rabbits with the mixture. Set aside.
2. Preheat a smoker to 225°F (107°C) with charcoal and hickory wood chips. Prepare indirect smoke.
3. Once the smoker has reached the desired temperature, place the seasoned rabbits in the smoker.
4. Check the smoke and add more wood chips if it is needed.
5. Smoke the rabbit for 3 hours and brush with beer every 15 minutes.
6. Once the rabbits are done, remove from the smoker then check whether the internal temperature has reached 165°F (74°C).
7. Take the rabbits out from the smoker then cut the smoked rabbits into pieces.
8. Transfer to a serving dish then serve.
9. Enjoy!
Nutrition:
Carbohydrates: 4g
Protein: 46 g
Fat: 16 g
Sodium: 28 mg
Cholesterol: 95 mg

84. Bacon-Wrapped Little Smokies

Preparation time: 30 minutes
Cooking Time: 6 Hours
Servings: 1
Ingredients:

- 1 lb. of bacon with strips cut into halves
- 14 oz. of cocktail sausages
- ½ cup of brown sugar

Directions:
1. Take a clean flat surface and lay bacon strips over it
2. Now use a rolling point and roll them out so that they get an even thickness
3. Now wrap every sausage in ½ strip of bacon and secure it firmly with a toothpick
4. Place this wrapped sausages in a casserole dish and cover it with brown sugar
5. Keep it in the fridge and let it sit for half an hour
6. When it is ready to cook, fire the grill and set the temperature to 350 degrees F
7. Now lay these sausages on the parchment-lined cookie sheet and place it on the grill grate
8. Cook it for almost half an hour until it is crisp
9. Serve and enjoy
Nutrition:
Carbohydrates: 4g
Protein: 46 g
Fat: 16 g
Sodium: 28 mg
Cholesterol: 95 mg

85. Grilled Lemon Pepper Pork Tenderloin

Preparation time: 30 minutes
Cooking Time: 5 Hours
Servings: 1
Ingredients:

- 2 lbs. of pork tenderloin
- 1 clove of minced garlic
- 1 teaspoon of minced fresh parsley
- 1 teaspoon of lemon juice
- ½ teaspoon of kosher salt
- 2 lemon zest
- 2 tablespoon of olive oil
- 1 teaspoon of black pepper

Directions:
1. Take a small bowl and whisk all ingredients except pork tenderloin
2. Now take the tenderloin and trim all the silver skin and get rid of the excess fat
3. Place it in a large zip lock bah
4. Now pour the marinade over the tenderloin and close the zip
5. Transfer it to the fridge and marinate it for approx. 2 hours
6. Set the grill to preheat and keep the temperature to 375 degrees F
7. Remove the tenderloins from the bag and then get rid of the marinade
8. When the grill has turned hot, put it on the grill grate and then cook for 20

minutes flipping it midway. Make sure the temperature reaches 145 degrees F

9. Remove from the heat, add sauce and let it rest for approx. 10 minutes

10. Slice and serve

Nutrition:

Carbohydrates: 4g

Protein: 46 g

Fat: 16 g

Sodium: 28 mg

Cholesterol: 95 mg

86. BBQ Baked Beans

Preparation time: 30 minutes

Cooking Time: 7 Hours

Servings: 1

Ingredients:

- 1 lb. of chopped bacon
- 4 cans of pork & beans
- 1 diced green bell pepper
- 1 diced yellow onion
- 1/2 tablespoon onion powder
- 1/2 tablespoon garlic powder
- 1 tablespoon black pepper
- 1/2 tablespoon kosher salt
- 2 tablespoon dry mustard
- 1 cup of ketchup

Directions:

1. Take a sauté pan and place bacon in it over medium heat

2. Cook it thoroughly until the bacon is crisp and the fat has been rendered

3. Strain the excess fat from bacon while keeping 2 tablespoons reserved and then set the bacon aside

4. Keep the reserved fat in the sauté pan and then add pepper along with onion

5. Now sauté it for 10 minutes approx. until the onions turn translucent and the peppers become tender

6. Remove from the heat source and set it aside

7. When it is ready to cook, prepare the grill for preheating and set the temperature to 350 degrees F

8. Take a casserole dish and mix cooked bacon, beans, peppers and onion along with their leftover ingredients. Mix well to combine thoroughly

9. Now cover the casserole with aluminum foil and place it on the grill grate

10. Cook for an hour making sure to stir it occasionally till the sauce has thickened

11. Let it rest for 15 minutes

12. Serve and enjoy

Nutrition:

Carbohydrates: 24g

Protein: 16 g

Fat: 66 g

Sodium: 38 mg

Cholesterol: 95 mg

87. Bacon Grilled Cheese Sandwich

Preparation time: 30 minutes

Cooking Time: 4 Hours

Servings: 1

Ingredients:

- 1 lb. of cooked apple wood bacon slices; smoked
- 9 slices of Texas toast
- 16 slices of cheddar cheese
- Mayonnaise

- Butter

Directions:

1. Set the grill on pre-heat by pushing the temperature to 350 degrees F

2. Now take the bread and lather it with mayonnaise

3. Place 1 piece of cheddar on a slice and then top it with two bacon slices

4. Now, again add another slice of cheese and then seal it with bread

5. Lather butter on the very top of the bread

6. When the grill has turned hot, place the grilled cheese on the grate with the buttered side facing down

7. Now spread butter on the top of the slice facing upwards

8. Cook on this side for 5 to 6 minutes until the grill marks begin to develop and the cheese starts to melt

9. Flip the sandwich and repeat it on the other side

10. Remove from the grill and serve immediately

Nutrition:

Carbohydrates: 24g

Protein: 16 g

Fat: 66 g

Sodium: 38 mg

Cholesterol: 95 mg

88. Baked Corn Dog Bites

Preparation time: 30 minutes

Cooking Time: 3 Hours

Servings: 2

Ingredients:

- 15 mini hot dogs
- 1 lightly beaten egg
- 2 cups of all-purpose flour

- 1 cup of milk at room temp
- 1/4 cup of vegetable oil
- 1 tablespoon of dried minced garlic
- 1/2 cup of yellow cornmeal
- 1 teaspoon of baking soda
- 1 tablespoon of coarse salt
- 4 teaspoons of active dry yeast
- 1/4 cup of granulated sugar
- 1/2 teaspoon of cayenne pepper
- 1/2 teaspoon of mustard powder
- Ketchup & mustard for serving

Directions:

1. Set the grill to preheat by keeping the temperature at 375 degrees F
2. Take a bowl and add yeast along with milk and sugar to it. Keep it aside for 5 minutes
3. Now, add oil along with salt, mustard powder, all-purpose flour, cayenne pepper, cornmeal, and baking soda. Mix well with a spoon and then knead to make a dough.
4. Transfer the dough to a bowl and cover it with plastic wrap to keep it aside for 45 minutes
5. The dough should approximately double in size
6. Remove the dough from the bowl and then divide it into 15 ounces

7. Keep it on a surface but make sure first to dust it with flour
8. Now make use of a rolling pin and roll the dough into 3x3" pieces.
9. Place the hot dog in the middle of the dough sheet
10. Roll it thoroughly in the dough and then press the edges to seal it and make 15 corn dog bites
11. Transfer these to a baking pan which is already lined with parchment paper
12. Brush each of them lightly with a beaten egg
13. Sprinkle minced garlic and salt
14. Bake in the smoker for approx. 30 minutes until they turn golden brownish
15. Serve with ketchup or mustard
16. Enjoy

Nutrition:
Carbohydrates: 24g
Protein: 16 g
Fat: 66 g
Sodium: 38 mg
Cholesterol: 95 mg

89. Smoked Sausage

Preparation time: 30 minutes
Cooking Time: 6 Hours
Servings: 1
Ingredients:

- 3 lbs. of ground pork
- 1 tablespoon of onion powder
- 1/2 tablespoon ground mustard
- 1/2 cup of ice water
- 1 tablespoon of garlic powder
- 1/2 tablespoon of salt

- 1 teaspoon of pink curing salt
- 4 teaspoons of black pepper
- Hog casings, soaked and rinsed in cold water

Directions:

Take a midsized bowl and combine both the meat and seasonings thoroughly in it

Now add ice water to the meat and mix with your hand making sure everything has been thoroughly mixed

Place this mixture in sausage stuffer and follow the given instructions for seamless operation

Do not overstuff the stuffer or else the casing may burst

When the meat has been stuffed, calculate the desired link length and then twist it a couple of times

Repeat the process for each link

Now set the smoker on pre-heat with the temperature reaching 225 degrees F

Place these links on the grill grate and cook for 2 or 3 hours till the temperature reaches 155 degrees F

Let the sausages rest for some time and then slice

Serve and enjoy

Nutrition:
Carbohydrates: 24g
Protein: 16 g
Fat: 66 g
Sodium: 38 mg
Cholesterol: 95 mg

90. Bacon and Sausage Bites

Preparation time: 30 minutes
Cooking Time: 45 minutes

Servings: 4
Ingredients:
- Smoked sausages - 1 pack
- Thick-cut bacon - 1 lb.
- Brown sugar - 2 cups

Directions:
1. Slice ⅓ of the sausages and wrap them around small pieces of sausage. Use a toothpick to secure them.
2. Line a baking tray with baking paper and place the small pieces of wrapped sausage on it.
3. Sprinkle brown sugar on top.
4. Preheat the wood pellet to 300 degrees.
5. Keep the baking tray with the wrapped sausages inside for 30 minutes.
6. Remove and let it stay outside for 15 minutes.
7. Serve warm with a dip of your choice.

Nutrition:
Carbohydrates: 61 g
Protein: 27 g
Fat: 30 g
Sodium: 1384 mg
Cholesterol: 82 mg

91. Grilled Pork Chops

Preparation time: 30 minutes
Cooking Time: 40 minutes
Servings: 4
Ingredients:
- Pork chops - 6, thickly cut
- Barbeque mix

Directions:
1. Preheat your wood pellet grill to 450 degrees.
2. Place the seasoned chops on the grill. Close the lid.
3. Cook for 6 minutes. The temperature should be around 145 degrees when you remove the lid.
4. Remove the pork chops.
5. Let it remain open for 5-10 minutes.
6. Serve with your choice of side dish.

Nutrition:
Carbohydrates: 0 g
Protein: 23 g
Fat: 7.8 g

92. Pigs in a Blanket

Preparation time: 10 minutes
Cooking Time: 45 minutes
Servings: 4
Ingredients:
- Pork sausages - 1 pack
- Biscuit dough - 1 pack

Directions:
1. Preheat your wood pellet grill to 350 degrees.
2. Cut the sausages and the dough into thirds.
3. Wrap the dough around the sausages. Place them on a baking sheet.
4. Grill with a closed lid for 20-25 minutes or until they look cooked.
5. Take them out when they are golden brown.
6. Serve with a dip of your choice.

Nutrition:
Protein: 9 g
Fat: 22 g
Sodium: 732 mg
Cholesterol: 44 mg

93. Smoked Bacon

Preparation time: 10 minutes
Cooking Time: 45 minutes
Servings: 4
Ingredients:
- Thick cut bacon - 1 lb.

Directions:
1. Preheat your wood pellet grill to 375 degrees.
2. Line a huge baking sheet. Place a single layer of thick-cut bacon on it.
3. Bake for 20 minutes and then flip it to the other side.
4. Cook for another 10 minutes or until the bacon is crispy.
5. Take it out and enjoy your tasty grilled bacon.

Nutrition:
Protein: 9 g
Fat: 10 g
Sodium: 500 mg
Cholesterol: 49 mg

94. Smoked, Candied, and Spicy Bacon

Preparation time: 10 minutes
Cooking Time: 45 minutes
Servings: 4
Ingredients:
- Center-cut bacon - 1 lb.
- Brown sugar - ½ cup
- Maple syrup - ½ cup
- Hot sauce - 1 tablespoon
- Pepper - ½ tablespoon

Directions:
1. Mix the maple syrup, brown sugar, hot sauce, and pepper in a bowl.
2. Preheat your wood pellet grill to 300 degrees.
3. Line a baking sheet and place the bacon slices on it.
4. Generously spread the brown sugar mix on both sides of the bacon slices.

5. Place the pan on the wood pellet grill for 20 minutes. Flip the bacon pieces.

6. Leave them for another 15 minutes until the bacon looks cooked and the sugar is melted.

7. Remove from the grill and let it stay for 10-15 minutes.

8. Voila! Your bacon candy is ready!

Nutrition:

Carbohydrates: 37 g

Protein: 9 g

Sodium: 565 mg

Cholesterol: 49 mg

95. St. Louis BBQ Ribs

Preparation time: 10 minutes

Cooking Time: 4 hours 5 minutes

Servings: 4

Ingredients:

• Pork as well as a poultry rubs - 6 oz.

• St. Louis bone in the form of pork ribs - 2 racks

• Sweet BBQ sauce - 1 bottle

• Apple juice - 8 oz.

Directions:

1. Trim the ribs and peel off their membranes from the back.

2. Apply an even coat of the poultry rub on the front and back of the ribs. Let the coat sit for at least 20 minutes. If you wish to refrigerate it, you can do so for up to 4 hours.

3. Once you are ready to cook it, preheat the pellet grill for around 15 minutes. Place the ribs on the grill grate, bone side down. Put the apple juice in an easy spray bottle and then spray it evenly on the ribs.

4. Smoke the meat for 1 hour.

5. Remove the ribs from the pellet grill and wrap them securely in aluminum foil. Ensure that there is an opening in the wrapping at one end. Pour the remaining 6 oz. of apple juice into the foil. Wrap it tightly.

6. Place the ribs on the grill again, meat side down. Smoke the meat for another 3 hours.

7. Once the ribs are done and cooked evenly, get rid of the foil. Gently brush a layer of the sauce on both sides of the ribs. Put them back on the grill to cook for another 10 minutes to ensure that the sauce is set properly.

8. Once the sauce sets, take the ribs off the pellet grill and let them rest for at least 10 minutes so that they can soak in all the juices.

9. Slice the ribs to serve and enjoy!

Nutrition:

Carbohydrates: 37 g

Protein: 9 g

Sodium: 565 mg

Cholesterol: 49 mg

Chapter 10. Lamb Recipes

96. Lamb Rack Wrapped In Apple Wood Walnut

Preparation Time: 25 Minutes
Cooking Time: 60 to 90 Minutes
Servings: 4
Ingredients:

• 3 tablespoons of Dijon mustard
• 2 pieces of garlic, chopped or 2 cups of crushed garlic
• ½ teaspoon of garlic
• ½ teaspoon kosher salt
• ½ teaspoon black pepper
• ½ teaspoon rosemary
• 1 (1½ pound) ram rack, French
• 1 cup crushed walnut

Directions:
1. Put mustard, garlic, garlic powder, salt, pepper and rosemary in a small bowl.
2. Spread the seasoning mix evenly on all sides of the lamb and sprinkle with crushed walnuts. Lightly press the walnuts by hand to attach the nuts to the meat.
3. Wrap the walnut-coated lamb rack loosely in plastic wrap and refrigerate overnight to allow the seasoning to penetrate the meat.
4. Remove the walnut-covered lamb rack from the refrigerator and let it rest for 30 minutes to reach room temperature.
5. Set the wood pellet r grill for indirect cooking and preheat to 225 ° F using apple pellets.
6. Lay the grill directly on the rack with the lamb bone down.
7. Smoke at 225 ° F until the thickest part of the ram rack reaches the desired internal temperature. This is measured with a digital instantaneous thermometer near the time listed on the chart.
8. Place the mutton under a loose foil tent for 5 minutes before eating

Nutrition: Calories: 165 Carbs: 0g Fat: 8g Protein: 20g

97. Roasted Lamb Leg

Preparation Time: 20 Minutes
Cooking Time: 1.5 Hours to 2 Hours
Servings: 6
Ingredients:

• 1 boneless leg of a lamb
• ½ cup of roasted garlic flavored extra virgin olive oil
• ¼ cup dried parsley
• 3 garlics, chopped
• 2 tablespoons of a fresh lemon juice or 1 tablespoon of lemon zest (from 1 medium lemon)
• 2 tablespoons of dried oregano
• 1 tablespoon dried rosemary
• ½ teaspoon black pepper

Directions:
1. Remove the net from the lamb's leg. Cut off grease, silver skin, and large pieces of fat.
2. In a small bowl, mix olive oil, parsley, garlic, lemon juice or zest, oregano, rosemary, and pepper.
3. Spice the inside and outside surfaces of the lamb's boneless legs.
4. Secure the boneless lamb leg using a silicone food band or butcher twine. Use a band or twine to form and maintain the basic shape of the lamb
5. Wrap the lamb loosely in plastic wrap and refrigerate overnight to allow the seasoning to penetrate the meat.
6. Remove the rum from the refrigerator and leave at room temperature for 1 hour.
7. Set up a wood pellet smoker and grill for indirect cooking and preheat to 400 ° F using selected pellets.
8. Remove the wrap from the ram.
9. Insert a wood pellet smoker and grill meat probe or remote meat probe into the thickest part of the lamb. If your grill does not have a meat probe or you do not have a remote meat probe, use an instant reading digital thermometer to read the internal temperature while cooking. Roast the lamb at 400 ° F until the internal temperature of the thickest part reaches the desired finish.
10. Place the lamb under the loose foil tent for 10 minutes, then cut it against the grain and eat.

Nutrition: Calories: 200 Carbs: 1g Fat: 13g Protein: 20g

98. Greek Leg of Lamb

Preparation Time: 15 minutes
Cooking Time: 25 minutes
Servings: 6
Ingredients:
- 2 tablespoons finely chopped fresh rosemary
- 1 tablespoon ground thyme
- 5 garlic cloves, minced
- 2 tablespoons sea salt
- 1 tablespoon freshly ground black pepper
- Butcher's string
- 1 whole boneless (6- to 8-pound) leg of lamb
- ¼ cup extra-virgin olive oil
- 1 cup red wine vinegar
- ½ cup canola oil

Directions:
1. In a container, combine the rosemary, thyme, garlic, salt, and pepper; set aside.
2. Using butcher's string, tie the leg of lamb into the shape of a roast. Your butcher should also be happy to truss the leg for you.
3. Rub the lamb generously with the olive oil and season with the spice mixture. Put it to a plate, cover with plastic wrap, and refrigerate for 4 hours.
4. Remove the lamb from the refrigerator but do not rinse.
5. Supply your smoker with wood pellets and follow the manufacturer's specific start-up procedure. Preheat, with the lid closed, to 325°F.

6. In a small bowl, combine the red wine vinegar and canola oil for basting.
7. Place the lamb directly on the grill, close the lid, and smoke for 20 to 25 minutes per pound (depending on desired doneness), basting with the oil and vinegar mixture every 30 minutes. Lamb is generally served medium-rare to medium, so it will be done when a meat thermometer where inserted in the thickest part reads 140°F to 145°F.
8. Let the lamb meat rest for about 15 minutes before slicing to serve.
Nutrition: Calories: 130 Carbs: 2g Fat: 5g Protein: 19g

99. Smoked Christmas Crown Roast of Lamb

Preparation Time: 1 hour
Cooking Time: 2 hours
Servings: 4
Ingredients:
- 2 racks of lamb, trimmed, drenched, and tied into a crown
- 1¼ cups extra-virgin olive oil, divided
- 2 tablespoons chopped fresh basil
- 2 tablespoons chopped fresh rosemary
- 2 tablespoons ground sage
- 2 tablespoons ground thyme
- 8 garlic cloves, minced
- 2 teaspoons salt
- 2 teaspoons freshly ground black pepper

Directions:

1. Set the lamb out in the counter to take the chill off, about an hour.
2. In a container, combine 1 cup of olive oil, the basil, rosemary, sage, thyme, garlic, salt, and pepper.
3. Baste the entire crown with the herbed olive oil and wrap the exposed drenched bones in aluminum foil.
4. Supply your smoker with wood pellets and follow the manufacturer's specific start-up procedure. Preheat, with the lid closed, to 275°F.
5. Put the lamb directly on the grill, close the lid, and smoke for 1 hour 30 minutes to 2 hours, or wait until a meat thermometer inserted in the thickest part reads 140°F.
6. Remove the lamb from the heat, tent with foil, and let rest for about 15 minutes before serving. The temperature will rise about 5°F during the rest period, for a finished temperature of 145°F.
Nutrition: Calories: 206 Carbs: 4g Fat: 9g Protein: 32g

100. Succulent Lamb Chops

Preparation Time: 15 minutes
Cooking Time: 20 minutes
Servings: 4
Ingredients:
- For The Marinade
- ½ cup rice wine vinegar
- 1 teaspoon liquid smoke
- 2 tablespoons extra-virgin olive oil
- 2 tablespoons dried minced onion

- 1 tablespoon chopped fresh mint
- For The Lamb Chops
- 8 (4-ounce) lamb chops
- ½ cup hot pepper jelly
- 1 tablespoon Sriracha
- 1 teaspoon salt
- 1 teaspoon freshly ground black pepper

Directions:

1. In a small container, whisk together the rice wine vinegar, liquid smoke, olive oil, minced onion, and mint.
2. Place the lamb chops in an aluminum roasting pan. Pour the marinade over the meat, turning to coat thoroughly. Cover it with a plastic wrapper and marinate in the refrigerator for 2 hours.
3. Supply your smoker with wood pellets and follow the manufacturer's specific start-up procedure. Preheat, with the lid closed, to 165°F, or the "Smoke" setting.
4. Put your saucepan top of the stove then low heat, combine the hot pepper jelly and Sriracha and keep warm.
5. When you are going to cook the chops, remove them from the marinade and pat dry. Discard the marinade.
6. Season all the chops with a salt and pepper, then place them directly on the grill grate, close the lid, and smoke for 5 minutes to "breathe" some smoke into them.
7. Remove the chops from the grill. Increase the pellet cooker temperature to 450°F, or the "High" setting. Once your griller is up to temperature, place the chops on the grill and sear, cooking for 2 minutes per side to achieve medium-rare chops. A meat thermometer that usually inserted in the thickest part of the meat should read 145°F. Continue grilling, if necessary, to your desired doneness.
8. Serve the chops with the warm Sriracha pepper jelly on the side.

Nutrition: Calories: 277 Carbs: 0g Fat: 26g Protein: 18g

101. Roasted Rosemary Lamb

Preparation Time: 15 minutes
Cooking Time: 4 hours
Servings: 2
Ingredients:

- 1 lamb rack
- 2 rosemary sprigs, chopped
- Salt and pepper to taste
- 12 baby potatoes
- 1/2 cup butter
- 1 bunch asparagus
- 2 tablespoons olive oil

Directions:

1. Set your wood pellet grill to 225 degrees F. Sprinkle the lamb with the rosemary, salt and pepper.
2. In a baking pan, add the potatoes and coat with the butter. Add the lamb to the grill.
3. Place the pan with potatoes beside the lamb. Roast for 3 hours.
4. Coat the asparagus with the olive oil. In your last twenty minutes of cooking, stir the asparagus into the potatoes.
5. Serve the lamb with the asparagus and baby potatoes.

Nutrition: Calories: 197 Carbs: 3g Fat: 14g Protein: 15g

102. Grilled Lamb

Preparation Time: 10 minutes
Cooking Time: 1 hour
Servings: 6
Ingredients:

- 2 racks of lamb, fat trimmed
- 2 tablespoons Dijon mustard
- Steak seasoning
- 1 teaspoon fresh rosemary, chopped
- 1 tablespoon fresh parsley, chopped

Directions:

1. Coat the lamb with the mustard.
2. Sprinkle all sides with the seasoning, rosemary and parsley.
3. Set your wood pellet grill to 400 degrees F.
4. Sear the meat side of the lamb for 6 minutes.
5. Reduce temperature to 300 degrees F.
6. Grill it for about 20 minutes, turning once or twice.
7. Let rest for 10 minutes before slicing and serving.

Nutrition: Calories: 241 Carbs: 0g Fat: 17g Protein: 21g

103. Chipotle Lamb

Preparation Time: 15 minutes
Cooking Time: 2 hours 30 minutes
Servings: 6
Ingredients:

- 1 rack lamb ribs
- 3/4 cup olive oil

- Pepper to taste
- 1 tablespoon chipotle powder
- 3 cloves, garlic
- 1/4 cup Apple wood bacon rub
- 2 tablespoons rosemary, chopped
- 2 tablespoons thyme, chopped
- 2 tablespoons sage, chopped
- 2 tablespoons parsley

Directions:

1. Coat the lamb ribs with olive oil. Season with the pepper and chipotle powder.
2. Marinate for 15 minutes. Set your wood pellet grill to 275 degrees F.
3. Combine the rest of the ingredients. Spread the mixture on all sides of the lamb.
4. Cook the lamb for 2 hours. Allow it to rest about ten minutes before carving and serving.

Nutrition: Calories: 210 Carbs: 0g Fat: 13g Protein: 22g

104. Hickory Rack of Lamb

Preparation Time: 10 minutes
Cooking Time: 2 hours
Servings: 3
Ingredients:

- 1 (3 pounds) rack of lamb (drenched)
- Marinade Ingredients:
- 1 lemon (juiced)
- 1 teaspoon ground black pepper
- 1 teaspoon thyme
- ¼ cup balsamic vinegar
- 1 teaspoon dried basil

- 2 tablespoons Dijon mustard
- 2 cloves garlic (crushed)

Rub Ingredients:

- ½ teaspoon cayenne pepper
- ½ teaspoon ground black pepper
- ¼ teaspoon Italian seasoning
- 1 teaspoon oregano
- 1 teaspoon dried mint
- 1 teaspoon paprika
- 1 teaspoon garlic powder
- 1 teaspoon onion powder
- 1 teaspoon dried parsley
- 1 teaspoon dried basil
- 1 teaspoon dried rosemary
- 4 tablespoons olive oil

Directions:

1. Put all the marinade ingredients in an empty container. Pour the marinade into a gallon zip-lock bag. Add the rack of lamb and massage the marinade into the rack. Seal the bag and place it in a refrigerator. Refrigerate for 8 hour or overnight.
2. When ready to roast, remove the rack of lamb from the marinade and let it sit for about 2 hour or until it is at room temperature.
3. Meanwhile, combine all the rub ingredients except the olive oil in a mixing bowl.
4. Rub the rub mixture over the rack of lamb generously. Drizzle rack with

the olive oil.
5. Start your grill on smoke with the lid opened until fire starts.
6. Close the lid and preheat grill to 225°F using hickory wood pellets.
7. Place the rack of your lamb on the grill grate, bone side down. Smoke it for about two hours or until the internal temperature of the meat reaches 140-145°F.
8. Take off the rack of lamb from the grill and let it rest for about 10 minutes to cool.

Nutrition: Calories: 800 Fat: 41.1g Carbs: 6.7g Protein 93.8g

105. Leg of Lamb

Preparation Time: 10 minutes
Cooking Time: 2 hours
Servings: 6
Ingredients:

- 1 (2 pounds) leg of lamb
- 1 teaspoon dried rosemary
- 2 teaspoon freshly ground black pepper
- 4 cloves garlic (minced)
- 2 teaspoon salt or more to taste
- ½ teaspoon paprika
- 1 teaspoon thyme
- 2 tablespoons olive oil
- 1 teaspoon brown sugar
- 2 tablespoons oregano

Directions:

1. Trim the meat of excess fat and remove silver-skin.
2. In a mixing bowl, combine the thyme, salt, sugar,

oregano, paprika, black pepper, garlic and olive oil.

3. Generously, rub the mixture over the leg of lamb. Cover seasoned leg of lamb with foil and let it sit for 1 hour to marinate.

4. Start your grill on smoke and leave the lid open for 5 minutes, or until fire starts. Cover the lid and preheat grill to 250°F using hickory, maple or apple wood pellets.

5. Remove the foil and place the leg of lamb on a smoker rack. Place the rack on the grill and smoke the leg of lamb for about 4 hours or until it reach the internal temperature of your meat 145°F. Take off the leg of lamb from the grill and let it rest for a few minutes to cool. Cut into sizes and serve.

Nutrition: Calories 334 Fat: 16g Carbs: 2.9g Protein 42.9g

106. Smoked Lamb chops

Preparation Time: 10 Minutes
Cooking Time: 50 Minutes
Servings: 4
Ingredients:

- 1 rack of lamb, fat trimmed
- 2 tablespoons rosemary, fresh
- 2 tablespoons sage, fresh
- 1 tablespoon garlic cloves, roughly chopped
- 1/2 tablespoon salt
- 1/2 tablespoon pepper, coarsely ground
- 1/4 cup olive oil
- 1 tablespoon honey
Directions:

1. Preheat your wood pellet smoker to 225°F using a fruitwood.

2. Put all your ingredients except the lamb in a food processor. Liberally apply the mixture on the lamb.

3. Place the lamb on the smoker for 45 minutes or until the internal temperature reaches 120°F.

4. Sear the lamb on the grill for 2 minutes per side. Let rest for 5 minutes before serving. Slice and enjoy.

Nutrition: Calories 704 Fat 56g Carbs 24g Protein 27g

107. Wood Pellet Smoked Lamb Shoulder

Preparation Time: 10 Minutes
Cooking Time: 1hour 30 Minutes
Servings: 7
Ingredients:

- For Smoked Lamb Shoulder
- 5 pound lamb shoulder, boneless and excess fat trimmed
- 2 tablespoons kosher salt
- 2 tablespoons black pepper
- 1 tablespoon rosemary, dried
- The Injection
- 1 cup apple cider vinegar
- The Spritz
- 1 cup apple cider vinegar
- 1 cup apple juice
Directions:

1. Preheat the wood pellet smoker with a water pan to 2250 F.

2. Rinse the lamb in cold water then pat it dry with a paper towel. Inject vinegar to the lamb.

3. Pat the lamb dry again and rub with oil, salt black pepper and rosemary. Tie with kitchen twine.

4. Smoke uncovered for 1 hour then spritz after every 15 minutes until the internal temperature reaches 1950 F.

5. Take off the lamb from the grill and place it on a platter. Let cool before shredding it and enjoying it with your favorite side.

Nutrition: Calories 243 Fat 19g Carbs 0g Protein 17g

108. Wood Pellet Smoked Pulled Lamb Sliders

Preparation Time: 10 Minutes
Cooking Time: 7 Hours
Servings: 7
Ingredients:
For the Lamb's shoulder

- 5 pound lamb shoulder, boneless
- 1/2 cup olive oil
- 1/4 cup dry rub
- 10 ounces spritz
- The Dry Rub
- 1/3 cup kosher salt
- 1/3 cup pepper, ground
- 1-1/3 cup garlic, granulated
- The Spritz
- 4 ounces Worcestershire sauce
- 6 ounces apple cider vinegar

Directions:
1. Preheat the wood pellet smoker with a water bath to 2500 F.
2. Trim any fat from the lamb then rub with oil and dry rub.
3. Place the lamb on the smoker for 90 minutes then spritz with a spray bottle every 30 minutes until the internal temperature reaches 1650 F.
4. Transfer the lamb shoulder to a foil pan with the remaining spritz liquid and cover tightly with foil.
5. Place back in the smoker and smoke until the internal temperature reaches 2000 F.
6. Remove from the smoker and let rest for 30 minutes before pulling the lamb and serving with slaw, bun, or aioli. Enjoy

Nutrition: Calories 339 Fat 22 Carbs 16g Protein 18g

109. Smoked Lamb Meatballs

Preparation Time: 10 Minutes
Cooking Time: 1 Hour
Servings: 5
Ingredients:

- 1 pound lamb shoulder, ground
- 3 garlic cloves, finely diced
- 3 tablespoons shallot, diced
- 1 tablespoon salt
- 1 egg
- 1/2 tablespoon pepper
- 1/2 tablespoon cumin
- 1/2 tablespoon smoked paprika
- 1/4 tablespoon red pepper flakes
- 1/4 tablespoon cinnamon, ground
- 1/4 cup panko breadcrumbs

Directions:
1. Set the wood pellet smoker to 2500 F using a fruitwood.
2. In a mixing bowl, combine all meatball ingredients until well mixed.
3. Form small-sized balls and place them on a baking sheet. Place the baking sheet in the smoker and smoke until the internal temperature reaches 1600 F.
4. Remove from the smoker and serve. Enjoy.

Nutrition: Calories 73 Fat 5.2g Carbs 1.5g Protein 4.9g

110. Crown Rack of Lamb

Preparation Time: 10 Minutes
Cooking Time: 30 Minutes
Servings: 6
Ingredients:

- 2 racks of lamb, drenched
- 1 tablespoon garlic, crushed
- 1 tablespoon rosemary, finely chopped
- 1/4 cup olive oil
- 2 feet twine

Directions:
1. Rinse the racks with cold water then pat them dry with a paper towel.
2. Lay the racks on a flat board then score between each bone, about ¼ inch down.
3. In a mixing bowl, mix garlic, rosemary, and oil then generously brush on the lamb.
4. Take each lamb rack and bend it into a semicircle forming a crown-like shape.
5. Use the twine to wrap the racks about 4 times starting from the base to the top. Make sure you tie the twine tightly to keep the racks together.
6. Preheat the wood pellet to 400-4500 F then place the lamb racks on a baking dish. Place the baking dish on the pellet grill.
7. Cook for 10 minutes then reduce temperature to 3000 F. cook for 20 more minutes or until the internal temperature reaches 1300 F.
8. Remove the lamb rack from the wood pellet and let rest for 15 minutes.
9. Serve when hot with veggies and potatoes. Enjoy.

Nutrition: Calories 390 Fat 35g Carbs 0g Protein 17g

111. Wood Pellet Smoked Leg of Lamb

Preparation Time: 15 Minutes
Cooking Time: 3hourss
Servings: 6
Ingredients:

- 1 leg lamb, boneless
- 4 garlic cloves, minced
- 2 tablespoons salt
- 1 tablespoon black pepper, freshly ground
- 2 tablespoons oregano
- 1 tablespoon thyme
- 2 tablespoons olive oil

Directions:
1. Cut off any excess of fat from the lamb and tie the

lamb using twine to form a nice roast.

2. In a mixing bowl, mix garlic, spices, and oil. Rub all over the lamb, wrap with a plastic bag then refrigerate for an hour to marinate.

3. Place the lamb on a smoker set at 2500 F. smoke the lamb for 4 hours or until the internal temperature reaches 1450 F.

4. Remove from the smoker and let rest to cool. Serve and enjoy.

Nutrition: Calories 356 Fat16g Carbs 3g Protein 49g

112. Wood Pellet Grilled Aussie Leg of Lamb Roast

Preparation Time: 30 Minutes
Cooking Time: 2 Hours
Serves: 8
Ingredients:

- 5 pounds Aussie leg of lamb, boneless
- Smoked Paprika Rub
- 1 tablespoon raw sugar
- 1 tablespoon kosher salt
- 1 tablespoon black pepper
- 1 tablespoon smoked paprika
- 1 tablespoon garlic powder
- 1 tablespoon rosemary, dried
- 1 tablespoon onion powder
- 1 tablespoon cumin
- 1/2 tablespoon cayenne pepper
- Roasted Carrots

- 1 bunch rainbow carrots
- Olive oil
- Salt
- Pepper

Directions:

1. Heat the wood pellet grill to 3750 F.

2. Trim any excess fat from the lamb.

3. Put all your rub ingredients and rub all over the lamb. Place the lamb on the grill and smoke for 2 hours.

4. Toss the carrots in oil, salt, and pepper then add to the grill after the lamb has cooked for 1 ½ hour.

5. Cook until the roast internal temperature reaches 1350 F. remove the lamb from the grill and cover with foil. Let rest for 30 minutes.

6. Remove the carrots from the grill once soft and serve with the lamb. Enjoy.

Nutrition: Calories 257 Fat 8g Carbs 6g Protein 37g

113. Simple Grilled Lamb Chops

Preparation Time: 10 Minutes
Cooking Time: 6 Minutes
Servings: 6
Ingredients:

- 1/4 cup distilled white vinegar
- 2 tablespoons salt
- 1/2 tablespoon black pepper
- 1 tablespoon garlic, minced
- 1 onion, thinly sliced
- 2 tablespoons olive oil
- 2 pounds lamb chops

Directions:

1. In a reseal able bag, mix vinegar, salt, black pepper, garlic, sliced onion, and oil until all salt has dissolved.

2. Add the lamb chops and toss until well coated. Place in the fridge to marinate for 2 hours.

3. Preheat the wood pellet grill to high heat.

4. Remove the lamb from the fridge and discard the marinade. Wrap any exposed bones with foil.

5. Grill your lamb meat for three minutes per side. You can also broil in a broiler for more crispness. Serve and enjoy

Nutrition: Calories 519 Fat 44.8g Carbs 2.3g Protein 25g

114. Wood Pellet Grilled Lamb with Brown Sugar Glaze

Preparation Time: 15 Minutes
Cooking Time: 10 Minutes
Servings: 4
Ingredients:

- 1/4 cup brown sugar
- 2 tablespoons ginger, ground
- 2 tablespoons tarragon, dried
- 1 teaspoon cinnamon, ground
- 1 tablespoons black pepper, ground
- 1 tablespoons garlic powder
- 1/2 tablespoons salt
- 4 lamb chops

Directions:

1. In a mixing bowl, mix sugar, ginger, dried tarragon,

cinnamon, black pepper, garlic, and salt.

2.   Rub the lamb chops with the seasoning and place it on a plate. Refrigerate for an hour to marinate.

3.   Preheat the grill to high heat then brush the grill grate with oil.

4.   Arrange the lamb chops on the grill grate in a single layer and cook for 5 minutes on each side. Serve and enjoy.

Nutrition: Calories 241 Fat 13.1g Carbs 15.8g Protein 14.6g

115. Grilled leg of lambs Steaks

Preparation Time: 10 Minutes
Cooking Time: 10 Minutes
Servings: 4
Ingredients:

- 4 lamb steaks, bone-in
- 1/4 cup olive oil
- 4 garlic cloves, minced
- 1 tablespoon rosemary, freshly chopped
- Salt and black pepper

Directions:

1.   Put the lamb in a shallow container in a single layer. Top with oil, garlic cloves, rosemary, salt, and black pepper then flip the steaks to cover on both sides.

2.   Let sit for 30 minutes to marinate.

3.   Preheat the wood pellet grill to high and brush the grill grate with oil.

4.   Place the lamb steaks on the grill grate and cook until browned and the internal are slightly pink. The internal temperature should be 1400 F.

5.   Let rest for 5 minutes before serving. Enjoy.

Nutrition: Calories 327 Fat 21.9g Carbs 1.7g Protein 29.6g

66

Chapter 11. Poultry Recipes

116. Herb Roasted Turkey

Preparation time: 15 minutes
Cooking time: 3 hours and 30 minutes
Servings: 12
Ingredients:
- 14 pounds turkey, cleaned
- 2 tablespoons chopped mixed herbs
- Pork and poultry rub as needed
- 1/4 teaspoon ground black pepper
- 3 tablespoons butter, unsalted, melted
- 8 tablespoons butter, unsalted, softened
- 2 cups chicken broth

Directions:
1. Clean the turkey by removing the giblets, wash it inside out, pat dry with paper towels, then place it on a roasting pan and tuck the turkey wings by tiring with butcher's string.
2. Switch on the Wood Pellet, fill the grill hopper with hickory flavored wood pellets, power the grill on by using the control panel, select 'smoke' on the temperature dial, or set the temperature to 325 degrees F and let it preheat for a minimum of 15 minutes.
3. Meanwhile, prepared herb butter and for this, take a small bowl, place the softened butter in it, add black pepper and mixed herbs and beat until fluffy.
4. Place some of the prepared herb butter underneath the skin of turkey by using a handle of a wooden spoon, and massage the skin to distribute butter evenly.
5. Then rub the exterior of the turkey with melted butter, season with pork and poultry rub, and pour the broth in the roasting pan.
6. When the grill has preheated, open the lid, place roasting pan containing turkey on the grill grate, shut the grill and smoke for 3 hours and 30 minutes until the internal temperature reaches 165 degrees F and the top has turned golden brown.
7. When done, transfer turkey to a cutting board, let it rest for 30 minutes, then carve it into slices and serve.

Nutrition:
Calories: 154.6
Fat: 3.1 g
Carbs: 8.4 g
Protein: 28.8 g
Fiber: 0.4 g

117. Turkey Legs

Preparation time: 24 hours
Cooking time: 5 hours
Servings: 4
Ingredients:
- 4 turkey legs

For the Brine:
- 1/2 cup curing salt
- 1 tablespoon whole black peppercorns
- 1 cup BBQ rub
- 1/2 cup brown sugar
- 2 bay leaves
- 2 teaspoons liquid smoke
- 16 cups of warm water
- 4 cups ice
- 8 cups of cold water

Directions:
1. Prepare the brine and for this, take a large stockpot, place it over high heat, pour warm water in it, add peppercorn, bay leaves, and liquid smoke, stir in salt, sugar, and BBQ rub and bring it to a boil.
2. Remove pot from heat, bring it to room temperature, then pour in cold water, add ice cubes and let the brine chill in the refrigerator.
3. Then add turkey legs in it, submerge them completely, and let soak for 24 hours in the refrigerator.
4. After 24 hours, remove turkey legs from the brine, rinse well and pat dry with paper towels.
5. When ready to cook, switch on the Wood Pellet, fill the grill hopper with hickory flavored wood pellets, power the grill on by using the control panel, select 'smoke' on the temperature dial, or set the temperature to 250 degrees F and let it preheat for a minimum of 15 minutes.
6. When the grill has preheated, open the lid, place turkey legs on the grill grate, shut the grill, and smoke for 5 hours until nicely browned and the internal temperature reaches 165 degrees F.
7. Serve immediately.

Nutrition:
Calories: 416
Fat: 13.3 g
Carbs: 0 g

Protein: 69.8 g
Fiber: 0 g

118. Turkey Breast

Preparation time: 12 hours
Cooking time: 8 hours
Servings: 6
Ingredients:
For the Brine:

- 2 pounds turkey breast, deboned
- 2 tablespoons ground black pepper
- 1/4 cup salt
- 1 cup brown sugar
- 4 cups cold water
- For the BBQ Rub:
- 2 tablespoons dried onions
- 2 tablespoons garlic powder
- 1/4 cup paprika
- 2 tablespoons ground black pepper
- 1 tablespoon salt
- 2 tablespoons brown sugar
- 2 tablespoons red chili powder
- 1 tablespoon cayenne pepper
- 2 tablespoons sugar
- 2 tablespoons ground cumin

Directions:
1. Prepare the brine and for this, take a large bowl, add salt, black pepper, and sugar in it, pour in water, and stir until sugar has dissolved.
2. Place turkey breast in it, submerge it completely and let it soak for a minimum of 12 hours in the refrigerator.
3. Meanwhile, prepare the BBQ rub and for this, take a small bowl, place all of its ingredients in it and then stir until combined, set aside until required.
4. Then remove turkey breast from the brine and season well with the prepared BBQ rub.
5. When ready to cook, switch on the Wood Pellet, fill the grill hopper with apple-flavored wood pellets, power the grill on by using the control panel, select 'smoke' on the temperature dial, or set the temperature to 180 degrees F and let it preheat for a minimum of 15 minutes.
6. When the grill has preheated, open the lid, place turkey breast on the grill grate, shut the grill, change the smoking temperature to 225 degrees F, and smoke for 8 hours until the internal temperature reaches 160 degrees F.
7. When done, transfer turkey to a cutting board, let it rest for 10 minutes, then cut it into slices and serve.
Nutrition:
Calories: 250
Fat: 5 g
Carbs: 31 g
Protein: 18 g
Fiber: 5 g

119. Hellfire Chicken Wings

Preparation time: 15 minutes
Cooking time: 40 minutes
Servings: 6
Ingredients:

- 3 pounds chicken wings, tips removed
- 2 tablespoons olive oil
- For the Rub:
- 1 teaspoon onion powder
- 1 teaspoon salt
- 1 teaspoon garlic powder
- 1 tablespoon paprika
- 1 teaspoon ground black pepper
- 1 teaspoon celery seed
- 1 teaspoon cayenne pepper
- 2 teaspoons brown sugar
- For the Sauce:
- 4 jalapeno peppers, sliced crosswise
- 8 tablespoons butter, unsalted
- 1/2 cup hot sauce
- 1/2 cup cilantro leaves

Directions:

- Switch on the Wood Pellet, fill the grill hopper with hickory flavored wood pellets, power the grill on by using the control panel, select 'smoke' on the temperature dial, or set the temperature to 350 degrees F and let it preheat for a minimum of 15 minutes.
- Prepare the chicken wings and for this, remove tips from the wings, cut each chicken wing through the joint into two pieces, and then place in a large bowl.
- Prepare the rub and for this, take a small bowl, place all of its ingredients in it and then stir until combined.

- Sprinkle prepared rub on the chicken wings and then toss until well coated.
- Meanwhile,
- When the grill has preheated, open the lid, place chicken wings on the grill grate, shut the grill and smoke for 40 minutes until golden brown and skin have turned crisp, turning halfway.
- Meanwhile, prepare the sauce and for this, take a small saucepan, place it over medium-low heat, add butter in it and when it melts, add jalapeno and cook for 4 minutes.
- Then stir in hot sauce and cilantro until mixed and remove the pan from heat.
- When done, transfer chicken wings to a dish, top with prepared sauce, toss until coated, and then serve.

Nutrition:
Calories: 250
Fat: 15 g
Carbs: 11 g
Protein: 19 g
Fiber: 1 g

120. Spicy BBQ Chicken

Preparation time: 8 hours and 10 minutes
Cooking time: 3 hours
Servings: 6
Ingredients:
- 1 whole chicken, cleaned
- For the Marinade:
- 1 medium white onion, peeled
- 6 Thai chilies
- 5 cloves of garlic, peeled
- 1 scotch bonnet

- 3 tablespoons salt
- 2 tablespoons sugar
- 2 tablespoons sweet paprika
- 4 cups Grapeseed oil

Directions:
1. Prepare the marinade, and for this, place all of its ingredients in a food processor and pulse for 2 minutes until smooth.
2. Smoother whole chicken with the prepared marinade and let it marinate in the refrigerator for a minimum of 8 hours.
3. When ready to cook, switch on the Wood Pellet, fill the grill hopper with apple-flavored wood pellets, power the grill on by using the control panel, select 'smoke' on the temperature dial, or set the temperature to 300 degrees F and let it preheat for a minimum of 15 minutes.
4. When the grill has preheated, open the lid, place chicken on the grill grate breast-side up, shut the grill and smoke for 3 hours until the internal temperature of chicken reaches 165 degrees F.
5. When done, transfer chicken to a cutting board, let it rest for 15 minutes, then cut into slices and serve.

Nutrition:
Calories: 100
Fat: 2.8 g
Carbs: 13 g
Protein: 3.5 g
Fiber: 2 g

121. BBQ Half Chickens

Preparation time: 15 minutes
Cooking time: 75 minutes

Servings: 4
Ingredients:
- 3.5-pound whole chicken, cleaned, halved
- Summer rub as needed
- Apricot BBQ sauce as needed

Directions:
1. Switch on the Wood Pellet, fill the grill hopper with apple-flavored wood pellets, power the grill on by using the control panel, select 'smoke' on the temperature dial, or set the temperature to 375 degrees F and let it preheat for a minimum of 15 minutes.
2. Meanwhile, cut chicken in half along with backbone and then season with summer rub.
3. When the grill has preheated, open the lid, place chicken halves on the grill grate skin-side up, shut the grill, change the smoking temperature to 225 degrees F, and smoke for 1 hour and 30 minutes until the internal temperature reaches 160 degrees F.
4. Then brush chicken generously with apricot sauce and continue grilling for 10 minutes until glazed.
5. When done, transfer chicken to cutting to a dish, let it rest for 5 minutes, and then serve.

Nutrition:
Calories: 435
Fat: 20 g
Carbs: 20 g
Protein: 42 g
Fiber: 1 g

122. Teriyaki Wings

Preparation time: 8 hours

69

Cooking time: 50 minutes
Servings: 8
Ingredients:
- 2 ½ pounds large chicken wings
- 1 tablespoon toasted sesame seeds
- For the Marinade:
- 2 scallions, sliced
- 2 tablespoons grated ginger
- ½ teaspoon minced garlic
- 1/4 cup brown sugar
- 1/2 cup soy sauce
- 2 tablespoon rice wine vinegar
- 2 teaspoons sesame oil
- 1/4 cup water

Directions:
1. Prepare the chicken wings and for this, remove tips from the wings, cut each chicken wing through the joint into three pieces, and then place in a large plastic bag.
2. Prepare the sauce and for this, take a small saucepan, place it over medium-high heat, add all of its ingredients in it, stir until mixed, and bring it to a boil.
3. Then switch heat to medium level, simmer the sauce for 10 minutes, and when done, cool the sauce completely.
4. Pour the sauce over chicken wings, seal the bag, turn it upside down to coat chicken wings with the sauce and let it marinate for a minimum of 8 hours in the refrigerator.
5. When ready to cook, switch on the Wood Pellet, fill the grill hopper with maple-flavored wood pellets, power

the grill on by using the control panel, select 'smoke' on the temperature dial, or set the temperature to 350 degrees F and let it preheat for a minimum of 15 minutes.
6. Meanwhile,
7. When the grill has preheated, open the lid, place chicken wings on the grill grate, shut the grill and smoke for 50 minutes until crispy and meat is no longer pink, turning halfway.
8. When done, transfer chicken wings to a dish, sprinkle with sesame seeds and then serve.

Nutrition:
Calories: 150
Fat: 7.5 g
Carbs: 6 g
Protein: 12 g
Fiber: 1 g

123. Korean Chicken Wings

Preparation time: 4 hours
Cooking time: 1 hour
Servings: 6
Ingredients:
- 3 pounds of chicken wings
- 2 tablespoons olive oil
- For the Brine:
- 1 head garlic, halved
- 1 lemon, halved
- 1/2 cup sugar
- 1 cup of sea salt
- 4 sprigs of thyme
- 10 peppercorns
- 16 cups of water

For the Sauce:
- 2 teaspoons minced garlic
- 1/2 cup gochujang hot pepper paste

- 1 tablespoon grated ginger
- 2 tablespoons of rice wine vinegar
- 1/3 cup honey
- 1/4 cup soy sauce
- 2 tablespoons lime juice
- 2 tablespoons toasted sesame oil
- 1/4 cup melted butter

Directions:
1. Prepare the brine and for this, take a large stockpot, place it over high heat, pour in water, stir in salt and sugar until dissolved, and bring to a boil.
2. Then remove the pot from heat, add the remaining ingredients for the brine, and bring the brine to room temperature.
3. Add chicken wings, submerge them completely, cover the pot and let wings soak for a minimum of 4 hours in the refrigerator.
4. When ready to cook, switch on the Wood Pellet, fill the grill hopper with flavored wood pellets, power the grill on by using the control panel, select 'smoke' on the temperature dial, or set the temperature to 375 degrees F and let it preheat for a minimum of 15 minutes.
5. Meanwhile, remove chicken wings from the brine, pat dry with paper towels, place them in a large bowl, drizzle with oil and toss until well coated.
6. When the grill has preheated, open the lid, place chicken wings on the grill grate,

shut the grill, and smoke for 1 hour until the internal temperature reaches 165 degrees F.

7. Meanwhile, prepare the sauce and for this, take a medium bowl, place all of the sauce ingredients in it and whisk until smooth.

8. When done, transfer chicken wings to a dish, top with prepared sauce, toss until coated, and then serve.

Nutrition:
Calories: 137
Fat: 9 g
Carbs: 4 g
Protein: 8 g
Fiber: 1 g

124. Garlic Parmesan Chicken Wings

Preparation time: 15 minutes
Cooking time: 20 minutes
Servings: 6
Ingredients:
- 5 pounds of chicken wings
- 1/2 cup chicken rub
- 3 tablespoons chopped parsley
- 1 cup shredded parmesan cheese
- For the Sauce:
- 5 teaspoons minced garlic
- 2 tablespoons chicken rub
- 1 cup butter, unsalted
Directions:
1. Switch on the Wood Pellet, fill the grill hopper with cherry flavored wood pellets, power the grill on by using the control panel, select 'smoke' on the temperature dial, or set the temperature to 450 degrees F and let it preheat for a minimum of 15 minutes.

2. Meanwhile, take a large bowl, place chicken wings in it, sprinkle with chicken rub and toss until well coated.

3. When the grill has preheated, open the lid, place chicken wings on the grill grate, shut the grill, and smoke for 10 minutes per side until the internal temperature reaches 165 degrees F.

4. Meanwhile, prepare the sauce and for this, take a medium saucepan, place it over medium heat, add all the ingredients for the sauce in it and cook for 10 minutes until smooth, set aside until required.

5. When done, transfer chicken wings to a dish, top with prepared sauce, toss until mixed, garnish with cheese and parsley and then serve.

Nutrition:
Calories: 180
Fat: 1 g
Carbs: 8 g
Protein: 0 g
Fiber: 0 g

125. Rosemary Orange Chicken

Preparation time: 2 hours
Cooking time: 45 minutes
Servings: 6
Ingredients:
- 4 pounds chicken, backbone removed
- For the Marinade:
- 2 teaspoons salt
- 3 tablespoons chopped rosemary leaves
- 2 teaspoons Dijon mustard
- 1 orange, zested
- 1/4 cup olive oil
- ¼ cup of orange juice
Directions:
1. Prepare the chicken and for this, rinse the chicken, pat dry with paper towels and then place in a large baking dish.

2. Prepare the marinade and for this, take a medium bowl, place all of its ingredients in it and whisk until combined.

3. Cover chicken with the prepared marinade, cover with a plastic wrap, and then marinate for a minimum of 2 hours in the refrigerator, turning halfway.

4. When ready to cook, switch on the Wood Pellet, fill the grill hopper with flavored wood pellets, power the grill on by using the control panel, select 'smoke' on the temperature dial, or set the temperature to 350 degrees F and let it preheat for a minimum of 5 minutes.

5. When the grill has preheated, open the lid, place chicken on the grill grate skin-side down, shut the grill and smoke for 45 minutes until well browned, and the internal temperature reaches 165 degrees F.

6. When done, transfer chicken to a cutting board, let it rest for 10 minutes, cut it into slices, and then serve.

Nutrition:
Calories: 258
Fat: 17.4 g
Carbs: 5.2 g

Protein: 19.3 g
Fiber: 0.3 g

126. Lemon Chicken Breast

Preparation time: 15 minutes
Cooking time: 30 minutes
Servings: 4
Ingredients:
- 6 chicken breasts, skinless and boneless
- ½ cup oil
- 1-3 fresh thyme sprigs
- 1 teaspoon ground black pepper
- 2 teaspoon salt
- 2 teaspoons honey
- 1 garlic clove, chopped
- 1 lemon, juiced and zested
- Lemon wedges

Directions:
1. Take a bowl and prepare the marinade by mixing thyme, pepper, salt, honey, garlic, lemon zest, and juice. Mix well until dissolved
2. Add oil and whisk
3. Clean breasts and pat them dry, place in a bag alongside marinade and let them sit in the fridge for 4 hours
4. Preheat your smoker to 400 degrees F
5. Drain chicken and smoke until the internal temperature reaches 165 degrees, for about 15 minutes
6. Serve and enjoy!

Nutrition: Calories: 230 Fats: 7g Carbs: 1g Fiber: 2g

127. Smokey Fried Chicken

Preparation Time: 10 minutes
Cooking time: 3 hours 30 minutes
Servings: 6-8
Ingredients:
The Meat
- 2 Whole fryer chickens – (3 – ½ lb.)

Other Ingredients
1. Coarse Kosher Salt
2. Vegetable oil
3. Black pepper.
4. Fresh buttermilk.
5. Hot sauce – 2 tbsp.
6. Brown sugar – 1 tbsp.
7. All-purpose flour – 2-1/2 cups.
8. Garlic powder – 2 tbsp.
9. Onion powder – 2 tbsp.
10. Poultry shake – 1 tbsp.
11. Peanut or Grapeseed oil

Directions:
1. Start the smoker with the lid open, after the fire has been established, then close the lid. Set the temperature at 200F. Preheat it at this temperature for about 15 minutes.
2. Use cold water to rinse the chicken. To dry it pat the chicken pieces and then place it on a baking sheet.
3. Use vegetable oil to rub outside the chicken and season it with salt and pepper.
4. Arrange the chicken on the grill grate. Smoke it for about 2-1/2 hours. The internal temperature for indicating that the chicken is done is about 150F.
5. Afterward, place the chicken on a baking sheet to cool down.
6. Start cutting the chicken now. Make about 20 pieces; 4 drumsticks, 4 wings, 4 thighs, and 8 breast quarters. Take two plastic bags and divide the chicken pieces evenly between them.
7. Take a mixing bowl and whisk the buttermilk with hot sauce and brown sugar. Pour half of this in each bag. Refrigerate these bags for an hour.
8. Take another bowl and whisk flour, 2 tablespoons each of salt and pepper, garlic powder, onion powder, and poultry seasoning in it.
9. Heat 2 inches of peanut or Grapeseed oil on a stovetop. The temperature should be medium-high at about 375 degrees. The pot for this purpose should be a heavy saucepan.
10. Now, drain the chicken pieces that were in the bag and put them in the flour mixture.
11. Fry the chicken in batches. After the color golden brown appears, then it means they done. It should take about 6 minutes for breast pieces and a little longer for others.
12. Put the chicken pieces on the paper towels to drain, and they are ready to serve.

Nutrition:
Calories: 321
Total Carbohydrate 15.5g 6%
Dietary Fiber: 0.3g 1%
Total Sugars 13.5g
Protein: 42.2g
Calcium: 25mg 2%
Iron: 4mg 24%
Potassium: 454mg 10%

128. Maple and Bacon Chicken

Preparation time: 20 minutes
Cooking time: 1 and ½ hours
Servings: 7
Ingredients:

- 4 boneless and skinless chicken breasts
- Salt as needed
- Fresh pepper
- 12 slices bacon, uncooked
- 1cup maple syrup
- ½ cup melted butter
- 1teaspoon liquid smoke

Directions:
1. Preheat your smoker to 250 degrees Fahrenheit
2. Season the chicken with pepper and salt
3. Wrap the breast with 3 bacon slices and cover the entire surface
4. Secure the bacon with toothpicks
5. Take a medium-sized bowl and stir in maple syrup, butter, liquid smoke, and mix well
6. Reserve 1/3rd of this mixture for later use
7. Submerge the chicken breast into the butter mix and coat them well
8. Place a pan in your smoker and transfer the chicken to your smoker
9. Smoker for 1 to 1 and a ½ hours
10. Brush the chicken with reserved butter and smoke for 30 minutes more until the internal temperature reaches 165 degrees Fahrenheit
11. Enjoy!

Nutrition: Calories: 458 Fats: 20g Carbs: 65g Fiber: 1g

129. Paprika Chicken

Preparation time: 20 minutes
Cooking time: 2 – 4 hours
Servings: 7
Ingredients:

- 4-6 chicken breast
- 4 tablespoons olive oil
- 2tablespoons smoked paprika
- ½ tablespoon salt
- ¼ teaspoon pepper
- 2teaspoons garlic powder
- 2teaspoons garlic salt
- 2teaspoons pepper
- 1teaspoon cayenne pepper
- 1teaspoon rosemary

Directions:
1. Preheat your smoker to 220 degrees Fahrenheit using your favorite wood Pellets
2. Prepare your chicken breast according to your desired shapes and transfer to a greased baking dish
3. Take a medium bowl and add spices, stir well
4. Press the spice mix over chicken and transfer the chicken to smoker
5. Smoke for 1-1 and a ½ hours
6. Turn-over and cook for 30 minutes more
7. Once the internal temperature reaches 165 degrees Fahrenheit
8. Remove from the smoker and cover with foil
9. Allow it to rest for 15 minutes
10. Enjoy!

Nutrition: Calories: 237 Fats: 6.1g Carbs: 14g Fiber: 3g

130. Sweet Sriracha BBQ Chicken

Preparation time: 30 minutes
Cooking time: 1 and ½-2 hours
Servings: 5
Ingredients:

- 1cup sriracha
- ½ cup butter
- ½ cup molasses
- ½ cup ketchup
- ¼ cup firmly packed brown sugar
- 1teaspoon salt
- 1teaspoon fresh ground black pepper
- 1whole chicken, cut into pieces
- ½ teaspoon fresh parsley leaves, chopped

Directions:
1. Preheat your smoker to 250 degrees Fahrenheit using cherry wood
2. Take a medium saucepan and place it over low heat, stir in butter, sriracha, ketchup, molasses, brown sugar, mustard, pepper and salt and keep stirring until the sugar and salt dissolves
3. Divide the sauce into two portions
4. Brush the chicken half with the sauce and reserve the remaining for serving
5. Make sure to keep the sauce for serving on the side, and keep the other portion for basting
6. Transfer chicken to your smoker rack and smoke for about 1 and a ½ to 2 hours

until the internal temperature reaches 165 degrees Fahrenheit

7. Sprinkle chicken with parsley and serve with reserved BBQ sauce

8. Enjoy!

Nutrition: Calories: 148 Fats: 0.6g Carbs: 10g Fiber: 1g

131. Smoked Chicken Drumsticks

Preparation time: 10 minutes
Cooking time: 2 hours 30 minutes
Servings: 5
Ingredients:

- 10 chicken drumsticks
- 2tsp garlic powder
- 1tsp salt
- 1tsp onion powder
- 1/2 tsp. ground black pepper
- ½ tsp. cayenne pepper
- 1tsp brown sugar
- 1/3 cup hot sauce
- 1tsp paprika
- ½ tsp. thyme

Directions:

1. In a large mixing bowl, combine the garlic powder, sugar, hot sauce, paprika, thyme, cayenne, salt, and ground pepper. Add the drumsticks and toss to combine.

2. Cover the bowl and refrigerate for 1 hour.

3. Remove the drumsticks from the marinade and let them sit for about 1 hour until they are at room temperature.

4. Arrange the drumsticks into a rack.

5. Start your pellet grill on smoke, leaving the lid open for 5 minutes for the fire to start.

6. Close the lid and preheat grill to 250°F, using hickory or apple hardwood pellets.

7. Place the rack on the grill and smoke drumsticks for 2 hours, 30 minutes, or until the drumsticks' internal temperature reaches 180°F.

8. Remove drumsticks from heat and let them rest for a few minutes.

9. Serve.

Nutrition: Calories: 167 Total Fat: 5.4 g Saturated Fat: 1.4 g Cholesterol: 81 mg Sodium: 946 mg Total Carbohydrate: 2.6 g Dietary Fiber: 0.5 g Total Sugars: 1.3 g Protein: 25.7 g

132. Chicken Cordon Bleu

Preparation time: 15 minutes
Cooking time: 40 minutes
Servings: 6
Ingredients:

- 6 boneless skinless chicken breasts
- 6 slices of ham
- 12 slices Swiss cheese
- 1cup panko breadcrumbs
- ½ cup all-purpose flour
- 1tsp ground black pepper or to taste
- 1tsp salt or to taste
- 4tbsp grated parmesan cheese
- 2tbsp melted butter
- ½ tsp. garlic powder
- ½ tsp. thyme
- ¼ tsp. parsley

Directions:

1. Butterfly the chicken breast with a pairing knife. Place the chicken breast in between 2 plastic wraps and pound with a mallet until the chicken breasts are ¼ inch thick.

2. Place a plastic wrap on a flat surface. Place one fat chicken breast on it.

3. Place one slice of Swiss cheese on the chicken. Place one slice of ham over the cheese and place another cheese slice over the ham.

4. Roll the chicken breast tightly. Fold both ends of the roll tightly. Pin both ends of the rolled chicken breast with a toothpick.

5. Repeat step 3 and 4 for the remaining chicken breasts

6. In a mixing bowl, combine the all-purpose flour, ½ tsp. salt, and ½ tsp. pepper. Set aside.

7. In another mixing bowl, combine breadcrumbs, parmesan, butter, garlic, thyme, parsley, ½ tsp. salt, and ½ tsp. pepper. Set aside.

8. Break the eggs into another mixing bowl and whisk. Set aside.

9. Grease a baking sheet.

10. Bake one chicken breast roll. Dip into the flour mixture, brush with eggs and dip into breadcrumb mixture. The chicken breast should be coated.

11. Place it on the baking sheet.

12. Repeat steps 9 and 10 for the remaining breast rolls.

13. Preheat your grill to 375°F with the lid closed for 15

minutes.

14. Place the baking sheet on the grill and cook for about 40 minutes, or until the chicken is golden brown.

15. Remove the baking sheet from the grill and let the chicken rest for a few minutes.

16. Slice cordon bleu and serve.

Nutrition: Calories: 560 Total Fat: 27.4 g Saturated Fat: 15.9 g Cholesterol: 156mg Sodium: 1158 mg Total Carbohydrate: 23.2 g Dietary Fiber: 1.1 g Total Sugars: 1.2 g Protein: 54.3 g

133. Smoked Whole Duck

Preparation time: 15 minutes
Cooking time: 2 hours 30 minutes
Servings: 6
Ingredients:

- 5 pounds whole duck (trimmed of any excess fat)
- 1small onion (quartered)
- 1apple (wedged)
- 1orange (quartered)
- 1tbsp freshly chopped parsley
- 1tbsp freshly chopped sage
- ½ tsp. onion powder
- 2tsp smoked paprika
- 1tsp dried Italian seasoning
- 1tbsp dried Greek seasoning
- 1tsp pepper or to taste
- 1tsp sea salt or to taste

Directions:

1. Remove giblets and rinse duck, inside and pour, under cold running water.

2. Pat dry with paper towels.

3. Use the tip of a sharp knife to cut the duck skin all over. Be careful not to cut through the meat. Tie the duck legs together with butcher's string.

4. To make a rub, combine the onion powder, pepper, salt, Italian seasoning, Greek seasoning, and paprika in a mixing bowl.

5. Insert the orange, onion, and apple to the duck cavity. Stuff the duck with freshly chopped parsley and sage.

6. Season all sides of the duck generously with rub mixture.

7. Start your pellet grill on smoke mode, leaving the lip open or until the fire starts.

8. Close the lid and preheat the grill to 325°F for 10 minutes.

9. Place the duck on the grill grate.

10. Roast for 2 to 21/2 hours, or until the duck skin is brown and the internal temperature of the thigh reaches 160°F.

11. Remove the duck from heat and let it rest for a few minutes.

12. Cut into sizes and serve.

Nutrition: Calories: 809 Total Fat: 42.9 g Saturated Fat: 15.8 g Cholesterol: 337 mg Sodium: 638 mg Total Carbohydrate: 11.7 g Dietary Fiber: 2.4 g Total Sugars: 7.5 g Protein: 89.6 g

134. Chicken Fajitas on a Wood Pellet Grill

Preparation time: 10 minutes
Cooking time: 20 minutes
Servings: 10
Ingredients:

- Chicken breast - 2 lb. thin sliced
- Red bell pepper - 1 large
- Onion - 1 large
- Orange bell pepper - 1 large
- Seasoning mix
- Oil - 2 tbsp.
- Onion powder - ½ tbsp.
- Granulated garlic - ½ tbsp.
- Salt - 1 tbsp.

Directions:

1. Preheat the grill to 450 degrees.

2. Mix the seasonings and oil.

3. Add the chicken slices to the mix.

4. Line a large pan with a non-stick baking sheet.

5. Let the pan heat for 10 minutes.

6. Place the chicken, peppers, and other vegetables in the grill.

7. Grill for 10 minutes or until the chicken is cooked.

8. Remove it from the grill and serve with warm tortillas and vegetables.

Nutrition: Carbohydrates: 5 g Protein: 29 g Fat: 6 g Sodium: 360 mg Cholesterol: 77 mg

135. Smoked Cornish Chicken in Wood Pellets

Preparation time: 0 minutes

Cooking time: 1 hour 10 minutes

Servings: 6

Ingredients:

- Cornish hens - 6
- Canola or avocado oil - 2-3 tbsp.
- Spice mix - 6 tbsp.

Directions:

1. Preheat your wood pellet grill to 275 degrees.
2. Rub the whole hen with oil and the spice mix. Use both of these ingredients liberally.
3. Place the breast area of the hen on the grill and smoke for 30 minutes.
4. Flip the hen, so the breast side is facing up. Increase the temperature to 400 degrees.
5. Cook until the temperature goes down to 165 degrees.
6. Pull it out and leave it for 10 minutes.
7. Serve warm with a side dish of your choice.

Nutrition: Carbohydrates: 1 g Protein: 57 g Fat: 50 g Sodium: 165 mg Cholesterol: 337 mg

Chapter 12. Fish And Seafood Recipes

136. Smoked Flatbread Salmon

Preparation time: 20 minutes
Cooking time: 45 minutes
Servings: 4-6
Ingredients:
- 1 pizza dough
- 1/4 cup crème fraiche
- 1/4 cup ricotta cheese
- Salt
- 1/2 chives, chopped
- 1/2 kg smoked salmon
- Capers, drained
- Extra-virgin olive oil

Directions:
1. Heat the oven to 200 F.
2. Spread a little of olive oil to the roasting pan.
3. Knead dough into a flat disk on a floured surface. Transfer dough to the prepared pan. Rub the top with olive oil and sprinkle with salt. Prick dough with a fork.
4. Bake the dough in a preheated oven for 5 minutes, then turn down the oven to 200 F. Bake for another 5-7 minutes until the crust is brown.
5. In the meantime, combine ricotta cheese, Crème Fraiche, and chopped chives. Season with salt. - Remove crust from oven and spread the mixture on top. Cover salmon with a thin layer of olive oil and place it on the bread. Bake at 200 F for 2 minutes.
6. Remove the bread from the oven, garnish with capers and drizzle with extra-virgin olive oil. Serve with a green salad.

Nutrition:
Energy (calories): 231 kcal
Protein: 19.56 g
Fat: 8.69 g
Carbohydrates: 11.81 g
Calcium: 204 mg
Magnesium: 29 mg
Phosphorus: 302 mg
Iron: 0.79 mg
Fiber: 0.2 g

137. Smoked Seafood Ceviche

Preparation time: 20 minutes
Cooking time: 45 minutes
Servings: 4-6
Ingredients:
- 1-pound Sea scallops
- 1-pound shrimp
- 1 tablespoon canola oil
- 1 lime, zested and juiced
- 1 lemon juice
- 1 orange, juiced
- 1 teaspoon garlic powder
- 1 teaspoon onion powder
- 2 teaspoon black pepper
- 1 teaspoon salt
- 1 avocado, diced
- 12 red onion
- 1 tablespoon cilantro
- 1 pinch red pepper flakes

Directions:
1. Smoke shrimp until crustaceans are just done, set aside to cool. Shuck scallops, dice and marinate with red onion and allow seafood to chill in the refrigerator for one hour.
2. Chill avocado and stir into the rest of the ingredients.

3. Serve it chilled.
Nutrition:
Energy (calories): 334 kcal
Protein: 34.5 g
Fat: 9.21 g
Carbohydrates: 30.69 g
Calcium: 181 mg
Magnesium: 90 mg
Phosphorus: 561 mg
Iron: 2.94 mg

138. Baked Halibut Fish Sticks with Spicy Coleslaw

Preparation time: 20 minutes
Cooking time: 35 minutes
Servings: 4-6
Ingredients:
- 1/2 cup mayonnaise
- 1/2 cup sour cream
- 1/2 tablespoon salt
- Black pepper
- 2 tablespoons dill seed
- 1 tablespoons sugar
- 2 tablespoons sriracha
- 2 tablespoons white wine vinegar
- 1 head cabbage, shredded
- 1 large carrot, peeled, shaved thin
- Olive oil
- 1 1/2-pound Halibut
- 1/2 cup all-purpose flour
- 1/2 breadcrumbs

Directions:
1. Make the spicy coleslaw by combining the sour cream, mayonnaise, salt, pepper, dill, sugar, sriracha, and vinegar together in a large bowl. Then mix in the cabbage and carrots. Cover the bowl and

keep it refrigerated until you are ready to serve.

2. Add the olive oil into a large skillet over medium-high heat until it is nice and hot.

3. Season the halibut fillets with salt and pepper on both sides.

4. Dip the fish into the batter and then dredge it into the flour. Remove any excess flour.

5. Lift the batter-coated fish out of the bowl and allow any excess batter to drip off.

6. Add the fish and cook it until it's opaque and firm to touch, about 2-4 minutes per side.

7. Serve it with a bed of spicy coleslaw and/or a lemon wedge.

Nutrition:
Energy (calories): 386 kcal
Protein: 21.05 g
Fat: 24.69 g
Carbohydrates: 20.63 g
Calcium: 123 mg
Magnesium: 67 mg
Phosphorus: 260 mg
Iron: 2.47 mg

139. Smoked Fish Chowder

Preparation time: 20 minutes
Cooking time: 35 minutes
Servings: 4
Ingredients:
- 12-ounces skin-on salmon fillet
- Traeger Fin and feather rub
- 2 corn husks
- 3 slices bacon
- 4 cans cream of potato soup, condensed
- 3 cups whole milk
- 8-ounces cream cheese
- 3 green onions
- 2 teaspoons hot sauce

Directions:
1. Soak corn husks in warm water for 20 minutes. Remove from water promptly and pat dry.

2. Add a small handful of the Traeger Fin and Feather Salmon Rub to coat both sides of the salmon.

3. Combine smoked salmon, cream of potato soup, milk, cream cheese, corn starch, and green onions in a saucepan on medium heat, stirring and cooking until thickened and bubbly, about 10 to 15 minutes.

4. Stir in bacon and add hot sauce. Cook for 1 minute, and then remove from heat.

5. Cut corn husks in half. Layer fish chowder in a circular design within one half of the husk.

6. Top with shredded cheddar cheese, fold in half and secure with a couple of toothpicks. Braais for 10 to 15 minutes or until the chowder is hot and cheese is melted.

7. Serve with a side of cornbread and enjoy it!

Nutrition:
Energy (calories): 839 kcal
Protein: 46.58 g
Fat: 45.25 g
Carbohydrates: 63.18 g
Calcium: 340 mg
Magnesium: 67 mg
Phosphorus: 597 mg
Iron: 4.79 mg

140. Roasted Clambake

Preparation time: 20 minutes
Cooking time: 1 hour and 10 minutes
Servings: 6-8
Ingredients:
- 8 small potatoes
- 1 potato, red
- 2 yellow onions, quartered
- 16 clams, in shell
- 16 mussels
- 4 pieces of ears fresh corn 4 mild Italian sausage
- 1 cup white wine
- 3 cloves garlic
- 2 whole lobsters
- 1/2 cup butter, melted
- 1 bread, French

Directions:
1. Clean the clams and mussels, but do not de-beard them, as it will make them taste like sand.

2. Place a heavy roasting pan in the oven, preheated to 300 degrees.

3. Prepare the sausage.

4. Add the wine and garlic.

5. Take the sausage and break it up into its individual pieces; add this to the roasting pan.

6. Bake in the oven for one hour.

7. When the hour is up, remove the roasting pan from the oven. Pour the butter over all the vegetables and meat. Return the roasting pan to the oven for another ten minutes.

8. During this time, bring a pot of water to a boil. Place the ears of corn in the boiling water for five minutes, or until they are cooked.

9. When ten minutes is up, take the corn out of the boiling water. Remove the outer husks from each ear. Remove the husks but do not scrape the corn off of the cobs.

10. Remove the roasting pan from the oven. Arrange each ear of corn in the center of a serving dish. Place the clam mixture and sausage around the corn. Sprinkle the lobster over the top. Serve with melted butter.

Nutrition:
Energy (calories): 763 kcal
Protein: 28.33 g
Fat: 21.44 g
Carbohydrates: 119.91 g
Calcium: 138 mg
Magnesium: 203 mg
Phosphorus: 587 mg
Iron: 6.89 mg
Fiber: 15.3 g
Sugars total: 9.2 g
Starch: 85.46 g

141. Grilled Blackened Saskatchewan Salmon

Preparation time: 20 minutes
Cooking time: 30 minutes
Servings: 4-6
Ingredients:
- 1 salmon fillet
- Zesty Italian Dressing
- Traeger Blackened Saskatchewan Rub
- Lemon wedges
Directions:
1. Rub the salmon thoroughly with the blackened Saskatchewan rub. Grill or barbecue to the desired doneness. In a glass, mix equal parts of basil pesto and Zesty Italian dressing.

2. Serve and enjoy it!
Nutrition:
Energy (calories): 351 kcal
Protein: 34.57 g
Fat: 20.24 g
Carbohydrates: 5.3 g
Calcium: 336 mg
Magnesium: 52 mg
Phosphorus: 542 m
Iron: 1.06 mg
Fiber: 1.87 g

142. Sweet Mandarin Salmon

Preparation time: 5 minutes
Cooking time: 10 minutes
Servings: 2
Ingredients:
- 1 whole lime juice
- 1 teaspoon sesame oil
- 1 Jar Traeger Mandarin Glaze
- 3/2 tablespoon soy sauce
- 2 tablespoon cilantro, finely chopped
- To taste cracked black pepper
- 1 pinch Jacobsen Salt Co. Pure Kosher Sea Salt
- 1 whole salmon, cut into fillets
Directions:
1. To prepare the marinade for the salmon fillets, you will need to take the Traeger Mandarin Glaze, rice vinegar, lime juice, soy sauce, cilantro, salt, and pepper in a small bowl and mix it until well combined. Place the cut salmon fillets in the marinade and cover them with plastic wrap. Place the salmon fillet in the refrigerator for at least an hour.

2. When the salmon fillets are ready, it is time to prepare them. Heat up your grill, preheating it to 350 degrees.

3. Clear the grates and spray them with cooking spray. Place the salmon fillets directly over the grill grates and turn on the salmon. Cook for about 6 minutes until the top is slightly charred. Carefully flip the salmon pieces with a spatula and cook for another four minutes.

4. Remove from heat and serve. Garnish with fresh cilantro and grate some extra lime zest over the top if desired. I like to serve mine along with some cauli-rice.

Nutrition:
Energy (calories): 114 kcal
Protein: 4.7 g
Fat: 5.63 g
Carbohydrates: 12.86 g
Calcium: 55 mg
Magnesium: 23 mg
Phosphorus: 83 mg
Iron: 0.58 mg

143. Baked Salmon Cakes

Preparation time: 20 minutes
Cooking time: 20 minutes
Servings: 4
Ingredients:
- 2-pounds salmon
- Salt
- Ground black pepper
- 1/2 small onion, diced
- 1 celery
- 1 bell pepper, red
- 1 tablespoon dill
- 1 teaspoon lemon zest
- 1/2 teaspoon black pepper

- 1/4 teaspoon coarse sea salt
- 1 1/2 tablespoons breadcrumbs
- 2 large egg
- 3 tablespoons Extra-virgin olive oil

Directions:
1. Preheat oven to 400 degrees F. Soak bread in 2 tablespoons water to prepare it for adding to the recipe.
2. Grate the salmon using the large grater, making sure that there are no bones in it.
3. Add diced onions, peppers, and celery.
4. Mix all of the ingredients.
5. Add the salmon mixture to the soaked and squeezed breadcrumbs.
6. Form salmon mixture into small patties.
7. In a 13"x9" baking dish, add the oil and place the salmon cakes onto the oil.
8. Bake for 20 minutes at 400 degrees F or until salmon is done.
9. Allow resting before serving.

Nutrition:
Energy (calories): 426 kcal
Protein: 48.64 g - Fat: 23.3 g
Carbohydrates: 2.73 g
Calcium: 491 mg
Magnesium: 75 mg
Phosphorus: 772 mg
Iron: 1.91 mg

144. Salmon Breakfast Pizza

Preparation time: 1 hour and 5 minutes
Cooking time: 30 minutes
Servings: 4

Ingredients:
- 4 1/2 cups all-purpose flour
- 1 1/2 tablespoon sugar
- 2 teaspoons yeast
- 3 tablespoons olive oil
- 15 fluid ounces water, lukewarm
- 2 tablespoons toasted sesame seeds
- 1 tablespoons sesame seed, black
- 1/2 cherry tomatoes
- 1 cup goat cheese
- 6 eggs
- 7-ounces smoked salmon
- 1 medium avocado
- 1/2 cup micro greens

Directions:
1. Mix 2 teaspoons of the flour with the yeast in half a cup lukewarm water and set aside for 10 minutes.
2. In a large bowl, place remaining flour and salt, pour the yeast-water mix, add the oil and pour over enough lukewarm water to make a sticky dough. Mix together for 5 minutes. Let it rise for 1 hour or until it doubles in size.
3. Spread the dough out into a round shape and add sesame seeds.
4. Bake the pizza on the top rack of the oven for 20 minutes or until the bottom becomes golden.
5. Meanwhile, fill a pan with water and boil it. Place eggs on top and simmer for 5 minutes. Cool eggs by placing them in a bowl of cold water.
6. Fry the salmon for 3 minutes on each side.
7. Wash micro greens.
8. Assemble your pizza by spreading goat cheese on top, then break eggs and place on top. Add tomatoes, salmon, avocado, and micro greens.

Nutrition:
Energy (calories): 1058 kcal
Protein: 43.2 g - Fat: 42.59 g
Carbohydrates: 123.98 g
Calcium: 268 mg
Magnesium: 109 mg
Phosphorus: 668 mg
Iron: 11.88 mg

145. Prosciutto Wrapped Grilled Shrimp with Peach Salsa

Preparation time: 20 minutes
Cooking time: 45 minutes
Servings: 6

Ingredients:
- 2-pounds shrimp
- 8 slices prosciutto ham
- Toothpicks
- 2 whole peaches, diced
- 2 tablespoons balsamic vinegar
- 2 tablespoons honey
- 1 chili
- 2 tablespoons basil
- Salt
- Black pepper

Directions:
1. In a small bowl, mix the peach salsa ingredients. Set aside.
2. In a large bowl, add the shrimp, 1/2 tablespoon olive oil, 1/2 tablespoon of salt, 1/2 tablespoon of pepper, basil, 1/4 cup of lemon juice, 1 tablespoon of honey, the juice

of the chili, and the cumin. Mix well.

3. Place 1 slice of prosciutto on a cutting board lay the shrimp along the length of the prosciutto. Roll the prosciutto to wrap the shrimp. Secure with a toothpick and repeat with remaining shrimp and prosciutto.

4. Place a grill pan on the stovetop over medium-high heat. When the pan is hot, add 1 tablespoon of oil. When the oil is hot, add the wrapped prosciutto-covered shrimp. Remove the seared shrimp to a plate lined with a paper towel. Place in the fridge to cool.

5. Peel and devein your shrimp. Thread the shrimp onto the toothpicks and serve.

Nutrition:
Energy (calories): 325 kcal
Protein: 39.09 g - Fat: 7.16 g
Carbohydrates: 25.91 g
Calcium: 281 mg
Magnesium: 66 mg
Phosphorus: 431 mg
Iron: 4.01 mg - Sodium: 914 mg

146. Pineapple Maple Glaze Fish

Preparation time: 10 minutes
Cooking time: 15 Minutes
Servings: 6 Servings
Ingredients:

• 3 pounds of fresh salmon
• 1/4 cup maple syrup
• 1/2 cup pineapple juice
Brine Ingredients:
• 3 cups of water
• Sea salt, to taste
• 2 cups of pineapple juice

• One-half cup of brown sugar
• 5 tablespoons of Worcestershire sauce
• 1 tablespoon of garlic salt
Directions:
1. Combine all the brine ingredients in a large cooking pan.
2. Place the fish into the brine and let it sit for 2 hours for marinating.
3. After 2 hours, take out the fish and pat dry with a paper towel, and set aside.
4. Preheat the smoker grill to 250 degrees Fahrenheit, until the smoke started to appear.
5. Put salmon on the grill and cook for 15 minutes.
6. Meanwhile, mix pineapple and maple syrup in a bowl and baste fish every 5 minutes.
7. Once the salmon is done, serve and enjoy it!

Nutrition:
Energy (calories): 538 kcal
Protein: 48.89 g - Fat: 16.98 g
Carbohydrates: 47.77 g
Calcium: 510 mg
Magnesium: 102 mg
Phosphorus: 782 mg
Iron: 2.67 mg - Fiber: 2.2 g
Sugars total: 34.79 g
Cholesterol: 60mg

147. Smoked Catfish Recipe

Preparation time: 10 minutes
Cooking time: 5 Minutes
Servings: 3 Servings
Ingredients:
The Rub:
• 2 tablespoons paprika

• 1/4 teaspoon salt
• 1 tablespoon garlic powder
• 1 tablespoon onion powder
• 1/2 tablespoon dried thyme
• 1/2 tablespoon cayenne
• 2 pounds fresh catfish fillets
• 4 tablespoons butter, soften
Directions:
1. Take a mixing bowl, and combine all the rub ingredients in it, including the paprika, salt, garlic powder, onion powder, and thyme and cayenne paper.
2. Rub the fillet with the butter, and then sprinkle a generous amount of rub on top
3. Coat fish well with the rub.
4. Preheat the smoker grill at 200 degrees Fahrenheit for 15 minutes.
5. Cook fish on the grill for 10 minutes, 5minutes per side.
6. Once done, serve and enjoy it!

Nutrition:
Energy (calories): 458 kcal
Protein: 51.24 g - Fat: 24.68 g
Carbohydrates: 7.24 g
Calcium: 72 mg
Magnesium: 85 mg
Phosphorus: 675 mg
Iron: 2.28 mg
Sodium: 28mg

148. Classic smoked Trout

Preparation time: 10 minutes

Cooking time: 1 Hour
Servings: 3 Servings
Ingredients:
- 4 cups of water - 1-2 cups dark-brown sugar
- 1 cup of sea salt - Ingredients for The Trout's
- 3 pounds of trout, backbone and pin bones removed
- 4 tablespoons of olive oil

Directions:
1. Preheat the electrical smoker grill, by setting the temperature to 250 degrees F, for 15 minutes by closing the lid.
2. Take a cooking pot, and combine all the brine ingredients, including water, sugar, and salt.
3. Submerged the fish in the brine mixture for a few hours.
4. Afterward, take out the fish, and pat dry with the paper towel.
5. Drizzle olive oil over the fish, and then place it over the grill grate for cooking.
6. Smoke the fish, until the internal temperature reaches 140 degrees Fahrenheit for 1 hour.
7. Then serve.

Nutrition:
Energy (calories): 1227 kcal
Protein: 94.34 g - Fat: 47.98 g
Carbohydrates: 102.48 g
Calcium: 315 mg
Magnesium: 114 mg
Phosphorus: 1115 mg
Iron: 7.97 mg - Sodium: 18 mg

149. Cajun smoked Shrimp

Preparation time: 10 minutes
Cooking time: 10 Minutes
Servings: 2 Servings
Ingredients:
- 2 tablespoons of virgin olive oil
- 1/2 lemon, juiced
- 3 cloves garlic, finely minced
- 2 tablespoons of Cajun spice
- Salt, to taste
- 1.5 pounds of shrimp, raw, peeled, deveined

Directions:
1. Take a zip lock bag and combine olive oil, lemon juice, garlic cloves, Cajun spice, salt, and shrimp.
2. Toss the ingredients well for fine coating.
3. Preheat the smoker grill for 10 minutes until the smoke starts to establish.
4. Put the fish on the grill grate and close the lid.
5. Turn the temperature to high and allow the fish to cook the shrimp for 10 minutes, 5 minutes per side.
6. Once done, serve.

Nutrition:
Energy (calories): 423 kcal
Protein: 70.18 g
Fat: 11.38 g
Carbohydrates: 6.2 g
Calcium: 540 mg
Magnesium: 122 mg
Phosphorus: 680 mg
Iron: 8.44 mg
Sodium: 48mg

150. Candied smoked Salmon with orange Ginger Rub

Preparation time: 10 minutes
Cooking time: 2 Hours 10 Minutes
Servings: 10 servings
Ingredients:
The Marinade:
- Brown sugar 1/4 cup
- Salt one-half teaspoon

The Rub:
- Minced garlic 2 tablespoons
- Grated fresh ginger 1 teaspoon
- Grated orange zest one-half teaspoon
- Chili powder one-half teaspoon
- Cayenne pepper one-half teaspoon

The Glaze:
- Red wine 2 tablespoons
- Dark rum 2 tablespoons
- Brown sugar 1 and one-half cups
- Honey 1 cup

Directions:
1. Mix salt with brown sugar then applies over the salmon fillet. Let it rest for approximately an hour or until the sugar is melted.
2. In the meantime, combine minced garlic with grated fresh ginger, orange zest, chili powder, and cayenne pepper. Mix well.
3. Rub the salmon fillet with the spice mixture then set aside.

4. Place the seasoned salmon in a wood pellet smoker and smoke for 2 hours.

5. Mix red wine with dark rum, brown sugar, and honey, then stir until dissolved.

6. During the smoking process, baste the honey mixture over the salmon fillet for several times.

7. Once the smoked salmon flakes, remove it from the wood pellet smoker and transfer it to a serving dish.

8. Serve and enjoy it!

Nutrition:
Energy (calories): 156 kcal
Protein: 0.29 g - Fat: 0.03 g
Carbohydrates: 41.35 g
Calcium: 6 mg
Magnesium: 2 mg
Phosphorus: 6 mg
Iron: 0.24 mg - Potassium: 39 mg

151. Juicy Lime smoked Tuna Belly

Preparation time: 10 minutes
Cooking time: 2 hours 10 Minutes
Servings: 10 servings
Ingredients:
• Tuna belly (3-lb., 1.4-kg.)
The Marinade:
• Fresh limes 2
• White sugar 2 tablespoons
• Brown sugar 3 tablespoons
• Pepper one-half teaspoon
• Soy sauce 1 tablespoon
• Sriracha sauce 2 tablespoons
Directions:

1. Cut the limes into halves then squeeze the juice over the tuna belly. Marinate the tuna belly with the juice for 10 minutes. Meanwhile, combine white sugar with brown sugar, pepper, soy sauce, and Sriracha sauce then mix well. Wash and rinse the tuna belly then pat it dry.

2. Set the wood pellet smoker.

3. Wait until the wood pellet smoker reaches the desired temperature then place the seasoned tuna belly in it. Smoke the tuna belly for 2 hours or until it flakes and once it is done, remove it from the wood pellet smoker.

4. Serve and enjoy it!

Nutrition:
Energy (calories): 63 kcal
Protein: 9.07 g
Fat: 0.74 g
Carbohydrates: 5.58 g
Calcium: 11 mg
Magnesium: 13 mg
Phosphorus: 68 mg
Iron: 0.81 mg
Fiber: 0 g

152. Lemon Butter smoked Mackerel with Juniper Berries Brine

Preparation time: 10 minutes
Cooking time: 2 hours 10 minutes
Servings: 10 servings
Ingredients:
• Mackerel fillet (4-lbs., 1.8-kg.)
The Brine:
• Coldwater 4 cups
• Mustard seeds 1 tablespoon
• Dried juniper berries 1 tablespoon
• Bay leaves 3
• Salt 1 tablespoon
The Glaze:
• Butter 2 tablespoons
• Lemon juice 2 tablespoons
Directions:

1. Pour cold water into a container, then season with salt, bay leaves, dried juniper berries, and mustard seeds, then stir well.

2. Add the mackerel fillet to the brine mixture, then soak for approximately 20 minutes, then wash and rinse it. Pat the mackerel dry.

3. Heat the pellet smoker for indirect heat then adjust the temperature to 225 °F (107 °C).

4. Place the seasoned mackerel on a sheet of aluminum foil then baste butter over it.

5. Drizzle lemon juice then wraps the mackerel fillet with the aluminum foil.

6. Smoke the wrapped mackerel for 2 hours or until it flakes and once it is done, remove from the wood pellet smoker. Unwrap the smoked mackerel and serve. Enjoy it!

Nutrition:
Energy (calories): 61 kcal
Protein: 8.3 g
Fat: 2.57 g
Carbohydrates: 0.74 g
Calcium: 25 mg
Magnesium: 17 mg
Phosphorus: 105 mg
Iron: 0.81 mg

153. Smoked Crab Paprika Garlic with Lemon Butter Flavor

Preparation time: 5 minutes
Cooking time: 30 Minutes
Servings: 10 servings
Ingredients:
- Fresh Crabs (7-lb., 3.2-kg.)

The Sauce:
- Salt 1 tablespoon
- Cayenne pepper 1 and one-half teaspoon
- Salted butter 2 cups
- Lemon juice one-half cup
- Worcestershire sauce 1 tablespoon
- Garlic powder 2 teaspoons
- Smoked paprika 2 teaspoons

Directions:
1. Preheat a saucepan over low heat then melt the butter. Let it cool.
2. Season the melted butter with salt, cayenne pepper, Worcestershire sauce, garlic powder, and smoked paprika, then pour lemon juice into the melted butter.
3. Stir until incorporated and set aside.
4. Arrange the crabs in a disposable aluminum pan then drizzle the sauce over the crabs.
5. Smoke the crabs for 30 minutes then remove from the wood pellet smoker.
6. Transfer the smoked crabs to a serving dish then serve.
7. Enjoy it!

Nutrition:
Energy (calories): 337 kcal
Protein: 1.07 g
Fat: 36.95 g
Carbohydrates: 2.33 g
Calcium: 18 mg
Magnesium: 5 mg
Phosphorus. 24 mg
Iron: 0.32 mg

154. Cayenne Garlic Smoked Shrimp

Preparation time: 5 minutes
Cooking time: 15 Minutes
Servings: 10 servings
Ingredients:
- Fresh Shrimps (3-lb., 1.4-kg.)

The Spices:
- Olive oil 2 tablespoons
- Lemon juice 2 tablespoons
- Salt three-fourth teaspoon
- Smoked paprika 2 teaspoons
- Pepper one-half teaspoon
- Garlic powder 2 tablespoons
- Onion powder 2 tablespoons
- Dried thyme 1 teaspoon
- Cayenne pepper 2 teaspoons

Directions:
1. Mix all the spices Set aside. Next, peel the shrimps and discard the head. Place in a disposable aluminum pan. Drizzle olive oil and lemon juice over the shrimps and shake to coat. Let the shrimps rest for approximately 5 minutes.
2. Prepare in advance the wood pellet smoker for indirect heat then adjust the temperature to 350 °F (177 °C).
3. Sprinkle the spice mixture over the shrimps then stir until the shrimps are completely seasoned.
4. Place the disposable aluminum pan with shrimps in the wood pellet smoker and smoke the shrimps for 15 minutes. The shrimps will be opaque and pink. Remove the smoked shrimps from the wood pellet smoker and transfer to a serving dish.
5. Serve and enjoy it!

Nutrition:
Energy (calories): 39 kcal
Protein: 0.7 g
Fat: 2.87 g
Carbohydrates: 3.4 g
Calcium: 10 mg
Magnesium: 5 mg
Phosphorus: 17 mg
Iron: 0.36 mg
Fiber: 0 g

155. Cinnamon Ginger juicy smoked Crab

Preparation time: 10 minutes
Cooking time: 30 Minutes
Servings: 10 servings
Ingredients:
- Fresh crabs (7-lb., 3.2-kg.)
- The Spices — Salt 1 tablespoon
- Ground celery seeds 3 tablespoons
- Ground mustard 2 teaspoons
- Cayenne pepper one-half teaspoon
- Black pepper one-half teaspoon

- Smoked paprika 1 and one-half teaspoon
- Ground clove a pinch
- Ground allspice three-fourth teaspoon
- Ground ginger 1 teaspoon
- Cardamom one-half teaspoon
- Cinnamon one-half teaspoon
- Bay leaves 2

Directions:

1. Combine the entire spices; salt, ground celery seeds, mustard, cayenne pepper, black pepper, smoked paprika, clove, allspice, ginger, cardamom, and cinnamon in a bowl then mix well.
2. Sprinkle the spice mixture over the crabs then wrap the crabs with aluminum foil.
3. Turn the switch on then adjust the temperature to 350 F (177 C). Place the wrapped crabs in the wood pellet smoker and smoke for 30 minutes.
4. Once it is done, remove the wrapped smoked carbs from the wood pellet smoker and let it rest for approximately 10 minutes.
5. Unwrap the smoked crabs and transfer it to a serving dish.
6. Serve and enjoy it!

Nutrition:
Energy (calories): 16 kcal
Protein: 1 g
Fat: 0.73 g
Carbohydrates: 1.91 g
Calcium: 42 mg
Magnesium: 13 mg
Phosphorus: 22 mg
Iron: 1.11 mg
Potassium: 64 mg
Fiber: 0 g

Chapter 13. Vegetable Recipes

156. Cajun Style Grilled Corn

Preparation Time: 5 minutes
Cooking Time: 25 minutes
Servings: 4
Ingredients:

- 4 ears corn, with husks
- 1 tsp. dried oregano
- 1 tsp. paprika
- 1 tsp. garlic powder
- 1 tsp. onion powder
- 1/2 tsp. kosher salt
- 1/2 tsp. ground black pepper
- 1/4 tsp. dried thyme
- 1/4 tsp. cayenne pepper
- 2 tsp. butter, melted

Directions:
1. Preheat pellet grill to 375°F.
2. Peel husks back but do not remove. Scrub and remove silks.
3. Mix oregano, paprika, garlic powder, onion powder, salt, pepper, thyme, and cayenne in a small bowl.
4. Brush melted butter over corn.
5. Rub seasoning mixture over each ear of corn. Pull husks up and place corn on grill grates. Grill for about 12-15 minutes, turning occasionally.
6. Remove from grill and allow to cool for about 5 minutes. Remove husks, then serve and enjoy!

Nutrition:
Calories: 278
Fat: 17.4 g
Cholesterol: 40.7 mg
Carbohydrate: 30.6 g
Fiber: 4.5 g
Sugar: 4.6 g
Protein: 5.4 g

157. Grilled Cherry Tomato Skewers

Preparation Time: 10 minutes
Cooking Time: 50 minutes
Servings: 4
Ingredients:

- 24 cherry tomatoes
- 1/4 cup olive oil
- 3 tbsp. balsamic vinegar
- 4 garlic cloves, minced
- 1 tbsp. fresh thyme, finely chopped
- 1 tsp. kosher salt
- 1 tsp. ground black pepper
- 2 tbsp. chives, finely chopped

Directions:
1. Preheat pellet grill to 425°F.
2. In a medium-sized bowl, mix olive oil, balsamic vinegar, garlic, and thyme. Add tomatoes and toss to coat.
3. Let tomatoes sit in the marinade at room temperature for about 30 minutes. Remove tomatoes from marinade and thread 4 tomatoes per skewer.
4. Season both sides of each skewer with kosher salt and ground pepper. Place on grill grate and grill for about 3 minutes on each side, or until each side is slightly charred.
5. Remove from grill and allow to rest for about 5 minutes. Garnish with chives, then serve and enjoy!

Nutrition:
Calories: 228 Fat: 10 g
Cholesterol: 70 mg
Carbohydrate: 7 g
Fiber: 2 g Sugar: 3 g Protein: 27g

158. Roasted Vegetable Medley

Preparation Time: 20 minutes
Cooking Time: 50 minutes
Servings: 4 to 6
Ingredients:

- 2 medium potatoes, cut into 1 inch wedges
- 2 red bell peppers, cut into 1 inch cubes
- 1 small butternut squash, peeled and cubed to 1 inch cube
- 1 red onion, cut into 1 inch cubes
- 1 cup broccoli, trimmed
- 2 tbsp. olive oil
- 1 tbsp. balsamic vinegar
- 1 tbsp. fresh rosemary, minced
- 1 tbsp. fresh thyme, minced
- 1 tsp. kosher salt
- 1 tsp. ground black pepper

Directions:
1. Preheat pellet grill to 425°F.
2. In a large bowl, combine potatoes, peppers, squash, and onion.
3. In a small bowl, whisk together olive oil, balsamic vinegar, rosemary, thyme, salt, and pepper.
4. Pour marinade over vegetables and toss to coat. Allow resting for about 15 minutes.

5. Place marinated vegetables into a grill basket, and place a grill basket on the grill grate. Cook for about 30-40 minutes, occasionally tossing in the grill basket.

6. Remove veggies from grill and transfer to a serving dish. Allow to cool for 5 minutes, then serve and enjoy!

Nutrition:

Calories: 158.6

Fat: 7.4 g

Cholesterol: 0

Carbohydrate: 22 g

Fiber: 7.2 g

Sugar: 3.1 g

Protein: 5.2 g

159. Grilled Corn with Honey Butter

Preparation Time: 15 minutes

Cooking Time: 10 minutes

Servings: 6

Ingredients:

- 6 pieces corn, husked
- 2 tablespoons olive oil
- Salt and pepper to taste
- ½ cup butter, room temperature
- ½ cup honey

Directions:

1. Fire the Traeger Grill to 350F. Use desired wood pellets when cooking. Keep lid unopened to preheat until 15 minutes

2. Coat corn with oil and add salt and pepper

3. Place the corn on the grill grate and cook for 10 minutes. Make sure to flip the corn halfway through the cooking time for even cooking.

4. Meanwhile, mix the butter and honey in a small bowl. Set aside.

5. Remove corn from grill and coat with honey butter sauce

Nutrition:

Calories: 387 Cal

Fat: 21.6 g

Carbohydrates: 51.2 g

Protein: 5 g

Fiber: 0 g

160. Smoked Mushrooms

Preparation Time: 20 minutes

Cooking Time: 2 hours

Servings: 6

Ingredients:

- 6-12 large Portobello mushrooms
- Sea salt
- black pepper
- Extra virgin olive oil
- Herbs de Provence

Directions:

1. Preheat the smoker to 200°F while adding water and wood chips to the smoker bowl and tray, respectively.

2. Wash and dry mushrooms

3. Rub the mushrooms with olive oil, salt and pepper seasoning with herbs in a bowl.

4. Place the mushrooms with the cap side down on the smoker rack. Smoke the mushrooms for 2 hours while adding water and wood chips to the smoker after every 60 minutes.

5. Remove the mushrooms and serve

Nutrition:

Calories: 106 Cal

Fat: 6 g

Carbohydrates: 5 g

Protein: 8 g

Fiber: 0.9 g

161. Smoked and Smashed New Potatoes

Preparation Time: 5 minutes

Cooking Time: 8 hours

Servings: 4

Ingredients:

- 1-1/2 pounds small new red potatoes or fingerlings
- Extra virgin olive oil
- Sea salt and black pepper
- 2 tbsp. softened butter

Directions:

1. Let the potatoes dry. Once dried, put in a pan and coat with salt, pepper, and extra virgin olive oil.

2. Place the potatoes on the topmost rack of the smoker.

3. Smoke for 60 minutes.

4. Once done, take them out and smash each one

5. Mix with butter and season

Nutrition:

Calories: 258 Cal

Fat: 2.0 g

Carbohydrates: 15.5 g

Protein: 4.1 g

Fiber: 1.5 g

162. Smoked Brussels Sprouts

Preparation Time: 15 minutes

Cooking Time: 45 minutes

Servings: 6

Ingredients:

- 1-1/2 pounds Brussels sprouts
- 2 cloves of garlic minced
- 2 tbsp. extra virgin olive oil
- Sea salt and cracked black pepper

Directions:
1. Rinse sprouts
2. Remove the outer leaves and brown bottoms off the sprouts.
3. Place sprouts in a large bowl, then coat with olive oil.
4. Add a coat of garlic, salt, and pepper and transfer them to the pan.
5. Add to the top rack of the smoker with water and woodchips.
6. Smoke for 45 minutes or until reaches 250°F temperature.
7. Serve
Nutrition:
Calories: 84 Cal
Fat: 4.9 g
Carbohydrates: 7.2 g
Protein: 2.6 g
Fiber: 2.9 g

163. Smokey Roasted Cauliflower

Preparation Time: 10 minutes
Cooking Time: 1 hour 20 minutes
Servings: 4 to 6
Ingredients:
• 1 head cauliflower
• 1 cup parmesan cheese
Spice ingredients:
• 1 tbsp. olive oil - 2 cloves garlic, chopped
• 1 tsp. kosher salt
• 1 tsp. smoked paprika
Directions:
1. Preheat pellet grill to 180°F. If applicable, set the smoke setting to high.
2. Cut cauliflower into bite-size flowerets and place in a grill basket. Place basket on the grill grate and smoke for an hour.

3. Mix spice ingredients in a small bowl while the cauliflower is smoking. Remove cauliflower from the grill after an hour and let cool. Change grill temperature to 425°F. After the cauliflower has cooled, put cauliflower in a resealable bag, and pour marinade in the bag. Toss to combine in the bag.
4. Place cauliflower back in a grill basket and return to grill. Roast in the grill basket for 10-12 minutes or until the outsides begin to get crispy and golden brown.
5. Remove from grill and transfer to a serving dish. Sprinkle parmesan cheese over the cauliflower and rest for a few minutes so the cheese can melt. Serve and enjoy!
Nutrition:
Calories: 70 Fat: 35 g
Cholesterol: 0 Carbohydrate: 7g
Fiber: 3 g Sugar: 3 g Protein: 3 g

164. Crispy Maple Bacon Brussels Sprouts

Preparation Time: 15 minutes
Cooking Time: 1 hour
Servings: 6
Ingredients:
• 1 lb. brussels sprouts, trimmed and quartered
• 6 slices thick-cut bacon
• 3 tbsp. maple syrup
• 1 tsp. olive oil
• 1/2 tsp. kosher salt
• 1/2 tsp. ground black pepper
Directions:
1. Preheat pellet grill to 425°F.

2. Cut bacon into 1/2 inch thick slices.
3. Place brussels sprouts in a single layer in the cast iron skillet. Drizzle with olive oil and maple syrup, then toss to coat. Sprinkle bacon slices on top, then season with kosher salt and black pepper.
4. Place skillet in the pellet grill and roast for about 40 to 45 minutes, or until the brussels sprouts are caramelized and brown.
5. Remove skillet from grill and allow brussels sprouts to cool for about 5 to 10 minutes. Serve and enjoy!
Nutrition:
Calories: 175.3 Fat: 12.1 g
Cholesterol: 6.6 mg
Carbohydrate: 13.6 g Fiber: 2.9g
Sugar: 7.6g Protein: 4.8g

165. Sweet Jalapeño Cornbread

Preparation Time: 20 minutes
Cooking Time: 50 minutes
Servings: 12
Ingredients:
• 2/3 cup margarine, softened
• 2/3 cup white sugar
• 2 cups cornmeal
• 1 1/3 cups all-purpose flour
• 4 tsp. baking powder
• 1 tsp. kosher salt
• 3 eggs
• 1 2/3 cups milk
• 1 cup jalapeños, deseeded and chopped
• Butter, to line baking dish
Directions:
1. Preheat pellet grill to

400°F.

2. Beat margarine and sugar together in a medium-sized bowl until smooth.

3. In another bowl, combine cornmeal, flour, baking powder, and salt.

4. In a third bowl, combine and whisk eggs and milk.

5. Pour 1/3 of the milk mixture and 1/3 of the flour mixture into the margarine mixture at a time, whisking just until mixed after each pour.

6. Once thoroughly combined, stir in chopped jalapeño.

7. Lightly butter the bottom of the baking dish. Pour the cornbread mixture evenly into the baking dish.

8. Place dish on grill grates and close the lid. Cook for about 23-25 minutes, or until thoroughly cooked. The way to test is by inserting a toothpick into the center of the cornbread - it should come out clean once removed.

9. Remove the dish from the grill and allow to rest for 10 minutes before slicing and serving.

Nutrition:
Calories: 160
Fat: 6 g
Cholesterol: 15 mg
Carbohydrate: 25 g
Fiber: 10 g
Sugar: 0.5 g
Protein: 3 g

166. Broccoli with Lemon and Pepper

Preparation Time: 15 minutes
Cooking Time: 3 Minutes
Servings: 1-2
Ingredients:
- 2 cups of broccoli, fresh
- 1 tablespoon of canola oil
- 1 teaspoon of lemon pepper

Directions:
1. Place the grill; grate inside the unit, and close the hood.
2. Preheat the grill by turning at high for 10 minutes.
3. Meanwhile, mix broccoli with lemon pepper and canola oil.
4. Toss well to coat the ingredients thoroughly.
5. Place it on a grill grade once add food appears.
6. Lock the unit and cook for 3 minutes at medium.
7. Take out and serve.

Nutrition:
Calories: 96
Total Fat: 7.3g
Saturated Fat: 0.5g
Cholesterol: 0mg
Sodium: 30mg
Total Carbohydrate: 6.7g
Dietary Fiber 2.7g
Total Sugars: 1.6g
Protein: 2.7g

167. Roasted Cauliflower

Preparation Time: 15 minutes
Cooking Time: 10 minutes
Servings: 4 to 6
Ingredients:
- 1 Cauliflower head, cut into florets
- 1 tbsp. Oil
- 1 cup grated Parmesan
- 2 Garlic cloves, cursed
- ½ Tsp. Black pepper
- ½ tsp. of Salt
- ¼ tsp. of Paprika

Directions:
1. Let the grill heat to 180F with the lid closed.
2. Place the cauliflower florets on the grill. Smoke for 1 hour. In the meantime, combine the remaining ingredients but not the cheese. Once done, remove the florets.
3. Increase the heat to 450F. Once heated, brush the florets with the mixture. Place on a cooking tray and on the grill. Roast for 10 minutes.
4. Sprinkle with cheese and let it sit on the grill with the lid closed until melted. Serve as it is or as a side dish. Enjoy!

Nutrition:
Calories: 45
Protein: 7g
Carbs: 7g
Fat: 2g

168. Roasted Asparagus

Preparation Time: 5 minutes
Cooking Time: 30 minutes
Servings: 4 to 6
Ingredients:
- 1 bunch of Asparagus
- Salmon seasoning as needed
- 2 tbsp. Oil, or as needed

Directions:
1. Season the asparagus with salmon seasoning and drizzle with oil. Make sure to coat well.
2. Let the grill heat to 350F with the lid closed.
3. Grill the asparagus for 30 minutes.
4. Serve and enjoy!

Nutrition:

Calories: 70g
Protein: 4g
Carbs: 7g
Fat: 4g

169. Grilled Mixed Veggies

Preparation Time: 15 minutes
Cooking Time: 20 minutes
Servings: 4 to 6
Ingredients:

- 1 Tomato, Large
- 1 Squash
- 1 Zucchini
- 1 Onion, red
- 1 Potato, Sweet
- Black pepper and Salt to taste
- Oil

Directions:
1. Let the grill heat with closed lit to high.
2. Slice the veggies into slices (1/4 inch).
3. Brush each slice with oil. Season with black pepper and salt.
4. First grill the squash, zucchini, onion, and sweet potato for 20min. turn them halfway.
5. Add the tomato slices 5 minutes before the cooking is done.
6. Serve them with your main dish and enjoy!
Nutrition:
Calories: 105
Protein: 5g
Carbs: 23g
Fat: 8g

170. Grilled Corn

Preparation Time: 15 minutes
Cooking Time: 25 minutes
Servings: 6
Ingredients:

- 6 fresh ears corn
- Salt
- Black pepper
- Olive oil
- Vegetable seasoning
- Butter for serving

Directions:
1. Let the grill heat to high with the lid closed.
2. Peel the husks. Remove the corn's silk. Rub with black pepper, salt, vegetable seasoning, and oil.
3. Close the husks and grill for 25 minutes. Turn them occasionally.
4. Serve topped with butter, and enjoy!
Nutrition:
Calories: 70
Protein: 3g
Carbs: 18g
Fat: 2g

171. Thyme - Rosemary Mash Potatoes

Preparation Time: 20 minutes
Cooking Time: 1 hour
Servings: 6
Ingredients:

- 4 ½ lbs. Potatoes, russet
- Salt
- 1 pint of Heavy cream
- 3 Thyme sprigs + 2 tbsp. for garnish
- 2 Rosemary sprigs
- 6 - 7 Sage leaves
- 6 - 7 Black peppercorns
- Black pepper to taste
- 2 stick Butter, softened
- 2 Garlic cloves, chopped

Directions:
1. Let the grill heat to 350F with the lid closed.
2. Peel the russet potatoes. Cut into small pieces and place them in a baking dish. Fill it with water (1 ½ cups). Place on the grill and cook with the lid closed for about 1 hour.
3. In the meantime, combine garlic, peppercorns, herbs and cream in a saucepan. Place on the grate and cook covered for about 15 minutes. Once done, strain to remove the garlic and herbs. Keep warm.
4. Drain the potatoes and place them in a stockpot. Rice them with a fork and pour 2/3 of the mixture.
5. Add 1 stick softened butter and salt. Add more cream to get the desired consistency.
6. Serve right away.
Nutrition:
Calories: 180
Protein: 4g
Carbs: 28g
Fat: 10g

172. Grilled Broccoli

Preparation Time: 15 minutes
Cooking Time: 10 minutes
Servings: 4 to 6
Ingredients:

- 4 bunches of Broccoli
- 4 tbsp. Olive oil
- Black pepper and salt to taste
- ½ Lemon, the juice
- ½ Lemon cut into wedges

Directions:
1. Let the grill heat to High with the lid closed.

2. In a bowl add the broccoli and drizzle with oil. Coat well. Season with salt.

3. Grill for 5 minutes and then flip. Cook for 3 minutes more.

4. Once done, transfer on a plate. Squeeze lemon on top and serve with lemon wedges. Enjoy!

Nutrition:

Calories: 35g

Protein: 2.5g

Carbs: 5g

Fat: 1g

173. The Best Potato Roast

Preparation Time: 15 minutes

Cooking Time: 35 minutes

Servings: 6

Ingredients:

- 4 Potatoes, large (scrubbed)
- 2 tbsp. Vegetable oil
- 1 ½ cups gravy (beef or chicken)
- Rib seasoning to taste
- 1 ½ cups Cheddar cheese
- Black pepper and salt to taste
- 2 tbsp. sliced Scallions

Directions:

1. Let the grill heat to high with the lid closed.

2. Slice each potato into wedges or fries. Transfer into a bowl and drizzle with oil. Season with Rib seasoning.

3. Spread the wedges/fries on a baking sheet (rimmed). Roast for about 20 minutes. Turn the wedges/fries and cook for 15 minutes more.

4. In the meantime, warm the chicken/beef gravy in a saucepan. Cut the cheese into small cubes.

5. Once done cooking, place the potatoes on a plate or into a bowl. Distribute the cut cheese and pour hot gravy on top.

6. Serve garnished with scallion. Season with pepper. Enjoy!

Nutrition:

Calories: 220

Protein: 3g

Carbs: 38g

Fat: 15g

Chapter 14. Party Recipes

174. Leek and Cheddar Cheese Sauce

Preparation time: 5 minutes
Cooking time: 10 minutes
Servings: 4
Ingredients:

- ·1 tablespoon of oil
- ·2 sliced leeks
- ·2 tablespoons of butter
- ·2 tablespoons of plain flour
- ·1 cup of semi-skimmed milk
- ·1 cup of grated Cheddar cheese

Directions:

1. To prepare this tasty sauce, heat a large, non-stick frying pan and add the oil; put in the leeks, cover, and fry for ten minutes
2. As the above process is going on, get a small saucepan and melt the butter in it before stirring in the flour; then cook for one or two minutes. Reduce the heat, and whisk in the milk slowly before bringing it to boil while still stirring until a thick mixture is achieved
3. Add seasoning taste after which the cheese is then stirred in until it melts
4. Once the grilled chicken is ready, the sauce can be poured over it and then place on the grill for another two or three minutes until it's golden and bubbling

Nutrition:
Calories 101.4
Carbohydrates 7.7g
Fiber 1g
Protein 4.2g
Fat 6.2g

175. Chocolate-Hazelnut and Strawberry Grilled Dessert Pizza

Preparation time: 10 minutes
Total cooking time: 6 minutes
Servings: 4
Ingredients:

- ·2 tablespoons all-purpose flour, plus more as needed
- ·½ store-bought pizza dough (about 8 ounces)
- ·1 tablespoon canola oil
- ·1 cup sliced fresh strawberries
- ·1 tablespoon sugar
- ·½ cup chocolate-hazelnut spread

Directions:

1. Insert the Grill Grate and close the hood. Select GRILL, set the temperature to MAX, and set the time to 6 minutes. Select START/STOP to begin preheating.
2. While the unit is preheating, dust a clean work surface with the flour. Place the dough on the floured surface and roll it out to a 9-inch round of even thickness. Dust your rolling pin and work surface with additional flour, as needed, to ensure the dough does not stick.
3. Brush the surface of the rolled-out dough evenly with half the oil. Flip the dough over, and brush with the remaining oil. Poke the dough with a fork 5 or 6 times across its surface to prevent air pockets from forming during cooking.
4. When the unit beeps to signify it has preheated, place the dough on the Grill Grate. Close the hood and cook for 3 minutes.
5. After 3 minutes, flip the dough. Close the hood and continue cooking for the remaining 3 minutes.
6. Meanwhile, in a medium mixing bowl, combine the strawberries and sugar.
7. Transfer the pizza to a cutting board and let cool. Top with the chocolate-hazelnut spread and strawberries. Cut into pieces and serve.

Nutrition:
Calories: 377
Total fat: 18g
Saturated fat: 4g
Cholesterol: 0mg
Sodium: 258mg
Carbohydrates: 53g
Fiber: 4g
Protein: 7g

176. Grilled Pound Cake with Fresh Mint and Berries

Preparation time: 10 minutes
Cooking time: 8 minutes
Servings: 6
Ingredients:

- ·3 tablespoons unsalted butter, at room temperature
- ·6 slices pound cake, sliced about 1-inch thick
- ·1 cup fresh raspberries
- ·1 cup fresh blueberries
- ·3 tablespoons sugar

- ·½ tablespoon fresh mint, minced

Directions:

1. Insert the Grill Grate and close the hood. Select GRILL, set the temperature to MAX, and set the time to 8 minutes. Select START/STOP to begin preheating.

2. While the unit is preheating, evenly spread the butter on both sides of each slice of pound cake.

3. When the unit beeps to signify it has preheated, place the pound cake on the Grill Grate. Close the hood and cook for 2 minutes.

4. After 2 minutes, flip the pound cake and cook for 2 minutes more, until golden brown. Repeat steps 3 and 4 for all of the pound cake slices.

5. While the pound cake cooks, in a medium mixing bowl, combine the raspberries, blueberries, sugar, and mint.

6. When cooking is complete, plate the cake slices and serve topped with the berry mixture.

Nutrition:

Calories: 215
Total fat: 12g
Saturated fat: 7g
Cholesterol: 82mg
Sodium: 161mg
Carbohydrates: 27g
Fiber: 2g
Protein: 2g

177. Sweet-Spicy Duck Breast

Preparation time: 10 minutes
Cooking time: 1 hour
Servings: 2
Ingredients:

- ·Your favorite spicy sauce (0.75 c.)
- ·Paprika, smoked
- ·(one teaspoon)
- ·Honey (0.25 C) Salt (one teaspoon)
- ·Thyme, fresh (two tsp.)
- ·Duck breasts (2)
- ·Pepper (half teaspoon)

Directions:

1. Chop the thyme and combine it with the pepper, salt, and smoked paprika.

2. Put the mixture liberally on the duck.

3. Put the duck in the smoker at 250 degrees F for at least 60 to 70 minutes.

4. Before slicing and serving the duck, let it rest for a few minutes. Mix the honey and spicy sauce together and drizzle over the duck.

Nutrition:

Protein: 44 g
Potassium: 628mg
Carbohydrates: 1 g
Cholesterol: 174 mg
Sodium: 1292 mg
Saturated fat: 2 g
Total fat: 9 g
Total calories: 313

178. Classic Smoked Duck Breast

Preparation time: 10 minutes
Cooking time: 1 hour
Servings: 2
Ingredients:

- ·Pepper (half teaspoon)
- ·Thyme, fresh (two tsp.)
- ·Duck breasts (2)
- ·Paprika, smoked (one teaspoon)
- ·Salt (one teaspoon)

Directions:

1. Chop the thyme and combine it with the pepper, salt, and smoked paprika.

2. Put the mixture liberally on the duck.

3. Put the duck in the smoker at 250 degrees F for at least 60 to 70 minutes.

4. Before slicing and serving the duck, let it rest for a few minutes.

Nutrition:

Protein: 44 g
Potassium: 628mg
Carbohydrates: 1 g
Cholesterol: 174 mg
Sodium: 1292 mg
Saturated fat: 2 g
Total fat: 9 g
Total calories: 282

179. BBQ Duck Breast

Preparation time: 10 minutes
Cooking time: 1 hour
Servings: 2
Ingredients:

- ·Your favorite BBQ sauce (1 c.)
- ·Thyme, fresh (two tsp.)
- ·Paprika, smoked (one teaspoon)
- ·Salt (one teaspoon)
- ·Pepper (half teaspoon)

Directions:

1. Chop the thyme and combine it with the pepper, salt, and smoked paprika.

2. Put the mixture liberally on the duck.

3. Put the duck in the smoker at 250 degrees F for at least 60 to 70 minutes.

4. Before slicing and serving the duck, let it rest for a few minutes. Then top with your favorite barbecue sauce.

Nutrition:

Protein: 44 g

Potassium: 628mg

Carbohydrates: 1 g

Cholesterol: 174 mg

Sodium: 1292 mg

Saturated fat: 2 g

Total fat: 9 g

Total calories: 299

180. Fresh Peach Crisp

Preparation Time: 5 minutes

Cooking time: 5 minutes

Servings: 4

Ingredients:

- ·2 peaches, halved
- ·Vanilla Ice Cream
- ·1 c. good quality granola

Directions:

1. Place the peach halves on a 400F grill and cover with the dome for 5 minutes

2. Remove the peaches and place them, cut side up, in a bowl. Top with vanilla ice cream and granola

Nutrition:

Calories: 163,

Fat: 5 g,

Carbohydrates: 25 g,

Protein: 3 g

181. Mustard Creamy Cheese Sauce

Preparation time: 10 minutes

Cooking time: 15 minutes

Servings: 5

Ingredients:

- ·2 tablespoons of butter
- ·2 tablespoons of all-purpose flour
- ·1/4 teaspoon of salt to taste
- ·A dash of pepper to taste
- ·1 cup of milk
- ·1/2 cup of cheddar cheese
- ·1/2 teaspoon of dry mustard
- ·A dash of garlic powder

Directions:

1. Place a saucepan over medium-low heat then add in the butter. Once the butter melts, add in the flour and cook for about one minute with a regular stir.

2. Add in the milk, salt, and pepper to taste, stir to combine, decrease the heat to low then cook for a few minutes until the sauce thickens.

3. Add in the rest of the ingredients on the list, stir to combine, and cook until the cheese melts completely.

4. Serve with your favorite grilled chicken

Nutrition:

Calories 289

Fat 19g

Carbohydrates 19g

Fiber 1g

Protein 11g

182. Grilled Pineapple Sundaes

Preparation Time: 30 minutes

Cooking time: 5 minutes

Servings: 4

Ingredients:

- ·4 fresh pineapple spears
- ·Vanilla Ice Cream
- ·Jarred Caramel Sauce
- ·Toasted Coconut

Directions:

1. Place pineapple spears on a 400F grill and close the dome for 2 minutes

2. Turn the pineapple and close the dome for another 2 minutes

3. Turn the pineapple once more and close the dome for another minute

4. Serve pineapple topped with ice cream, caramel sauce, and toasted coconut

Nutrition:

Calories: 112

Fat: 1 g

Carbohydrates: 29 g

Protein: 0.4g

183. Grilled Steak with American cheese Sandwich

Preparation Time: 20 minutes

Cooking time: 55 minutes

Servings: 4

Ingredients:

- ·1 pound of beef steak.
- ·1/2 teaspoon of salt to taste.
- ·1/2 teaspoon of pepper to taste.
- ·1 tablespoon of Worcestershire sauce.
- ·2 tablespoons of butter.
- ·1 chopped onion.
- ·1/2 chopped green bell pepper.
- ·Salt and pepper to taste.

- ·8 slices of American cheese.
- ·8 slices of white bread.
- ·4 tablespoons of butter.

Directions:

1. Turn your Wood Pellet Smoker and Grill to smoke and fire up for about four to five minutes. Set the temperature of the grill to 450 degrees F and let it preheat for about ten to fifteen minutes with its lid closed.

2. Next, place a non-stick skillet on the griddle and preheat for about fifteen minutes until it becomes hot. Once hot, add in the butter and let melt. Once the butter melts, add in the onions and green bell pepper then cook for about five minutes until they become brown, set aside.

3. Next, still using the same pan on the griddle, add in the steak, Worcestershire sauce, salt, and pepper to taste then cook for about five to six minutes until it is cooked through. Add in the cooked bell pepper mixture; stir to combine then heat for another three minutes, set aside.

4. Use a sharp knife to slice the bread in half, butter each side then grill for about three to four minutes with its sides down. To assemble, add slices of cheese on each bread slice, top with the steak mixture then your favorite toppings, close the sandwich with another bread slice then serve.

Nutrition:
Calories 589g
Carbohydrates 28g
Protein 24g
Fat 41g
Fiber 2g

184. Blueberry Cobbler
Preparation time: 15 minutes
Cooking time: 30 minutes
Servings: 6
Ingredients:
- ·4 cups fresh blueberries
- ·1 teaspoon grated lemon zest
- ·1 cup sugar, plus 2 tablespoons
- ·1 cup all-purpose flour, plus 2 tablespoons
- ·Juice of 1 lemon
- ·2 teaspoons baking powder
- ·¼ teaspoon salt
- ·6 tablespoons unsalted butter
- ·¾ cup whole milk
- ·⅛ teaspoon ground cinnamon

Directions:

1. In a medium bowl, combine the blueberries, lemon zest, 2 tablespoons of sugar, 2 tablespoons of flour, and lemon juice.

2. In a medium bowl, combine the remaining 1 cup of flour and 1 cup of sugar, baking powder, and salt. Cut the butter into the flour mixture until it forms an even crumb texture. Stir in the milk until a dough form.

3. Select BAKE, set the temperature to 350°F, and set the time to 30 minutes. Select START/STOP to begin preheating.

4. Meanwhile, pour the blueberry mixture into the Multi-Purpose Pan, spreading it evenly across the pan. Gently pour the batter over the blueberry mixture, and then sprinkle the cinnamon over the top.

5. When the unit beeps to signify it has preheated, place the pan directly in the pot. Close the hood and cook for 30 minutes, until lightly golden.

6. When cooking is complete, serve warm.

Nutrition:
Calories: 408
Total fat: 13g
Saturated fat: 8g
Cholesterol: 34mg
Sodium: 194mg
Carbohydrates: 72g
Fiber: 3g
Protein: 5g

185. Rack of Lamb
Preparation Time: 20 minutes
Cooking Time: 75 minutes
Servings: 4
Ingredients:
For Paste
- ·1/2 cup olive oil - ½ cup dry mustard - ¼ cup hot chili powder
- ·2 tablespoons freshly squeezed lemon juice - 2 tablespoon onion, minced
- ·1 tablespoon paprika - 1 tablespoon dried thyme - 1 tablespoon salt
- ·1 American rack of lamb, 7-9 chops
·Mint Sauce
- ·¼ cup fresh mint leaves, chopped
- ·¼ cup hot water

- ·2 tablespoons apple cider vinegar
- ·2 tablespoons brown sugar
- ·½ teaspoon salt
- ·½ teaspoon fresh ground pepper

Directions:

1. Take a small bowl and mix in olive oil, mustard, chili powder, lemon juice, onion, paprika, thyme, Worcestershire sauce, salt
2. Pre-heat your smoker to 200 degrees F
3. Rub the paste all over the lamb and transfer to the smoker, smoke for 75 minutes until internal temperature reaches 145 degrees F
4. Remove lamb from heat and let it rest for a few minutes, serve with mint sauce
5. Enjoy!

Nutrition:
Calories: 920
Fats: 83g
Carbs: 11g
Fiber: 1g

186. Mouthwatering Lamb Chops

Preparation Time: 15 minutes + marinate time
Cooking Time: 10-20 minutes
Servings: 4
Ingredients:
For Marinade

- ·½ cup of rice wine vinegar
- ·1 teaspoon liquid smoke
- ·2 tablespoons extra virgin olive oil
- ·2 tablespoons dried onion, minced
- ·1 tablespoon fresh mint, chopped
- ·Lamb Chops
- ·8 (4 ounces0 lamb chops
- ·½ cup hot pepper jelly
- ·1 tablespoon Sriracha
- ·1 teaspoon salt
- ·1 teaspoon freshly ground black pepper

Directions:

1. Take a small bowl and whisk in rice wine vinegar, liquid smoke, olive oil, minced onion, and mint
2. Add lamb chops in an aluminum roasting pan, pour marinade over meat and turn well to coat
3. Cover with plastic wrap and marinate for 2 hours
4. Pre-heat your smoker to 165 degrees F
5. Take a small saucepan and place it over low heat, add hot pepper jelly and sriracha keep it warm
6. Once ready to cook chops, remove them from marinade and pat dry
7. Discard marinade
8. Season chops with salt, pepper, and transfer to the grill grate
9. Close and smoke for 5 minutes
10. Remove chops from grill and increase the temperature to 450 degrees F
11. Transfer chops to grill and sear for 2 minutes per side until the internal temperature reaches 145 degrees F
12. Serve chops and enjoy!

Nutrition:

Calories: 227 - Fats: 21g
Carbs: 0g - Fiber: 2g

187. Spicy Lamb Sausage with Honey Mustard

Preparation Time: 15 minutes
Cooking Time: 3 hours
Servings: 10
Ingredients:
Meat

- ·2 and ½ pounds of spicy lamb sausages, at room temp
- ·Honey Mustard
- ·¼ cup honey
- ·¼ cup mayonnaise
- ·¼ cup mustard
- ·1 tablespoon white vinegar
- ·¼ teaspoon cayenne pepper

Directions:

1. Pre-heat your smoker to 250 degrees F
2. Arrange sausages on the smoker with a little gap between them
3. Smoke for about 3 hours until the internal temperature reaches 165 degrees F
4. Take a bowl and add honey, mustard, mayonnaise, vinegar, cayenne pepper, and mix well
5. Serve cooked sausages with the honey mustard sauce
6. Enjoy!

Nutrition:
Calories: 682
Fats: 47g
Carbs: 7g
Fiber: 3g

188. Smoked Lamb Shoulder Chops

Preparation Time: 15 minutes + 3-4 hours marinate time
Cooking Time: 25-30 minutes
Servings: 10
Ingredients:
Meat

- ·4 thick lamb shoulder chops
- ·Olive oil as needed
- ·The Texas-style rub of your choice

For Brine

- ·4 cups buttermilk
- ·1 cup of cold water
- ·¼ cup coarse kosher salt

Directions:
1. Pre-heat your smoker to 240 degrees F
2. Prepare the smoker according to manufacturer instructions and add wood pellets
3. Prepare the brine by mixing buttermilk, water to a large jug and add salt, stir for 30 seconds
4. Add chops to zip bag and add buttermilk mixture over chops
5. Transfer the zip lock bag to the fridge and let it chill for 3-4 hours
6. Remove chops from zip bag and discard bring, rinse chops with cold water
7. Keep it on the side
8. Drizzle drop of oil over top and cover well
9. Scatter a generous amount of Texas rub on top
10. Turn meat over and repeat the oiling and rubbing process
11. Add lamb chops to smoker and smoke for 25 minutes
12. Once the internal temperature reaches 110 degrees F, serve and enjoy!
Nutrition:
Calories: 342
Fats: 29g
Carbs: 1g
Fiber: 0g

189. Cornish Game Hen

Preparation Time: 30 minutes
Cooking Time: 2 -3 hours
Servings: 4
Ingredients:

- ·2 Cornish Game Hens
- ·Salt as needed
- ·Fresh ground pepper as needed
- ·1 cup quick-cooking seasoned browned rice
- ·1 small onion, chopped
- ·½ cup orange juice, squeezed
- ·½ cup apricot jelly

Directions:
1. Pre-heat your smoker to 275 degrees Fahrenheit
2. Season the birds with pepper and salt
3. Take a small saucepan over low heat and add 2 tablespoons of butter melt the butter and stir in rice and onion
4. Stuff the hens with the rice mix and secure the legs with twine
5. Rinse the saucepan and put it back to low heat
6. Melt remaining 2 tablespoons of butter and stir in orange juice alongside apricot jelly
7. Whisk until smooth
8. Baste the hen with the jelly glaze
9. Transfer the birds to your smoker and smoke for 2-3 hours until the internal temperature reaches 170 degrees Fahrenheit
10. Brush with more jelly and enjoy it!
Nutrition:
Calories: 552
Fats: 41g
Carbs: 4g
Fiber: 2g

190. Baba Ghanoush

Preparation Time: 25-30 minutes
Cooking Time: 60-90 minutes
Servings: 4
Ingredients:

- ·1 eggplant, halved lengthwise
- ·1 tablespoon olive oil
- ·2 and ½ teaspoon salt
- ·2 and ½ tablespoon tahini
- ·Juice of 1 lemon
- ·1 garlic clove, minced
- ·2 tablespoons fresh parsley, chopped

Directions:
1. Pre-heat your smoker to 200 degrees Fahrenheit
2. Rub eggplant halves with olive oil and sprinkle 2 teaspoons of salt
3. Place the halves o smoker rack and smoker for about 1 and ½ hours
4. Remove and peel off the skin, discard it

5. Transfer eggplant flesh to a food processor
6. Add tahini, garlic, lemon juice, 1/ a teaspoon of salt and blend well
7. Transfer to a storage
8. Stir in parsley and serve with pita Pellets
9. Enjoy!

Nutrition:
Calories: 335
Fats: 25g
Carbs: 28g
Fiber: 3g

191. Smoked Peach Parfait

Preparation Time: 20 minutes
Cooking Time: 35-45 minutes
Servings: 4
Ingredients:
- ·4 barely ripe peaches, halved and pitted
- ·1 tablespoon firmly packed brown sugar
- ·1-pint vanilla ice cream
- ·3 tablespoons honey

Directions:
1. Pre-heat your smoker to 200 degrees Fahrenheit
2. Sprinkle cut peach halves with brown sugar
3. Transfer them to smoker and smoke for 33-45 minutes
4. Transfer the peach halves to dessert plates and top with vanilla ice cream
5. Drizzle honey and serve!

Nutrition:
Calories: 309
Fats: 27g
Carbs: 17g
Fiber: 2g

192. Fancy Bologna

Preparation Time: 20 minutes
Cooking Time: 60 minutes
Servings: 4
Ingredients:
- ·2 tablespoons chili powder
- ·2 tablespoons packed brown sugar
- ·1 teaspoon ground coriander
- ·1 teaspoon ground nutmeg
- ·1 teaspoon garlic powder
- ·5 pounds all-beef bologna club
- ·¼ cup homemade yellow mustard
- ·Salt and pepper to taste

Directions:
1. Pre-heat your smoker to 250 degrees Fahrenheit using your preferred wood
2. Take a small bowl and add chili powder, coriander, brown sugar, nutmeg, and garlic powder
3. Keep it on the side
4. Cut the bologna into ½ inch slices and make few small cuts all around the edges of the slices
5. Coat both sides with the mustard mix
6. Season with salt, pepper and spice mix
7. Transfer the slices to smoker and smoke for 60 minutes. Enjoy!

Nutrition:
Calories: 819
Fats: 46g
Carbs: 1g
Fiber: 2g

193. Baked Peach Cobbler

Preparation time: 10 minutes
Cooking Time: 3 Hours
Servings: 3 Servings
Ingredients:
- ·4 teaspoons of butter, melted
- ·2 pounds of peaches, sliced
- ·½ cup maple syrup
- ·1 cup flour, self-rising flour
- ·3/4 teaspoon baking powder
- ·1 pinch cinnamon
- ·1 pinch salt
- ·1/2 cup unsalted butter, cut into small cubes
- ·1/2 cup white sugar
- ·4 eggs
- ·1/3 teaspoon vanilla

Directions:
1. Preheat the smoker grill at 220 degrees Fahrenheit until the smoke started to form
2. Take a heatproof pan and coat it with melted butter
3. In an aluminium pan, combine peaches along with maple syrup
4. In a separate bowl, combine flour, baking powder, salt, and cinnamon
5. In a small glass bowl mixed with sugar and butter, then add whisk eggs and vanilla into the butter
6. Fold this mixture into the flour mixture
7. Place the aluminium pan onto the smoker grill grate and cook 3 hours at 250 degrees Fahrenheit
8. Once done, serve

Nutrition:
Calories 477
Total Fat 8.8g
Saturated Fat 8.5g
Cholesterol 45mg

194. Chocolate Pudding

Preparation time: 10 minutes
Cooking Time: 1 Hour
Servings: 2 Servings
Ingredients:

- ·1 cup chocolate, chopped
- ·1 cup whipping cream, side serving (topping)
- ·Cobbler Topping Ingredients
- ·2 cups all-purpose flour
- ·8 tablespoons of sugar
- ·2 teaspoons of baking powder
- ·1 tablespoon of cocoa powder
- ·1 cup sour cream

Directions:
1. The first step is to preheat the smoker grill at 350 degrees Fahrenheit until the smoke establish
2. Take a medium bowl and combine sugar, flour, baking soda, and cocoa powder
3. Mix sour cream to the bowl
4. Mix the ingredients well
5. Now add in the chocolate and pour it into the aluminum pan
6. Put the aluminum pan on top of the grill grate and close the lid
7. Smoke it for 60 minutes or until the top gets brown and bubbly
8. Served with whipping cream

Nutrition:
Calories 784
Total Fat 8.9g
Saturated Fat 3.5g
Cholesterol 56mg

Chapter 15. Light Recipes (Without Heavy Ingredients)

195. Egg and Ham "Muffins"

Preparation Time: 10 minutes
Cooking Time: 20 minutes
Servings: 4
Ingredients:

- 12 whole eggs
- 12 slices of ham
- Paprika
- Pepper and salt as needed

Directions:
1. Preheat your oven to 375 degrees Fahrenheit
2. Take 12 muffin tins and line with 1 ham
3. Crack an egg into each muffin tin
4. Season muffin with paprika, salt, and paprika
5. Place in your oven and bake for 20 minutes
6. Enjoy once ready!
Nutrition:
Calories: 210
Fat: 6g
Carbohydrates: 27g
Protein: 14g

196. Scrambled Turkey Eggs

Preparation Time: 15 minutes
Cooking Time: 15 minutes
Servings: 2
Ingredients:

- 1 tablespoon coconut oil
- 1 medium red bell pepper, diced
- ½ medium yellow onion, diced
- ¼ teaspoon hot pepper sauce
- 3 large free-range eggs
- ¼ teaspoon black pepper, freshly ground
- ¼ teaspoon salt

Directions:
1. Set a pan to medium-high heat and add coconut oil, let it heat up
2. Add onions and Sauté
3. Add turkey and red pepper
4. Cook until turkey is cooked
5. Take a bowl and beat eggs, stir in salt and pepper
6. Pour eggs in the pan with turkey and gently cook and scramble eggs
7. Top with hot sauce and enjoy!
Nutrition:
Calories: 435
Fat: 30g
Carbohydrates: 34g
Protein: 16g

197. Baked Carrot Chips

Preparation Time: 10 minutes
Cooking Time: 10 minutes
Servings: 4
Ingredients:

- 3 cups carrots, sliced paper-thin rounds
- 2 tablespoons olive oil
- 2 teaspoons ground cumin
- ½ teaspoon smoked paprika
- Pinch of salt

Directions:
1. Preheat your oven to 400 degrees Fahrenheit
2. Slice carrot into paper-thin shaped coins using a peeler
3. Place slices in a bowl and toss with oil and spices
4. Layout the slices on a parchment paper-lined baking sheet in a single layer
5. Sprinkle salt
6. Transfer to oven and bake for 8-10 minutes
7. Remove and serve
8. Enjoy!
Nutrition:
Calories: 434
Fat: 35g
Carbohydrates: 31g
Protein: 2g

198. Cauliflower with Bacon Wrap

Preparation Time: 5 minutes
Cooking Time: 20-25 minutes
Servings: 4
Ingredients:

- Salt and pepper as needed
- 2 teaspoons olive oil
- 3 strips bacon, cut into bite-sized portions
- 6 garlic cloves, sliced thinly
- 1 head cauliflower, cut into florets

Directions:
1. Preheat your oven to 375 degrees Fahrenheit
2. Toss olive oil, bacon, garlic slices and cauliflower on a baking sheet and mix
3. Roast for 20-25 minutes until the cauliflower is cooked and bacon is crisp
4. Season roasted cauliflower with salt and pepper
5. Serve and enjoy!
Nutrition:
Calories: 299
Fat: 23g
Carbohydrates: 15g

Protein: 12g

199. Pistachio and Brussels

Preparation Time: 15 minutes
Cooking Time: 15 minutes
Servings: 4
Ingredients:
- 1 pound Brussels sprouts, sturdy bottom trimmed and halved lengthwise
- 4 shallots, peeled and quartered
- 1 tablespoon extra-virgin olive oil
- Sea salt
- Freshly ground black pepper
- ½ cup roasted pistachios, chopped
- Zest of ½ lemon
- Juice of ½ lemon

Directions:
1. Preheat your oven to 400 degrees F
2. Take a baking sheet and line it with aluminum foil
3. Keep it on the side
4. Take a large bowl and add Brussels, shallots and dress them with olive oil
5. Season with salt, pepper and spread veggies on a sheet
6. Bake for 15 minutes until slightly caramelized
7. Remove the oven and transfer to a serving bowl
8. Toss with lemon zest, lemon juice, and pistachios
9. Serve and enjoy!

Nutrition:
Calories: 126
Fat: 7g
Carbohydrates: 14g
Protein: 6g

200. Crispy Kale

Preparation Time: 10 minutes
Cooking Time: 25 minutes
Servings: 4
Ingredients:
- 3 cups kale, stemmed and thoroughly washed, torn in 2-inch pieces
- 1 tablespoon extra-virgin olive oil
- ½ teaspoon chili powder
- ¼ teaspoon of sea salt

Directions:
1. Prepare your oven by pre-heating to 300 degrees F
2. Line 2 baking sheets with parchment paper and keep them on the side
3. Dry kale and transfer to a large bowl
4. Add olive oil and toss, making sure to cover the leaves well
5. Season kale with salt, chili powder, and toss
6. Divide kale between baking sheets and spread into a single layer
7. Bake for 25 minutes until crispy
8. Let them cool for 5 minutes, serve
9. Enjoy!

Nutrition:
Calories: 56
Fat: 4g
Carbohydrates: 5g
Protein: 2g

201. Avocado and Cilantro Mix

Preparation Time: 10 minutes
Cooking Time: nil
Servings: 2
Ingredients:
- 2 avocados, peeled, pitted and diced
- 1 sweet onion, chopped
- 1 green bell pepper, chopped
- 1 large ripe tomato, chopped
- ¼ cup of fresh cilantro, chopped
- ½ a lime, juiced
- Salt and pepper as needed

Directions:
1. Take a medium-sized bowl and add onion, tomato, avocados, bell pepper, lime, and cilantro
2. Give the whole mixture a toss
3. Season accordingly and serve chilled
4. Enjoy!

Nutrition:
Calories: 126
Fat: 10g
Carbohydrates: 10g
Protein: 2g

202. Side Dish Mushroom Sauté

Preparation Time: 4 minutes
Cooking Time: 9 minutes
Servings: 4
Ingredients:
- 2 tablespoons clarified butter
- 1 tablespoon olive oil
- 1 and1/2 pound gourmet mushrooms
- 4 garlic cloves, diced
- 1/3 cup white wine vinegar
- Salt as needed

Directions:

1. Take a heavy pan and place it over medium heat
2. Add olive oil and ½ butter
3. When smoking, add mushrooms and keep stirring until browned
4. Add another ½ butter and garlic
5. Stir everything well
6. Add white wine vinegar and cook until the liquid is absorbed
7. Season with salt and enjoy!
Nutrition:
Calories: 256
Fat: 18g
Carbohydrates: 16g
Protein: 14g

203. Garlic and Tomato Meal

Servings: 4
Preparation Time: 10 minutes
Cooking Time: 50 minutes
Ingredients:
- 4 garlic cloves, crushed
- 1 pound mixed cherry tomatoes
- 3 thyme sprigs, chopped
- Pinch of salt
- Black pepper as needed
- ¼ cup olive oil
Directions:
1. Take a baking dish and add tomatoes, olive oil, and thyme
2. Season with salt and pepper and mix
3. Bake at 325 degrees Fahrenheit for 50 minutes
4. Divide tomatoes and pan juices and serve
5. Enjoy!

Nutrition:
Calories: 100
Fat: 0g
Carbohydrates: 1g
Protein: 6g

204. Potato and Tuna Salad

Preparation Time: 10 minutes
Cooking Time: nil
Servings: 4
Ingredients:
- 1 pound baby potatoes, scrubbed, boiled
- 1 cup tuna chunks, drained
- 1 cup cherry tomatoes, halved
- 1 cup medium onion, thinly sliced
- 8 pitted black olives
- 2 medium hard-boiled eggs, sliced
- 1 head Romaine lettuce
- ¼ cup olive oil
- 2 tablespoons lemon juice
- 1 tablespoon Dijon mustard
- 1 teaspoon dill weed, chopped
- Salt as needed
- Pepper as needed
Directions:
1. Take a small glass bowl and mix in your olive oil, lemon juice, Dijon mustard and dill
2. Season the mix with pepper and salt
3. Add in the tuna, baby potatoes, cherry tomatoes, red onion, green beans, black olives and toss everything nicely
4. Arrange your lettuce leaves on a beautiful serving

dish to make the base of your salad
5. Top them up with your salad mixture and place the egg slices
6. Drizzle it with the previously prepared Salad Dressing
7. Serve hot
Nutrition:
Calories: 406
Fat: 22g
Carbohydrates: 28g
Protein: 26g

205. Big Avocado Egg

Preparation Time: 5 minutes
Cooking Time: 20 minutes
Servings: 1
Ingredients:
- 2 ripe avocados
- 4 eggs
- Salt
- Pepper, to taste
Directions:
1. Preheat the oven 350 degrees F
2. Slice the avocado and remove the seed
3. Crack one egg into the hollow depression of the avocado where the seed has been
4. Season with salt and pepper to taste
5. Bake in the oven for 20 minutes
6. Serve and enjoy!
Nutrition:
Calories: 290
Fat: 24g
Carbohydrates: 10g
Protein: 11g

206. Awesome Buffalo Cashew Mix

Preparation Time: 10 minutes
Cooking Time: 55 minutes
Servings: 4
Ingredients:

- 2 cups raw cashews
- ¾ cup red hot sauce
- 1/3 cup avocado oil
- ½ teaspoon garlic powder
- ¼ teaspoon turmeric

Directions:

1. Take a bowl and mix wet ingredients in a bowl and stir in seasoning
2. Add cashews to the pan and mix
3. Soak cashews in hot sauce mix for 2-4 hours
4. Preheat your oven to 325 degrees F
5. Spread cashews onto a baking sheet
6. Bake for 35-55 minutes, making user turn after every 10-15 minutes
7. Let them cool and serve!

Nutrition:
Calories: 268
Fat: 16g
Carbohydrates: 20g
Protein: 14g

207. Quick Bite Island Sardine

Preparation Time: 10 minutes
Cooking Time: 8 minutes
Servings: 4
Ingredients:

- ½ pound sardines gutted and scales removed
- 1 Roma tomatoes, diced
- 1 clove garlic, minced
- ¼ cup onion, sliced
- 1 teaspoon cayenne pepper flakes
- 2 tablespoons olive oil
- 1 tablespoon lemon juice, freshly squeezed
- A dash of rosemary
- A dash of sage
- Salt and pepper, to taste

Directions:

1. Add all ingredients into your slow cooker and mix them well
2. Cover and cook on low for 8 hours
3. Adjust seasoning as you prefer
4. Serve and enjoy!

Nutrition:
Calories: 195
Fat: 2g
Carbohydrates: 3g
Protein: 15g

208. Shrimp and Avocado Platter

Preparation Time: 10 minutes
Cooking Time: nil
Servings: 8
Ingredients:

- 2 green onions, chopped
- 2 avocados, pitted, peeled and cut into chunks
- 2 tablespoons cilantro, chopped
- 1 cup shrimp, cooked, peeled and deveined
- Pinch of pepper

Directions:

1. Take a bowl and add cooked shrimp, avocado, green onions, cilantro, pepper
2. Toss well and serve
3. Enjoy!

Nutrition:
Calories: 160
Fat: 2g
Net Carbohydrates: 5g
Protein: 6g

209. Juicy Calamari

Preparation Time: 10 minutes +1 hour marinating
Cooking Time: 8 minutes
Servings: 4
Ingredients:

- 2 tablespoons extra virgin olive oil
- 1 teaspoon chili powder
- ½ teaspoon ground cumin
- Zest of 1 lime
- Juice of 1 lime
- Dash of sea sunflower seeds
- 1 and ½ pounds squid, cleaned and split open, with tentacles cut into ½ inch rounds
- 2 tablespoons cilantro, chopped
- 2 tablespoons red bell pepper, minced

Directions:

1. Take a medium bowl and stir in olive oil, chili powder, cumin, lime zest, sea sunflower seeds, lime juice, and pepper
2. Add squid and let it marinade and stir to coat, coat and let it refrigerate for 1 hour
3. Pre-heat your oven to broil
4. Arrange squid on a baking sheet, broil for 8 minutes turn once until tender
5. Garnish the broiled calamari with cilantro and red

bell pepper
6.   Serve and enjoy!
Nutrition:
Calories: 159
Fat: 13g
Carbohydrates: 12g
Protein: 3g

210. Creamy Coconut Shrimp

Preparation Time: 10 minutes
Cooking Time: nil
Servings: 4
Ingredients:
- 1 pound shrimp, cooked, peeled and deveined
- 1 tablespoon coconut cream
- ¼ teaspoon jalapeno, chopped
- ½ teaspoon lime juice
- 1 tablespoon parsley, chopped
- Pinch of pepper
Directions:
1.   Take a bowl and add shrimp, cream, jalapeno, lime juice, parsley, pepper
2.   Toss well and divide into small bowls
3.   Serve and enjoy!
Nutrition:
Calories: 183
Fat: 5g
Net Carbohydrates: 12g
Protein: 8g

211. Garlic and Almond Butter Shrimp

Preparation Time: 15 minutes
Cooking Time: 30 minutes
Servings: 4
Ingredients:
- 4 pounds shrimp
- 1-2 tablespoons garlic, minced

- ½ cup almond butter
- 1 tablespoon lemon pepper seasoning
- ½ teaspoon garlic powder
Directions:
1.   Preheat your oven to 300 degrees F
2.   Take a bowl and mix in garlic and almond butter
3.   Place shrimp in a pan and dot with almond butter garlic mix
4.   Sprinkle garlic powder and lemon pepper
5.   Bake for 30 minutes
6.   Enjoy!
Nutrition:
Calories: 749
Fat: 30g
Net Carbohydrates: 7g
Protein: 74g

212. Grilled Salmon Teriyaki

Preparation Time: 5 minutes
Cooking Time: 6 minutes
Servings: 2
Ingredients:
- 2 piece(8 ounces each) salmon fillets
- 2 tablespoons teriyaki sauce
- ½ teaspoon black pepper, coarsely and grounded
Directions:
1.   Take a shallow dish and add salmon
2.   Add teriyaki sauce and marinate in room temperature for 10 minutes
3.   Preheat your grill to medium-high heat and grease grate
4.   Add rubbed pepper on the fleshy part of salmon

5.   Place on grate skin part touching the grate
6.   Grill for 4 minutes
7.   Then turn off the heat wait for 2 minutes to cook properly
8.   Serve and enjoy!
Nutrition:
Calories: 365
Fat: 16g
Carbohydrates: 3g
Protein: 48g

213. Stir-Fried Ground Beef

Preparation Time: 10 minutes
Cooking Time: 15 minutes
Servings: 4
Ingredients:
- 1 pound beef, grounded
- ½ medium-sized onion, chopped
- 1 tablespoon coconut oil
- 1 tablespoon Chinese five spices
- 5 medium mushrooms, sliced
- 2 kale leaves, chopped
- ½ cup broccoli, chopped
- ½ red bell pepper, chopped
- 1 tablespoon cayenne pepper, optional
Directions:
1.   Take a skillet, add coconut oil
2.   Heat the oil over medium-high heat
3.   Sauté the onion for one minute and add vegetables
4.   Keep stirring constantly

5. Add the ground beef and the spices
6. Cook for 2 minutes and lower the heat
7. Cover the skillet and cook for 10 minutes
8. Once done, now ready to serve
9. Enjoy!

Nutrition:
Calories: 304
Fat: 17g
Carbohydrates: 6g
Protein: 32g

214. Fancy Garlic Scallops

Preparation Time: 10 minutes
Cooking Time: 5 minutes
Servings: 4
Ingredients:

- 1 tablespoon olive oil
- 1 and ¼ pounds dried scallops
- 2 tablespoons all-purpose flour
- ¼ teaspoon sunflower seeds
- 4-5 garlic cloves, minced
- 1 scallion, chopped
- 1 pinch of ground sage
- 1 lemon juice
- 2 tablespoons parsley, chopped

Directions:
1. Take a non-stick skillet and place it over medium-high heat
2. Add oil and allow the oil to heat up
3. Take a medium-sized bowl and add scallops alongside sunflower seeds and flour

4. Place the scallops in the skillet and add scallions, garlic, and sage
5. Sauté for 3-4 minutes until they show an opaque texture
6. Stir in lemon juice and parsley
7. Remove heat and serve hot!

Nutrition:
Calories: 151
Fat: 4g
Carbohydrates: 10g
Protein: 18g

Chapter 16. Dessert Recipes

215. Ice Cream Bread

Preparation time: 20 minutes
Cooking time: 1 hour
Servings: 8
Ingredients:

- 1 ½ quart full-fat butter pecan ice cream, softened
- 1 tbsp. salt
- 2 cups semisweet chocolate chips
- 1 cup sugar
- 1 stick melted butter
- Butter, for greasing
- 4 cups self-rising flour

Directions:

1. Add wood pellets to your smoker and follow your cooker's startup procedure. Preheat your smoker, with your lid closed, until it reaches 350.
2. Mix together the salt, sugar, flour, and ice cream with an electric mixer set to medium for two minutes.
3. As the mixer is still running, add in the chocolate chips, beating until everything is blended.
4. Spray a Bundt pan or tube pan with cooking spray. If you choose to use a pan that is solid, the center will take too long to cook. That's why a tube or Bundt pan works best.
5. Add the batter to your prepared pan.
6. Set the cake on the grill, cover, and smoke for 50 minutes to an hour. A toothpick should come out clean.
7. Take the pan off the grill. For 10 minutes, cool the bread.
8. Remove carefully the bread from the pan and then drizzle it with some melted butter.

Nutrition:
Calories: 148
Fat: 3g
Cholesterol: 9mg
Carbs: 27g
Protein: 3g

216. Blackberry Pie

Preparation time: 20 minutes
Cooking time: 40 minutes
Servings: 8
Ingredients:

- Butter, for greasing
- 1/2 cup all-purpose flour
- 1/2 cup milk
- 2 pints blackberries
- 2 cups sugar, divided
- 1 box refrigerated piecrusts
- 1 stick melted butter
- 1 stick of butter
- Vanilla ice cream

Directions:

1. Add wood pellets to your smoker and follow your cooker's startup procedure. Preheat your smoker, with your lid closed, until it reaches 375. Butter a cast iron skillet.
2. Unroll a piecrust and lay it in the bottom and up the sides of the skillet. Use a fork to poke holes in the crust.
3. Lay the skillet on the grill and smoke for five minutes, or until the crust is browned. Set off the grill.
4. Mix together 1 ½ cup of sugar, the flour, and the melted butter together. Add in the blackberries and toss everything together.
5. The berry mixture should be added to the skillet. The milk should be added on the top afterward. Sprinkle on half of the diced butter.
6. Unroll the second pie crust and lay it over the skillet. You can also slice it into strips and weave it on top to make it look like a lattice. Place the rest of the diced butter over the top. Sprinkle the rest of the sugar over the crust and place it skillet back on the grill.
7. Lower the lid and smoke for 15 to 20 minutes or until it is browned and bubbly. You may want to cover with some foil to keep it from burning during the last few minutes of cooking.
8. Serve the hot pie with some vanilla ice cream.

Nutrition:
Calories: 370
Fat: 14g
Cholesterol: 4mg
Carbs: 60g
Protein: 4g

217. S'mores Dip

Preparation time: 10 minutes
Cooking time: 15 minutes
Servings: 8
Ingredients:

- 12 ounces semisweet chocolate chips
- 1/4 cup milk

- 2 tbsp. melted salted butter
- 16 ounces marshmallows
- Apple wedges
- Graham Crackers

Directions:

1. Add wood pellets to your smoker and follow your cooker's startup procedure. Preheat your smoker, with your lid closed, until it reaches 450.
2. Put a cast iron skillet on your grill and add in the milk and melted butter. Stir together for a minute.
3. Once it has heated up, top with the chocolate chips, making sure it makes a single layer. Place the marshmallows on top, standing them on their end and covering the chocolate.
4. Cover, and let it smoke for five to seven minutes. The marshmallows should be toasted lightly.
5. Take the skillet off the heat and serve with apple wedges and graham crackers.

Nutrition:
Calories: 350
Fat: 10g
Carbs: 60g
Protein: 4g

218. Butternut Squash
Preparation time: 15 minutes
Cooking time: 2 hours
Servings: 6
Ingredients:

- Brown sugar
- Maple syrup
- 6 tbsp. butter
- Butternut squash

- Egg-Free

Directions:

1. Add wood pellets to your smoker and follow your cooker's startup procedure. Preheat your smoke, with your lid closed, until it reaches 300.
2. Slice the squash in half, lengthwise. Clean out all the seeds and membrane.
3. Place this cut side down on the grill and smoke for 30 minutes. Flip the squash over and cook for another 30 minutes.
4. Place each half of the squash onto aluminum foil. Sprinkle each half with brown sugar and maple syrup and put 3 tbsp. of butter onto each. Wrap foil around to create a tight seal.
5. Increase temperature to 400 and place onto the grill for another 35 minutes.
6. Carefully unwrap each half making sure to reserve juices in the bottom. Place onto serving platter and drizzle juices over each half. Use a spoon to scoop out and enjoy.

Nutrition:
Calories: 80
Carbs: 20g
Protein: 2g
Fiber: 7g

219. Apple Cobbler
Preparation time: 20 minutes
Cooking time: 1 hour and 50 minutes
Servings: 8
Ingredients:

- 8 Granny Smith apples
- 1 cup sugar

- 1 stick melted butter
- 1 tbsp. cinnamon
- Pinch salt
- ½ cup brown sugar
- 2 eggs
- 2 tbsp. baking powder
- 2 cups plain flour
- 1 ½ cup sugar

Directions:

1. Peel and quarter apples, place into a bowl. Add in the cinnamon and one cup sugar. Stir well to coat and let it set for one hour.
2. Add wood pellets to your smoker and follow your cooker's startup procedure. Preheat your smoker, with your lid closed, until it reaches 350°.
3. In a large bowl add the salt, baking powder, eggs, brown sugar, sugar, and flour. Mix until it forms crumbles.
4. Place apples into a Dutch oven. Add the crumble mixture on top and drizzle with melted butter.
5. Place on the grill and cook for 50 minutes.

Nutrition:
Calories: 330
Fat: 3g
Carbs: 77g
Protein: 2g

220. Peach Popsicle
Preparation time: 15 minutes
Cooking time: 3 hours and 15 minutes
Servings: 6
Ingredients:

- 1 cup cream, divided
- 1 vanilla bean

- 1 cup plain yogurt
- 1/2 cup honey
- 4 peaches

Directions:

1.   Add wood pellet to your smoker and follow your cooker's start up procedure. Preheat your smoker, with the lid closed, until it reaches 450°.
2.   Slice the peaches in half and remove pits. Put about two tablespoons of honey onto each cut side of the peach. Place on grill and cook for ten minutes.
3.   Take off the grill and put into a blender. Process until smooth. Put to the side.
4.   In a bowl, put vanilla, beans, honey, milk, and yogurt. Whisk until they are well-combined.
5.   Place some peach puree into a Popsicle mold. Layer with the yogurt mixture. Continue to layer until molds are filled ¾ of the way. Place sticks into each mold and freeze for four hours.

Nutrition:
Calories: 87
Fat: 3g
Carbs: 11g
Protein: 1g

221. Roasted Pumpkin Seeds

Preparation time: 10 minutes
Cooking time: 50 minutes
Servings: 12
Ingredients:

- Seeds from a pumpkin
- Favorite dry rub
- 2 cups melted butter

Directions:

1.   Add wood pellets to your smoker and follow your cooker's startup procedure. Preheat your smoker, with your lid closed, until it reaches 300°.
2.   Clean the seeds and dry. Toss them in the melted butter and then toss in the dry rub. Spread them across a baking sheet. Place on the grill and cook for 45 minutes.

Nutrition:
Calories: 126 Fat: 6g
Carbs: 15g Protein: 5g

222. Sweet Cheese Muffins

Preparation time: 20 minutes
Cooking time: 30 minutes
Servings: 10
Ingredients:

- 2 room temp beaten eggs
- 2 ¼ cups buttermilk
- One c. self-rising flour
- 1/4 cup packed brown sugar
- 3 ½ cup shredded cheddar
- 1 ½ stick softened butter
- 1 stick melted butter
- Butter, for greasing
- 1 package corn muffin mix
- 1 package butter cake mix

Directions:

1.   Add wood pellets to your smoker and follow your cooker's startup procedure. Preheat your smoker, with your lid closed, until it reaches 375.
2.   Mix together the flour, corn muffin mix, and cake mix.
3.   Slice up the softened butter and cut into the flour mixture.
4.   Beat together the buttermilk and the eggs and mix into the flour mixture until everything has come together.
5.   Grease three 12-c. mini muffin pans. Spoon in a quarter cup of the batter into the cup
6.   Place them on the grill, cover, and smoke for 12 to 15 minutes. Make sure that you monitor the muffins closely. They should be lightly browned.
7.   As they are cooking, mix together the brown sugar and the melted butter.
8.   Take the muffins off the grill and brush with the sweet butter. Serve.

Nutrition:
Calories: 130
Fat: 2g
Cholesterol: 3mg
Carbs: 24g
Protein: 5g

223. Cinnamon Almonds

Preparation time: 15 minutes
Cooking time: 1 hour
Servings: 6
Ingredients:

- 1/2 cup brown sugar
- Salt
- 1 egg white
- 1 tbsp. cinnamon
- 1/2 cup sugar
- 1-pound almonds

Directions:

1.   Beat the egg white until frothy. Mix in the salt,

cinnamon, and sugars. Toss in the almonds to coat.

2. Add wood pellets to your smoker and follow your cooker's startup procedure. Preheat your smoker, with your lid closed, until it reaches 225.

3. Lay the almonds on a cookie sheet and place on the grill, cover. Cook for 90 minutes. Stir every ten minutes.

4. Serve.

Nutrition:

Calories: 135

Fat: 8g

Carbs: 15g

Protein: 3g

224. Pomegranate Lemonade

Preparation time: 10 minutes

Cooking time: 45 minutes

Servings: 1

Ingredients:

- 1 cup pomegranate seeds
- 1 small bottle pom juice
- 2-3 smoked ice cubes
- 4-ounce lemonade
- 1 ½ ounces vodka

Directions:

1. Add wood pellets to your smoker and follow your cooker's startup procedure. Preheat your smoker, with your lid closed, until it reaches 180.

2. To make the ice cubes, add the pom juice and pomegranate seeds to a sheet pan and smoke for 45 minutes. Remove and chill. Pour into an ice mold and freeze.

3. Place the ice in a tall glass and add in the lemonade

and vodka.

4. Serve.

Nutrition:

Calories: 120

Carbs: 30g

Glucose: 28g

225. Sweet Plums

Preparation time: 10 minutes

Cooking time: 25 minutes

Servings: 10

Ingredients:

- 1/2 cup brown sugar
- 1/2 cup balsamic vinegar
- 10 black plums

Directions:

1. Add wood pellet to your smoker and follow your cooker's startup procedure. Preheat your smoker, with the lid closed, until it reaches 350.

2. Cut the plums in half and remove pits.

3. Place plums on grill cut side down and grill for ten minutes.

4. Place the balsamic vinegar and brown sugar into a pot and simmer for ten minutes until thick.

5. Turn plum over and baste with balsamic vinegar mixture and cook for another five minutes.

Nutrition:

Calories: 30

Fat: 1g

Carbs: 7g

Protein: 1g

226. Blueberry Bread Muffin

Preparation time: 20 minutes

Cooking time: 1 hour and 35 minutes

Servings: 12

Ingredients:

- Salt - 2 ½ cup milk - 1 ½ tbsp. vanilla
- 1 tbsp. cinnamon - 1 ½ c. sugar
- 5 eggs
- 3 cups blueberries
- Bread, cut into one-inch cubes

Directions:

1. Mix together the salt, cinnamon, vanilla, sugar, milk, and eggs.

2. Mix the blueberries and bread together.

3. Pour egg mixture over bread mixture and allow to set for 30 minutes. Place paper liners into a muffin tin.

4. Add wood pellet to your smoker and follow your cooker's startup procedure. Preheat your smoker, with the lid closed, until it reaches 225.

5. Spoon the bread mixture into the prepared muffin tin. Sprinkle with sugar.

6. Place on the grill for 30 minutes. Increase temperature to 350 and allow it to smoke for 25 minutes or until golden.

Nutrition:

Calories: 370

Fat: 15g

Carbs: 50g

Protein: 5g

227. Bacon Chocolate Chip Cookies

Preparation time: 30 minutes

Cooking time: 30 minutes

Servings: 12

Ingredients:

- 8 slices cooked and crumbled bacon
- 2 ½ t. apple cider vinegar
- 1 tbsp. vanilla
- 2 cups semisweet chocolate chips
- 2 room temp eggs
- 1 ½ tbsp. baking soda
- 1 cup granulated sugar
- 1/2 tbsp. salt
- 2 ¾ cup all-purpose flour
- 1 cup light brown sugar
- 1 ½ stick softened butter

Directions:

1. Mix together salt, baking soda and flour.
2. Cream the sugar and the butter together. Lower the speed. Add in the eggs, vinegar, and vanilla.
3. Still on low, slowly add in the flour mixture, bacon pieces, and chocolate chips.
4. Add wood pellets to your smoker and follow your cooker's startup procedure. Preheat your smoker, with your lid closed, until it reaches 375.
5. Place some parchment on a baking sheet and drop a teaspoonful of cookie batter on the baking sheet. Let them cook on the grill, covered, for approximately 12 minutes or until they are browned.
6. Enjoy.

Nutrition:
Calories: 130
Fat: 9g
Carbs: 11g
Protein: 3g

228. Pineapple Cake

Preparation time: 30 minutes
Cooking time: 1 hour and 20 minutesServings: 8
Ingredients:

- 1 cup sugar
- 1 tbsp. baking powder
- 1 cup buttermilk
- 1/2 tbsp. salt
- 1 jar maraschino cherry
- 1 stick butter, divided
- 3/4 cup brown sugar
- 1 can pineapple slices
- 1 ½ cup flour

Directions:

1. Add wood pellets to your smoker and follow your cooker's startup procedure. Preheat your smoker, with your lid closed, until it reaches 350.
2. Take a medium-sized cast iron skillet and melt one half stick butter. Be sure to coat the entire skillet. Sprinkle brown sugar into a cast iron skillet.
3. Lay the sliced pineapple on top of the brown sugar. Put a cherry into each individual pineapple ring.
4. Mix together the salt, baking powder, flour, and sugar. Add in the eggs, one-half stick melted butter, and buttermilk. Whisk to combine.
5. Put the cake on the grill and cook for an hour.
6. Take off from the grill and let it set for ten minutes. Flip onto serving platter.

Nutrition:
Calories: 120
Protein: 1g

Carbs: 18g
Fat: 5g

229. Caramel Bananas

Preparation time: 15 minutes
Cooking time: 15 minutes
Servings: 4
Ingredients:

- 1/3 cup chopped pecans
- 1/2 cup sweetened condensed milk
- 4 slightly green bananas
- 1/2 cup brown sugar
- 2 tbsp. corn syrup
- 1/2 cup butter

Directions:

1. Add wood pellet to your smoker and follow your cooker's startup procedure. Preheat your smoker, with the lid closed, until it reaches 350.
2. Place the milk, corn syrup, butter, and brown sugar into a heavy saucepan and bring to boil. For five minutes simmer the mixture in low heat. Stir frequently.
3. Place the bananas with their peels on and let them grill for 5 minutes. Flip and cook for 5 minutes more. Peels will be dark and might split.
4. Place on serving platter. Cut the ends off the bananas and split peel down the middle. Take the peel off the bananas and spoon caramel on top. Sprinkle with pecans.

Nutrition:
Calories: 340
Protein: 10g
Carbs: 75g
Fat: 1g

230. Chocolate Chip Cookies

Preparation time: 30 minutes
Cooking time: 30 minutes
Servings: 12
Ingredients:

- 1 ½ cup chopped walnuts
- 1 tbsp. vanilla
- 2 cups chocolate chips
- 1 tbsp. baking soda
- 2 ½ cups plain flour
- 1/2 tbsp. salt
- 1 ½ stick softened butter
- 2 eggs
- 1 cup brown sugar
- 1/2 cup sugar

Directions:

1. Add wood pellets to your smoker and follow your cooker's startup procedure. Preheat your smoker, with your lid closed, until it reaches 350.
2. Mix together the baking soda, salt, and flour.
3. Cream the brown sugar, sugar, and butter. Mix in the vanilla and eggs until it comes together.
4. Slowly add in the flour while continuing to beat. Once all flour has been incorporated, add in the chocolate chips and walnuts. Using a spoon, fold into batter.
5. Place an aluminum foil onto grill. In an aluminum foil, drop spoonful of dough and bake for 17 minutes.

Nutrition:
Calories: 66
Protein: 2g
Carbs: 5g

Fat: 4g

231. Pork Maple Doughnut Sliders

Preparation time: 20 minutes
Cooking time: 30 minutes
Servings: 12
Ingredients:

- 12 doughnut holes, plain, yeast or cake
- 1 cup of sugar, powdered
- 4 tbsp. of syrup, maple + extra if needed
- 1 1/2 cups of pulled pork in barbeque sauce, warm, store-bought
- 3/4 cup of store-bought coleslaw

Directions:

1. Whisk 2 tbsp. syrup and the powdered sugar in shallow bowl. Add additional syrup as needed to create a glaze-y, thick texture.
2. Roll the doughnut holes in glaze. Place on wire racks to set up. Once the glaze has set, cut the doughnut holes in halves. Brush both sides of doughnut halves with the rest of the syrup.
3. Place 2 tbsp. pulled pork + 1 tbsp. coleslaw on a doughnut half.
4. Top with the other doughnut half. Secure with toothpicks.
5. Repeat with remaining ingredients.
6. Serve.

Nutrition:
Calories: 140
Fat: 8g
Cholesterol: 14mg

Carbs: 15g
Protein: 4g

232. Banana Bacon S'mores

Preparation time: 15 minutes
Cooking time: 15 minutes
Servings: 2
Ingredients:

- 2 halved graham crackers
- 1 x 1 1/2-oz. pkg. of peanut butter cups
- 2 slices of bacon, cooked
- 4 toasted marshmallows, large
- 4 slices of banana

Directions:

1. Top each of two graham cracker halves using one peanut butter cup, 1 bacon slice and two toasted marshmallows.
2. Add banana slices and the remainder of crackers.
3. Press gently to close and serve promptly.

Nutrition:
Calories: 250
Fat: 16g
Cholesterol: 50mg
Carbs: 35g
Protein: 3g

233. Pumpkin Bacon Pie

Preparation time: 25 minutes
Cooking time: 2 hours and 10 minutes
Servings: 12
Ingredients:

- 1/2 cup of pumpkin, fresh, cubed

- 1 1/2 cups of softened cream cheese, reduced fat
- 1 cup of brown sugar, packed
- 3 eggs, medium
- 1 tsp. of vanilla extract, pure
- 1 tsp. of cinnamon, ground
- 1/2 tsp. ground each of ginger, cloves and allspice
- 2 x 10" pie crust, graham cracker, prepared
- 16 bacon slices, maple cured

Directions:

1. Preheat the oven to 425°F.
2. Bring small sized pot of lightly salted water to boil. Add pumpkin. Cook till soft enough that it can be easily pierced with fork, 8-10 minutes. Drain the water off.
3. Mash cooked pumpkin in large sized bowl. Mix brown sugar and cream cheese in. Whisk in eggs, one after another. Add the vanilla, cloves, allspice, ginger and cinnamon.
4. Stir till the batter is thin, a bit thinner than typical pancake batter. Pour into pie crusts.
5. Place the bacon in large sized skillet on medium heat till browned evenly. Trim the fatty, soft bits from slices. Press seven bacon pieces per pie in batter with fork.
6. Bake pies at 425°F for 15-18 minutes, then decrease heat to 375°F.
7. Top pies with 2 pieces of bacon each. Bake for 1/2 hour longer.
8. Allow the pies to completely cool, then serve.

Nutrition:
Calories: 200
Fat: 17g
Cholesterol:
Carbs: 2g
Protein: 19g

234. Chocolate Salami

Preparation time: 15 minutes
Cooking time: 25 minutes
Servings: 2
Ingredients:

- 2 x 12-oz. cups of chopped chocolate or chocolate chips
- 2/3 cup of cream, heavy
- 3/4 cup of nuts, chopped
- 12 to 14 oz. of chopped shortbread cookies
- 1/4 cup of sugar, powdered
- 1/2 cup of dates or raisins, if desired

Directions:

1. Place the chocolate in medium sized bowl.
2. Heat the cream in saucepan till it steams but does not boil.
3. Pour hot cream over chocolate. Allow to set for several minutes, allowing chocolate chops to melt. Stir cream and chocolate together till you have a smooth texture.
4. Add chopped cookies, nuts and, if using, dried fruit pieces.
5. Allow mixture to sit and cool for 12-15 minutes, till it has slightly cooled.
6. Divide mixture into halves. Spoon onto two pieces of plastic wrap. Use wrap to form mixture into two logs. Twist ends up.
7. Place in fridge to completely chill for three to four hours. You can leave it overnight if you like.
8. When chocolate has cooled, dust with the powdered sugar on each side.
9. Slice, then serve.

Nutrition:
Calories: 180
Fat: 12g
Carbs: 15g
Protein: 3g

Chapter 17. Mixed Recipes

235. Formaggi Macaroni and Cheese

Preparation time: 30 minutes
Cooking time: 1 hour
Servings: 8
Ingredients:

- ¼ c. all-purpose flour
- ½ stick butter
- Butter, for greasing
- One-pound cooked elbow macaroni
- One c. grated Parmesan
- 8 ounces cream cheese
- Two c. shredded Monterey Jack
- 3 t. garlic powder
- Two t. salt
- One t. pepper
- Two c. shredded Cheddar, divided
- 3 c. milk

Directions:
1. Add the butter to a pot and melt. Mix in the flour. Stir constantly for a minute. Mix in the pepper, salt, garlic powder, and milk. Let it boil.
2. After lowering the heat, let it simmer for about 5 minutes, or until it has thickened. Remove from the heat.
3. Mix in the cream cheese, parmesan, Monterey jack, and 1 ½ c. of cheddar. Stir everything until melted. Fold in the pasta.
4. Add wood pellets to your smoker and follow your cooker's startup procedure.
Preheat your smoker, with your lid closed, until it reaches 225.
5. Butter a 9" x 13" baking pan. Pour the macaroni mixture to the pan and lay on the grill. Cover and allow it to smoke for an hour, or until it has become bubbly. Top the macaroni with rest of the cheddar during the last
6. Serve.
Nutrition:
Calories: 180
Carbs: 19g
Fat: 8g
Protein: 8g

236. Spicy Barbecue Pecans

Preparation time: 15 minutes
Cooking time: 1 hour
Servings: 2
Ingredients:

- 2 ½ t. garlic powder
- 16 ounces raw pecan halves
- One t. onion powder
- One t. pepper
- Two t. salt
- One t. dried thyme
- Butter, for greasing
- 3 T. melted butter

Directions:
1. Add wood pellets to your smoker and follow your cooker's startup procedure. Preheat your smoker, with your lid closed, until it reaches 225.
2. Cover and smoke for an hour, flipping the nuts one. Make sure the nuts are toasted and heated. They should be removed from the grill. Set aside to cool and dry.
Nutrition:
Calories: 150

Carbs: 16g
Fat: 9g
Protein: 1g

237. Greek Meatballs

Preparation time: 10 minutes
Cooking time: 40 minutes
Servings: 6
Ingredients:

- Pepper
- Salt
- Two chopped green onions
- One T. almond flour
- Two eggs
- ½ pound ground pork
- 2 ½ pound ground beef

Directions:
1. Mix all the ingredients together using your hands until everything is incorporated evenly. Form mixture into meatballs until all meat is used.
2. Add wood pellets to your smoker and follow your cooker's startup procedure. Preheat your smoker, with your lid closed, until it reaches 380.
3. Brush the meatballs with olive oil and place onto grill. Cook for ten minutes on all sides.
Nutrition:
Calories: 161
Carbs: 10g
Fat: 6g
Protein: 17g

238. Smo-Fried Chicken

Preparation time: 30 minutes
Cooking time: 55 minutes
Servings: 4 to 6

Ingredients:

- 1 egg, beaten
- ½ cup milk
- 1 cup all-purpose flour
- 2 tablespoons salt
- 1 tablespoon freshly ground black pepper
- 2 teaspoons freshly ground white pepper
- 2 teaspoons cayenne pepper
- 2 teaspoons garlic powder
- 2 teaspoons onion powder
- 1 teaspoon smoked paprika
- 8 tablespoons (1 stick) unsalted butter, melted
- 1 whole chicken, cut up into pieces

Directions:

1. Supply your smoker with wood pellets and follow the manufacturer's specific start-up procedure. Preheat, with the lid closed, to 375°F.
2. Smoke the chicken in the pan of butter ("smo-fry") on the grill, with the lid closed, for 25 minutes, then reduce the heat to 325°F and turn the chicken pieces over.
3. Continue smoking with the lid closed for about 30 minutes, or until a meat thermometer inserted in the thickest part of each chicken piece reads 165°F.
4. Serve immediately.

Nutrition:
Calories: 166
Carbs: 0g
Fat: 8g
Protein: 23g

239. Roasted Vegetables

Preparation time: 20 minutes
Cooking time: 20-40 minutes
Servings: 4
Ingredients:

- 1 cup cauliflower floret
- 1 cup small mushroom, half
- 1 medium zucchini, sliced in half
- 1 medium yellow squash, sliced in half
- One medium-sized red pepper, chopped to 1.5-2 inches
- 1 small red onion, chopped to 1½-2 inch
- 6 oz. small baby carrot
- Six mid-stem asparagus spears, cut into 1-inch pieces
- 1 cup cherry or grape tomato
- ¼ Extra virgin olive oil with cup roasted garlic flavor
- 2 tablespoons of balsamic vinegar
- 3 garlics, chopped
- 1 tsp. dry time
- 1 tsp. dried oregano
- 1 teaspoon of garlic salt
- 1/2 teaspoon black pepper

Directions:

1. Put cauliflower florets, mushrooms, zucchini, yellow pumpkin, red peppers, red onions, carrots, asparagus and tomatoes in a large bowl.
2. Add olive oil, balsamic vinegar, garlic, thyme, oregano, garlic salt, and black hu add to the vegetables.
3. Gently throw the vegetables by hand until

completely covered with olive oil, herbs and spices.
4. Spread the seasoned vegetables evenly on a non-stick grill tray / bread / basket (about 15 x 12 inches).
5. Use of wood pellet smokers and grills
6. Set the wood pellet smoker grill for indirect cooking and preheat to 425 degrees Fahrenheit using all types of wood pellets.
7. Transfer the grill tray to a preheated smoker grill and roast the vegetables for 20-40 minutes or until the vegetables are al dente. Please put it out immediately.

Nutrition:
Calories: 80
Carbs: 7g
Fat: 6g
Protein: 1g

240. Bacon Cheddar Slider

Preparation time: 30 minutes
Cooking time: 15 minutes
Servings: 6-10
Ingredients:

- 1-pound ground beef (80% lean)
- 1/2 teaspoon of garlic salt
- 1/2 teaspoon salt
- 1/2 teaspoon of garlic
- 1/2 teaspoon onion
- 1/2 teaspoon black pepper
- 6 bacon slices, cut in half
- ½Cup mayonnaise
- 2 teaspoons of creamy wasabi (optional)

- 6 (1 oz.) sliced sharp cheddar cheese, cut in half (optional)
- Sliced red onion
- ½Cup sliced kosher dill pickles
- 12 mini breads sliced horizontally
- Ketchup

Directions:

1. Place ground beef, garlic salt, seasoned salt, garlic powder, onion powder and black hupe pepper in a medium bowl.
2. Set up a wood pellet smoker grill for direct cooking to use griddle accessories.
3. Spray a cooking spray on the griddle cooking surface for best non-stick results.
4. Preheat wood pellet smoker grill to 350 ° F using selected pellets. Griddle surface should be approximately 400 ° F.
5. Grill the putty for 3-4 minutes each until the internal temperature reaches 160 ° F.
6. Place a small amount of mayonnaise mixture, a slice of red onion, and a hamburger pate in the lower half of each roll. Pickled slices, bacon and ketchup

Nutrition:

Calories: 80

Carbs: 0g

Fat: 5g

Protein: 0g

241. Wild West Wings

Preparation time: 10 minutes

Cooking time: 50 minutes

Servings: 4

Ingredients:

- 2 pounds chicken wings
- 2 tablespoons extra-virgin olive oil
- 2 packages ranch dressing mix (such as Hidden Valley brand)
- ¼ cup prepared ranch dressing (optional)

Directions:

1. Supply your smoker with wood pellets and follow the manufacturer's specific start-up procedure. Preheat, with the lid closed, to 350°F.
2. Flip and smoke for 20 to 35 minutes more, or until a meat thermometer inserted in the thickest part of the wings reads 165°F and the wings are crispy. (Note: The wings will likely be done after 45 minutes, but an extra 10 to 15 minutes makes them crispy without drying the meat.)
3. Serve warm with ranch dressing (if using).

Nutrition:

Calories: 660

Carbs: 54g

Fat: 34g

Protein: 35g

242. Garlic Parmesan Wedge

Preparation time: 15 minutes

Cooking time: 30-35 minutes

Servings: 3

Ingredients:

- 3 large russet potatoes
- ¼ cup of extra virgin olive oil
- 1 tsp. salt
- ¾ teaspoon black hu pepper
- 2 tsp. garlic powder

- ¾ cup grated parmesan cheese
- 3 tablespoons of fresh coriander or flat leaf parsley (optional)
- ½ cup blue cheese or ranch dressing per serving, for soaking (optional)

Directions:

1. Gently rub the potatoes with cold water using a vegetable brush to dry the potatoes.
2. Cut the potatoes in half vertically and cut them in half.
3. Wipe off any water released when cutting potatoes with a paper towel. Moisture prevents wedges from becoming crunchy.
4. Put the potato wedge, olive oil, salt, pepper and garlic powder in a large bowl and shake lightly by hand to distribute the oil and spices evenly.
5. Place the wedges on a single layer of non-stick grill tray / pan / basket (about 15 x 12 inches).
6. Use of wood pellet smokers and grills
7. Set the wood pellet r grill for indirect cooking and use all types of wood pellets to preheat to 425 degrees Fahrenheit.
8. Put the grill tray in the preheated smoker grill, roast the potato wedge for 15 minutes, and turn. Roast the potato wedge for an additional 15-20 minutes until the potatoes are soft inside and crispy golden on the outside.
9. Sprinkle potato wedge with parmesan cheese and add

coriander or parsley as needed. If necessary, add blue cheese or ranch dressing for the dip.
Nutrition:
Calories: 110
Carbs: 2g
Fat: 7g
Protein: 10g

243. Mediterranean Meatballs

Preparation time: 15 minutes
Cooking time: 35 minutes
Servings: 8
Ingredients:
- Pepper
- Salt
- One t. vinegar
- Two T. olive oil
- Two eggs
- One chopped onion
- One soaked slice of bread
- ½ t. cumin
- One T. chopped basil
- 1 ½ T. chopped parsley
- 2 ½ pounds ground beef

Directions:
1. Use your hands to combine everything together until thoroughly combined. If needed, when forming meatballs, dip your hands into some water. Shape into 12 meatballs.
2. Add wood pellets to your smoker and follow your cooker's startup procedure. Preheat your smoker, with your lid closed, until it reaches 380.
3. Place the meatballs onto the grill and cook on all sides for eight minutes. Take off the grill and let sit for five minutes.

4. Serve with favorite condiments or a salad.
Nutrition:
Calories: 33
Carbs: 6g
Fat: 0g
Protein: 1g

244. Twice-Baked Spaghetti Squash

Preparation time: 15 minutes
Cooking time: 45-60 minutes
Servings: 6-10
Ingredients:
- 1 medium spaghetti squash
- 1 tbsp. extra virgin olive oil
- 1 tsp. salt
- 1/2 teaspoon pepper
- ½Chop shredded mozzarella cheese, split
- 1/2 cup of parmesan cheese, split

Directions:
1. Using a large, sharp knife, carefully cut the pumpkin in half lengthwise. Use a spoon to remove each half of the seeds and pulp.
2. Raise wood pellet smoker grill temperature to 425 ° F.
3. Transfer the strand to a large bowl. Add half the mozzarella cheese and parmesan cheese and mix.
4. Fill half the squash shell with the mixture and sprinkle the remaining mozzarella and parmesan cheese on top.
5. Bake the packed spaghetti squash halves at 425 ° F for another 15 minutes or until the cheese is brown.

Nutrition:
Calories: 230
Carbs: 9g
Fat: 17g
Protein: 12g

245. Traditional BBQ Chicken

Preparation time: 10 minutes
Cooking time: 1 hour 30 minutes
Servings: 8
Ingredients:
- 8 boneless, skinless chicken breasts
- 2 teaspoons salt
- 2 teaspoons freshly ground black pepper
- 2 teaspoons garlic powder
- 2 cups Bill's Best BBQ Sauce or your preferred barbecue sauce, divided

Directions:
1. Supply your smoker with wood pellets and follow the manufacturer's specific start-up procedure. Preheat, with the lid closed, to 250°F.
2. Place the roasting pan on the grill, close the lid, and smoke for 1 hour 30 minutes to 2 hours, or until a meat thermometer inserted in the thickest part of each breast reads 165°F. During the last 15 minutes of cooking, cover the chicken with 1 cup of barbecue sauce.
3. Serve the chicken warm with the remaining 1 cup of barbecue sauce.

Nutrition:
Calories: 273
Carbs: 25g
Fat: 5g
Protein: 32g

246. Smoked Airline Chicken

Preparation time: 4 hours 20 minutes
Cooking time: 2 hours
Servings: 2
Ingredients:
- 2 boneless chicken breasts with drumettes attached
- ½ cup soy sauce
- ½ cup teriyaki sauce
- ¼ cup canola oil
- ¼ cup white vinegar
- 1 tablespoon minced garlic
- ¼ cup chopped scallions
- 2 teaspoons freshly ground black pepper
- 1 teaspoon ground mustard

Directions:
1. Place the chicken in a baking dish.
2. In a bowl, whisk together the soy sauce, teriyaki sauce, canola oil, vinegar, garlic, scallions, pepper and ground mustard, then pour this marinade over the chicken, coating both sides.
3. Arrange the chicken directly on the grill, close the lid, and smoke for 1 hour 30 minutes to 2 hours, or until a meat thermometer inserted in the thickest part of the meat reads 165°F.
4. Let the meat rest for 3 minutes before serving.

Nutrition:
Calories: 430
Carbs: 0g
Fat: 23g
Protein: 53g

247. Cinnamon Sugar Pumpkin Seeds

Preparation time: 12 minutes
Cooking time: 30 minutes
Servings: 8-12
Ingredients:
- Two T. sugar
- Seeds from a pumpkin
- One t. cinnamon
- Two T. melted butter

Directions:
1. Add wood pellets to your smoker and follow your cooker's startup procedure. Preheat your smoker, with your lid closed, until it reaches 350.
2. Clean the seeds and toss them in the melted butter. Add them to the sugar and cinnamon. Spread them out on a baking sheet, place on the grill, and smoke for 25 minutes.
3. Serve.

Nutrition:
Calories: 160
Carbs: 5g
Fat: 12g
Protein: 7g

248. Mushrooms Stuffed with Crab Meat

Preparation time: 20 minutes
Cooking time: 45 minutes
Servings: 4-6
Ingredients:
- 6 medium-sized Portobello mushrooms
- Extra virgin olive oil
- ⅓Grated parmesan cheese cup
- Club Beat Staffing:
- 8 oz. fresh crab meat or canned or imitation crab meat
- 2 tablespoons extra virgin olive oil
- ⅓Chopped celery
- Chopped red peppers
- ½ cup chopped green onion
- ½ cup Italian breadcrumbs
- ½Cup mayonnaise
- 8 oz. cream cheese at room temperature
- 1/2 teaspoon of garlic
- 1 tablespoon dried parsley
- Grated parmesan cheese cup
- 1 1 teaspoon of Old Bay seasoning
- ¼ teaspoon of kosher salt
- ¼ teaspoon black pepper

Directions:
1. Clean the mushroom cap with a damp paper towel. Cut off the stem and save it.
2. Remove the brown gills from the bottom of the mushroom cap with a spoon and discard.
3. Prepare crab meat stuffing.
4. Gently pour the chilled sautéed vegetables and the remaining ingredients into a large bowl.
5. Cover and refrigerate crab meat stuffing until ready to use.
6. Use the pellets to set the wood pellet smoker grill to indirect heating and preheat to 375 ° F.
7. Bake for 30-45 minutes until the filling becomes hot.

Nutrition:
Calories: 31
Carbs: 4g
Fat: 0g
Protein: 2g

249. Feta Cheese Stuffed Meatballs

Preparation time: 12 minutes
Cooking time: 35 minutes
Servings: 6
Ingredients:
- Pepper
- Salt
- ¾ c. Feta cheese
- ½ t. thyme
- Two t. chopped oregano
- Zest of one lemon
- One-pound ground pork
- One-pound ground beef
- One T. olive oil

Directions:
1. Place the pepper, salt, thyme, oregano, olive oil, lemon zest, and ground meats into a large bowl.
2. Combine thoroughly the ingredients using your hands.
3. Cut the Feta into little cubes and begin making the meatballs. Take a half tablespoon of the meat mixture and roll it around a piece of cheese. Continue until all meat has been used.
4. Add wood pellets to your smoker and follow your cooker's startup procedure. Preheat your smoker, with your lid closed, until it reaches 350.
5. Brush the meatballs with more olive oil and put onto the grill. Grill for ten minutes until browned.

Nutrition:
Calories: 390
Carbs: 8g
Fat: 31g
Protein: 20g

250. Brisket Baked Beans

Preparation time: 20 minutes
Cooking time: 2 hours
Servings: 10-12
Ingredients:
- 2 tablespoons extra virgin olive oil
- 1 large diced onion
- 1 diced green pepper
- 1 red pepper diced
- 2-6 jalapeno peppers diced
- Texas style brisket flat chopped 3 pieces
- 1 (28 oz.) baked beans, like Bush's country style baked beans
- 1 (28 oz.) pork and beans
- 1 (14 oz.) red kidney beans, rinse, drain
- 1 cup barbecue sauce like Sweet Baby Ray's barbecue sauce
- ½ cup stuffed brown sugar
- 3 garlics, chopped
- 2 teaspoons of mustard
- 1/2 tsp. kosher salt
- 1/2 teaspoon black pepper

Directions:
1. Heat the olive oil in a skillet over medium heat and add the diced onion, peppers and jalapeno. Cook, stirring occasionally, for about 8-10 minutes until the onion is translucent.
2. Using the selected pellets, configure a wood pellet smoking grill for indirect cooking and preheat to 325 ° F. Cook the beans baked in the brisket for 1.5 to 2 hours until they become bare beans. Rest for 15 minutes before eating

Nutrition:
Calories: 199
Carbs: 35g
Fat: 2g
Protein: 9g

251. Apple Wood Smoked Cheese

Preparation time: 1 hour 15 minutes
Cooking time: 3 hours
Servings: 10
Ingredients:
- Gouda
- Sharp cheddar
- Very sharp 3-year cheddar
- Monterey Jack
- Pepper jack
- Swiss

Directions:
1. Preheat the wood pellet smoker grill to 180 ° F or use apple pellets and smoke settings, if any, to get a milder smoke flavor.
2. Place the cheese on a Teflon-coated fiberglass non-stick grill mat and let cool for 2 hours.
3. Leave the cheese on the counter for one hour to form a fragile skin or crust, which acts as a heat barrier, but allows smoke to penetrate.

4. After labeling the smoked cheese with a vacuum seal, refrigerate for 2 weeks or more, then smoke will permeate, and the cheese flavor will become milder.

Nutrition:
Calories: 102
Carbs: 0g
Fat: 9g
Protein: 6g

252. Jamaican Jerk Chicken Quarters

Preparation time: 15 minutes
Cooking time: 1 hour 30 minutes
Servings: 4
Ingredients:

- 4 chicken leg quarters, scored
- ¼ cup canola oil
- ½ cup Jamaican Jerk Paste
- 1 tablespoon whole allspice (pimento) berries

Directions:
1. Supply your smoker with wood pellets and follow the manufacturer's specific start-up procedure. Preheat, with the lid closed, to 275°F.
2. Arrange the chicken on the grill, close the lid, and smoke for 1 hour to 1 hour 30 minutes, or until a meat thermometer inserted in the thickest part of the thigh reads 165°F.
3. Let the meat rest for 5 minutes and baste with the reserved jerk paste before serving.

Nutrition:
Calories: 335
Carbs: 7g
Fat: 20g
Protein: 31g

253. Apple wood-Smoked Whole Turkey

Preparation time: 10 minutes
Cooking time: 6 hours
Servings: 6 to 8
Ingredients:

- 1 (10- to 12-pound) turkey, giblets removed
- Extra-virgin olive oil, for rubbing
- ¼ cup poultry seasoning
- 8 tablespoons (1 stick) unsalted butter, melted
- ½ cup apple juice
- 2 teaspoons dried sage
- 2 teaspoons dried thyme

Directions:
1. Supply your smoker with wood pellets and follow the manufacturer's specific start-up procedure. Preheat, with the lid closed, to 250°F.
2. Rub the turkey with oil and season with the poultry seasoning inside and out, getting under the skin.
3. Put the turkey in a roasting pan, place on the grill, close the lid, and grill for 5 to 6 hours, basting every hour, until the skin is brown and crispy, or until a meat thermometer inserted in the thickest part of the thigh reads 165°F.
4. Let the bird rest for 15 to 20 minutes before carving.

Nutrition:
Calories: 120
Carbs: 4g
Fat: 1g
Protein: 20

Chapter 18. Conclusion

Thank you for making it to the end. The Wood Pellet Smoker and Grill will also be an advantage for those who have limited space or are not looking for something that will take a lot of space. This is because a small wood pellet smoker can be placed on a balcony. It will also allow you to regulate the temperature through the two dampers that can be controlled for both the intake and exhaust. It is also an advantage that it takes a minimum amount of time to get heated up. This can be anywhere from fifteen to twenty minutes. This is insignificant when compared to the amount of time taken by a gas smoker to heat up.

There is almost no chance of flaring up when using a wood pellet smoker as it features a controlled ventilation system. The system will automatically assist in releasing the heat and replacing it with air and smoke void for maintaining the temperature.

When it comes to using the wood pellets smoker, you will not have to seal the lid and the coals. This smoker also features an automatic safety that when you turn the unit on, you will be reminded with a beeping sound.

You will also immediately catch a good smell after turning on the wood pellet smoker as the smokeproof cover is made with chemical paint that will trigger the nose, especially if you have pets or children in the house.

When it comes to choosing your wood pellets, it will be an advantage for you if you have other smokers on hand that you can use for comparison. Generally, you will want to choose your wood pellets for the type of food that you want. For instance, if you are going to be using it for pork, then you will want to have the high quality and good tasting hickory pellets. This type of wood will leave the pork nice and flavorful. However, you may want to consider the type of wood pellet you will be using when you are being eaten by yataghan or the Burmese python. This is because a wood pellet can be caught in its bill, or it can also bite you! You can use the hickory wood pellets for you if the python is somewhere away from the area.

Wood pellet smokers are among the most popular smokers available today. They are among the best smoking food is simple. They are also easier to use than other smokers because the intake and exhaust ports are all within easy reach. You will also be using the wood pellet smoker at an affordable cost. They also come with many advantages for a variety of indoor and outdoor cooking with great results.

The wood pellets that were used in the Mythwood pellet smoker you are now reading that will be a good smoke output. They will produce heavier smoke, therefore, better flavor. You will also be using the wood pellets for a maximum of fifteen minutes. This is much better than the time it would take for the smoke to reach its consistency with gas, wood-burning, and pellet smokers.

As mentioned, we have many pellet smokers being offered by different entities. You will want to make sure that the reviews are good on this product. Of course, you will also want to make sure that the cost is under $100. This is to eliminate the unnecessary expenses you may incur for the product.

The wood pellets will be more than likely, a great smell. The wood pellets will also be a great taste that will add to the flavor of already great food.

The wood pellets will leave behind no used smoking products to clean up any mess that will be left behind in the smoker. You will, therefore, be able to cook without having to clean the smoker or worrying about the place you will be cooking. This is another advantage that wood pellets have..

The Mythwood pellet smoker uses red oak ribs and is used for grilling. It also creates a beautiful, glowing briquette that can be used for smoking or grilling indoors or outdoors. These wood pellets can also be lit only on your money!

Mythwood pellet smoker does not use propane, and it is not necessary for you to use lighting so that you will be saving on electricity bills, and you will be able to cook great food and smoke it with the same effortless behavior.

The Mythwood pellet smoker also features an automatic ignition. This is a safety feature that will prevent things from burning if you decide to change temperature settings without knowing about it.

Some of the wood pellets that are available from this unit are kettle wood, lignum, and heartwood. These wood pellets are sold for their natural essence, and because they offer high smoking output, therefore, burning with the wood pellets will not be necessary. You will be able to set up a smoke output that will give you an ideal cooking experience.

I hope you have learned something!

TRAEGER GRILL & SMOKER COOKBOOK

250 WAYS IN TERMS OF OUTSTANDING WOOD PELLET SMOKER RECIPES TO BECOME "THE-REAL-DEAL" BBQ CHEF IN YOUR VERY OWN YARD REGARDLESS OF YOUR CURRENT COOKING SKILLS

BY

BOB FRANKLIN

Chapter 19. Introduction

A Wood Pellet barbecue is an ideal product for those who want to give their dishes the taste of wood without excessively getting their hands dirty with coal or firewood. For those who love the taste of dishes cooked over a flame but do not want to manage the drawbacks of temperature regulation or subsequent cleaning. Pellet grills also offer the convenience of combining several cooking options into one unit. Although it is not able to reach the same temperatures as the coal, it still manages to heat the plate or the grill in a few minutes, making the barbecue ready for use in a time much less than that required for the preparation of the barbecue charcoal

With so many grills available in the market, the Traeger Grill is considered one of the top-of-the-line grills that you can ever invest in for your outdoor kitchen. This innovative grill allows you to cook authentic grilled foods. Yet, you do not deviate with the tradition of cooking using wood pellets so you do not get that distasteful aftertaste you get from cooking in a gas grill.

Made by an Oregon-based company, the Traeger Grill has been around for many decades. This type of smoker grill is known to cook food using all-nature wood pellets so that foods smell and taste great and healthy. However, unlike traditional smokers, the Traeger Grill has been innovated to provide convenience even to grill and barbecue neophytes. It comes with a motor that turns the drill thereby consistently feeding the burn pot so you can achieve even cooking.

Pellet grills give you even more as if that were not enough. With your new pellet grill, you have the absolute convenience of combining several varied cooking options. Old-time smokers only smoke their food, so if you want to grill, bake, and roast your food, you would need to purchase separate units for each process.

Pellet Grills are different from propane or gas grills in that they offer more control. Pellet grills and gas grills both offer their own set of convenient features to the outdoor chef but look more closely, and you will see some major differences. Gas grills are very good when cooking chores, but due to poor insulation, they do not typically perform very well at all at low cooking temperatures. In addition, the older style of propane grills needs to be set up so that they receive the proper degree of ventilation. This, alone, makes them a poor choice for smokers. The Pellet Grill is a no brainer in today's world!

Pellet grills provide the chef with more flavor options. With pellet grills, the wood pellets are available in many different flavors. This provides you with the ability to cook all the foods on your Pellet Smoker Grill. In the end, sure, they both cook your food, but the pellet grill is exponentially better on so many levels. For me, there is no choice but to the Pellet Smoker Grill!

Then there is the question of using a Pellet Grill or staying with the highly coveted charcoal method of barbecuing your fine foods.

Charcoal grills have long been considering the king of the backyard barbecue area. There are several choices of configurations for charcoal grills but with two choices for fuel: lump charcoal or charcoal briquettes. Grilling using a charcoal grill is definitely a labor of love. I know several people who defend them to the ends of the earth, and that is fine. We are different, and thank goodness for that, too. However, cooking on a charcoal grill is not so easy. It takes quite a lot of practice to get all the elements just right and is difficult to control temperatures.

The way pellet grills are used when grilling and smoking are infinitely simpler. This is exactly why they have become the nation's number one seller. As for the cleanup, have you ever seen a charcoal grill the next morning? You may need to carry them out to the trash or recycling. It is not the same with your pellet grill, though.

Chapter 20. The advantages of the Traeger grill

The Traeger Grill is not only limited to, well, grilling. It is an essential outdoor kitchen appliance as it allows you also to bake, roast, and smoke, braise, and barbecue. Nevertheless, more than it being a useful kitchen appliance, below are the advantages of getting your very own Traeger Grill:

➢ Better flavor: The Traeger Grill uses all-natural wood, so food comes out better tasting than when you cook them in a gas or charcoal grill. You can impart 14 different flavors to your food.

➢ No flare-ups: No flare-ups mean that food is cook evenly on all sides. This made possible by using indirect heat. Because there are no flare-ups, you can smoke, bake, and rose without some areas or sides of your food burning.

➢ Mechanical parts are well designed and protected: The mechanical parts of the Traeger Grill protected particularly from fats and drippings, so it is not stuck over time.

➢ Exceptional temperature control: The Traeger Grill has exceptional temperature control. The thing is that all you need is to set up the heat and the grill will maintain a consistent temperature even if the weather goes bad. Moreover, having a stable temperature control allows you to cook food better and tastier minus the burnt taste.

➢ Built-in Wi-Fi: All Traeger Grills have built-in Wi-Fi to set them up even if you are not physically present in front of your grill. Moreover, the grill also alerts you once your food is ready. With this setting, you will be able to do other important things instead of slaving in front of your grill. Lastly, it also comes with an app that allows you to check many recipes from their website.

➢ Environmentally friendly: Perhaps the main selling point of the Traeger Grill is that it is environmentally friendly. Traeger Grill uses all-natural wood pellets, so your grill does not produce harmful chemicals when you are using it… only smoky goodness.

The thing is that the Traeger Grill is more than just your average grill. It is one of the best and you will get your money's worth with this grill.

Some special aspects of the Traeger Grills are:

1. The fuel

Most other types of grills make use of charcoal, natural gas, or propane as a source of fuel. In the case of these fuel sources, the user needs to have a bit of knowledge of the grill type and be present to 'babysit' the grill.

On the other hand, Traeger grills use wood pellets that are all-natural and all-wood. These pellets can burn well in a controlled environment and provide flavorful food. Additionally, these pellets are FDA-approved and safe for home and outdoor uses.

The pellets are available in 14 distinct flavors. They can be used to create a new range of individual flavors and do not harm the environment when burned.

2. Flavor

Traeger pellets are available in 14 different types of pellets like pecan, apple, mesquite, hickory, etc. Apart from infusing delicious flavor to the meat, you can also use them for baking sweets like pie and cookies.

3. No flare-up

There are no flare-ups in roasting, baking, smoking, or grilling when you are using indirect electric heat, not gas. This is because electric heat (indirect) does not lead to flare-ups. The appliances are also not exposed to dripping temperatures.

4. Control of the temperature

One of the best aspects of the Traeger Grill is total control of the temperature. Once you set it, the grill is capable of maintaining consistent heat, even if the weather may not look favorable.

The Traeger grills can be set in 5-degree increments, which is a feature not seen in many grills, especially charcoal and gas ones. All you need to do is cook the food using the recipe and not worry about the appliance dropping down the temperature.

Additionally, since pellets are essentially electric, you are not tied to your grill like a gas grill. For instance, you do not have to keep checking the grill from time-to-time to ensure that the food has not burned.

5. Environmentally-friendly

Grills manufactured by Traeger make use of all-natural and real wood pellets that can burn within a controlled system, thereby offering flavor, ease of use, and convenience.

These grills are also approved by the FDA and the flavors of the pellets can be blended to create a mix of flavors. Additionally, burning these pellets will not cause any harm to the environment, as mentioned before.

Chapter 21. Tips and tricks for using a Traeger Grill

If you are looking for some tips and tricks that can help you better utilize your Traeger grill, they are listed for you. If you already have the appliance, you are already on the sweet side of life. Whether you are a grill newbie or a master, there are always things that you can learn to become the ultimate grill and smoker master.

Some of the top tricks, tips, and hacks that can make your barbequing, smoking, and grilling experience better include:

1.   Always use disposable drip bucket liners

If you get tired of cleaning up that slimy residue every time you decide to grill or smoke some steak or are prone to bumping the bucket off accidentally when putting on the cover, it is recommended that you look for bucket liners - disposable ones of course. With the help of these disposable drip bucket liners, cleaning will become much easier.

2.   Grill lights to light the way

If you plan on cooking at night or are always bumping around the grill in the dark, you can look for some grill lights. If you are a serious smoker but are busy dealing with the headlamp or flashlight, these grill lights will come in very handy.

No wonder this device is one of the top-sellers on several online shopping sites. The grill lights are fitted with a magnetic base and can clamp and bend according to the shape of the grill.

3.   Drip tray liners for easier cleaning

If you want to get serious, then it is time to dump the aluminum foil. Once you have the drip tray liners, you will not have to deal with wadded up, oily, blackened, or small tears in the foil.

The overall idea here is to make the cleaning process easier so that you can redirect your focus on the more important things, such as smoking and grilling.

4.   Meat temperature and meat smoking magnets to measure the temperature accurately

One of the worst things that can happen while grilling and smoking meat is guessing the cooking temperature. With the help of meat smoking and temperature magnets, you can now leave all the frantic web searches behind.

With these devices, you will know the internal temperature that you need to cook meat safely. Then, you will always have perfectly cooked pieces of meat all the time.

5.   Wireless thermometer or Tappecue for the perfect temperature

You have already spent hundreds of dollars on a perfect grill. However, you can still end up spending tens and thousands of dollars more each time you decide to cook on it.

If you want to protect your important investment from harm, you need to ensure that you do not have to 'peek' while cooking. With the Tappecue, you will get the internal temperature that you are looking for.

6. Swap out pellets with bucket head vacuum

Imagine that you need to move from the apple to the hickory flavor. However, you see that the grill is more than half-full of apple pellets. What can do you in this scenario? Of course, you can choose to wait until the pellets cool down and then remove them. Another solution to this issue is using a bucket head vacuum.

Get the appropriate bucket head for a 5-gallon bucket and simply vacuum out the pellets. Once done, you will be left with storage that you can use any time. Additionally, you do not even need a specialized bucket for this purpose; you can use a simple bucket and storage lid kit that is fitted with a filter.

7. Add extra smoke on any type of cooking with an A-maze-n Smoker Tube

If you love smoking, you should definitely buy a dedicated smoker tube – like the A-maze-n Smoker Tube. Known for its great simplicity, this tube is one of the best tools for a seasoned smoker. All you need to do is to add some pellets and light it at just one end. Then, leave it on the grates.

A smoker tube is a great option for cold smoking fish, nuts, and cheese; of course, it can also be used for some extra smoke on meats, like brisket, pulled pork, etc.

Chapter 22.   Common FAQs

How We Chose Your Selection of the Best Wood Pellet Grills

Mark - The pellet grill has only been around for about 30 years and has only attracted public attention for 10 to 15 years. As such, there are actually only a relative handful of companies that produce premium pellet grills. The number of entries on this list including the number of corresponding brands is therefore limited. In fact, it's likely that whatever list of "best grills" you read will include more or less the same brands. Again, it's not because these brands are paying critics not to have the competition on their lists, but simply because there are only a small number of companies doing this product well. Just like there are only a limited number of companies that does well in supercars or high-end watches.

Reviews - Few products tend to elicit the kind of polarizing appraisals from customers like pellet grills. It's hard to understand exactly why people love or hate them, but it might have something to do with the price. If you're going to drop $8 or $ 800 on an electric pellet smoker, you want and expect it to perform flawlessly. If not, you may well turn to the internet to express your rage. With that said, we certainly do take into account what people say about their pellet grills, but at the ending of the day, as always, our opinions and choices are based primarily on our own experience with these products.

Price - Let's put something aside first: there is no such thing as a "cheap" wood smoker. The price of the items on this list varies between approximately € 400 and € 1,000 and more. That's why we have our eyes open for value when we can find it. In this case, the price-performance ratio is the best price-performance ratio. This is one of the reasons the Green Mountain Grills Davy Crockett Pellet tend Grill tops our list as our top pick. Because it offers an irresistible mix of features at a reasonable price and the quality of craft guarantees that it will be on your patio for many years to come, it is a value.

Features to Look for In Pellet Grills

When it comes to the cooking mechanics of your choice, pellet grills of meat and garden-fresh produce all share more or less the same characteristics. And of course, all the grills on our list produce exceptional results with a high degree of reliability. What often separates one pellet grill from the other is all of the features. Here are features you'll want to consider when purchasing your pellet grill, along with other practical considerations to keep in mind.

Temperature Control - If you are familiar with cooking, you are aware of the importance of temperature control. Of course, you can always lay a chicken right on a campfire, and in about 10 minutes, you will be able to eat something. But will it be succulent? Will it be juicy and delicious? Of course not. It will be a charred, dry, tasteless piece of meat that no one wants. The fine temperature of your pellet grill allows you to access a wide range of culinary possibilities. It's up to you to choose the fineness you want, but if your grill also allows you to control the internal temperature of the meat, even better.

Types of Temperature Controllers - With the above in mind, you will probably want to learn more about pellet grill temperature controllers. Here are some basics:

- Three Position Regulators - When you see or hear about a three-position system, it is a system that offers low, medium including high settings. While three settings are better than what you get with charcoal, the control may not be enough for the type of cooking you have in mind.

- Multi-position controllers - With a multi-position controller, you can adjust the temperature up or down at 25-degree intervals. This provides a high degree of control than the three-position controllers, and for some people who use their grill primarily for burgers and sausages, it may be sufficient.

- PID Regulators - A PID (Proportional Integrative Derivative) regulator incorporates digital technology to maintain a more stable temperature in the grill. Rather than having a continuous cranked auger like most other pellet grills, the PID relies on an algorithm that continually monitors internal temperatures and only releases pellets when circumstances demand it.

- Pellet Capacity - No one wants a pellet grill that runs out of fuel halfway through cooking. Therefore, think about the number of people who are likely to attend your parties and meetings, and make sure you buy a grill with a large enough cooking surface and sufficient fuel capacity to keep going until the end. The fuel capacity of the above-profiled pellet grates ranges from 9 to over 20 pounds. Make sure you choose the right capacity to meet your needs.

- Heated stand - A heated stand is a great feature to have, especially when dealing with large gatherings. You want to keep in line and make sure everyone's food is good and hot. The heating floors are perfect for this. It's also a nice thing to have when someone asks me, "Can you keep this warm while I go for a swim in the pool?" »Not all wood smokers have a heated grill. So, if that's a feature you're interested in, you're not just assuming that the grill you've got your eye on will have one. Make sure to check it out.

- Searing Box - In a nutshell, that's what creates these iconic grilling lines on food. Food research also offers contrasts in taste and texture that make the dining experience more complete. Searing foods can also lock in flavors and juices and prevent the meat from turning to dry ash when cooked at high heat.

Additional Considerations

The Ease of Use of the Grill - Some of the best pellet grills are basically plugged in and play business. They also feature automatic temperature control as well as automatic ash cleaning and automatic grease capture and removal. Others require a little more work. If you don't mind cleaning up any drippings or ash yourself or you don't mind buying a separate thermometer to keep the temperature inside the grill and the meat, you can save a few dollars in giving you a simpler grille. If, however, convenience including ease of use is of paramount importance to you, then you'll want to look for features that make it easy to start and clean.

Your Budget - Since, as said earlier, pellet grills don't come cheap, you'll want to make sure that the one you've got your eyes on falls within your budget. There are a few cheaper pellet grills that aren't on this list that we wouldn't buy with someone else's money. Why? Because they're so poorly built that they're likely to collapse a year later. In this case, you require going back to your bank account to purchase another. When you are considering a grill, think about the value. In This: A slightly more expensive grill that burns pellets efficiently, is well constructed and meets all of your cooking needs is a better value than an inexpensive grill that ends up on the sidewalk a year after purchase.

Chapter 23. Breakfast recipes

254. Mini Quiches

Preparation Time: 15 minutes
Cooking Time: 20 minutes
Servings: 8-12
Ingredients:

- ¼ cup Fresh Basil, chopped
- oz. Mozzarella cheese, shredded
- 10 Eggs
- cups of Baby Spinach
- ½ Onion, diced
- 1 tbsp. Olive oil
- Cooking Spray
- Black pepper and Salt to taste

Directions:

1 Spray a muffin tin (12) with a cooking spray.
2 Turn on medium heat and heat the oil in a skillet. Add onion. Cook 7 minutes and then add the spinach. Cook for 1 more minute.
3 Once done transfer the mixture to a board. Once cooled chop.
4 Preheat the grill to 350F with the lid closed.
5 In the meantime, break the eggs in a bowl and whisk them until frothy. Add the spinach, onion, basil, and cheese. Add pepper and salt to season
6 Pour the mixture into the muffin tin cups.
7 Place the tin on the preheated grill and bake for 20 minutes.
8 Serve right away or let them cool and refrigerate. They can last for 4 days in the fridge.

Nutrition:
Calories: 280 Cal
Fat: 6 g
Carbohydrates: 21 g
Protein: 11 g
Fiber: 1g

255. Breakfast Sausage

Preparation Time: 5 minutes
Cooking Time: 30 minutes
Servings: 6-8
Ingredients:

- 12 Breakfast Links
- 1 tbsp. Mustard, Dijon - style
- ½ cup Apricot Jam

Directions:

1 Open the grill and start on Smoke. Once you have a fire close the lid and let it preheat to 350F.
2 In a saucepan warm the Apricot Jam mixed with the mustard.
3 Place the sausages on the grate and cook 15 minutes turning them 2 times. Use tongs and rill the sausages a few times in the sauce mixture and grill for 3 more minutes.
4 Serve with the sauce mixture and enjoy!

Nutrition:
Calories: 180 Cal
Fat: 20 g
Carbohydrates: 18 g
Protein: 15 g
Fiber: 1g

256. Cinnamon Pancakes

Preparation Time: 20 minutes
Cooking Time: 10 minutes
Servings: 2-4
Ingredients:

- 1 Egg, beaten lightly
- 1 tbsp. oil
- 1 cup of Milk
- 1 cup Flour
- 2 tsp. of Baking powder
- 2 tbsp. Sugar
- ½ tsp. of Salt
- 1 tsp. of Vanilla
- 1 tsp. Vanilla
- 1 ¼ cups of Powdered Sugar
- 2 oz. of Cream cheese

tbsp. unsalted butter

- 1 tbsp. Cinnamon, ground
- ¾ cup Brown sugar, packed
- ½ cup melted Butter

Directions:

1. Make the filling: In a bowl combine the cinnamon, brown sugar and butter. Mix. Scoop into a zip lock bag. Set aside.
2. Make the batter: Whisk together the sugar, salt, baking powder, and flour. Whisk in the egg, milk, and vanilla until combined.
3. Prepare the glaze: In a bowl heat cream cheese and butter until melted.

Whisk well until smooth. Add vanilla and powdered sugar. Whisk and set aside.

4. Heat a skillet on the grill and spray with a cooking spray. Scoop a ½ cup of the batter and pour on the skillet.

5. The grill should be ready before you start cooking. Open the lid and start the smoke and once there is a fire set to high temperature. Close the lid and let it preheat for 15 minutes.

6. Cut the zip lock bag's corner and squeeze out the filling on the pancake.

7. When bubbles start to appear flip and cook for about 2 minutes.

8. Serve with the glaze and enjoy.

Nutrition:
Calories: 550 Cal
Fat: 15 g
Carbohydrates: 80 g
Protein: 11 g
Fiber: 5 g

257. Peanut Butter Cookies

Preparation Time: 5 minutes
Cooking Time: 25 minutes
Servings: 24
Ingredients:
- 1 egg
- 1 cup sugar
- 1 cup peanut butter

Directions:
1 Set your wood pellet grill to smoke.
2 Preheat to high.
3 Mix all the ingredients in one bowl
4 Form cookies from the mixture.
5 Place in a baking pan.
6 Bake in the grill for 20 minutes.
7 Let cool for 5 minutes before serving.

Nutrition:
Calories: 166 Cal
Fat: 8 g
Carbohydrates: 20 g
Protein: 3 g
Fiber: 0 g

258. Pretzels

Preparation Time: 30 minutes
Cooking Time: 1 hour and 30 minutes
Servings: 6
Ingredients:
- 1 packet active instant dry yeast
- 1 tablespoon sugar
- 1 1/2 cups warm water
- 2 oz. melted butter
- 4 ½ cups all-purpose flour
- Cooking spray
- 1/2 cups baking soda
- 10 cups boiling water
- Egg yolks, beaten
- Sea salt

Directions:
1 In a bowl, add the yeast, sugar and warm water.
2 Combine using a mixer.
3 Let sit for 10 minutes.
4 Once it bubbles, stir in the butter and flour.
5 Mix for 3 minutes.
6 Transfer to a bowl.
7 Spray with oil.
8 Add a clean towel on top of the bowl.
9 Let it rise for 1 hour.
10 Roll the dough into long strips.
11 Form a knot to create a pretzel shape.
12 Start your wood pellet grill.
13 Set it to 350 degrees F.
14 Add the baking soda to the boiling water.
15 Drop the pretzels into the boiling water.
16 Transfer to a baking sheet.
17 Brush the top with the egg yolk and sprinkle with the salt.
18 Bake in the wood pellet grill for 20 minutes.

Nutrition:
Calories: 110 Cal
Fat: 1 g
Carbohydrates: 23 g
Protein: 3 g
Fiber: 1 g

259. Roasted Pumpkin Seeds

Preparation Time: 15 minutes
Cooking Time: 45 minutes
Servings: 10
Ingredients:
- 10 cups pumpkin seeds
- 4 teaspoons melted butter
- Java steak dry rub

Directions:
1 Set your wood pellet grill to smoke.
2 Preheat it to 300 degrees F.
3 Toss the seeds in steak rub and butter.
4 Place seeds

5   Cook for 45 minutes, stirring occasionally.

Nutrition:
Calories: 170 Cal
Fat: 15 g
Carbohydrates: 4 g
Protein: 9 g
Fiber: 2g

260.   Cinnamon Pumpkin Seeds

Preparation Time: 5 minutes
Cooking Time: 20-25 minutes
Servings: 8
Ingredients:

- 8 cups pumpkin seeds
- 2 tablespoons melted butter
- 2 tablespoons sugar
- 1 teaspoon ground cinnamon

Directions:

1   Set your wood pellet grill to smoke.
2   Preheat it to 350 degrees F.
3   Toss the pumpkin seeds in the butter, sugar and cinnamon.
4   Spread in a baking pan.
5   Roast for 20 to 25 minutes.

Nutrition:
Calories: 285 Cal
Fat: 12 g
Carbohydrates: 34 g
Protein: 12 g
Fiber: 12 g

261. Cilantro and Lime Corn

Preparation Time: 15 minutes
Cooking Time: 15 minutes
Servings: 4
Ingredients:

- 4 corn cobs
- 1 tablespoon lime juice
- 2 tablespoons melted butter
- Smoked paprika
- 1 cup cilantro, chopped

Directions:

1   Preheat your wood pellet grill to 400 degrees F.
2   Grill for 15 minutes, rotating every 5 minutes.
3   Brush the corn cobs with a mixture of lime juice and butter.
4   Season with the paprika.

Nutrition:
Calories: 100 Cal
Fat: 2 g
Carbohydrates: 19 g
Protein: 3 g
Fiber: 2 g

262.   Roasted Trail Mix

Preparation Time: 10 minutes
Cooking Time: 15 minutes
Servings: 6
Ingredients:

- 1 cup pretzels
- 1 cup crackers
- 1 cup mixed nuts and seeds
- 3 tablespoons butter
- 1 teaspoon smoked paprika

Directions:

1   Start your wood pellet grill.
2   Preheat it to 225 degrees F.
3   Toss all the ingredients in a roasting pan.
4   Smoke for 15 minutes.
5   Let cool and serve.

Nutrition:

Calories: 150 Cal
Fat: 11 g
Carbohydrates: 11 g
Protein: 5 g
Fiber: 2 g

263.   Grilled Watermelon

Preparation Time: 5 minutes
Cooking Time: 6 minutes
Servings: 8
Ingredients:

- 1 watermelon, sliced
- Feta cheese
- Mint leaves, chopped

Directions:

1   Preheat your wood pellet grill to 450 degrees F.
2   Grill the watermelon for 3 minutes per side.
3   Slice into cubes.
4   Transfer to a bowl.
5   Top with the cheese and mint leaves.

Nutrition:
Calories: 14 Cal
Fat: 0 g
Carbohydrates: 3 g
Protein: 0 g
Fiber: 0 g

264.   Grilled Peaches

Preparation Time: 5 minutes
Cooking Time: 10 minutes
Servings: 6
Ingredients:

- 1/2 tablespoon ground cinnamon
- 3 tablespoons brown sugar
- 3 peaches, sliced in half and pitted
- 1 tablespoon melted butter

Directions:

1. Turn on your wood pellet grill.
2. Set it to smoke.
3. Establish fire in the burn pot for 5 minutes.
4. Set it to 400 degrees F.
5. In a bowl, mix the cinnamon and brown sugar.
6. Coat the peaches with the butter.
7. Grill for 6 minutes.
8. Flip and sprinkle with the sugar mixture.
9. Grill for 2 minutes.

Nutrition:
Calories: 98 Cal
Fat: 6 g
Carbohydrates: 12 g
Protein: 1 g
Fiber: 1 g

265.   Grilled Strawberries

Preparation Time: 5 minutes
Cooking Time: 5 minutes
Servings: 4
Ingredients:

- 1 tablespoon lemon juice
- 4 tablespoons honey
- 16 strawberries

Directions:

1. Turn on your wood pellet grill.
2. Set it to 450 degrees F.
3. Thread the strawberries into skewers.
4. Brush with the honey and lemon juice.
5. Grill for 5 minutes.

Nutrition:
Calories: 53 Cal
Fat: 0 g
Carbohydrates: 12 g

Protein: 1 g
Fiber: 3 g

266.   Smoked Crepes

Preparation Time: 10 minutes
Cooking Time: 2 hours
Servings: 6
Ingredients:

- 2-pound apples, sliced into wedges
- Apple butter seasoning
- 1/2 cup apple juice
- 2 teaspoon lemon juice
- 5 tablespoon butter
- 3/4 teaspoon cinnamon, ground
- 2 tablespoon brown sugar
- 3/4 teaspoon cornstarch
- 6 crepes

Directions:

1. Preheat your wood pellet grill to 225 degrees F.
2. Season the apples with the apple butter seasoning.
3. Add to the grill.
4. Smoke for 1 hour.
5. Let cool and slice thinly.
6. Add to a baking pan.
7. Stir in the rest of the ingredients except the crepes. Roast for 15 minutes.
8. Add the apple mixture on top of the crepes. Roll and serve.

Nutrition:
Calories: 130 Cal
Fat: 5 g
Carbohydrates: 14 g
Protein: 7 g

Fiber: 1 g

267.   Apple Crumble

Preparation Time: 30 minutes
Cooking Time: 1 hour and 30 minutes
Servings: 8
Ingredients:

- 2 cups and 2 tablespoons flour, divided
- 1/2 cup shortening
- Pinch salt
- 1/4 cup cold water
- 8 cups apples, sliced into cubes
- 3 teaspoons lemon juice
- 1/2 teaspoon ground nutmeg
- 1 teaspoon apple butter seasoning
- 1/8 teaspoon ground cloves
- 1 teaspoon cinnamon
- 1/4 cup butter

Directions:

1. Set your wood pellet grill to smoke.
2. Preheat it to 350 degrees F.
3. Mix 1 1/2 cups flour, shortening and salt in a bowl until crumbly .
4. Slowly add cold water. Mix gently.
5. Wrap the dough in plastic and refrigerate for 20 to 30 minutes.
6. Place the apples in a bowl.
7. Toss in lemon juice. Take the dough out.
8. Press into a pan.

9   In a bowl, combine the 2 tablespoons flour, nutmeg, apple butter seasoning, ground cloves and cinnamon.
10 Add this to the bowl with apples.
11 Add the butter and mix with a mixer until crumbly.
12 Spread this on top of the dough.
13 Bake for 1 hour.

Nutrition:
Calories: 283 Cal
Fat: 6 g
Carbohydrates: 55 g
Protein: 1 g
Fiber: 0 g

268.   Fruits on Bread

Preparation Time: 30 minutes
Cooking Time: 1 hour and 30 minutes
Servings: 8
Ingredients:
- 1/2 cup milk
- 1 teaspoon sugar
- 1/4 cup warm water
- 2 1/2 teaspoon active yeast, instant
- 2 1/2 cups all-purpose flour
- 2 tablespoon melted butter
- 1 egg
- 1/2 teaspoon vanilla
- 1/2 teaspoon salt
- Vegetable oil
- 1 tablespoon ground cinnamon
- Chocolate spread
- Fruits, sliced

Directions:
1   Add the milk, sugar, water and yeast in a bowl. Let sit for 10 minutes.
2   In another bowl, add the flour.
3   Create a well in the center.
4   Add the sugar mixture, butter, egg, vanilla and salt.
5   Mix and knead.
6   Place in a bowl.
7   Cover with clean towel.
8   Let rise for 1 hour.
9   Start your wood pellet grill.
10 Set it to 450 degrees F.
11 Grease a cast iron skillet with the oil.
12 Create balls from the mixture.
13 Press and sprinkle with the cinnamon.
14 Fry for 1 minute per side.
15 Spread with chocolate and top with sliced fruits.

Nutrition:
Calories: 110 Cal
Fat: 2 g
Carbohydrates: 21 g
Protein: 5 g
Fiber: 2 g

269.   Grill a Burger Without Flipping Them

Preparation Time: 15 Minutes
Cooking Time: 50 Minutes
Servings: 6
Ingredients:
- 1 Ground Beef Patties
- Beef Rub
- Cheese
- Pretzel buns

Directions:
1   Start with cold but not frozen patties and sprinkle on the Beef Rub, and massage into both sides of the patty.
2   Preheat grill to 250 degrees and cook for 45 minutes
3   Add cheese and other topic varieties of your liking
4   Close the grill back up and let them finish for another 10 minutes before removing

Nutrition:
Calories: 696 Cal
Fat: 54 g
Carbohydrates: 11 g
Protein: 38 g

270.   Reversed Baked Flank Steak

Preparation Time: 10 Minutes
Cooking Time: 20 Minutes
Servings: 2
Ingredients:
- 3-pound flank steaks
- 1 tbsp salt
- 1/2 tbsp onion powder
- 1/4 tbsp garlic powder
- 1/2 black pepper, coarsely ground

Directions:
1   Preheat the Traeger to 2250F.
2   Add the steaks and rub them generously with the rub mixture.
3   Place the steak
4   Let cook until its internal temperature is 100F under your desired temperature. 1150F for rare, 1250F

138

for the medium rear, and 1350F for medium.

5. Wrap the steak with foil and raise the grill temperature to high.
6. Place back the steak and grill for 3 minutes on each side.
7. Pat with butter and serve when hot.

Nutrition:
Calories: 112 Cal
Fat: 5 g
Carbohydrates: 1 g
Protein: 16 g
Fiber: 0 g

271. Traeger New York Strip

Preparation Time: 5 Minutes
Cooking Time: 15 Minutes
Servings: 6
Ingredients:

- 3 New York strips
- Salt and pepper

Directions:

1. If the steak is in the fridge, remove it 30 minutes before cooking.
2. Preheat the Traeger to 4500F.
3. Meanwhile, season the steak generously with salt and pepper.
4. Place it on the grill and let it cook for 5 minutes per side or until the internal temperature reaches 1280F.
5. Rest for 10 minutes.

Nutrition:
Calories: 198 Cal
Fat: 14 g
Carbohydrates: 0 g
Protein: 17 g

Chapter 24. Basic recipes

272. Smoked Hot Paprika Pork Tenderloin

Preparation Time: 20-35 minutes
Cooking Time: 2 ½ to 3 hours
Servings: 6
Ingredients:

- 2-pound pork tenderloin
- 3/4 cup chicken stock
- 1/2 cup tomato-basil sauce
- 2 tbsp smoked hot paprika (or to taste)
- 1 tbsp oregano
- Salt and pepper to taste

Directions:
1. In a bowl, combine the chicken stock, tomato-basil sauce, paprika, oregano, salt, and pepper together.
2. Brush over tenderloin.
3. Smoke grill for 4-5 minutes. Pre head, lid closed for 10-14 minutes
4. Place pork for 2 ½ to 3 hours.
5. Rest for 10 minutes.

Nutrition:
Calories: 360.71 Cal
Fat: 14.32 g
Carbohydrates: 3.21 g
Protein: 52.09 g
Fiber: 1.45 g

273. Smoked Pork Tenderloin with Mexican Pineapple Sauce

Preparation Time: 10-15 minutes
Cooking Time: 3 hours and 55 minutes
Servings: 6
Ingredients:

- Pineapple Sauce
- 1 can (11 oz) unsweetened crushed pineapple
- 1 can (11 oz) roasted tomato or tomatillo
- 1/2 cup port wine
- 1/4 cup orange juice
- 1/4 cup packed brown sugar
- 1/4 cup lime juice
- 2 tbsp Worcestershire sauce
- 1 tsp garlic powder
- 1/4 tsp cayenne pepper
- PORK
- 2 pork tenderloin (1 pound each)
- 1 tsp ground cumin
- 1/2 tsp pepper
- 1/4 tsp cayenne pepper
- 2 tbsp lime juice (freshly squeezed)

Directions:
1. Combine cumin, pepper, cayenne pepper and lime juice and rub over tenderloins.
2. Smoke grill for 4-5 minutes. Preheat, lid closed for 10-15 minutes
3. Smoke tenderloin for 2 ½ to 3 hours.
4. Rest for 5 minutes
5. For Sauce:
6. Combine ingredients and boil for 25 minutes
7. Remove from heat and cool.
8. Serve pork slices with pineapple sauce and lime wedges.

Nutrition:
Calories: 277.85 Cal
Fat: 3.49 g
Carbohydrates: 24.31 g
Protein: 32.42 g
Fiber: 0.67 g

274. Garlic Aioli and Smoked Salmon Sliders

Preparation Time: 15 minutes
Cooking Time: 1 hour and 30 minutes
Servings: 12
Ingredients:

- For Brine:
- Water as needed
- ½ a cup of salt
- 1 tablespoon of dried tarragon
- 1 and a ½ pound of salmon fillets
- For Aioli:
- 1 cup of mayonnaise
- 3 tablespoon of fresh lemon juice
- 3 minced garlic cloves
- 1 and a ½ teaspoon of ground black pepper
- ½ a teaspoon of lemon zest
- Salt as needed
- ½ a cup of apple wood chips
- 12 slide burger buns

Directions:

1. Take a large sized baking dish and add ½ a cup of salt alongside about half water
2. Add tarragon, salmon in the brine mix and keep adding more water
3. Cover up the dish and freeze for 2-12 hours. Take a small bowl and add lemon juice, mayonnaise, pepper, garlic, 1 pinch of salt and lemon zest.
4. Mix and chill for 30 minutes
5. Remove your Salmon from the brine and place it on a wire rack and let it sit for about 30 minutes.
6. Smoke them over low heat for 1 and a ½ to 2 hours. Assemble sliders by dividing the salmon among 12 individual buns.
7. Top each of the pieces with a spoonful of aioli and place another bun on top

Nutrition:
Calories: 320 Cal
Fat: 22 g
Carbohydrates: 13 g
Protein: 22 g
Fiber: 0 g

275.   Texas Styled Smoked Flounder

Preparation Time: 20 minutes
Cooking Time: 20 minutes
Servings: 6
Ingredients:

- 1 whole flounder
- 1 halved lemon
- Ground black pepper as needed
- 2 tablespoons of chopped up fresh dill
- 1 tablespoon of olive oil
- 1 cup of soaked wood chips

Directions:

1. Preheat your smoker to a temperature of 350 degrees Fahrenheit.
2. Slice half of your lemon and place them into the slices. Rub the fish with a coating of olive oil. Squeeze another half of the lemon all over the fish. Season with some black pepper.
3. Rub 1 tablespoon of dill into the slits and insert the lemon slices firmly. Place the flounder on top of a large piece of aluminum foil and fold the sides all around the fish.
4. Place the fish in your smoker and throw a couple handful of soaked wood chips into the coals. And smoke for 10 minutes
5. Once done, seal up the foil and smoke it until it is fully done. Remove fish and garnish with some extra dill

Nutrition:
Calories: 226 Cal
Fat: 4 g
Carbohydrates: 28 g
Protein: 28 g
Fiber: 0 g

276.   Fire and Ice Smoked Salmon

Preparation Time: 6 hours
Cooking Time: 50 minutes
Servings: 7
Ingredients:

- ½ a cup of brown sugar
- 2 tablespoons of salt
- 2 tablespoon of crushed red pepper flakes
- Mint leaves
- ¼ cup of brandy
- 1 (4 pounds) salmon side with bones removed
- 2 cups of alder wood chips, soaked up in water

Directions:

1. Take a medium bowl and mix in the brown sugar, crushed red pepper flakes, salt, mint leaves and brandy until a paste form. Coat the paste on all sides of the salmon and wrap the Salmon up in plastic wrap.
2. Let it refrigerate for at least 4 hours or overnight. Preheat your smoker to high heat and oil up the grate. Add soaked alder chips to your heat box and wait until smoke starts to appear.
3. Turn the heat to your lowest setting and place the salmon on the grate. Lock up the lid

and let your Salmon smoke for about 45 minutes.

Nutrition:
Calories: 370 Cal
Fat: 28 g
Carbohydrates: 1 g
Protein: 23 g
Fiber: 0 g

277. Bradley Maple Cure Smoked Salmon

Preparation Time: 2 hours
Cooking Time: 1 hour and 30 minutes
Servings: 6
Ingredients:

- 1 large sized salmon fillet
- 1 quart of water
- ½ a cup of pickling and canning salt
- ½ a cup of maple syrup
- ¼ cup of dark rum
- ¼ cup of lemon juice
- 10 whole cloves
- 10 whole allspice berries
- 1 bay leaf

Directions:

1   Take a medium sized bowl and add the brine ingredients. Mix them well. Place the salmon fillet in a cover with brine.
2   Cover it up and let it refrigerate for about 2 hours. Remove the Salmon and pat dry then air dry for 1 hour.
3   Preheat your smoker to a temperature of 180 degrees Fahrenheit and add Bradley Maple-

Flavored briquettes. Smoke the salmon for about 1 and a ½ hour.

Nutrition:
Calories: 223 Cal
Fat: 7 g
Carbohydrates: 15 g
Protein: 21 g
Fiber: 0 g

278. Smoked Teriyaki Tuna

Preparation Time: 5-7 hours
Cooking Time: 2 hours
Servings: 4
Ingredients:

- Tuna steaks, 1 oz.
- 2 c. marinade, teriyaki
- Alder wood chips soaked in water

Directions:

1   Slice tuna into thick slices of 2 inch. Place your tuna slices and marinade then set in your fridge for about 3 hours
2   After 3 hours, remove the tuna from the marinade and pat dry. Let the tuna air dry in your fridge for 2-4 hours. Preheat your smoker to 180 degrees Fahrenheit
3   Place the Tuna on a Teflon-coated fiberglass and place them directly on your grill grates. Smoke the Tuna for about an hour until the internal temperature reaches 145 degrees Fahrenheit.
4   Remove the tuna from your grill and let them

rest for 10 minutes. Serve!

Nutrition:
Calories: 249 Cal
Fat: 3 g
Carbohydrates: 33 g
Protein: 21 g
Fiber: 0 g

279. Cold Hot Smoked Salmon

Preparation Time: 16 hours
Cooking Time: 8 hours
Servings: 4
Ingredients:

- 5 pound of fresh sockeye (red) salmon fillets
- For trout Brine
- 4 cups of filtered water
- 1 cup of soy sauce
- ½ a cup of pickling kosher salt
- ½ a cup of brown sugar
- 2 tablespoon of garlic powder
- 2 tablespoon of onion powder
- 1 teaspoon of cayenne pepper

Directions:

1   Combine all of the ingredients listed under trout brine in two different 1-gallon bags. Store it in your fridge. Cut up the Salmon fillets into 3-4-inch pieces. Place your salmon pieces into your 1-gallon container of trout brine and let it keep in your fridge for 8 hours.
2   Rotate the Salmon and pat them dry using a

kitchen towel for 8 hours

3　Configure your pellet smoker for indirect cooking. Remove your salmon pieces of from your fridge Preheat your smoker to a temperature of 180 degrees Fahrenheit

4　Once a cold smoke at 70 degrees Fahrenheit starts smoke your fillets

5　Keep smoking it until the internal temperature reaches 145 degrees Fahrenheit.

6　Remove the Salmon from your smoker and let it rest for 10 minutes

Nutrition:
Calories: 849 Cal
Fat: 45 g
Carbohydrates: 51 g
Protein: 46 g
Fiber: 0 g

280.　　Smoked Up Salmon and Dungeness Crab Chowder

Preparation Time: 30 minutes
Cooking Time: 45 minutes
Servings: 6
Ingredients:

- 4 gallons of water
- 3 fresh Dungeness crabs
- 1 cup of rock salt
- 3 cups of Cold-Hot Smoked Salmon
- 3 cups of ocean clam juice
- 5 diced celery stalks
- 1 yellow diced onion
- 2 peeled and diced large sized russet potatoes
- 14 ounces of sweet corn
- 12 ounce of clam chowder dry soup mix
- 4 bacon slices crumbled and cooked

Directions:

1　Bring 4 gallons of water and rock salt to a boil. Add the Dungeness crab and boil for 20 minutes

2　Remove the crabs , let it cool and clean the crabs and pick out crab meat. Place it over high heat.

3　Add clam juice, 5 cups of water, diced potatoes, diced celery, and onion. Bring the mix to a boil as well. Add corn to the liquid and boil.

4　Whisk in the clam chowder and keep mixing everything. Simmer on low for about 15 minutes and add the crumbled bacon. Add bacon, garnish with ½ cup flaked smoked salmon and ½ cup Dungeness crabmeat. Serve!

Nutrition:
Calories: 174 Cal
Fat: 5 g
Carbohydrates: 12 g
Protein: 8 g
Fiber: 0 g

281. Alder Wood Smoked Bony Trout

Preparation Time: 4 hours
Cooking Time: 2 hours
Servings: 4
Ingredients:

- 4 fresh boned whole trout with their skin on
- For trout Brine
- 4 cups of filtered water
- 1 cup of soy sauce
- ½ a cup of pickling kosher salt
- ½ a cup of brown sugar
- 2 tablespoon of garlic powder
- 2 tablespoon of onion powder
- 1 teaspoon of cayenne pepper

Directions:

1　Combine all of the ingredients listed under trout brine in two different 1-gallon bags.

2　Store it in your fridge.

3　Place your trout in the sealable bag with trout brine and place the bag in a shallow dish.

4　Let it refrigerate for about 2 hours, making sure to rotate it after 30 minutes.

5　Remove them from your brine and pat them dry using kitchen towels.

6　Air Dry your brine trout in your fridge uncovered for about 2 hours.

7　Preheat your smoker to a temperature of 180 degrees Fahrenheit using alder pellets.

8   The pit temperature of should be 180 degrees Fahrenheit and the cold smoke should be 70 degrees Fahrenheit.

9   Cold smoke your prepared trout for 90 minutes.

10 After 90 minutes transfer the cold smoked boned trout pellets to your smoker grill are and increase the smoker temperature to 225 degrees Fahrenheit.

11 Keep cooking until the internal temperature reaches 145 degrees Fahrenheit in the thickest parts.

12 Remove the trout from the grill and let them rest for 5 minutes.

13 Serve!

Nutrition:

Calories: 508 Cal

Fat: 23 g

Carbohydrates: 47 g

Protein: 15 g

Fiber: 0 g

Chapter 25. Beef Recipes

282. Smoked and Pulled Beef

Preparation Time: 10 Minutes
Cooking Time: 6 Hours
Servings: 6
Ingredients:

- 4 lb. beef sirloin tip roast
- 1/2 cup BBQ rub
- Two bottles of amber beer
- One bottle barbecues sauce

Directions:
1. Turn your wood pellet grill onto smoke setting, then trim excess fat from the steak.
2. Coat the steak with BBQ rub and let it smoke on the grill for 1 hour.
3. Continue cooking and flipping the steak for the next 3 hours. Transfer the steak to a braising vessel. Add the beers.
4. Braise the beef until tender, then transfer to a platter reserving 2 cups of cooking liquid.
5. Use a pair of forks to shred the beef and return it to the pan. Add the reserved liquid and barbecue sauce. Stir well and keep warm before serving.
6. Enjoy.

Nutrition:
Calories 829
Total fat 46g
Total carbs 4g
Protein 86g
Sodium: 181mg

283. Wood Pellet Smoked Beef Jerky

Preparation Time: 15 Minutes
Cooking Time: 5 Hours
Servings: 10
Ingredients:

- 3 lb. sirloin steaks, sliced into 1/4-inch thickness
- 2 cups soy sauce
- 1/2 cup brown sugar
- 1 cup pineapple juice
- 2 tbsp sriracha
- 2 tbsp red pepper flake
- 2 tbsp hoisin
- 2 tbsp onion powder
- 2 tbsp rice wine vinegar
- 2 tbsp garlic, minced

Directions:
1. Mix all the fixings in a Ziplock bag.
2. Seal the bag and mix until the beef is well coated.
3. Put the bag in the fridge overnight to let marinate. Remove the bag from the fridge 1 hour before cooking.
4. Startup your wood pallet grill and set it to smoke setting. You need to layout the meat on the grill with a half-inch space between them.
5. Let them cook for 5 hours while turning after every 2-1/2 hours.
6. Transfer from the grill and let cool for 30 minutes before serving.
7. Enjoy.

Nutrition:
Calories 80
Total fat 1g
Total carbs 5g
Protein 14g
Sugar 5g
Sodium: 650mg

284. Reverse Seared Flank Steak

Preparation Time: 10 Minutes
Cooking Time: 10 Minutes
Servings: 2
Ingredients:

- 1.5 lb. Flanks steak
- 1 tbsp salt
- 1/2 onion powder
- 1/4 tbsp garlic powder
- 1/2 black pepper, coarsely ground

Directions:
1. Preheat your wood pellet grill to 225°F.
2. In a mixing bowl, mix salt, onion powder, garlic powder, and pepper. Generously rub the steak with the mixture.
3. Place the steaks on the preheated grill, close the lid, and let the steak cook.
4. Crank up the grill to high, then let it heat. The steak should be off the grill and tented with foil to keep it warm.
5. Once the grill is heated up to 450°F, place the steak back and grill for 3 minutes per side.

6. Remove from heat, pat with butter, and serve. Enjoy.

Nutrition:
Calories 112
Total fat 5g
Total carbs 1g
Protein 16g
Sodium: 737mg

285. Smoked Midnight Brisket

Preparation Time: 15 Minutes
Cooking Time: 12 Minutes
Servings: 6
Ingredients:

- 1 tbsp Worcestershire sauce
- 1 tbsp Traeger beef Rub
- 1 tbsp Traeger Chicken rub
- 1 tbsp Traeger Blackened Saskatchewan rub
- 5 lb. flat cut brisket
- 1 cup beef broth

Directions:

1. Rub the sauce and rubs in a mixing bowl, then rub the mixture on the meat.
2. Preheat your grill to 180°F with the lid closed for 15 minutes. You can use super smoke if you desire.
3. Place the meat on the grill and grill for 6 hours or until the internal temperature reaches 160°F.
4. Remove the meat from the grill and double wrap it with foil.

5. Add beef broth and return to grill, with the temperature increased to 225°F. Cook for 4 hours or until the internal temperature reaches 204°F.
6. Remove from grill and let rest for 30 minutes. Serve and enjoy with your favorite BBQ sauce.

Nutrition:
Calories 200
Total fat 14g
Total carbs 3g
Protein 14g
Sodium: 680mg

286. Cocoa Crusted Grilled Flank Steak

Preparation Time: 15 Minutes
Cooking Time: 6 Minutes
Servings: 7
Ingredients:

- 1 tbsp cocoa powder
- 2 tbsp chili powder
- 1 tbsp chipotle chili powder
- 1/2 tbsp garlic powder
- 1/2 tbsp onion powder
- 1-1/2 tbsp brown sugar
- 1 tbsp cumin
- 1 tbsp smoked paprika
- 1 tbsp kosher salt
- 1/2 tbsp black pepper
- Olive oil
- 4 lb. Flank steak

Directions:

1. Whisk together cocoa, chili powder, garlic powder, onion powder, sugar, cumin, paprika,

salt, and pepper in a mixing bowl.
2. Drizzle the steak with oil, then rub with the cocoa mixture on both sides.
3. Preheat your wood pellet grill for 15 minutes with the lid closed.
4. Cook the meat on the grill grate for 5 minutes or until the internal temperature reaches 135°F.
5. Remove the meat from the grill and cool for 15 minutes to allow the juices to redistribute.
6. Slice the meat against the grain and on a sharp diagonal.
7. Serve and enjoy.

Nutrition:
Calories 420
Total fat 26g
Total carbs 21g
Protein 3g
Sugar 7g,
Fiber 8g
Sodium: 2410mg

287. Wood Pellet Grill Prime Rib Roast

Preparation Time: 5 Minutes
Cooking Time: 4 Hours
Servings: 10
Ingredients:

- 7 lb. bone prime rib roast
- Traeger prime rib rub

Directions:

1. Coat the roast generously with the rub, then wrap in a plastic wrap. Let sit in

the fridge for 24 hours to marinate.

2. Set the temperatures to 500°F.to to preheat with the lid closed for 15 minutes.

3. Place the rib directly on the grill fat side up and cook for 30 minutes.

4. Decrease the temperature to 300°F and cook for 4 hours or until the internal temperature is 120°F-rare, 130°F-medium rare, 140°F-medium and 150°F-well done.

5. Remove from the grill and let rest for 30 minutes, then serve and enjoy.

Nutrition:
Calories 290
Total fat 23g
Total carbs 0g
Protein 19g
Sodium: 54mg
Potassium 275mg

288. Smoked Longhorn Cowboy Tri-Tip

Preparation Time: 15 Minutes
Cooking Time: 4 Hours
Servings: 7
Ingredients:
3 lb. tri-tip roast
1/8 cup coffee, ground
1/4 cup Traeger beef rub
Directions:

1. Preheat the grill to 180°F with the lid closed for 15 minutes.

2. Meanwhile, rub the roast with coffee and beef rub. Place the

roast on the grill grate and smoke for 3 hours.

3. Remove the roast from the grill and double wrap it with foil. Increase the temperature to 275°F.

4. Return the meat to the grill and cook for 90 minutes or until the internal temperature reaches 135°F.

5. Remove from the grill, unwrap it and let rest for 10 minutes before serving.

6. Enjoy.

Nutrition:
Calories 245
Total fat 14g
Total Carbs 0g
Protein 23g
Sodium: 80mg

289. Wood Pellet Grill Teriyaki Beef Jerky

Preparation Time: 15 Minutes
Cooking Time: 5 Hours
Servings: 10
Ingredients:

- 3 cups soy sauce
- 2 cups brown sugar
- Three garlic cloves
- 2-inch ginger knob, peeled and chopped
- 1 tbsp sesame oil
- 4 lb. beef, skirt steak

Directions:

1. Place all the fixings except the meat in a food processor. Pulse until well mixed.

2. Trim any extra fat from the meat and slice into 1/4-inch slices. Add

the steak with the marinade into a zip lock bag and let marinate for 12-24 hours in a fridge.

3. Set the wood pellet grill to smoke and let preheat for 5 minutes.

4. Arrange the steaks on the grill, leaving a space between each. Let smoke for 5 hours.

5. Remove the steak from the grill and serve when warm.

Nutrition:
Calories 80
Total fat 1g
Total Carbs 7g
Protein 11g
Sugar 6g
Sodium: 390mg

290. Grilled Butter Basted Rib-eye

Preparation Time: 20 Minutes
Cooking Time: 20 Minutes
Servings: 4
Ingredients:

- Two rib-eye steaks, bone-in
- Salt to taste
- Pepper to taste
- 4 tbsp butter, unsalted

Directions:

1. Mix steak, salt, and pepper in a Ziplock bag. Seal the bag and mix until the beef is well coated. Ensure you get as much air as possible from the Ziplock bag.

2. Set the wood pellet grill temperature to high with a closed lid for 15

minutes. Place a cast-iron into the grill.

3. Place the steaks on the grill's hottest spot and cook for 5 minutes with the lid closed.
4. Open the lid and add butter to the skillet. When it's almost melted, place the steak on the skillet with the grilled side up.
5. Cook for 5 minutes while busting the meat with butter. Close the lid and cook until the temperature is 130°F.
6. Remove the steak from the skillet and let rest for 10 minutes before enjoying with the reserved butter.

Nutrition:
Calories 745
Total fat 65g
Total Carbs 5g
Net Carbs 5g
Protein 35g

291. Wood Pellet Smoked Ribeye Steaks

Preparation Time: 15 Minutes
Cooking Time: 35 Minutes
Servings: 1
Ingredients:
- 2-inch thick ribeye steaks
- Steak rub of choice

Directions:
1. Preheat your pellet grill to low smoke.
2. Sprinkle the steak with your favorite steak rub and place it on the grill. Let it smoke for 25 minutes.

3. Remove the steak from the grill and set the temperature to 400°F.
4. Return the steak to the grill and sear it for 5 minutes on each side.
5. Cook until the desired temperature is achieved; 125°F-rare, 145°F-Medium, and 165°F.-Well done.
6. Wrap the steak with foil and let rest for 10 minutes before serving. Enjoy.

Nutrition:
Calories 225
Total fat 10.4g
Total Carbs 0.2g
Protein 32.5g
Sodium: 63mg,
Potassium 463mg

292. Smoked Trip Tip with Java Chophouse

Preparation Time: 10 Minutes
Cooking Time: 90 Minutes
Servings: 4
Ingredients:
- 2 tbsp olive oil
- 2 tbsp java chophouse seasoning
- 3 lb. trip tip roast, fat cap, and silver skin removed

Directions:
1. Startup your wood pellet grill and smoker and set the temperature to 225°F.
2. Rub the roast with olive oil and seasoning, then place it on the smoker rack.

3. Smoke until the internal temperature is 140°F.
4. Remove the tri-tip from the smoker and let rest for 10 minutes before serving. Enjoy.

Nutrition:
Calories 270
Total fat 7g
Total Carbs 0g
Protein 23g
Sodium: 47mg
Potassium 289mg

293. Supper Beef Roast

Preparation Time: 5 Minutes
Cooking Time: 3 Hours
Servings: 7
Ingredients:
- 3-1/2 beef top round
- 3 tbsp vegetable oil
- Prime rib rub
- 2 cups beef broth
- One russet potato, peeled and sliced
- Two carrots, peeled and sliced
- Two celery stalks, chopped
- One onion, sliced
- Two thyme sprigs

Directions:
1. Rub the roast with vegetable oil and place it on the roasting fat side up. Season with prime rib rub, then pours the beef broth.
2. Set the temperature to 500°F and preheat the wood pellet grill for 15 minutes with the lid closed.

3. Cook for 30 minutes or until the roast is well seared.
4. Reduce temperature to 225°F. Add the veggies and thyme and cover with foil. Cook for three more hours or until the internal temperature reaches 135°F.
5. Remove from the grill and let rest for 10 minutes. Slice against the grain and serve with vegetables and the pan drippings.
6. Enjoy.

Nutrition:
Calories 697
Total fat 10g
Total Carbs 127g
Protein 34g
Sugar 14g
Fiber 22g
Sodium: 3466mg
Potassium 2329mg

294. Wood Pellet Grill Deli-Style Roast Beef

Preparation Time: 15 Minutes
Cooking Time: 4 Hours
Servings: 2
Ingredients:
- 4lb round-bottomed roast
- 1 tbsp coconut oil
- 1/4 tbsp garlic powder
- 1/4 tbsp onion powder
- 1/4 tbsp thyme
- 1/4 tbsp oregano
- 1/2 tbsp paprika
- 1/2 tbsp salt
- 1/2 tbsp black pepper

Directions:
1. Combine all the dry hubs to get a dry rub.
2. Roll the roast in oil, then coat with the rub.
3. Set your grill to 185°F and place the roast on the grill.
4. Smoke for 4 hours or until the internal temperature reaches 140°F.
5. Remove the roast from the grill and let rest for 10 minutes.
6. Slice thinly and serve.

Nutrition:
Calories 90
Total fat 3g
Total Carbs 0g
Protein 14g
Sodium: 420mg

295. Bacon-Swiss Cheesesteak Meatloaf

Preparation Time: 15 minutes
Cooking Time: 2 hours
Servings: 8-10
Ingredients:
- 1 tablespoon canola oil
- 2 garlic cloves, finely chopped
- 1 medium onion, finely chopped
- 1 poblano chile, stemmed, seeded, and finely chopped
- 2 pounds extra-lean ground beef
- 2 tablespoons Montreal steak seasoning
- 1 tablespoon A.1. Steak Sauce
- ½ pound bacon, cooked and crumbled
- 2 cups shredded Swiss cheese
- 1 egg, beaten
- 2 cups breadcrumbs
- ½ cup Tiger Sauce

Directions:
1 On your stove top, heat the canola oil in a medium sauté pan over medium-high heat. Add the garlic, onion, and poblano, and sauté for 3 to 5 minutes, or until the onion is just barely translucent.
2 Supply your smoker with wood pellets and follow the manufacturer's specific start-up procedure. Preheat, with the lid closed, to 225°F.
3 In a large bowl, combine the sautéed vegetables, ground beef, steak seasoning, steak sauce, bacon, Swiss cheese, egg, and breadcrumbs. Mix with your hands until well incorporated, then shape into a loaf.
4 Put the meatloaf in a cast iron skillet and place it on the grill. Insert meat thermometer inserted in the loaf reads 165°F.
5 Top with the meatloaf with the Tiger Sauce, remove from the grill, and let rest for about 10 minutes before serving.

Nutrition:
Calories: 120 Cal
Fat: 2 g
Carbohydrates: 0 g
Protein: 23 g
Fiber: 0 g

296.   London Broil

Preparation Time: 20 minutes
Cooking Time: 12-16 minutes
Servings: 3-4
Ingredients:

- 1 (1½- to 2-pound) London broil or top round steak
- ¼ cup soy sauce
- 2 tablespoons white wine
- 2 tablespoons extra-virgin olive oil
- ¼ cup chopped scallions
- 2 tablespoons packed brown sugar
- 2 garlic cloves, minced
- 2 teaspoons red pepper flakes
- 1 teaspoon freshly ground black pepper

Directions:

1 Using a meat mallet, pound the steak lightly all over on both sides to break down its fibers and tenderize. You are not trying to pound down the thickness.
2 In a medium bowl, make the marinade by combining the soy sauce, white wine, olive oil, scallions, brown sugar, garlic, red pepper flakes, and black pepper.

3 Put the steak in a shallow plastic container with a lid and pour the marinade over the meat. Cover and refrigerate for 4 hours.
4 Supply your smoker with wood pellets and follow the manufacturer's specific start-up procedure. Preheat, with the lid closed, to 350°F.
5 Place the steak directly on the grill, close the lid, and smoke for 6 minutes. Flip, then smoke with the lid closed for 6 to 10 minutes more, or until a meat thermometer inserted in the meat reads 130°F for medium-rare.
6 The meat's temperature will rise by about 5 degrees while it rests.

Nutrition:
Calories: 316 Cal
Fat: 3 g
Carbohydrates: 0 g
Protein: 54 g
Fiber: 0 g

297.   French Onion Burgers

Preparation Time: 35 minutes
Cooking Time: 20-25 minutes
Servings: 4
Ingredients:

- 1-pound lean ground beef
- 1 tablespoon minced garlic
- 1 teaspoon Better Than Bouillon Beef Base

- 1 teaspoon dried chives
- 1 teaspoon freshly ground black pepper
- 8 slices Gruyère cheese, divided
- ½ cup soy sauce
- 1 tablespoon extra-virgin olive oil
- 1 teaspoon liquid smoke
- 3 medium onions, cut into thick slices (do not separate the rings)
- 1 loaf French bread, cut into 8 slices
- 4 slices provolone cheese

Directions:

1 In a large bowl, mix together the ground beef, minced garlic, beef base, chives, and pepper until well blended.
2 Divide the meat mixture and shape into 8 thin burger patties.
3 Top each of 4 patties with one slice of Gruyère, then top with the remaining 4 patties to create 4 stuffed burgers.
4 Supply your smoker with wood pellets and follow the manufacturer's specific start-up procedure. Preheat, with the lid closed, to 425°F.
5 Arrange the burgers directly on one side of the grill, close the lid, and smoke for 10 minutes. Flip and smoke with the lid

150

closed for 10 to 15 minutes more, or until a meat thermometer inserted in the burgers reads 160°F. Add another Gruyère slice to the burgers during the last 5 minutes of smoking to melt.

6 Meanwhile, in a small bowl, combine the soy sauce, olive oil, and liquid smoke.

7 Arrange the onion slices on the grill and paste on both sides with the soy sauce mixture. Smoke with the lid closed for 20 minutes, flipping halfway through.

8 Lightly toast the French bread slices on the grill. Layer each of 4 slices with a burger patty, a slice of provolone cheese, and some of the smoked onions. Top each with another slice of toasted French bread. Serve immediately.

Nutrition:
Calories: 704 Cal
Fat: 43 g
Carbohydrates: 28 g
Protein: 49 g
Fiber: 2 g

298. Beef Shoulder Clod

Preparation Time: 10 minutes
Cooking Time: 12-16 hours
Servings: 16-20
Ingredients:

- ½ cup sea salt
- ½ cup freshly ground black pepper
- 1 tablespoon red pepper flakes
- 1 tablespoon minced garlic
- 1 tablespoon cayenne pepper
- 1 tablespoon smoked paprika
- 1 (13- to 15-pound) beef shoulder clod

Directions:
1 Combine spices
2 Generously apply it to the beef shoulder.
3 Supply your smoker with wood pellets and follow the manufacturer's specific start-up procedure. Preheat, with the lid closed, to 250°F.
4 Put the meat on the grill grate, close the lid, and smoke for 12 to 16 hours, or until a meat thermometer inserted deeply into the beef reads 195°F. You may need to cover the clod with aluminum foil toward the end of smoking to prevent overbrowning.
5 Let the meat rest and serve

Nutrition:
Calories: 290 Cal
Fat: 22 g
Carbohydrates: 0 g
Protein: 20 g
Fiber: 0 g

299. Corned Beef and Cabbage

Preparation Time: 30 minutes
Cooking Time: 4-5 hours
Servings: 6-8
Ingredients:

- 1-gallon water
- 1 (3- to 4-pound) point cut corned beef brisket with pickling spice packet
- 1 tablespoon freshly ground black pepper
- 1 tablespoon garlic powder
- ½ cup molasses
- 1 teaspoon ground mustard
- 1 head green cabbage
- 4 tablespoons (½ stick) butter
- 2 tablespoons rendered bacon fat
- 1 chicken bouillon cube, crushed

Directions:
1 Refrigerate overnight, changing the water as often as you remember to do so—ideally, every 3 hours while you're awake—to soak out some of the curing salt initially added.
2 Supply your smoker with wood pellets and follow the manufacturer's specific start-up procedure. Preheat, with the lid closed, to 275°F.
3 Remove the meat from the brining liquid, pat it dry, and generously rub with the black pepper and garlic powder.

4   Put the seasoned corned beef directly on the grill, fat-side up, close the lid, and grill for 2 hours. Remove from the grill when done.

5   In a small bowl, combine the molasses and ground mustard and pour half of this mixture into the bottom of a disposable aluminum pan.

6   Transfer the meat to the pan, fat-side up, and pour the remaining molasses mixture on top, spreading it evenly over the meat. Cover tightly with aluminum foil.

7   Transfer the pan to the grill, close the lid, and continue smoking the corned beef for 2 to 3 hours, or until a meat thermometer inserted in the thickest part reads 185°F.

8   Rest meat

9   Serve.

Nutrition:
Calories: 295 Cal
Fat: 17 g
Carbohydrates: 19 g
Protein: 18 g
Fiber: 6 g

300. Cheeseburger Hand Pies

Preparation Time: 35 minutes
Cooking Time: 10 minutes
Servings: 6
Ingredients:

- ½ pound lean ground beef
- 1 tablespoon minced onion
- 1 tablespoon steak seasoning
- 1 cup cheese
- 8 slices white American cheese, divided
- 2 (14-ounce) refrigerated prepared pizza dough sheets, divided
- 2 eggs
- 24 hamburger dill pickle chips
- 2 tablespoons sesame seeds
- 6 slices tomato, for garnish
- Ketchup and mustard, for serving

Directions:

1   Supply your smoker with wood pellets and follow the manufacturer's specific start-up procedure. Preheat, with the lid closed, to 325°F.

2   On your stove top, in a medium sauté pan over medium-high heat, brown the ground beef for 4 to 5 minutes, or until cooked through. Add the minced onion and steak seasoning.

3   Toss in the shredded cheese blend and 2 slices of American cheese and stir until melted and fully incorporated.

4   Remove the cheeseburger mixture from the heat and set aside.

5   Make sure the dough is well chilled for easier handling. Working quickly, roll out one prepared pizza crust on parchment paper and brush with half of the egg wash.

6   Arrange the remaining 6 slices of American cheese on the dough to outline 6 hand pies.

Nutrition:
Calories: 325 Cal
Fat: 21 g
Carbohydrates: 11 g
Protein: 23 g
Fiber: 0 g

301. Pastrami

Preparation Time: 10 minutes
Cooking Time: 4-5 hours
Servings: 12
Ingredients:

- 1-gallon water, plus ½ cup
- ½ cup packed light brown sugar
- 1 (3- to 4-pound) point cut corned beef brisket with brine mix packet
- 2 tablespoons freshly ground black pepper
- ¼ cup ground coriander

Directions:

1   Cover and refrigerate overnight, changing the water as often as you remember to do so—ideally, every 3 hours while you're awake—to soak out some of the curing salt originally added.

2   Supply your smoker with wood pellets and

follow the manufacturer's specific start-up procedure. Preheat, with the lid closed, to 275°F.

3 In a small bowl, combine the black pepper and ground coriander to form a rub.

4 Drain the meat, pat it dry, and generously coat on all sides with the rub.

5 Place the corned beef directly on the grill, fat-side up, close the lid, and smoke for 3 hours to 3 hours 30 minutes, or until a meat thermometer inserted in the thickest part reads 175°F to 185°F.

6 Add the corned beef, cover tightly with aluminum foil, and smoke on the grill with the lid closed for an additional 30 minutes to 1 hour.

7 Remove the meat

8 Refrigerate

Nutrition:
Calories: 123 Cal
Fat: 4 g
Carbohydrates: 3 g
Protein: 16 g
Fiber: 0 g

302. Traeger Beef Jerky

Preparation Time: 15 minutes
Cooking Time: 5 hours
Servings: 10
Ingredients:

- 3 pounds sirloin steaks
- 2 cups soy sauce
- 1 cup pineapple juice
- 1/2 cup brown sugar
- 2 tbsp sriracha
- 2 tbsp hoisin
- 2 tbsp red pepper flake
- 2 tbsp rice wine vinegar
- 2 tbsp onion powder

Directions:

1 Mix the marinade in a zip lock bag and add the beef. Mix until well coated and remove as much air as possible.

2 Place the bag in a fridge and let marinate overnight or for 6 hours. Remove the bag from the fridge an hour prior to cooking

3 Startup the Traeger and set it on the smoking settings or at 1900F.

4 Lay the meat on the grill leaving a half-inch space between the pieces. Let cool for 5 hours and turn after 2 hours.

5 Remove from the grill and let cool. Serve or refrigerate

Nutrition:
Calories: 309 Cal
Fat: 7 g
Carbohydrates: 20 g
Protein: 34 g
Fiber: 1 g

303. Traeger Smoked Beef Roast

Preparation Time: 10 minutes
Cooking Time: 6 hours
Servings: 6
Ingredients:

- 1-3/4 pounds beef sirloin tip roast
- 1/2 cup barbeque rub
- 2 bottles amber beer
- 1 bottle BBQ sauce

Directions:

1 Turn the Traeger onto the smoke setting.

2 Rub the beef with barbeque rub until well coated then place on the grill. Let smoke for 4 hours while flipping every 1 hour.

3 Transfer the beef to a pan and add the beer. The beef should be 1/2 way covered.

4 Braise the beef until fork tender. It will take 3 hours on the stovetop and 60 minutes on the instant pot.

5 Remove the beef from the ban and reserve 1 cup of the cooking liquid.

6 Use 2 forks to shred the beef into small pieces then return to the pan with the reserved braising liquid. Add BBQ sauce and stir well then keep warm until serving. You can also reheat if it gets cold.

Nutrition:
Calories: 829 Cal
Fat: 18 g
Carbohydrates: 4 g
Protein: 86 g
Fiber: 0 g

Chapter 26. Pork recipes

304. Smoked Avocado Pork Ribs

Preparation Time: 20 Minutes
Cooking Time: 3 Hours
Servings: 5
Ingredients:

- 2 lbs. of pork spare ribs
- 1 cup of avocado oil
- One teaspoon of garlic powder
- One teaspoon of onion powder
- One teaspoon of sweet pepper flakes
- Salt and pepper, to taste

Directions:

1. In a bowl, combine the avocado oil, garlic salt, garlic powder, onion powder, sweet pepper flakes, and salt and pepper.
2. Place pork chops in a shallow container and pour evenly avocado mixture.
3. Cover and refrigerate for at least 4 hours or overnight.
4. Start pellet grill on, lid open until the fire is established (4-5 minutes).
5. Increase the temperature to 225 and pre-heat for 10 - 15 minutes.
6. Arrange pork chops on the grill rack and smoke for 3 to 4 hours.
7. Transfer pork chops on serving plate, let them rest for 15 minutes, and serve.

Nutrition:
Calories: 677 call
Carbohydrates: 0.9g
Fat: 64g
Fiber: 0.14g
Protein: 28.2g

305. Smoked Honey - Garlic Pork Chops

Preparation Time: 15 Minutes
Cooking Time: 60 Minutes
Servings: 4
Ingredients:

- 1/4 cup of lemon juice freshly squeezed
- 1/4 cup honey (preferably a darker honey)
- Three cloves garlic, minced
- Two tablespoons of soy sauce (or tamari sauce)
- Salt and pepper to taste
- 24 ounces center-cut pork chops boneless

Directions:

1. Combine honey, lemon juice, soy sauce, garlic, and salt and pepper in a bowl.
2. Place pork in a container and pour marinade over pork.
3. Cover and marinate in a fridge overnight.
4. Remove pork from marinade and pat dry on kitchen paper towel. (Reserve marinade)
5. Start your pellet on Smoke with the lid open until the fire is established (4 - 5 minutes).
6. Increase temperature to 450 and preheat, lid closed, for 10 - 15 minutes.
7. Arrange the pork chops on the grill racks and smoke for about one hour (depending on the thickness)
8. In the meantime, heat the remaining marinade in a small saucepan over medium heat to simmer.
9. Transfer pork chops on a serving plate, pour with the marinade, and serve hot.

Nutrition:
Calories: 301.5 call
Carbohydrates: 17g
Fat: 6.5g
Fiber: 0.2g
Protein: 41g

306. Smoked Pork Burgers

Preparation Time: 15 Minutes
Cooking Time: 1 Hour and 45 Minutes
Servings: 4
Ingredients:

- 2 lb. ground pork
- 1/2 of onion finely chopped
- 2 Tablespoon fresh sage, chopped
- One teaspoon garlic powder
- One teaspoon cayenne pepper
- Salt and pepper to taste

Directions:

1. Start the pellet grill on

SMOKE wait until the fire is established.
2. Set the temperature to 225 and warm-up, lid closed, for 10 to 15 minutes.
3. In a bowl, combine ground pork with all remaining ingredients.
4. Use your hands to mix thoroughly—form mixture into eight evenly burgers.
5. Place the hamburgers on the racks.
6. Smoke the burgers for 60 minutes until they reach an internal temperature of 150 to 160.
7. Serve hot.

Nutrition:
Calories: 588.7 call
Carbohydrates: 1g
Fat: 48.2g
Fiber: 0.5g
Protein: 38.4g

307. Smoked Pork Chops Marinated with Tarragon

Preparation Time: 20 Minutes
Cooking Time: 3 Hours
Servings: 4
Ingredients:
- 1/2 cup olive oil
- 4 Tablespoon of fresh tarragon chopped
- Two teaspoons fresh thyme, chopped
- Salt and grated black pepper
- Two teaspoon apple cider vinegar
- Four pork chops or fillets

Directions:
1. Whisk the olive oil, tarragon, thyme, salt, pepper, apple cider, and stir well.
2. Place the pork chops in a container and pour it with a tarragon mixture.
3. Refrigerate for 2 hours.
4. Start pellet grill on, lid open, until the discharge is established (4-5 minutes). Increase the temperature to 225 and allow to pre-heat, lid closed, for 10 - 15 minutes.
5. Remove chops from marinade and pat dry on kitchen towel.
6. Arrange pork chops on the grill rack and smoke for 2 to 3 hours.
7. Transfer chops on a serving platter and lets it rest 15 minutes before serving.

Nutrition:
Calories: 528.8 Cal
Carbohydrates: 0.6g
Fat: 35g
Fiber: 0.14g
Protein: 51g

308. Smoked Pork Cutlets in Citrus-Herbs Marinade

Preparation Time: 4 Hours
Cooking Time: 1 Hour and 45 Minutes
Servings: 4
Ingredients:
- Four pork cutlets
- One fresh orange juice
- Two large lemons freshly squeezed
- Ten twigs of coriander chopped
- 2 Tablespoon of fresh parsley finely chopped
- Three cloves of garlic minced
- 2 Tablespoon of olive oil
- Salt and ground black pepper

Directions:
1. Place the pork cutlets in a large container along with all remaining ingredients; toss to cover well.
2. Refrigerate at least 4 hours or overnight.
3. When ready, remove the pork cutlets from marinade and pat dry on a kitchen towel.
4. Start pellet grill on, lid open until the fire is established (4-5 minutes). Upsurge the temperature to 250 and allow to pre-heat, lid closed, for 10 - 15 minutes.
5. Place pork cutlets on grill grate and smoke for 1 1/2 hours.
6. Serve hot.

Nutrition:
Calories: 260 Cal
Carbohydrates: 5g
Fat: 12g
Fiber: 0.25g
Protein: 32.2g

309. Smoked Pork Cutlets with Caraway and Dill

Preparation Time: 4 Hours
Cooking Time: 1 Hour and 45 Minutes
Servings: 4
Ingredients:

- Four pork cutlets
- Two lemons freshly squeezed
- Two tablespoons fresh parsley finely chopped
- 1 Tablespoon of ground caraway
- 3 Tablespoon of fresh dill finely chopped
- 1/4 cup of olive oil
- Salt and ground black pepper

Directions:

1. Place the pork cutlets in a large resealable bag and all remaining ingredients; shake to combine well.
2. Refrigerate for at least 4 hours.
3. Remove the pork cutlets from marinade and pat dry on a kitchen towel.
4. Start the pellet grill (recommended maple pellet) on SMOKE with the lid open until the fire is established.
5. Set the temperature to 250 and preheat for 10 to 15 minutes.
6. Arrange pork cutlets on the grill rack and smoke for about 1 1/2 hours.
7. Allow cooling at room temperature before serving.

Nutrition:
Calories: 308 Cal
Carbohydrates: 2.4g
Fat: 18.5g
Fiber: 0.36g
Protein: 32g

310. Smoked Pork Loin in Sweet-Beer Marinade

Preparation Time: 15 Minutes
Cooking Time: 3 Hours
Servings: 6
Ingredients:
Marinade

- One onion finely diced
- 1/4 cup honey (preferably a darker honey)
- 1 1/2 cups of dark beer
- 4 Tablespoon of mustard
- 1 Tablespoon fresh thyme finely chopped
- Salt and pepper

Pork

- 3 1/2 lbs. of pork loin

Directions:

1. Combine all fixings for the marinade in a bowl.
2. Place the pork along with marinade mixture in a container, and refrigerate overnight.
3. Remove the pork from the marinade and dry on a kitchen towel.
4. Prepare the grill on Smoke with the lid open until the fire is established.
5. Set the temperature to 250F and preheat, lid closed, for 10 to 15 minutes.
6. Place the meat on the grill rack and smoke until the pork's internal temperature is at least 145-150 (medium-rare), 2-1/2 to 3 hours.
7. Remove meat from the smoker and let rest for 15 minutes before slicing.
8. Serve hot or cold.

Nutrition:
Calories: 444.6 Cal
Carbohydrates: 17g
Fat: 12.7g
Fiber: 0.8g
Protein: 60.5g

311. Smoked Pork Ribs with Fresh Herbs

Preparation Time: 20 Minutes
Cooking Time: 3 Hours
Servings: 6
Ingredients:

- 1/4 cup olive oil
- 1 Tablespoon garlic minced
- 1 Tablespoon crushed fennel seeds
- One teaspoon of fresh basil leaves finely chopped
- One teaspoon fresh parsley finely chopped
- One teaspoon fresh rosemary finely chopped
- One teaspoon fresh sage finely chopped
- Salt and ground black pepper to taste
- 3 lbs. pork rib roast bone-in

Directions:

1. Combine the olive oil, garlic, fennel seeds, parsley, sage, rosemary, salt, and pepper in a bowl; stir well.
2. Coat each chop on equal sides with the herb mixture.
3. Start the pellet grill (recommended hickory pellet) on SMOKE with the lid open until the fire is established. Set the temperature to 225 and heat up, lid closed, for 10 to 15 minutes.
4. Smoke the ribs for 3 hours.
5. Transfer the ribs to a platter and serve hot.

Nutrition:
Calories: 459.2 Cal
Carbohydrates: 0.6g
Fat: 31.3g
Fiber: 0.03g
Protein: 41g

312. Smoked Pork Side Ribs with Chives

Preparation Time: 15 Minutes
Cooking Time: 3 Hours and 20 Minutes
Servings: 6
Ingredients:

- 1/3 cup of olive oil (or garlic-infused olive oil)
- 3 Tablespoon of ketchup
- 3 Tablespoon chives finely chopped
- 3 lbs. of pork side ribs
- Salt and black pepper to taste

Directions:

1. In a bowl, stir together olive oil, finely chopped chives, ketchup, salt, and pepper.
2. Cut pork into individual ribs and generously coat with chives mixture.
3. Flinch the pellet grill on SMOKE with the lid open until the discharge is established.
4. Set the temperature to 250 and preheat for 10 to 15 minutes.
5. Arrange pork chops on the grill rack and smoke for about 3 to 4 hours.
6. Allow resting 15 minutes before serving.

Nutrition:
Calories: 689.7 Cal
Carbohydrates: 2g
Fat: 65g
Fiber: 0.1g
Protein: 35.2g

313. Smoked Spicy Pork Medallions

Preparation Time: 15 Minutes
Cooking Time: 1 Hour and 45 Minutes
Servings: 6
Ingredients:

- 2 lb. pork medallions
- 3/4 cup chicken stock
- 1/2 cup tomato sauce (organic)
- 2 Tablespoon of smoked hot paprika (or to taste)
- 2 Tablespoon of fresh basil finely chopped

- 1 Tablespoon oregano
- Salt and pepper to taste

Directions:

1. In a bowl, blend the chicken stock, tomato sauce, paprika, oregano, salt, and pepper.
2. Brush bigheartedly over the outside of the tenderloin.
3. Twitch the pellet grill on Smoke with the lid open until the fire is established (4 to 5 minutes). Set the temperature to 250 and preheat, lid closed, for 10 to 15 minutes.
4. Place the pork on the grill grate and smoke until the pork's internal temperature is at minimum medium-rare (about 145) for 1 1/2 hours.
5. Let meat rest for 15 minutes and serve.

Nutrition:
Calories: 364.2 Cal
Carbohydrates: 4g
Fat: 14.4g
Fiber: 2g
Protein: 52.4g

314. Applewood Smoked Mango Pork Quesadillas

Preparation Time: 10 Minutes
Cooking Time: 15 Minutes
Servings: 4
Ingredients:

- One tablespoon olive oil
- 1.7 pounds Smithfield Applewood Smoked Bacon Pork Loin Filet

cut into little scaled-down pieces

- One teaspoon chipotle stew powder pretty much to your taste
- One teaspoon smoked paprika
- 4-inch flour tortillas 6-8
- One ready yet firm mango, stripped + diced
- 1 cup cooked rice or quinoa
- 2 cups destroyed sharp cheddar
- Cherry tomato salsa:
- 2 cup cherry tomatoes
- One jalapeno seeded + hacked
- 1/4 cup new basil cleaved
- 1/4 cup fresh cilantro cleaved
- Juice from 1/2 a lime
- Salt to taste

Directions:
1. Warmth a heavy skillet over medium heat and include olive oil, contain the pork, and season with chipotle bean stew pepper and paprika. Cook, regularly mixing until the pork is caramelized, all finished around 8 minutes. Expel from the warmth. Expel the pork to a plate.
2. Utilizing a similar skillet, over medium warmth, include a touch of olive oil. Spot 4 tortillas down on a

perfect counter, sprinkle each with destroyed cheddar, at that point equally appropriate the rice, and top with the hacked mango pieces. Presently include the pork, cut into little scaled-down pieces. Sprinkle with somewhat more of the cheddar. Spot the tortilla onto the hot frying pan or skillet and spread with the other tortilla. Cook until the base is firm and brilliant dark-colored. At that point, tenderly flip and cook for another 2-3 minutes until fresh and bright.
3. Present with the tomato salsa and cut avocado.

Nutrition:
Calories: 477 Cal
Carbohydrates: 4.5g
Fat: 14g
Fiber: 2.4g
Protein: 50g

315. Maple Baby Backs
Preparation Time: 25 minutes
Cooking Time: 4 hours
Servings: 4-6
Ingredients:

- 2 (2- or 3-pound) racks baby back ribs
- 2 tablespoons yellow mustard
- 1 batch Sweet Brown Sugar Rub
- ½ cup plus 2 tablespoons maple syrup, divided

- 2 tablespoons light brown sugar
- 1 cup Pepsi or other non-diet cola
- ¼ cup Bill's Best BBQ Sauce

Directions:
1. Supply your smoker with wood pellets and follow the manufacturer's specific start-up procedure. Preheat the grill
2. Eradicate the membrane. This can be done by cutting just through the membrane in an X pattern and working a paper towel between the membrane and the ribs to pull it off.
3. Coat the ribs on both sides with mustard and season them with the rub. Rub into meat.
4. Grill ribs and smoke for 3 hours.
5. Remove grill and place bone-side up, on enough aluminum foil to wrap the ribs completely. Add maple syrup over the ribs and sprinkle them with 1 tablespoon of brown sugar. Flip the ribs and repeat the maple syrup and brown sugar application on the meat side.
6. Increase the grill's temperature to 300°F.
7. Fold in three sides of the foil around the ribs and add the cola. Fold in the last side,

completely enclosing the ribs and liquid. Place ribs back to the grill for 30 to 45 minutes.

8 Remove the ribs from the grill and unwrap them from the foil.

9 In a small bowl, stir together the barbecue sauce and remaining 6 tablespoons of maple syrup. Use this to baste the ribs. Return the ribs to the grill, without the foil, and cook for 15 minutes to caramelize the sauce.

10 Cut into individual ribs and serve immediately.

Nutrition:
Calories: 330 Cal
Fat: 24 g
Carbohydrates: 11 g
Protein: 17 g
Fiber: 0 g

316. Simple Smoked Baby Backs

Preparation Time: 25 minutes
Cooking Time: 4-6 hours
Servings: 4-8
Ingredients:

- 2 (2- or 3-pound) racks baby back ribs
- 2 tablespoons yellow mustard
- 1 batch Not-Just-for-Pork Rub

Directions:

1 Supply your smoker with wood pellets and follow the manufacturer's specific start-up procedure. Preheat grill

2 Eradicate the membrane from the backside of the ribs. This can be done by cutting just through the membrane in an X pattern and working a paper towel between the membrane and the ribs to pull it off.

3 Coat the ribs on both sides with mustard and season them with the rub. Work rubs onto meat.

4 smoke until their internal temperature reaches between 190°F and 200°F.

5 Remove the racks from the grill and cut into individual ribs. Serve immediately.

Nutrition:
Calories: 245 Cal
Fat: 12 g
Carbohydrates: 10 g
Protein: 22 g
Fiber: 0 g

317. Smoked Spare Ribs

Preparation Time: 25 minutes
Cooking Time: 4-6 hours
Servings: 4-8
Ingredients:

- 2 (2- or 3-pound) racks spare ribs
- 2 tablespoons yellow mustard
- 1 batch Sweet Brown Sugar Rub
- ¼ cup Bill's Best BBQ Sauce

Directions:

1 Supply your smoker with wood pellets and follow the

manufacturer's specific start-up procedure. With lid closed, preheat grill

2 The membrane must be removed. This can be done by cutting just through the membrane in an X pattern and working a paper towel between the membrane and the ribs to pull it off.

3 Coat the ribs on both sides with mustard and season with the rub. Work rubs onto meat.

4 Put the ribs on the grill and smoke until their internal temperature reaches between 190°F and 200°F.

5 Drizzle barbeque sauce.

6 Increase the grill's temperature to 300°F and continue to cook the ribs for 15 minutes more.

7 Remove the racks from the grill, cut them into individual ribs, and serve immediately.

Nutrition:
Calories: 318 Cal
Fat: 24 g
Carbohydrates: 0 g
Protein: 23 g
Fiber: 0 g

318. Sweet Smoked Country Ribs

Preparation Time: 25 minutes
Cooking Time: 4 hours
Servings: 2-4
Ingredients:

- 2 pounds country-style

ribs

- 1 batch Sweet Brown Sugar Rub
- 2 tablespoons light brown sugar
- 1 cup Pepsi or other cola
- ¼ cup Bill's Best BBQ Sauce

Directions:

1   Supply your smoker with wood pellets and follow the manufacturer's specific start-up procedure. With the lid closed, preheat the grill until the temperature is 180 degrees

2   Sprinkle the ribs with the rub and use your hands to work the rub into the meat.

3   Place the ribs directly on the grill grate and smoke for 3 hours.

4   Remove the ribs from the grill and place them on enough aluminum foil to wrap them completely. Dust the brown sugar over the ribs.

5   Increase the grill's temperature to 300°F.

6   Fold in three sides of the foil around the ribs and add the cola. Fold in the last side, completely enclosing the ribs and liquid. Return the ribs to the grill and cook for 45 minutes.

7   Remove the ribs from the foil and place them

on the grill grate. Baste all sides of the ribs with barbecue sauce. Cook for 15 minutes more to caramelize the sauce.

8   Remove the ribs from the grill and serve immediately.

Nutrition:
Calories: 230 Cal
Fat: 17 g
Carbohydrates: 0 g
Protein: 20 g
Fiber: 0 g

319. Classic Pulled Pork

Preparation Time: 15 minutes
Cooking Time: 16-20 hours
Servings: 8-12
Ingredients:

- 1 (6- to 8-pound) bone-in pork shoulder
- 2 tablespoons yellow mustard
- 1 batch Not-Just-for-Pork Rub

Directions:

1   Supply your smoker with wood pellets and follow the manufacturer's specific start-up procedure.

2   Coat the pork shoulder all over with mustard and season it with the rub.

3   Place the shoulder on the grill grate and smoke until its internal temperature reaches 195°F.

4   Pull the shoulder from the grill and wrap it completely in aluminum foil or butcher paper. Place it in a cooler, cover the

cooler, and let it rest for 1 or 2 hours.

5   Remove the pork shoulder from the cooler and unwrap it. Remove the shoulder bone and pull the pork apart using just your fingers. Serve immediately as desired. Leftovers are encouraged.

Nutrition:
Calories: 414 Cal
Fat: 29 g
Carbohydrates: 1 g
Protein: 38 g
Fiber: 0 g

320.   Rub-Injected Pork Shoulder

Preparation Time: 15 minutes
Cooking Time: 16-20 hours
Servings: 8-12
Ingredients:

- 1 (6- to 8-pound) bone-in pork shoulder
- 2 cups Tea Injectable made with Not-Just-for-Pork Rub
- 2 tablespoons yellow mustard
- 1 batch Not-Just-for-Pork Rub

Directions:

1   Supply your smoker with wood pellets and follow the manufacturer's specific start-up procedure.

2   Inject the pork shoulder throughout with the tea injectable.

3   Coat the pork shoulder all over with mustard and season it with the rub. Work rub onto

4   Place the shoulder directly on the grill grate and smoke until its internal temperature reaches 160°F and a dark bark has formed on the exterior.

5   Pull the shoulder from the grill and wrap it completely in aluminum foil or butcher paper.

6   Increase the grill's temperature to 350°F.

7   Return the pork shoulder to the grill and cook until its internal temperature reaches 195°F.

8   Pull the shoulder from the grill and place it in a cooler. Cover the cooler and let the pork rest for 1 or 2 hours.

9   Remove the pork shoulder from the cooler and unwrap it. Remove the shoulder bone and pull the pork apart using just your fingers. Serve immediately.

10 Nutrition:

11 Calories: 257 Cal

12 Fat: 15 g

13 Carbohydrates: 0 g

14 Protein: 29 g

15 Fiber: 0 g

321. Maple-Smoked Pork Chops

Preparation Time: 10 minutes
Cooking Time: 55 minutes
Servings: 4
Ingredients:

- 4 (8-ounce) pork chops, bone-in or boneless (I use boneless)
- Salt
- Freshly ground black pepper

Directions:

1   Supply your smoker with wood pellets and follow the manufacturer's specific start-up procedure.

2   Drizzle pork chop with salt and pepper to season.

3   Place the chops directly on the grill grate and smoke for 30 minutes.

4   Increase the grill's temperature to 350°F. Continue to cook the chops until their internal temperature reaches 145°F.

5   Remove the pork chops from the grill and let them rest for 5 minutes before serving.

Nutrition:
Calories: 130 Cal
Fat: 12 g
Carbohydrates: 3 g
Protein: 20 g
Fiber: 0 g

322. Apple-Smoked Pork Tenderloin

Preparation Time: 15 minutes
Cooking Time: 4-5 hours
Servings: 4-6
Ingredients:
2 (1-pound) pork tenderloins
1 batch Not-Just-for-Pork Rub
Directions:
Supply your smoker with wood pellets and follow the manufacturer's specific start-up procedure. Preheat the grill Generously season the tenderloins with the rub. W Put tenderloins on the grill and smoke for 4 or 5 hours, until their internal temperature reaches 145°F.
The tenderloins must be put out of the grill and let it rest for 5-10 minutes then begin slicing into thin pieces before serving
Nutrition:
Calories: 180 Cal
Fat: 8 g
Carbohydrates: 3 g
Protein: 24 g
Fiber: 0 g

323. Teriyaki Pork Tenderloin

Preparation Time: 30 minutes
Cooking Time: 1 ½ hours to 2 hours
Servings: 4-6
Ingredients:

- 2 (1-pound) pork tenderloins
- 1 batch Easy Teriyaki Marinade
- Smoked salt

Directions:

1   In a large zip-top bag, combine the tenderloins and marinade. Seal the bag, turn to coat, and refrigerate the pork for at least 30 minutes—I recommend up to overnight.

2   Supply your smoker with wood pellets and follow the manufacturer's specific start-up procedure.

Preheat the grill, with the lid closed, to 180°F.

3   As you get the tenderloins from the marinade begin seasoning them with smoked salt

4   Place the tenderloins directly on the grill grate and smoke for 1 hour.

5   Increase the grill's temperature to 300°F and continue to cook until the pork's internal temperature reaches 145°F.

6   With the tenderloins removed from the grill, let it cool for at least 5-10 minutes before slicing and serving

Nutrition:
Calories: 110 Cal
Fat: 3 g
Carbohydrates: 2 g
Protein: 18 g
Fiber: 0 g

324.   Barbecued Tenderloin

Preparation Time: 5 minutes
Cooking Time: 3o minutes
Servings: 4-6
Ingredients:

- 2 (1-pound) pork tenderloins
- 1 batch Sweet and Spicy Cinnamon Rub

Directions:

1   Supply your smoker with wood pellets and follow the manufacturer's specific start-up procedure. Preheat the grill

2   Generously season the tenderloins with the rub. Work rubs onto meat.

3   Place the tenderloins and smoke internal temperature reaches 145°F.

4   As you put out the tenderloins from the grill, let it cool down for 5-10 minutes before slicing it up and serving it

Nutrition:
Calories: 186 Cal
Fat: 4 g
Carbohydrates: 8 g
Protein: 29 g
Fiber: 1 g

Chapter 27. Lamb recipes

325. Grilled Lamb Burgers

Preparation Time: 10 minutes
Cooking Time: 15 minutes
Servings: 5
Ingredients:

- 1 1/4 pounds of ground lamb.
- 1 egg.
- 1 teaspoon of dried oregano.
- 1 teaspoon of dry sherry.
- 1 teaspoon of white wine vinegar.
- 4 minced cloves of garlic.
- Red pepper
- 1/2 cup of chopped green onions.
- 1 tablespoon of chopped mint.
- 2 tablespoons of chopped cilantro.
- 2 tablespoons of dry bread crumbs.
- 1/8 teaspoon of salt to taste.
- 1/4 teaspoon of ground black pepper to taste.
- 5 hamburger buns.

Directions:

1. Preheat a Wood Pellet Smoker or Grill to 350-450 degrees F then grease it grates.
2. Using a large mixing bowl, add in all the ingredients on the list aside from the buns then mix properly to combine with clean hands.
3. Make about five patties out of the mixture then set aside.
4. Place the lamb patties on the preheated grill and cook for about seven to nine minutes turning only once until an inserted thermometer reads 160 degrees F.
5. Serve the lamb burgers on the hamburger, add your favorite toppings and enjoy.

Nutrition:
Calories: 376 Cal
Fat: 18.5 g
Carbohydrates: 25.4 g
Protein: 25.5 g
Fiber: 1.6 g

326. Grilled Lamb Sandwiches

Preparation Time: 5 minutes
Cooking Time: 50 minutes
Servings: 6
Ingredients:

- 1 (4 pounds) boneless lamb.
- 1 cup of raspberry vinegar.
- 2 tablespoons of olive oil.
- 1 tablespoon of chopped fresh thyme.
- 2 pressed garlic cloves.
- 1/4 teaspoon of salt to taste.
- 1/4 teaspoon of ground pepper.
- Sliced bread.

Directions:

1. Using a large mixing bowl, add in the raspberry vinegar, oil, and thyme then mix properly to combine. Add in the lamb, toss to combine then let it sit in the refrigerator for about eight hours or overnight.
2. Next, discard the marinade the season the lamb with salt and pepper to taste. Preheat a Wood Pellet Smoker and grill t0 400-500 degrees F, add in the seasoned lamb and grill for about thirty to forty minutes until it attains a temperature of 150 degrees F.
3. Once cooked, let the lamb cool for a few minutes, slice as desired then serve on the bread with your favorite topping.

Nutrition:
Calories: 407 Cal
Fat: 23 g
Carbohydrates: 26 g
Protein: 72 g
Fiber: 2.3 g

327. Lamb Chops

Preparation Time: 10 minutes
Cooking Time: 12 minutes
Servings: 6
Ingredients:

- 6 (6-ounce) lamb chops
- 3 tablespoons olive oil
- Ground black pepper

Directions:

1. Preheat the pallet grill to 450 degrees F.

2   Coat the lamb chops with oil and then, season with salt and black pepper evenly.

3   Arrange the chops in pallet grill grate and cook for about 4-6 minutes per side.

Nutrition:
Calories: 376 Cal
Fat: 19.5 g
Carbohydrates: 0 g
Protein: 47.8 g
Fiber: 0 g

328.   Lamb Ribs Rack

Preparation Time: 10 minutes
Cooking Time: 2 hours
Servings: 2
Ingredients:

- 2 tablespoons fresh sage
- 2 tablespoons fresh rosemary
- 2 tablespoons fresh thyme
- 2 peeled garlic cloves
- 1 tablespoon honey
- Black pepper
- ¼ cup olive oil
- 1 (1½-pound) trimmed rack lamb ribs

Directions:
1   Combine all ingredients

2   While motor is running, slowly add oil and pulse till a smooth paste is formed.

3   Coat the rib rack with paste generously and refrigerate for about 2 hours.

4   Preheat the pallet grill to 225 degrees F.

5   Arrange the rib rack in pallet grill and cook for about 2 hours.

6   Remove the rib rack from pallet grill and transfer onto a cutting board for about 10-15 minutes before slicing.

7   With a sharp knife, cut the rib rack into equal sized individual ribs and serve.

Nutrition:
Calories: 826 Cal
Fat: 44.1 g
Carbohydrates: 5.4 g
Protein: 96.3 g
Fiber: 1 g

329.   Lamb Shank

Preparation Time: 10 minutes
Cooking Time: 4 hours
Servings: 6
Ingredients:

- 8-ounce red wine
- 2-ounce whiskey
- 2 tablespoons minced fresh rosemary
- 1 tablespoon minced garlic
- Black pepper
- 6 (1¼-pound) lamb shanks

Directions:
1   In a bowl, add all ingredients except lamb shank and mix till well combined.

2   In a large resealable bag, add marinade and lamb shank.

3   Seal the bag and shake to coat completely.

4   Refrigerate for about 24 hours.

5   Preheat the pallet grill to 225 degrees F.

6   Arrange the leg of lamb in pallet grill and cook for about 4 hours.

Nutrition:
Calories: 1507 Cal
Fat: 62 g
Carbohydrates: 68.7 g
Protein:163.3 g
Fiber: 6 g

330.   Leg of a Lamb

Preparation Time: 10 minutes
Cooking Time: 2 hours and 30 minutes
Servings: 10
Ingredients:

- 1 (8-ounce) package softened cream cheese
- ¼ cup cooked and crumbled bacon
- 1 seeded and chopped jalapeño pepper
- 1 tablespoon crushed dried rosemary
- 2 teaspoons garlic powder
- 1 teaspoon onion powder
- 1 teaspoon paprika
- 1 teaspoon cayenne pepper
- Salt, to taste
- 1 (4-5-pound) butterflied leg of lamb
- 2-3 tablespoons olive oil

Directions:
1   For filling in a bowl, add all ingredients and mix till well combined.

2   For spice mixture in another small bowl, mix together all ingredients.

3 Place the leg of lamb onto a smooth surface. Sprinkle the inside of leg with some spice mixture.

4 Place filling mixture over the inside surface evenly. Roll the leg of lamb tightly and with a butcher's twine, tie the roll to secure the filling

5 Coat the outer side of roll with olive oil evenly and then sprinkle with spice mixture.

6 Preheat the pallet grill to 225-240 degrees F.

7 Arrange the leg of lamb in pallet grill and cook for about 2-2½ hours. Remove the leg of lamb from pallet grill and transfer onto a cutting board.

8 With a piece of foil, cover leg loosely and transfer onto a cutting board for about 20-25 minutes before slicing.

9 With a sharp knife, cut the leg of lamb in desired sized slices and serve.

Nutrition:
Calories: 715 Cal
Fat: 38.9 g
Carbohydrates: 2.2 g
Protein: 84.6 g
Fiber: 0.1 g

331. Lamb Breast
Preparation Time: 10 minutes
Cooking Time: 2 hours and 40 minutes
Servings: 2

Ingredients:
- 1 (2-pound) trimmed bone-in lamb breast
- ½ cup white vinegar
- ¼ cup yellow mustard
- ½ cup BBQ rub

Directions:
1 Preheat the pallet grill to 225 degrees F.
2 Rinse the lamb breast with vinegar evenly.
3 Coat lamb breast with mustard and the, season with BBQ rub evenly.
4 Arrange lamb breast in pallet grill and cook for about 2-2½ hours.
5 Remove the lamb breast from the pallet grill and transfer onto a cutting board for about 10 minutes before slicing.
6 With a sharp knife, cut the lamb breast in desired sized slices and serve.

Nutrition:
Calories: 877 Cal
Fat: 34.5 g
Carbohydrates: 2.2 g
Protein: 128.7 g
Fiber: 0 g

332.   Smoked Lamb Shoulder Chops
Preparation Time: 4 hours
Cooking Time: 25-30 minutes
Servings: 4

Ingredients:
- 4 lamb shoulder chops
- 4 cups buttermilk
- 1 cup cold water

- ¼ cup kosher salt
- 2 tablespoons olive oil
- 1 tablespoon Texas style rub

Directions:
1 In a large bowl, add buttermilk, water and salt and stir till salt is dissolved.
2 Add chops and coat with mixture evenly.
3 Refrigerate for at least 4 hours. Remove the chops from bowl and rinse under cold water.
4 Coat the chops with olive oil and then sprinkle with rub evenly. Preheat the pallet grill to 240 degrees F.
5 Arrange the chops in pallet grill grate and cook for about 25-30 minute or till desired doneness.
6 Meanwhile preheat the broiler of oven.
7 Cook the chops under broiler till browned.

Nutrition:
Calories: 328 Cal
Fat: 18.2 g
Carbohydrates:11.7 g
Protein: 30.1 g
Fiber: 0 g

333.   Lamb Skewers
Preparation Time: 5 minutes
Cooking Time: 8-12 minutes
Servings: 6
Ingredients:
- One lemon, juiced
- Two crushed garlic cloves

- Two chopped red onions
- One t. chopped thyme
- Pepper
- Salt
- One t. oregano
- 1/3 c. oil
- ½ t. cumin
- Two pounds cubed lamb leg

Directions:
1 Refrigerate the chunked lamb.
2 The remaining ingredients should be mixed together. Add in the meat. Refrigerate overnight.
3 Pat the meat dry and thread onto some metal or wooden skewers. Wooden skewers should be soaked in water.
4 Add wood pellets to your smoker and follow your cooker's startup procedure. Preheat your smoker, with your lid closed, until it reaches 450.
5 Grill, covered, for 4-6 minutes on each side.
6 Serve.

Nutrition:
Calories: 201 Cal
Fat: 9 g
Carbohydrates: 3 g
Protein: 24 g
Fiber: 1 g

334. Brown Sugar Lamb Chops

Preparation Time: 2 hours
Cooking Time: 10-15 minutes
Servings: 4

Ingredients:
- Pepper
- One t. garlic powder
- Salt
- Two t. tarragon
- One t. cinnamon
- ¼ c. brown sugar
- 4 lamb chops
- Two t. ginger

Directions:
1 Combine the salt, garlic powder, pepper, cinnamon, tarragon, ginger, and sugar. Coat the lamb chops in the mixture and chill for two hours.
2 Add wood pellets to your smoker and follow your cooker's startup procedure. Preheat your smoker, with your lid closed, until it reaches 450.
3 Place the chops on the grill, cover, and smoke for 10-15 minutes per side.
4 Serve.

Nutrition:
Calories: 210 Cal
Fat: 11 g
Carbohydrates: 3 g
Protein: 25 g
Fiber: 1 g

335. Traeger Smoked Lamb Chops

Preparation Time: 10 Minutes
Cooking Time: 50 Minutes
Servings: 4

Ingredients:
- One rack lamb
- 2 tbsp rosemary, fresh
- 2 tbsp sage, fresh

- 1 tbsp thyme, fresh
- Two garlic cloves, roughly chopped
- 2 tbsp shallots, roughly chopped
- 1/2 tbsp salt
- 1/2 tbsp ground pepper
- 1/4 cup olive oil
- 1 tbsp honey

Directions:
1. Preheat the Traeger to 2250F
2. Trim any excess fat and silver skin from the lamb.
3. Combine the rest of the ingredients in the food processor and generously rub the lamb with the seasoning.
4. Place the seasoned lamb on the Traeger and cook for 45 minutes or until the internal temperature reaches 1200F.
5. Sear the lamb on the Traeger for 2 minutes per side or until the internal temperature reaches 1250F for medium-rare or 1450F for medium.
6. Let rest for 5 minutes beforehand slicing it. Enjoy

Nutrition:
Calories 916
Total fat 78.3g
Total carbs 2.7g
Protein 47g
Sugars 0.1g
Fiber 0.5g
Sodium 1324mmg

166

336. Traeger Smoked Lamb Shoulder

Preparation Time: 20 Minutes
Cooking Time: 3 Hours
Servings: 7
Ingredients:

- 5 lb. lamb shoulder
- 1 cup cider vinegar
- 2 tbsp. oil
- 2 tbsp. kosher salt
- 2 tbsp. black pepper, freshly ground
- 1 tbsp. dried rosemary

For the Spritz

- 1 cup apple cider vinegar
- 1 cup apple juice

Directions:

1. Preheat the Traeger to 2250F with a pan of water for moisture.
2. Trim any extra fat from the lamb and rinse the meat in cold water. Pat dry with a paper towel.
3. Inject the cider vinegar in the meat, then pat dry with a clean paper towel.
4. Rub the meat with oil, salt, black pepper, and dried rosemary. Tie the lamb shoulder with a twine.
5. Place in the smoker for an hour, then spritz after every 15 minutes until the internal temperature reaches 1650F.
6. Remove from the Traeger and let rest for 1 hour before shredding and serving.

Nutrition:
Calories 472
Total Fat 37g
Total carbs 3g
Protein 31g
Sodium 458mg

337. Traeger Smoked Pulled Lamb Sliders

Preparation Time: 10 Minutes
Cooking Time: 9 Hours
Servings: 7
Ingredients:

- 5 lb. lamb shoulder, boneless
- 1/2 cup olive oil
- 1/3 cup kosher salt
- 1/3 cup pepper, coarsely ground
- 1/3 cup granulated garlic

For the spritz

- 4 oz Worcestershire sauce
- 6 oz apple cider vinegar

Directions:

1. Preheat the Traeger to 2250F with a pan of water for moisture.
2. Trim any excess fat from the lamb, then pat it dry with some paper towel. Rub with oil, salt, pepper, and garlic.
3. Place the lamb in the Traeger smoker for 90 minutes, then spritz every 30 minutes until the internal temperature reaches 1650F.
4. Transfer the lamb to a foil pan, then add the remaining spritz liquid. Cover with a foil and place back in the Traeger.
5. Smoke until the internal temperature reaches 2050F.
6. Remove from the smoker and let rest in a cooler without ice for 30 minutes before pulling it.
7. Serve with slaw or bun and enjoy.

Nutrition:
Calories 235
Total Fat 6g
Total Carbs 22g
Protein 20g
Sugars 7g
Fiber 1g
Sodium 592mg
Potassium 318mg

338. Traeger Smoked Lamb Meatballs

Preparation Time: 10 Minutes
Cooking Time: 1 Hour
Servings: 20 Meatballs
Ingredients:

- 1 lb. lamb shoulder, ground
- Three garlic cloves, finely diced
- 3 tbsp. shallot, diced
- 1 tbsp. salt
- One egg
- 1/2 tbsp. pepper
- 1/2 tbsp. cumin
- 1/2 tbsp. smoked paprika
- 1/4 tbsp. red pepper flakes
- 1/4 tbsp. cinnamon
- 1/4 cup panko breadcrumbs

Directions:

1. Set your Traeger to 2500F.
2. Combine all the fixings in a small bowl, then mix thoroughly using your hands.
3. Form golf ball-sized meatballs and place them on a baking sheet.
4. Place the baking sheet in the smoker and smoke until the internal temperature reaches 1600F.
5. Remove the meatballs from the smoker and serve when hot.

Nutrition:
Calories 93
Total fat 5.9g
Total carbs 4.8g
Protein 5g
Sugars 0.3g
Fiber 0.3g
Sodium 174.1mg
Potassium 82.8mg

339. Traeger Crown Rack of Lamb

Preparation Time: 30 Minutes
Cooking Time: 30 Minutes
Servings: 6
Ingredients:

- Two racks of lamb. Frenched
- 1 tbsp garlic, crushed
- 1 tbsp rosemary
- 1/2 cup olive oil
- Kitchen twine

Directions:

1. Preheat your Traeger to 4500F.
2. Rinse the lab with clean cold water, then pat it dry with a paper towel.
3. Lay the lamb even on a chopping board and score a ¼ inch down between the bones. Repeat the process between the bones on each lamb rack. Set aside.
4. In a small mixing bowl, combine garlic, rosemary, and oil. Brush the lamb rack generously with the mixture.
5. Bend the lamb rack into a semicircle, then place the racks together such that the bones will be up and will form a crown shape.
6. Wrap around four times, starting from the base moving upward. Tie tightly to keep the racks together.
7. Place the lambs on a baking sheet and set in the Traeger. Cook on high heat for 10 minutes. Reduce the temperature to 3000F and cook for 20 more minutes or until the internal temperature reaches 1300F.
8. Remove the lamb rack from the Traeger and let rest while wrapped in a foil for 15 minutes.
9. Serve when hot.

Nutrition:
Calories 390
Total fat 35g
Total carbs 0g
Protein 17g
Sodium 65mg

340. Traeger Smoked Leg

Preparation Time: 15 Minutes
Cooking Time: 3 Hours
Servings: 6
Ingredients:

- One leg of lamb, boneless
- 2 tbsp oil
- Four garlic cloves, minced
- 2 tbsp oregano
- 1 tbsp thyme
- 2 tbsp salt
- 1 tbsp black pepper, freshly ground

Directions:

1. Trim excess fat from the lamb, ensuring you keep the meat in an even thickness for even cooking.
2. In a mixing bowl, mix oil, garlic, and all spices. Rub the mixture all over the lamb, then cover with a plastic wrap.
3. Place the lamb in a fridge and let marinate for an hour.
4. Transfer the lamb on a smoker rack and set the Traeger to smoke at 2500F.
5. Smoke the meat for 4 hours or until the internal temperature reaches 1450F
6. Remove from the Traeger and serve immediately.

Nutrition:
Calories 356
Total fat 16g
Total carbs 3g

Protein 49g
Sugars 1g
Fiber 1g
Sodium 2474mg

341. Traeger Grilled Aussie Leg of Lamb

Preparation Time: 30 Minutes
Cooking Time: 2 Hours
Servings: 8
Ingredients:

- 5 lb. Aussie Boneless Leg of lamb

Smoked Paprika Rub

- 1 tbsp raw sugar
- 1 tbsp salt
- 1 tbsp black pepper
- 1 tbsp smoked paprika
- 1 tbsp garlic powder
- 1 tbsp rosemary
- 1 tbsp onion powder
- 1 tbsp cumin
- 1/2 tbsp cayenne pepper

Roasted Carrots

- One bunch of rainbow carrots
- Olive oil
- Salt and pepper

Directions:

1 Preheat your Traeger to 3500F and trim any excess fat from the meat.
2 Combine the paprika rub ingredients and generously rub all over the meat.
3 Place the lamb on the preheated Traeger over indirect heat and smoke for 2 hours.
4 Meanwhile, toss the carrots in oil, salt, and pepper.

5 Add the carrots to the grill after 1 ½ hour or until the internal temperature has reached 900F.
6 Cook until the internal meat temperature reaches 1350F.
7 Remove the lamb from the Traeger and cover it with foil for 30 minutes.
8 Once the carrots are cooked, serve with the meat and enjoy it.

Nutrition:
Calories 257
Total fat 8g
Total carbs 6g
Protein 37g
Sugars 3g
Fiber 1g
Sodium 431mg
Potassium 666mg

342. Simple Traeger Grilled Lamb Chops

Preparation Time: 10 Minutes
Cooking Time: 20 Minutes
Servings: 6
Ingredients:

- 1/4 cup white vinegar, distilled
- 2 tbsp olive oil
- 2 tbsp salt
- 1/2 tbsp black pepper
- 1 tbsp minced garlic
- One onion, thinly sliced
- 2 lb. lamb chops

Directions:

1 In a resealable bag, mix vinegar, oil, salt, black pepper, garlic, and

sliced onions until all salt has dissolved.
2 Add the lamb and toss until evenly coated. Place in a fridge to marinate for 2 hours.
3 Preheat your Traeger.
4 Remove the lamb from the resealable bag and leave any onion that is stuck on the meat. Use an aluminum foil to cover any exposed bone ends.
5 Grill until the desired doneness is achieved. Serve and enjoy when hot.

Nutrition:
Calories 519
Total fat 44.8g
Total carbs 2.3g
Protein 25g
Sugars 0.8g
Fiber 0.4g
Sodium 861mg
Potassium 358.6mg

343. Traeger Grilled Lamb with Sugar Glaze

Preparation Time: 15 Minutes
Cooking Time: 20 Minutes
Servings: 4
Ingredients:

- 1/4 cup sugar
- 2 tbsp ground ginger
- 2 tbsp dried tarragon
- 1/2 tbsp salt
- 1 tbsp black pepper, ground
- 1 tbsp ground cinnamon
- 1 tbsp garlic powder
- Four lamb chops

Directions:

1. In a mixing bowl, mix sugar, ground ginger, tarragon, salt, pepper, cinnamon, and garlic.
2. Rub the lamb chops with the mixture and refrigerate for an hour.
3. Meanwhile, preheat your Traeger.
4. Brush the grill grates with oil and place the marinated lamb chops on it—Cook for 5 minutes on each side.
5. Serve and enjoy.

Nutrition:
Calories 241
Total fat 13.1g
Total carbs 15.8g
Protein 14.6g
Sugars 13.6g
Fiber 0.7g
Sodium 339.2mg
Potassium 256.7mg

344. Traeger Grilled Leg of Lamb Steak

Preparation Time: 10 Minutes
Cooking Time: 10 Minutes
Servings: 4
Ingredients:

- 4 reaches lamb steaks, bone-in
- 1/4 cup olive oil
- Four garlic cloves, minced
- 1 tbsp rosemary, freshly chopped
- Salt and pepper to taste

Directions:

1. Arrange the steak in a dish in a single layer. Cover the meat with oil, garlic, fresh

rosemary, salt, and pepper.

2. Flip the meat to coat on all sides and let it marinate for 30 minutes.
3. Preheat your Traeger and lightly oil the grates. Cook the meat on the grill until well browned on both sides, and the internal temperature reaches 1400F.
4. Serve and enjoy.

Nutrition:
Calories 327.3
Total fat 21.9g
Total carbs 1.7g
Protein 29.6g
Sugars 0.1g
Fiber 0.2g
Sodium 112.1mg
Potassium 409.8mg

345. Traeger Garlic Rack Lamb

Preparation Time: 45 Minutes
Cooking Time: 3 Hours
Servings: 4
Ingredients:

- Lamb Rack
- Basil – 1 teaspoon
- Oregano – 1 teaspoon
- Peppermill – 10 cranks
- Marsala wine – 3 oz.
- Cram Sherry – 3 oz.
- Olive oil
- Madeira wine – 3 oz
- Balsamic vinegar – 3 oz.
- Rosemary – 1 teaspoon

Directions:

1. Add all of the ingredients into a zip

bag the mix well to form an emulsion.

2. Place the rack lamb into the bag the release all of the air as you rub the marinade all over the lamb.
3. Let it stay in the bag for about 45 minutes
4. Get the wood pellet grill preheated to 2500F, then cook the lamb for 3 hours as you turn on both sides.
5. Ensure that the internal temperature is at 1650F before removing from the grill.
6. Allow to cool for a few minutes, then serve and enjoy.

Nutrition:
Calories: 291 Cal
Protein: 26 g
Fat: 21 g

346. Traeger Braised Lamb Shank

Preparation Time: 20 Minutes
Cooking Time: 4 Hours
Servings: 6
Ingredients:

- Lamb shanks – 4
- Olive oil as required
- Beef broth – 1 cup
- Red wine – 1 cup
- Fresh thyme and sprigs – 4

Directions:

1. Season lamb shanks with prime rib rub, then allow resting.
2. Get the wood pellet grill temperature set to high, then cook the lamb shanks for about 30 minutes.

3. Place the shanks directly on the grill grate, then cook for another 20 minutes until browned on the outside.
4. Transfer the cooked lamb shanks into a Dutch oven, then pour beef broth, the herbs, and wine. Cover it with a fitting lid, then place it back on the grill grate and allow it to cook at a reduced temperature of 3250F.
5. Brace the lamb shanks for about 3 hours or until the internal temperature gets to 1800F.
6. Remove the lid once ready, then serve on a platter together with the accumulated juices and enjoy.

Nutrition:
Calories: 312 Cal
Protein: 27 g
Fat: 24 g

Chapter 28. Poultry recipes

347. Buffalo Chicken Wings

Preparation Time: 15 Minutes
Cooking Time: 25 Minutes
Servings: 6
Ingredients:

- 2 lb. chicken wings
- 1/2 cup sweet, spicy dry rub
- 2/3 cup buffalo sauce
- Celery, chopped

Directions:

1. Start your wood pellet grill.
2. Set it to 450 degrees F.
3. Sprinkle the chicken wings with the dry rub.
4. Place on the grill rack.
5. Cook for 10 minutes per side.
6. Brush with the buffalo sauce.
7. Grill for another 5 minutes.
8. Dip each wing in the buffalo sauce.
9. Sprinkle the celery on top.

Nutrition:
Calories 935
Total fat 53g
Saturated fat 15g
Protein 107g
Sodium 320mg

348. Sweet and Sour Chicken

Preparation Time: 30 Minutes
Cooking Time: 5 Hours
Servings: 4
Ingredients:

- Eight chicken drumsticks
- 1/4 cup soy sauce
- 1 cup ketchup
- Two tablespoons rice wine vinegar
- Two tablespoons lemon juice
- Two tablespoons honey
- Two tablespoons garlic, minced
- Two tablespoons ginger, minced
- One tablespoon sweet-spicy dry rub
- Three tablespoons brown sugar

Directions:

1. Combine all the sauce fixings in a bowl.
2. Mix well.
3. Take half of the mixture, transfer to another bowl and refrigerate.
4. Add the chicken to the bowl with the remaining sauce.
5. Toss to coat evenly.
6. Cover and refrigerate for 4 hours.
7. When ready to cook, take the chicken out of the refrigerator.
8. Discard the marinade.
9. Turn on your wood pellet grill.
10. Set it to smoke.
11. Set the temperature to 225 degrees F.
12. Smoke the chicken for 3 hours.
13. Serve the chicken with the reserved sauce.

Nutrition:
Calories 935
Total fat 53g

Saturated fat 15g
Protein 107g
Sodium 320mg

349. Honey Glazed Whole Chicken

Preparation Time: 30 Minutes
Cooking Time: 4 Hours
Servings: 4
Ingredients:

- One tablespoon honey
- Four tablespoons butter
- Three tablespoons lemon juice
- One whole chicken, giblets trimmed
- Four tablespoons chicken seasoning

Directions:

1. Set your wood pellet grill to smoke.
2. Set it to 225 degrees F.
3. In a pan over low heat, increase the honey and butter. Pour in the lemon juice.
4. Add the seasoning.
5. Cook for 1 minute, stirring.
6. Add the chicken to the grill.
7. Smoke for 8 minutes.
8. Flip the chicken and brush with the honey mixture.
9. Smoke for 3 hours, brushing the sauce every 40 minutes.
10. Let rest for 5 minutes before serving.

Nutrition:
Calories 935
Total fat 53g
Saturated fat 15g
Protein 107g

Sodium 320mg

350. Chicken Lollipops

Preparation Time: 30 Minutes
Cooking Time: 2 Hours
Servings: 6
Ingredients:

- 12 chicken lollipops
- Chicken seasoning
- Ten tablespoons butter, sliced into 12 cubes
- 1 cup barbecue sauce
- 1 cup hot sauce

Directions:

1. Turn on your wood pellet grill.
2. Set it to 300 degrees F.
3. Then season, the chicken with the chicken seasoning.
4. Arrange the chicken in a baking pan.
5. Put the butter cubes on top of each chicken.
6. Cook the chicken lollipops for 2 hours, basting with the melted butter in the baking pan every 20 minutes.
7. Pour in the barbecue sauce and hot sauce over the chicken.
8. Grill for 15 minutes.

Nutrition:
Calories 935
Total fat 53g
Saturated fat 15g
Protein 107g
Sodium 320mg

351. Asian Wings

Preparation Time: 30 Minutes
Cooking Time: 3 Hours
Servings: 6
Ingredients:

- One teaspoon honey
- One teaspoon soy sauce
- Two teaspoon rice vinegar
- 1/2 cup hoisin sauce
- Two teaspoon sesame oil
- One teaspoon ginger, minced
- One teaspoon garlic, minced
- One teaspoon green onion, chopped
- 1 cup hot water
- 2 lb. chicken wings

Directions:

1. Combine all the sauce fixings in a large bowl. Mix well.
2. Transfer 1/3 of the sauce to another bowl and refrigerate.
3. Add the chicken wings to the remaining sauce.
4. Cover and refrigerate for 2 hours.
5. Turn on your wood pellet grill.
6. Set it to 300 degrees F.
7. Add the wings to a grilling basket.
8. Cook for 1 hour.
9. Heat the reserved sauce in a pan.
10. Bring to a boil and then simmer for 10 minutes.
11. Brush the chicken with the remaining sauce.
12. Grill for another 10 minutes.
13. Let rest for 5 minutes before serving.

Nutrition:
Calories 935
Total fat 53g

Saturated fat 15g
Protein 107g
Sodium 320mg

352. Lemon Chicken in Foil Packet

Preparation Time: 5 Minutes
Cooking Time: 25 Minutes
Servings: 4
Ingredients:

- Four chicken fillets
- Three tablespoons melted butter
- One garlic, minced
- 1-1/2 teaspoon dried Italian seasoning
- Salt and pepper to taste
- One lemon, sliced

Directions:

1. Turn on your wood pellet grill.
2. Keep the lid open while burning for 5 minutes.
3. Preheat it to 450 degrees F.
4. Add the chicken fillet on top of foil sheets.
5. In a bowl, mix the butter, garlic, seasoning, salt, and pepper.
6. Brush the chicken with this mixture.
7. Put the lemon slices on top.
8. Wrap the chicken with the foil.
9. Grill each side for 7 to 10 minutes per side.

Nutrition:
Calories 935
Total fat 53g
Saturated fat 15g
Protein 107g

Sodium 320mg

353. Sweet and Spicy Chicken

Preparation Time: 30 Minutes
Cooking Time: 1 Hour and 30 Minutes
Servings: 4
Ingredients:

- 16 chicken wings
- Three tablespoons lime juice
- A sweet, spicy rub

Directions:

1. Arrange the chicken wings in a baking pan.
2. Pour the lime juice over the wings.
3. Sprinkle the wings with the seasoning.
4. Set your wood pellet grill to 350 degrees F.
5. Add the chicken wings to the grill.
6. Grill for 20 minutes per side.

Nutrition:
Calories 935
Total fat 53g
Saturated fat 15g
Protein 107g
Sodium 320mg

354. Teriyaki Turkey

Preparation Time: 30 Minutes
Cooking Time: 4 Hours
Servings: 10
Ingredients:
Glaze

- 1/4 cup melted butter
- 1/2 cup apple cider
- Two cloves garlic, minced
- 1/2 teaspoon ground ginger

- Two tablespoons soy sauce
- Two tablespoons honey

Turkey

- Two tablespoons chicken seasoning
- One whole turkey

Thickener

- One tablespoon cold water
- One teaspoon cornstarch

Directions:

1. Add the glaze ingredients to a pan over medium heat.
2. Bring to a boil and then simmer for 5 minutes.
3. Reserve 5 tablespoons of the mixture.
4. Add the remaining to a marinade injection.
5. Place the turkey in a baking pan.
6. Season with the chicken seasoning.
7. Turn on the wood pellet grill.
8. Set it to 300 degrees F.
9. Add the turkey to the grill.
10. Cook for 3 hours.
11. Add the thickener to the reserved mixture.
12. Brush the turkey with this sauce.
13. Cook for another 1 hour.

Nutrition:
Calories 935
Total fat 53g
Saturated fat 15g
Protein 107g
Sodium 320mg

355. Cheesy Turkey Burger

Preparation Time: 20 Minutes
Cooking Time: 3 Hours
Servings: 8
Ingredients:

- 3 lb. ground turkey
- Burger seasoning
- 7 oz. brie cheese, sliced into cubes
- Eight burger buns, sliced
- Blueberry jam
- Two roasted bell peppers, sliced

Directions:

1. Season the turkey with the burger seasoning.
2. Mix well.
3. Form 8 patties from the mixture.
4. Press cheese into the patties.
5. Cover the top with more turkey.
6. Preheat your wood pellet grill to 350 degrees F.
7. Cook the turkey burgers for 30 to 40 minutes per side.
8. Spread the burger buns with blueberry jam.
9. Add the turkey burger on top.
10. Top with the bell peppers.

Nutrition:
Calories 935
Total fat 53g
Saturated fat 15g
Protein 107g
Sodium 320mg

356.   Turkey Sandwich

Preparation Time: 5 Minutes
Cooking Time: 25 Minutes
Servings: 4
Ingredients:

- Eight bread slices
- 1 cup gravy
- 2 cups turkey, cooked and shredded

Directions:

1. Set your wood pellet grill to smoke.
2. Preheat it to 400 degrees F.
3. Place a grill mat on top of the grates.
4. Add the turkey on top of the mat.
5. Cook for 10 minutes.
6. Toast the bread in the flame broiler.
7. Top the bread with the gravy and shredded turkey.

Nutrition:
Calories 935
Total fat 53g
Saturated fat 15g
Protein 107g
Sodium 320mg

357.   Smoked Turkey

Preparation Time: 30 Minutes
Cooking Time: 6 Hours and 30 Minutes
Servings: 8
Ingredients:

- 1 cup butter
- 1/2 cup maple syrup
- Two tablespoons chicken seasoning
- One whole turkey

Directions:

1. Add the butter to a pan over low heat.
2. Stir in the maple syrup.
3. Simmer for 5 minutes, stirring.
4. Turn off the stove and let cool.
5. Add to a marinade injection.
6. Inject into the turkey.
7. Add the turkey to the wood pellet grill.
8. Set it smoke.
9. Smoke at 275 degrees F for 6 hours.

Nutrition:
Calories 935
Total fat 53g
Saturated fat 15g
Protein 107g
Sodium 320mg

358.   Texas Turkey

Preparation Time: 30 Minutes
Cooking Time: 4 Hours and 30 Minutes
Servings: 8
Ingredients:

- One pre-brined turkey
- Salt and pepper to taste
- 1 lb. butter

Directions:

1. Preheat your wood pellet grill to 300 degrees F.
2. Season the turkey with salt and pepper.
3. Grill for 3 hours.
4. Add the turkey to a roasting pan.
5. Cover the turkey with the butter.
6. Cover with foil.
7. Add to the grill and cook for another 1 hour.
8. Let rest for 20 minutes before carving and serving.

Nutrition:
Calories 935
Total fat 53g
Saturated fat 15g
Protein 107g
Sodium 320mg

359.   Traeger Grilled Chicken

Preparation Time: 10 Minutes
Cooking Time: 1 Hour and 10 Minutes
Servings: 6
Ingredients:

- 5 lb. whole chicken
- 1/2 cup oil
- Traeger chicken rub

Directions:

1. Preheat the Traeger on the smoke setting with the lid open for 5 minutes. Close the lid, and let it warm for 15 minutes or until it reaches 450.
2. Use bakers' twine to tie the chicken legs together, then rub it with oil. Coat the chicken with the rub and place it on the grill.
3. Grill for 70 minutes with the lid closed or until it reaches an internal temperature of 1650F.
4. Remove the chicken from the Traeger and let rest for 15 minutes. Cut and serve.

Nutrition:
Calories 935
Total fat 53g
Saturated fat 15g
Protein 107g

Sodium 320mg

360. Traeger Chicken Breast

Preparation Time: 10 Minutes
Cooking Time: 15 Minutes
Servings: 6
Ingredients:

- Three chicken breasts
- 1 tbsp avocado oil
- 1/4 tbsp garlic powder
- 1/4 tbsp onion powder
- 3/4 tbsp salt
- 1/4 tbsp pepper

Directions:

1. Preheat your Traeger to 3750F
2. Cut the chicken breast into halves lengthwise, then coat with avocado oil.
3. Season with garlic powder, onion powder, salt, and pepper.
4. Place the chicken on the grill and cook for 7 minutes on each side or until the internal temperature reaches 1650F

Nutrition:
Calories 120
Total fat 4g
Saturated fat 1g
Protein 19g
Sodium 309mg

361. Trager Smoked Spatchcock Turkey

Preparation Time: 30 Minutes
Cooking Time: 1 Hour and 15 Minutes
Servings: 8
Ingredients:

- One turkey
- 1/2 cup melted butter
- 1/4 cup Traeger chicken rub
- 1 tbsp onion powder
- 1 tbsp garlic powder
- 1 tbsp rubbed sage

Directions:

1. Preheat your Traeger to high temperature.
2. Put the turkey on a chopping board with the breast side down and the legs pointing towards you.
3. Cut either side of the turkey backbone to remove the spine. Flip the turkey and place it on a pan
4. Season both sides with the seasonings and place it on the grill skin side up on the grill.
5. Cook for 30 minutes, reduce temperature, and cook for 45 more minutes until the internal temperature reaches 1650F.
6. Remove from the Traeger and let rest for 15 minutes before slicing and serving.

Nutrition:
Calories 156
Total fat 16g
Saturated fat 2g
Total carbs 1g
Net carbs 1g
Protein 2g
Sodium 19mg

362. Chicken Wings

Preparation Time: 10 minutes
Cooking Time: 15 minutes
Servings: 4
Ingredients:

- Fresh chicken wings
- Salt to taste
- Pepper to taste
- Garlic powder
- Onion powder
- Cayenne
- Paprika
- Seasoning salt
- Barbeque sauce to taste

Directions:

1. Preheat the wood pellet grill to low.
2. Mix seasoning and coat on chicken
3. Put the wings on the grill and cook
4. Place the wings on the grill and cook for 20 minutes or until the wings are fully cooked.
5. Let rest to cool for 5 minutes then toss with barbeque sauce.
6. Serve with orzo and salad. Enjoy.

Nutrition:
Calories: 311 Cal
Fat: 22 g
Carbohydrates: 22 g
Protein: 22 g
Fiber: 3 g

363. Wood Pellet Grilled Chicken Kabobs

Preparation Time: 45 minutes
Cooking Time: 12 minutes
Servings: 6
Ingredients:

- 1/2 cup olive oil
- 2 tbsp white vinegar
- 1 tbsp lemon juice
- 1-1/2 tbsp salt
- 1/2 tbsp pepper, coarsely ground

- 2 tbsp chives, freshly chopped
- 1-1/2 tbsp thyme, freshly chopped
- 2 tbsp Italian parsley freshly chopped
- 1tbsp garlic, minced
- Kabobs
- 1 each orange, red, and yellow pepper
- 1-1/2 pounds chicken breast, boneless and skinless
- 12 mini mushrooms

Directions:

1 In a mixing bowl, add all the marinade ingredients and mix well. Toss the chicken and mushrooms in the marinade then refrigerate for 30 minutes.
2 Meanwhile, soak the skewers in hot water. Remove the chicken from the fridge and start assembling the kabobs.
3 Preheat your wood pellet to 450°F.
4 Grill the kabobs in the wood pellet for 6 minutes, flip them and grill for 6 more minutes.
5 Remove from the grill and let rest. Heat up the naan bread on the grill for 2 minutes.
6 Serve and enjoy.

Nutrition:
Calories: 165 Cal
Fat: 13 g
Carbohydrates: 1 g
Protein: 33 g

Fiber: 0 g

364. Wood Pellet Grilled Chicken

Preparation Time: 10 minutes
Cooking Time: 1 hour and 10 minutes
Servings: 6
Ingredients:

- 5 pounds whole chicken
- 1/2 cup oil
- Chicken rub

Directions:

1 Preheat your wood pellet on smoke with the lid open for 5 minutes. Close the lid, increase the temperature to 450°F and preheat for 15 more minutes.
2 Tie the chicken legs together with the baker's twine then rub the chicken with oil and coat with chicken rub.
3 Place the chicken on the grill with the breast side up.
4 Grill the chicken for 70 minutes without opening it or until the internal temperature reaches 165°F.
5 Once the chicken is out of the grill let it cool down for 15 minutes
6 Enjoy.

Nutrition:
Calories: 935 Cal
Fat: 53 g
Carbohydrates: 0 g
Protein: 107 g
Fiber: 0 g

365. Wood Pellet Chicken Breasts

Preparation Time: 10 minutes
Cooking Time: 15 minutes
Servings: 6
Ingredients:

- 3 chicken breasts
- 1 tbsp avocado oil
- 1/4 tbsp garlic powder
- 1/4 tbsp onion powder
- 3/4 tbsp salt
- 1/4 tbsp pepper

Directions:

1 Preheat your pellet to 375°F.
2 Half the chicken breasts lengthwise then coat with avocado oil.
3 With the spices, drizzle it on all sides to season
4 Drizzle spices to season the chicken
5 Put the chicken on top of the grill and begin to cook until its internal temperature approaches 165 degrees Fahrenheit
6 Put the chicken on top of the grill and begin to cook until it rises to a temperature of 165 degrees Fahrenheit
7 Serve and enjoy.

Nutrition:
Calories: 120 Cal
Fat: 4 g
Carbohydrates: 0 g
Protein: 19 g
Fiber: 0 g

366. Wood Pellet Smoked Spatchcock Turkey

Preparation Time: 30 minutes
Cooking Time: 1 hour and 45 minutes
Servings: 6
Ingredients:

- 1 whole turkey
- 1/2 cup oil
- 1/4 cup chicken rub
- 1 tbsp onion powder
- 1 tbsp garlic powder
- 1 tbsp rubbed sage

Directions:

1 Preheat your wood pellet grill to high.
2 Meanwhile, place the turkey on a platter with the breast side down then cut on either side of the backbone to remove the spine.
3 Flip the turkey and season on both sides then place it on the preheated grill or on a pan if you want to catch the drippings.
4 Grill on high for 30 minutes, reduce the temperature to 325°F, and grill for 45 more minutes or until the internal temperature reaches 165°F
5 Remove from the grill and let rest for 20 minutes before slicing and serving. Enjoy.

Nutrition:
Calories: 156 Cal
Fat: 16 g
Carbohydrates: 1 g
Protein: 2 g
Fiber: 0 g

367. Wood Pellet Smoked Cornish Hens

Preparation Time: 10 minutes
Cooking Time: 1 hour
Servings: 6
Ingredients:

- 6 Cornish hens
- 3 tbsp avocado oil
- 6 tbsp rub of choice

Directions:

1 Fire up the wood pellet and preheat it to 275°F.
2 Rub the hens with oil then coat generously with rub. Place the hens on the grill with the chest breast side down.
3 Smoke for 30 minutes. Flip the hens and increase the grill temperature to 400°F. Cook until the internal temperature reaches 165°F.
4 Remove from the grill and let rest for 10 minutes before serving. Enjoy.

Nutrition:
Calories: 696 Cal
Fat: 50 g
Carbohydrates: 1 g
Protein: 57 g
Fiber: 0 g

368. Smoked and Fried Chicken Wings

Preparation Time: 10 minutes
Cooking Time: 2 hours
Servings: 6
Ingredients:

- 3 pounds chicken wings
- 1 tbsp Goya adobo all-purpose seasoning
- Sauce of your choice

Directions:

1 Fire up your wood pellet grill and set it to smoke.
2 Meanwhile, coat the chicken wings with adobo all-purpose seasoning. Place the chicken on the grill and smoke for 2 hours.
3 Remove the wings from the grill.
4 Preheat oil to 375°F in a frying pan. Drop the wings in batches and let fry for 5 minutes or until the skin is crispy.
5 Drain the oil and proceed with drizzling preferred sauce
6 Drain oil and drizzle preferred sauce
7 Enjoy.

Nutrition:
Calories: 755 Cal
Fat: 55 g
Carbohydrates: 24 g
Protein: 39 g
Fiber: 1 g

369. Wood Pellet Grilled Buffalo Chicken Leg

Preparation Time: 5 minutes
Cooking Time: 25 minutes
Servings: 6
Ingredients:

- 12 chicken legs
- 1/2 tbsp salt
- 1 tbsp buffalo seasoning
- 1 cup buffalo sauce

Directions:

1 Preheat your wood pellet grill to 325°F.

2 Toss the legs in salt and buffalo seasoning then place them on the preheated grill.

3 Grill for 40 minutes ensuring you turn them twice through the cooking.

4 Brush the legs with buffalo sauce and cook for an additional 10 minutes or until the internal temperature reaches 165°F.

5 Remove the legs from the grill, brush with more sauce, and serve when hot.

Nutrition:
Calories: 956 Cal
Fat: 47 g
Carbohydrates: 1 g
Protein: 124 g
Fiber: 0 g

370. Wood Pellet Chile Lime Chicken

Preparation Time: 2 minutes
Cooking Time: 15 minutes
Servings: 1
Ingredients:
- 1 chicken breast
- 1 tbsp oil
- 1 tbsp chile-lime seasoning

Directions:
1 Preheat your wood pellet to 400°F.

2 Brush the chicken breast with oil on all sides.

3 Sprinkle with seasoning and salt to taste.

4 Grill for 7 minutes per side or until the

internal temperature reaches 165°F.

5 Serve when hot or cold and enjoy.

Nutrition:
Calories: 131 Cal
Fat: 5 g
Carbohydrates: 4 g
Protein: 19 g
Fiber: 1 g

371. Wood Pellet Sheet Pan Chicken Fajitas

Preparation Time: 10 minutes
Cooking Time: 10 minutes
Servings: 10
Ingredients:
- 2 tbsp oil
- 2 tbsp chile margarita seasoning
- 1 tbsp salt
- 1/2 tbsp onion powder
- 1/2 tbsp garlic, granulated
- 2-pound chicken breast, thinly sliced
- 1 red bell pepper, seeded and sliced
- 1 orange bell pepper
- 1 onion, sliced

Directions:
1 Preheat the wood pellet to 450°F.

2 Meanwhile, mix oil and seasoning then toss the chicken and the peppers.

3 Line a sheet pan with foil then place it in the preheated grill. Let it heat for 10 minutes with the grill's lid closed.

4 Open the grill and place the chicken with

the veggies on the pan in a single layer.

5 Cook for 10 minutes or until the chicken is cooked and no longer pink.

6 Remove from grill and serve with tortilla or your favorite fixings.

Nutrition:
Calories: 211 Cal
Fat: 6 g
Carbohydrates: 5 g
Protein: 29 g
Fiber: 1 g

372. Buffalo Chicken Flatbread

Preparation Time: 5 minutes
Cooking Time: 30 minutes
Servings: 6
Ingredients:
- 6 mini pita bread
- 1-1/2 cups buffalo sauce
- 4 cups chicken breasts, cooked and cubed
- 3 cups mozzarella cheese
- Blue cheese for drizzling

Directions:
1 Preheat the wood pellet grill to 375-400°F.

2 Place the breads on a flat surface and evenly spread sauce over all of them.

3 Toss the chicken with the remaining buffalo sauce and place it on the pita breads.

4 Top with cheese then place the breads on the grill but indirectly from

the heat. Close the grill lid.

5   Cook for 7 minutes or until the cheese has melted and the edges are toasty.

6   Remove from grill and drizzle with blue cheese. Serve and enjoy.

Nutrition:
Calories: 254 Cal
Fat: 13 g
Carbohydrates: 4 g
Protein: 33 g
Fiber: 3 g

373.   Wood Pellet Grilled Buffalo Chicken

Preparation Time: 5 minutes
Cooking Time: 20 minutes
Servings: 6
Ingredients:

- 5 chicken breasts, boneless and skinless
- 2 tbsp homemade barbeque rub
- 1 cup homemade Cholula buffalo sauce

Directions:

1   Preheat the wood pellet grill to 400°F.
2   Slice the chicken into long strips and season with barbeque rub.
3   Place the chicken on the grill and paint both sides with buffalo sauce.
4   Cook for 4 minutes with the grill closed. Cook while flipping and painting with buffalo sauce every 5 minutes until the

internal temperature reaches 165°F.

5   Remove from the grill and serve when warm. Enjoy.

Nutrition:
Calories: 176 Cal
Fat: 4 g
Carbohydrates: 1 g
Protein: 32 g
Fiber: 0 g

374.   Beer Can Chicken

Preparation Time: 10 minutes
Cooking Time: 1 hour and 15 minutes
Servings: 6
Ingredients:

- 5-pound chicken
- 1/2 cup dry chicken rub
- 1 can beer

Directions:

1   Preheat your wood pellet grill on smoke for 5 minutes with the lid open.
2   The lid must then be closed and then preheated up to 450 degrees Fahrenheit
3   Pour out half of the beer then shove the can in the chicken and use the legs like a tripod.
4   Place the chicken on the grill until the internal temperature reaches 165°F.
5   Remove from the grill and let rest for 20 minutes before serving. Enjoy.

Nutrition:
Calories: 882 Cal
Fat: 51 g

Carbohydrates: 2 g
Protein: 94 g
Fiber: 0 g

375.   Wood Pellet Chicken Wings with Spicy Miso

Preparation Time: 15 minutes
Cooking Time: 25 minutes
Servings:6
Ingredients:

- 2-pound chicken wings
- 3/4 cup soy
- 1/2 cup pineapple juice
- 1 tbsp sriracha
- 1/8 cup miso
- 1/8 cup gochujang
- 1/2 cup water
- 1/2 cup oil
- Togarashi

Directions:

1   Mix all ingredients then toss the chicken wings until well coated. Refrigerate for 12 minutes.
2   Preheat your wood pellet grill to 375°F.
3   Place the chicken wings on the grill grates and close the lid. Cook until the internal temperature reaches 165°F.
4   Remove the wings from the grill and sprinkle with togarashi.
5   Serve when hot and enjoy.

Nutrition:
Calories: 704 Cal
Fat: 56 g
Carbohydrates: 24 g
Protein: 27 g
Fiber: 1 g

376. Bacon-wrapped Chicken Tenders

Preparation Time: 25 minutes
Cooking Time: 30 minutes
Servings: 6
Ingredients:

- 1-pound chicken tenders
- 10 strips bacon
- 1/2 tbsp Italian seasoning
- 1/2 tbsp black pepper
- 1/2 tbsp salt
- 1 tbsp paprika
- 1 tbsp onion powder
- 1 tbsp garlic powder
- 1/3 cup light brown sugar
- 1 tbsp chili powder

Directions:

1. Preheat your wood pellet smoker to 350°F.
2. Mix seasonings
3. Sprinkle the mixture on all sides of chicken tenders
4. Wrap each chicken tender with a strip of bacon
5. Place them on the smoker and smoker for 30 minutes with the lid closed or until the chicken is cooked.
6. Serve and enjoy.

Nutrition:
Calories: 206 Cal
Fat: 7.9 g
Carbohydrates: 1.5 g
Protein: 30.3 g
Fiber: 0 g

Chapter 29. Fish and seafood

377. Swordfish Steaks with Corn Salsa

Preparation Time: 10 Minutes
Cooking Time: 30 Minutes
Servings: 4
Ingredients:

- Four whole ears corn, husked
- Olive oil, as needed
- Salt and black pepper, to taste
- 1-pint cherry tomatoes
- One whole serrano chile, chopped
- One whole red onion, diced
- One whole lime, juiced
- Four whole swordfish fillets

Directions:

1. When ready to cook, put the Traeger to High and preheat for 15 minutes.
2. Brush the corn with the olive oil and season with salt and pepper. Place the corn on the grill grate and grill for 12 to 15 minutes, or until cooked through and lightly browned. Set aside to cool.
3. Once the corn has cooled, cut the kernels from the corn and transfer to a medium bowl. Stir in the tomatoes, serrano, red onion, and lime juice.
4. Brush the swordfish fillets with the olive oil and season with salt and pepper.
5. Arrange the fillets on the grill grate and grill for about 18 minutes, or until the fish is opaque and flakes when pressed with a fork.
6. Serve the grilled swordfish topped with the corn salsa.

Nutrition:
Calories 270
Total fat 17g
Saturated fat 9g
Total carbs 2g
Net carbs 2g
Protein 28g
Sodium 381mg

378. Grilled Oysters with Veggie Sauce

Preparation Time: 20 Minutes
Cooking Time: 25 Minutes
Servings: 4
Ingredients:

- Five tablespoons extra-virgin olive oil
- Two medium onions, chopped
- One medium red bell pepper, chopped
- Two lemons, juiced
- Three dried bay leaves
- Five tablespoons minced garlic
- Three tablespoons Traeger Chicken Rub
- Three teaspoons dried thyme
- ¼ cup white wine
- Five tablespoons hot pepper sauce
- Three tablespoons Worcestershire Sauce
- Four butter sticks
- 12 whole oysters, cleaned and shucked
- Italian cheese blend, as needed

Directions:

1. When ready to cook, put the Traeger to High and preheat, lid closed for 15 minutes.
2. Heat the olive oil in a cast-iron pan over medium heat. Add the onions, bell peppers, lemon juice, bay leaves, garlic, Traeger Chicken Rub, and thyme to the pan. Sauté the vegetable mixture for 5 to 7 minutes, or until the onions are translucent and peppers are tender.
3. Add the white wine, hot pepper sauce, Worcestershire Sauce, and butter to the pan. Sauté for another 15 minutes.
4. Place the oysters and top with the sauce— Cook for 5 minutes.
5. Top with Italian cheese and serve hot.

Nutrition:
Calories 261
Total fat 14g
Saturated fat 5g
Total carbs 5g
Net carbs 5g
Protein 28g
Sodium 1238mg

379. Crispy Fried Halibut Fish Sticks

Preparation Time: 10 Minutes
Cooking Time: 3 to 4 Minutes
Servings: 4
Ingredients:

- Extra-virgin olive oil, as needed
- 1½ pounds (680 g) halibut, rinsed, patted dry, and cut into 1-inch strips
- ½ cup all-purpose flour
- 1½ teaspoons salt
- One teaspoon ground black pepper
- Two large eggs
- 1½ cups panko bread crumbs
- Two tablespoons dried parsley
- One teaspoon dried dill weed

Directions:

1. When ready to cook, put Traeger temperature to 500°F (260°C) and preheat, lid closed for 15 minutes.
2. Place a Dutch oven inside the grill to preheat for about 10 minutes, with enough olive oil to fry the fish.
3. In a bowl, stir together the all-purpose flour, salt, and pepper.
4. In a separate bowl, beat the eggs. In a third bowl, combine the panko, parsley, and dill.
5. Dredge the fish fillets in the flour mixture, then the eggs, and then the panko mixture.
6. Place the coated fish fillets in the oil and fry for about 3 to 4 minutes, or until they reach an internal temperature of 130°F (54°C).
7. Serve warm.

Nutrition:
Calories 245
Total fat 2g
Total carbs 2g
Protein 52g
Sugars 1g
Fiber 1g
Sodium 442mg

380. White Fish Steaks with Orange Basil Pesto

Preparation Time: 10 Minutes
Cooking Time: 15 Minutes
Servings: 4
Ingredients:

- One orange, juiced
- 2 cups fresh basil
- 1 cup chopped flat-leaf parsley
- ½ cup toasted walnuts
- Two teaspoons orange zest
- ½ cup olive oil
- 1 cup grated Parmesan cheese
- Four white fish steaks rinsed and patted dry
- ½ teaspoon coarse sea salt
- ½ teaspoon black pepper

Directions:

1. Make the pesto: In a food processor, combine the orange juice, basil, parsley, walnuts, and orange zest and pulse until finely chopped. With the machine running, slowly drizzle in the olive oil until the mixture is emulsified.
2. Scrape the pesto into a bowl and stir in the Parmesan cheese.
3. Brush the fish steaks with olive oil on both sides and season with salt and pepper.
4. Arrange the fish steaks on the grill grate. Grill for 12 to 15 minutes, turning once with a thin-bladed metal spatula, or until the fish is opaque and breaks into chunks when pressed with a fork.
5. Transfer the steaks to a platter. Drizzle with the prepared pesto and serve immediately.

Nutrition:
Calories 245
Total fat 2g
Total carbs 2g
Protein 52g
Sugars 1g
Fiber 1g
Sodium 442mg

381. Lemony Salmon Fillets

Preparation Time: 10 Minutes
Cooking Time: 20 Minutes
Servings: 2
Ingredients:

- Two tablespoons butter softened
- Two teaspoons fresh chopped dill, plus more for garnish

- One teaspoon lemon juice
- ½ teaspoon lemon zest
- ½ teaspoon salt
- Black pepper, to taste
- 4 (8-ounce / 227-g) salmon fillets, skin on
- One lemon, thinly sliced

Directions:

1. When fit to cook, set Traeger temperature to 350°F (177°C) and preheat for 15 minutes.
2. Meanwhile, stir together all the ingredients, except for the salmon and lemon, in a bowl.
3. Generously spread the lemon-dill butter over the top of the salmon fillets and top with a slice of lemon.
4. Place the salmon fillets on the grill grate, skin-side facing down. Cook for 15 to 20 minutes, for a medium-rare salmon, or until the salmon is done to your liking.
5. Serve garnished with the fresh dill.

382. Grilled Salmon Teriyaki Sauce

Preparation Time: 10 Minutes
Cooking Time: 15 Minutes
Servings: 2
Ingredients:

- 1 cup of soy sauce
- Six tablespoons brown sugar

- One tablespoon minced ginger
- Four cloves garlic
- Juice and zest of 2 whole oranges
- 4 (6-ounce / 170-g) pieces salmon fillets
- One tablespoon sesame seed
- Toasted sesame seeds, as needed
- Chopped scallions, as needed

Directions:

1. In a saucepan, place the soy sauce, brown sugar, ginger, garlic, orange juice, and zest. Bring to a boil and slowly boil for 1o minutes, or until a syrupy consistency is achieved, about a 50 percent reduction. Let cool completely. Add the salmon and sesame seeds and marinate for 1 hour.
2. Remove the salmon from the marinade and bring the sauce to a boil.
3. Place the salmon fillets straight on the grill grate, skin-side up— Cook for about 3 to 5 minutes per side, or until they are done until your liking. Occasionally, then brush the salmon with the sauce.
4. Remove the salmon from the grill and serve topped with the toasted sesame seeds and chopped scallions.

Nutrition:
Calories 119
Total fat 10g
Saturated fat 2g
Sodium 720mg

383. Roasted Stuffed Rainbow Trout

Preparation Time: 10 Minutes
Cooking Time: 15 Minutes
Servings: 1
Ingredients:

- Four tablespoons butter
- Lemon juice, as needed
- One whole rainbow trout, rinsed
- One tablespoon salt
- One teaspoon chipotle pepper
- Two whole oranges, sliced
- Four sprigs thyme sprigs
- Three whole bay leaves
- One clove garlic, chopped

Directions:

1. When ready to cook, custom Traeger temperature to 400°F (204°C) and preheat, lid closed for 15 minutes.
2. Melt the butter in a pot over medium-high heat. After the butter melts completely, it will begin to foam, and the milk solids will start to brown. After all, foam subsides, and the butter looks golden brown, remove the pan from the heat and drizzle in a

bit of lemon juice to stop the browning process. Set aside.

3. Then layout a piece of foil 3 inches longer on each end than the fish. Drizzle the fish's exterior and cavity with the brown butter and season with salt and chipotle powder. Stuff the hole with the remaining ingredients and fold the foil into a packet.

4. Place the packet directly on the grill grate and cook for about 15 minutes, or until the internal temperature has reached 145ºF (63ºC).

5. Remove from the grill and serve hot.

Nutrition:
Calories 305
Total fat 14g
Saturated fat 8g
Total carbs 5g
Net carbs 5g
Protein 38g
Sodium 684mg

384. Buttery Crab Legs

Preparation Time: 10 Minutes
Cooking Time: 30 Minutes
Servings: 4
Ingredients:

- 3 pounds (1.4 kg) crab legs, thawed and halved
- 1 cup butter, melted
- Two tablespoons fresh lemon juice
- Two cloves garlic, minced

- One tablespoon Traeger Fin & Feather Rub
- Chopped Italian parsley, for garnish

Directions:

1. When ready to cook, custom Traeger temperature to 350ºF (177ºC) and preheat, lid closed for 15 minutes.

2. Split the crab shells open lengthwise. Transfer to the roasting pan.

3. In a small bowl, stick together the butter, lemon juice, and garlic.

4. Spread the butter mixture over the crab legs, turning the legs to coat. Sprinkle the Traeger Fin & Feather Rub over the legs.

5. Place the pan on the grill grate—Cook the meat for 20 to 30 minutes, or until warmed. Then, basting once or twice with the butter sauce from the pan's bottom.

6. Transfer the crab legs to a large platter and divide the sauce and accumulated juices between 4 dipping bowls. Serve topped with the parsley.

Nutrition:
Calories 305
Total fat 14g
Saturated fat 8g
Total carbs 5g
Net carbs 5g
Protein 38g

Sodium 684mg

385. Grilled Buttery BBQ Oysters

Preparation Time: 10 Minutes
Cooking Time: 6 Minutes
Servings: 4
Ingredients:

- 1 pound (454 g) unsalted butter, softened
- One bunch green onion, chopped, plus more for garnish
- Two cloves garlic, minced
- One tablespoon Meat Church Holy Gospel BBQ Rub
- 12 oysters, shucked, juice reserved
- ¼ cup seasoned bread crumbs
- 8 ounces (227 g) shredded Pepper Jack cheese
- Traeger Sweet & Heat BBQ Sauce, as needed

Directions:

1. Make the compound butter: Stir together the butter, green onions, garlic, and Meat Church Holy Gospel BBQ Rub in a medium bowl.

2. Lay the butter on parchment paper. Roll it up to form a log and tie each end with cooking twine. Place in the freezer for an hour to solidify.

3. Sprinkle the bread crumbs over the

oysters and place directly on the grill. Cook for 5 minutes, or until the edge of the oyster starts to curl slightly.

4. After 5 minutes, place a spoonful of compound butter in the oysters. After the butter melts, add a pinch of Pepper Jack cheese. Cook for one more minute.

5. Remove the oysters from the grill. Then top the oysters with a squirt of Traeger Sweet & Heat BBQ Sauce and a few chopped onions. Let cool for 5 minutes before serving.

Nutrition:
Calories 261
Total fat 14g
Saturated fat 5g
Total carbs 5g
Net carbs 5g
Protein 28g
Sodium 1238mg

386. Smoked Vodka Salmon

Preparation Time: 5 Minutes
Cooking Time: 1 Hour
Servings: 4
Ingredients:

- 1 cup brown sugar
- 1 cup vodka
- ½ cup coarse salt
- One tablespoon black pepper
- One wild-caught salmon (1½ to 2 pounds / 680 to 907 g)
- One lemon, wedged, for serving

- Capers for serving

Directions:

1. In a small bowl, whisk together the brown sugar, vodka, salt, and pepper.

2. Place the salmon in a large resealable bag. Pour in the marinade and massage into the salmon. Refrigerate for 2 to 4 hours.

3. Remove the salmon from the bag, rinse and pat dry with paper towels.

4. Set Traeger temperature to 180°F (82°C) and preheat, lid closed for 15 minutes.

5. Place the salmon on the grill, skin-side down, and smoke for 30 minutes.

6. Increase the temperature to 225°F. Then continue to cook the salmon for 60 minutes. Or you may wait until the fish flakes easily when pressed with a fork.

7. Serve with the lemons and capers.

Nutrition:
Calories 119
Total fat 10g
Saturated fat 2g
Sodium 720mg

387. Grilled Lobster Tail

Preparation Time: 10 minutes
Cooking Time: 15 minutes
Servings: 4
Ingredients:

- 2 (8 ounces each) lobster tails
- 1/4 tsp old bay seasoning
- ½ tsp oregano
- 1 tsp paprika
- Juice from one lemon
- 1/4 tsp Himalayan salt
- 1/4 tsp freshly ground black pepper
- 1/4 tsp onion powder
- 2 tbsp freshly chopped parsley
- ¼ cup melted butter

Directions:

1. Slice the tail in the middle with a kitchen shear. Pull the shell apart slightly and run your hand through the meat to separate the meat partially

2. Combine the seasonings

3. Drizzle lobster tail with lemon juice and season generously with the seasoning mixture.

4. Preheat your wood pellet smoker to 450°F, using apple wood pellets.

5. Place the lobster tail directly on the grill grate, meat side down. Cook for about 15 minutes.

6. The tails must be pulled off and it must cool down for a few minutes

7. Drizzle melted butter over the tails.

8. Serve and garnish with fresh chopped parsley.

Nutrition:

Calories: 146 Cal
Fat: 11.7 g
Carbohydrates: 2.1 g
Protein: 9.3 g
Fiber: 0.8 g

388. Halibut

Preparation Time: 10 minutes
Cooking Time: 3o minutes
Servings: 4
Ingredients:

- 1-pound fresh halibut filet (cut into 4 equal sizes)
- 1 tbsp fresh lemon juice
- 2 garlic cloves (minced)
- 2 tsp soy sauce
- ½ tsp ground black pepper
- ½ tsp onion powder
- 2 tbsp honey
- ½ tsp oregano
- 1 tsp dried basil
- 2 tbsp butter (melted)
- Maple syrup for serving

Directions:

1 Combine the lemon juice, honey, soy sauce, onion powder, oregano, dried basil, pepper and garlic.
2 Brush the halibut filets generously with the filet the mixture. Wrap the filets with aluminum foil and refrigerate for 4 hours.
3 Remove the filets from the refrigerator and let them sit for about 2 hours, or until they are at room temperature.
4 Activate your wood pellet grill on smoke, leaving the lid opened for 5 minutes or until fire starts.
5 The lid must not be opened for it to be preheated and reach 275°F 15 minutes, using fruit wood pellets.
6 Place the halibut filets directly on the grill grate and smoke for 30 minutes
7 Remove the filets from the grill and let them rest for 10 minutes.
8 Serve and top with maple syrup to taste

Nutrition:
Calories: 180 Cal
Fat: 6.3 g
Carbohydrates: 10 g
Protein: 20.6 g
Fiber: 0.3 g

389. Grilled Salmon

Preparation Time: 10 minutes
Cooking Time: 4o minutes
Servings: 8
Ingredients:

- 2 pounds salmon (cut into fillets)
- 1/2 cup low sodium soy sauce
- 2 garlic cloves (grated)
- 4 tbsp olive oil
- 2 tbsp honey
- 1 tsp ground black pepper
- ½ tsp smoked paprika
- ½ tsp Italian seasoning
- 2 tbsp chopped green onion

Directions:

1 Incorporate pepper, paprika, Italian seasoning, garlic, soy sauce and olive oil. Add the salmon fillets and toss to combine. Cover the bowl and refrigerate for 1 hour.
2 Remove the fillets from the marinade and let it sit for about 2 hours, or until it is at room temperature.
3 Start the wood pellet on smoke, leaving the lid opened for 5 minutes, or until fire starts.
4 Keep lid unopened and preheat grill to a temperature 350°F for 15 minutes.
5 Do not open lid for 4 minutes or until cooked
6 Flip the fillets and cook for additional 25 minutes or until the fish is flaky.
7 Remove the fillets from heat and let it sit for a few minutes.
8 Serve warm and garnish with chopped green onion.

Nutrition:
Calories: 317 Cal
Fat: 18.8 g
Carbohydrates: 8.3 g
Protein: 30.6 g
Fiber: 0.4 g

390. Barbeque Shrimp

Preparation Time: 20 minutes
Cooking Time: 8 minutes
Servings: 6
Ingredients:

- 2-pound raw shrimp (peeled and deveined)
- ¼ cup extra virgin olive oil
- ½ tsp paprika
- ½ tsp red pepper flakes
- 2 garlic cloves (minced)
- 1 tsp cumin
- 1 lemon (juiced)
- 1 tsp kosher salt
- 1 tbsp chili paste
- Bamboo or wooden skewers (soaked for 30 minutes, at least)

Directions:
1. Combine the pepper flakes, cumin, lemon, salt, chili, paprika, garlic and olive oil. Add the shrimp and toss to combine.
2. Transfer the shrimp and marinade into a zip-lock bag and refrigerate for 4 hours.
3. Let shrimp rest in room temperature after pulling it out from marinade
4. Start your grill on smoke, leaving the lid opened for 5 minutes, or until fire starts. Use hickory wood pellet.
5. Keep lid unopened and preheat the grill to "high" for 15 minutes.
6. Thread shrimps onto skewers and arrange the skewers on the grill grate.
7. Smoke shrimps for 8 minutes, 4 minutes per side.
8. Serve and enjoy.

Nutrition:
Calories: 267 Cal
Fat: 11.6 g
Carbohydrates: 4.9 g
Protein: 34.9 g
Fiber: 0.4 g

391. Grilled Tuna
Preparation Time: 5 minutes
Cooking Time: 4 minutes
Servings: 4
Ingredients:

- 4 (6 ounce each) tuna steaks (1 inch thick)
- 1 lemon (juiced)
- 1 clove garlic (minced)
- 1 tsp chili
- 2 tbsp extra virgin olive oil
- 1 cup white wine
- 3 tbsp brown sugar
- 1 tsp rosemary

Directions:
1. Combine lemon, chili, white wine, sugar, rosemary, olive oil and garlic. Add the tuna steaks and toss to combine.
2. Transfer the tuna and marinade to a zip-lock bag. Refrigerate for 3 hours.
3. Remove the tuna steaks from the marinade and let them rest for about 1 hour
4. Start your grill on smoke, leaving the lid opened for 5 minutes, or until fire starts.
5. Do not open lid to preheat until 15 minutes to the setting "HIGH"
6. Grease the grill grate with oil and place the tuna on the grill grate. Grill tuna steaks for 4 minutes, 2 minutes per side.
7. Remove the tuna from the grill and let them rest for a few minutes.

Nutrition:
Calories: 137 Cal
Fat: 17.8 g
Carbohydrates: 10.2 g
Protein: 51.2 g
Fiber: 0.6 g

392. Oyster in Shells
Preparation Time: 25 minutes
Cooking Time: 8 minutes
Servings: 4
Ingredients:

- 12 medium oysters
- 1 tsp oregano
- 1 lemon (juiced)
- 1 tsp freshly ground black pepper
- 6 tbsp unsalted butter (melted)
- 1 tsp salt or more to taste
- 2 garlic cloves (minced)
- 2 ½ tbsp grated parmesan cheese
- 2 tbsp freshly chopped parsley

Directions:
1. Remove dirt
2. Open the shell completely. Discard the top shell.
3. Gently run the knife under the oyster to loosen the oyster foot from the bottom shell.

4 Repeat step 2 and 3 for the remaining oysters.

5 Combine melted butter, lemon, pepper, salt, garlic and oregano in a mixing bowl.

6 Pour ½ to 1 tsp of the butter mixture on each oyster.

7 Start your wood pellet grill on smoke, leaving the lid opened for 5 minutes, or until fire starts.

8 Keep lid unopened to preheat in the set "HIGH" with lid closed for 15 minutes.

9 Gently arrange the oysters onto the grill grate.

10 Grill oyster for 6 to 8 minutes or until the oyster juice is bubbling and the oyster is plump.

11 Remove oysters from heat. Serve and top with grated parmesan and chopped parsley.

Nutrition:
Calories: 200 Cal
Fat: 19.2 g
Carbohydrates: 3.9 g
Protein: 4.6 g
Fiber: 0.8 g

393. Grilled King Crab Legs

Preparation Time: 10 minutes
Cooking Time: 25 minutes
Servings: 4
Ingredients:

- 4 pounds king crab legs (split)
- 4 tbsp lemon juice
- 2 tbsp garlic powder
- 1 cup butter (melted)
- 2 tsp brown sugar
- 2 tsp paprika
- Black pepper (depends to your liking)

Directions:

1 In a mixing bowl, combine the lemon juice, butter, sugar, garlic, paprika and pepper.

2 Arrange the split crab on a baking sheet, split side up.

3 Drizzle ¾ of the butter mixture over the crab legs.

4 Configure your pellet grill for indirect cooking and preheat it to 225°F, using mesquite wood pellets.

5 Arrange the crab legs onto the grill grate, shell side down.

6 Cover the grill and cook 25 minutes.

7 Remove the crab legs from the grill.

8 Serve and top with the remaining butter mixture.

Nutrition:
Calories: 480 Cal
Fat: 53.2 g
Carbohydrates: 6.1 g
Protein: 88.6 g
Fiber: 1.2 g

394. Cajun Smoked Catfish

Preparation Time: 15 minutes
Cooking Time: 2 hours
Servings: 4
Ingredients:

- 4 catfish fillets (5 ounces each)
- ½ cup Cajun seasoning
- 1 tsp ground black pepper
- 1 tbsp smoked paprika
- 1 /4 tsp cayenne pepper
- 1 tsp hot sauce
- 1 tsp granulated garlic
- 1 tsp onion powder
- 1 tsp thyme
- 1 tsp salt or more to taste
- 2 tbsp chopped fresh parsley

Directions:

1 Pour water into the bottom of a square or rectangular dish. Add 4 tbsp salt. Arrange the catfish fillets into the dish. Cover the dish and refrigerate for 3 to 4 hours.

2 Combine the paprika, cayenne, hot sauce, onion, salt, thyme, garlic, pepper and Cajun seasoning in a mixing bowl.

3 Remove the fish from the dish and let it sit for a few minutes, or until it is at room temperature. Pat the fish fillets dry with a paper towel.

4 Rub the seasoning mixture over each fillet generously.

5 Start your grill on smoke, leaving the lid opened for 5 minutes, or until fire starts.

6 Keep lid unopened and preheat to 200°F, using

mesquite hardwood pellets.

7 Arrange the fish fillets onto the grill grate and close the grill. Cook for about 2 hours, or until the fish is flaky.

8 Remove the fillets from the grill and let the fillets rest for a few minutes to cool.

9 Serve and garnish with chopped fresh parsley.

Nutrition:
Calories: 204 Cal
Fat: 11.1 g
Carbohydrates: 2.7 g
Protein: 22.9 g
Fiber: 0.6 g

395. Smoked Scallops

Preparation Time: 10 minutes
Cooking Time: 15 minutes
Servings: 6
Ingredients:

- 2 pounds sea scallops
- 4 tbsp salted butter
- 2 tbsp lemon juice
- ½ tsp ground black pepper
- 1 garlic clove (minced)
- 1 kosher tsp salt
- 1 tsp freshly chopped tarragon

Directions:

1 Let the scallops dry using paper towels and drizzle all sides with salt and pepper to season

2 Place you're a cast iron pan in your grill and preheat the grill to 400°F with lid closed for 15 minutes.

3 Combine the butter and garlic in hot cast iron pan. Add the scallops and stir. Close grill lid and cook for 8 minutes.

4 Flip the scallops and cook for an additional 7 minutes.

5 Remove the scallop from heat and let it rest for a few minutes.

6 Stir in the chopped tarragon. Serve and top with lemon juice.

Nutrition:
Calories: 204 Cal
Fat: 8.9 g
Carbohydrates: 4 g
Protein: 25.6 g
Fiber: 0.1 g

396. Grilled Tilapia

Preparation Time: 10 minutes
Cooking Time: 2o minutes
Servings: 6
Ingredients:

- 2 tsp dried parsley
- ½ tsp garlic powder
- 1 tsp cayenne pepper
- ½ tsp ground black pepper
- ½ tsp thyme
- ½ tsp dried basil
- ½ tsp oregano
- 3 tbsp olive oil
- ½ tsp lemon pepper
- 1 tsp kosher salt
- 1 lemon (juiced)
- 6 tilapia fillets
- 1 ½ tsp creole seafood seasoning

Directions:

1 In a mixing bowl, combine spices

2 Brush the fillets with oil and lemon juice.

3 Liberally, season all sides of the tilapia fillets with the seasoning mix.

4 Preheat your grill to 325°F

5 Place a non-stick BBQ grilling try on the grill and arrange the tilapia fillets onto it.

6 Grill for 15 to 20 minutes

7 Remove fillets and cool down

Nutrition:
Calories: 176 Cal
Fat: 9.6 g
Carbohydrates: 1.5 g
Protein: 22.3 g
Fiber: 0.5 g

397. Traeger Salmon with Togarashi

Preparation Time: 5 Minutes
Cooking Time: 20 Minutes
Servings: 3
Ingredients:

- One salmon fillet
- 1/4 cup olive oil
- 1/2 tbsp kosher salt
- 1 tbsp Togarashi seasoning

Directions:

1. Preheat your Traeger to 4000F.

2. Place the salmon on a sheet lined with non-stick foil with the skin side down.

3. Rub the oil into the meat, then sprinkle salt and Togarashi.

4. Place the salmon on the grill and cook for

20 minutes or until the internal temperature reaches 1450F with the lid closed.

5. Remove from the Traeger and serve when hot.

Nutrition:
Calories 119
Total fat 10g
Saturated fat 2g
Sodium 720mg

398. Trager Rockfish

Preparation Time: 10 Minutes
Cooking Time: 20 Minutes
Servings: 6
Ingredients:

- Six rockfish fillets
- One lemon, sliced
- 3/4 tbsp salt
- 2 tbsp fresh dill, chopped
- 1/2 tbsp garlic powder
- 1/2 tbsp onion powder
- 6 tbsp butter

Directions:

1. Preheat your Traeger to 4000F.
2. Season the fish with salt, dill, garlic, and onion powder on both sides, then place it in a baking dish.
3. Place a pat of butter and a lemon slice on each fillet. Place the baking dish in the Traeger and close the lid.
4. Cook for 20 minutes or until the fish is no longer translucent and is flaky.

5. Remove from Traeger and let rest before serving.

Nutrition:
Calories 270
Total fat 17g
Saturated fat 9g
Total carbs 2g
Net carbs 2g
Protein 28g
Sodium 381mg

399. Traeger Grilled Lingcod

Preparation Time: 10 Minutes
Cooking Time: 15 Minutes
Servings: 6
Ingredients:

- 2 lb. lingcod fillets
- 1/2 tbsp salt
- 1/2 tbsp white pepper
- 1/4 tbsp cayenne pepper
- Lemon wedges

Directions:

1. Preheat your Traeger to 3750F.
2. Place the lingcod on a parchment paper or a grill mat
3. Season the fish with salt, pepper, and top with lemon wedges.
4. Cook the fish for 15 minutes or until the internal temperature reaches 1450F.

Nutrition:
Calories 245
Total fat 2g
Total carbs 2g
Protein 52g
Sugars 1g
Fiber 1g
Sodium 442mg

400. Crab Stuffed Lingcod

Preparation Time: 20 Minutes
Cooking Time: 30 Minutes
Servings: 6
Ingredients:
Lemon cream sauce

- Four garlic cloves
- One shallot
- One leek
- 2 tbsp olive oil
- 1 tbsp salt
- 1/4 tbsp black pepper
- 3 tbsp butter
- 1/4 cup white wine
- 1 cup whipping cream
- 2 tbsp lemon juice
- 1 tbsp lemon zest

Crab mix

- 1 lb. crab meat
- 1/3 cup mayo
- 1/3 cup sour cream
- 1/3 cup lemon cream sauce
- 1/4 green onion, chopped
- 1/4 tbsp black pepper
- 1/2 tbsp old bay seasoning

Fish

- 2 lb. lingcod
- 1 tbsp olive oil
- 1 tbsp salt
- 1 tbsp paprika
- 1 tbsp green onion, chopped
- 1 tbsp Italian parsley

Directions:
Lemon cream sauce

1. Chop garlic, shallot, and leeks, then add to a saucepan with oil, salt, pepper, and butter.

2. Sauté over medium heat until the shallot is translucent.
3. Deglaze with white wine, then add whipping cream. Bring the sauce to boil, reduce heat, and simmer for 3 minutes.
4. Remove from heat and add lemon juice and lemon zest. Transfer the sauce to a blender and blend until smooth.
5. Set aside 1/3 cup for the crab mix

Crab mix
1. Add all the fixings to a mixing bowl and mix thoroughly until well combined.
2. Set aside

Fish
1. Fire up your Traeger to high heat, then slice the fish into 6-ounce portions.
2. Lay the fish on its side on a cutting board and slice it 3/4 way through the middle leaving a 1/2 inch on each end to have a nice pouch.
3. Rub the oil into the fish, then place them on a baking sheet. Sprinkle with salt.
4. Stuff crab mix into each fish, then sprinkle paprika and place it on the grill.
5. Cook for 15 minutes or more if the fillets are more than 2 inches thick.

6. Remove the fish and transfer to serving platters. Pour the remaining lemon cream sauce on each fish and garnish with onions and parsley.

Nutrition:
Calories 476
Total fat 33g
Saturated fat 14g
Total carbs 6g
Net carbs 5g
Protein 38g
Sugars 3g
Fiber 1g
Sodium 1032mg

401. Traeger Smoked Shrimp

Preparation Time: 10 Minutes
Cooking Time: 10 Minutes
Servings: 6
Ingredients:
- 1 lb. tail-on shrimp, uncooked
- 1/2 tbsp onion powder
- 1/2 tbsp garlic powder
- 1/2 tbsp salt
- 4 tbsp teriyaki sauce
- 2 tbsp green onion, minced
- 4 tbsp sriracha mayo

Directions:
1. Peel the shrimp shells leaving the tail on, then wash well and rise.
2. Drain well and pat dry with a paper towel.
3. Preheat your Traeger to 4500F.
4. Season the shrimp with onion powder, garlic powder, and salt. Place the shrimp in the

Traeger and cook for 6 minutes on each side.
5. Remove the shrimp from the Traeger and toss with teriyaki sauce, then garnish with onions and mayo.

Nutrition:
Calories 87
Total carbs 2g
Net carbs 2g
Protein 16g
Sodium 1241mg

402. Grilled Shrimp Kabobs

Preparation Time: 5 Minutes
Cooking Time: 10 Minutes
Servings: 4
Ingredients:
- 1 lb. colossal shrimp, peeled and deveined
- 2 tbsp. oil
- 1/2 tbsp. garlic salt
- 1/2 tbsp. salt
- 1/8 tbsp. pepper
- Six skewers

Directions:
1. Preheat your Traeger to 3750F.
2. Pat the shrimp dry with a paper towel.
3. In a mixing bowl, mix oil, garlic salt, salt, and pepper
4. Toss the shrimp in the mixture until well coated.
5. Skewer the shrimps and cook in the Traeger with the lid closed for 4 minutes.
6. Open the lid, flip the skewers, cook for another 4 minutes, or wait until the shrimp is

pink and the flesh is opaque.

7. Serve.

Nutrition:
Calories 325
Protein 20g
Sodium 120mg

403. Bacon-Wrapped Shrimp

Preparation Time: 20 Minutes
Cooking Time: 10 Minutes
Servings: 12
Ingredients:

- 1 lb. raw shrimp
- 1/2 tbsp salt
- 1/4 tbsp garlic powder
- 1 lb. bacon, cut into halves

Directions:

1. Preheat your Traeger to 3500F.
2. Remove the shells and tails from the shrimp, then pat them dry with the paper towels.
3. Sprinkle salt and garlic on the shrimp, then wrap with bacon and secure with a toothpick.
4. Place the shrimps on a baking rack greased with cooking spray.
5. Cook for 10 minutes, flip and cook for another 10 minutes, or until the bacon is crisp enough.
6. Remove from the Traeger and serve.

Nutrition:
Calories 204
Total fat 14g
Saturated fat 5g
Total carbs 1g
Net carbs 1g

Protein 18g
Sodium 939mg

404. Traeger Spot Prawn Skewers

Preparation Time: 10 Minutes
Cooking Time: 10 Minutes
Servings: 6
Ingredients:

- 2 lb. spot prawns
- 2 tbsp oil
- Salt and pepper to taste

Directions:

1. Preheat your Traeger to 4000F.
2. Skewer your prawns with soaked skewers, then generously sprinkle with oil, salt, and pepper.
3. Place the skewers on the grill, then cook with the lid closed for 5 minutes on each side.
4. Remove the skewers and serve when hot.

Nutrition:
Calories 221
Total fat 7g
Saturated fat 1g
Total carbs 2g
Net carbs 2g
Protein 34g
Sodium 1481mg

405. Traeger Bacon-wrapped Scallops

Preparation Time: 15 Minutes
Cooking Time: 20 Minutes
Servings: 8
Ingredients:

- 1 lb. sea scallops
- 1/2 lb. bacon
- Sea salt

Directions:

1. Preheat your Traeger to 3750F.
2. Pat dry the scallops with a towel, then wrap them with a piece of bacon and secure with a toothpick.
3. Lay the scallops on the grill with the bacon side down. Close the lid and cook for 5 minutes on each side.
4. Keep the scallops on the bacon side so that you will not get grill marks on the scallops.
5. Serve and enjoy.

Nutrition:
Calories 261
Total fat 14g
Saturated fat 5g
Total carbs 5g
Net carbs 5g
Protein 28g
Sodium 1238mg

406. Traeger Lobster Tail

Preparation Time: 10 Minutes
Cooking Time: 15 Minutes
Servings: 2
Ingredients:

- 10 oz lobster tail
- 1/4 tbsp old bay seasoning
- 1/4 tbsp Himalayan salt
- 2 tbsp butter, melted
- 1 tbsp fresh parsley, chopped

Directions:

1. Preheat your Traeger to 4500F.
2. Slice the tail down the middle, then season it

with bay seasoning and salt.

3. Place the tails directly on the grill with the meat side down. Grill for 15 minutes or until the internal temperature reaches 1400F.
4. Remove from the Traeger and drizzle with butter.
5. Serve when hot garnished with parsley.

Nutrition:
Calories 305
Total fat 14g
Saturated fat 8g
Total carbs 5g
Net carbs 5g
Protein 38g
Sodium 684mg

407.   Roasted Honey Salmon

Preparation Time: 5 Minutes
Cooking Time: 1 Hour
Servings: 4
Ingredients:

- Two cloves garlic, grated
- Two tablespoon ginger, minced
- One teaspoon honey
- One teaspoon sesame oil
- Two tablespoon lemon juice
- One teaspoon chili pastes
- Four salmon fillets
- Two tablespoon soy sauce

Directions:

1 Set your wood pellet grill to smoke while the lid is open.
2 Do this for 5 minutes.
3 Preheat your wood pellet grill to 400 degrees F.
4 Combine all the ingredients except salmon in a sealable plastic bag.
5 Shake to mix the ingredients.
6 Add the salmon.
7 Marinate inside the refrigerator for 30 minutes.
8 Add the salmon to a roasting pan and place it on top of the grill.
9 Close the lid and cook for 3 minutes.
10 Flip the salmon and cook for another 3 minutes.

Nutrition:
Calories 119
Total fat 10g
Saturated fat 2g
Sodium 720mg

408.   Blackened Salmon

Preparation Time: 10 Minutes
Cooking Time: 20 Minutes
Servings: 4
Ingredients:

- 2 lb. salmon, fillet, scaled and deboned
- Two tablespoons olive oil
- Four tablespoons sweet dry rub
- One tablespoon cayenne pepper
- Two cloves garlic, minced

Directions:

1. Turn on your wood pellet grill.
2. Set it to 350 degrees F.
3. Brush the salmon with the olive oil.
4. Sprinkle it with the dry rub, cayenne pepper, and garlic.
5. Grill for 5 minutes per side.

Nutrition:
Calories 119
Total fat 10g
Saturated fat 2g
Sodium 720mg

409.   Grilled Cajun Shrimp

Preparation Time: 5 Minutes
Cooking Time: 25 Minutes
Servings: 8
Ingredients:
Dip

- 1/2 cup mayonnaise
- One teaspoon lemon juice
- 1 cup sour cream
- One clove garlic, grated
- One tablespoon Cajun seasoning
- One tablespoon hickory bacon rub
- One tablespoon hot sauce
- Chopped scallions

Shrimp

- 1/2 lb. shrimp, peeled and deveined
- Two tablespoons olive oil
- 1/2 tablespoon hickory bacon seasoning
- One tablespoon Cajun seasoning

Directions:

1. Turn on your wood pellet grill.
2. Set it to 350 degrees F.
3. Mix the dip ingredients in a bowl.
4. Transfer to a small pan.
5. Cover with foil.
6. Place on top of the grill.
7. Cook for 10 minutes.
8. Coat the shrimp with the olive oil and sprinkle with the seasonings.
9. Grill for 5 minutes per side.
10. Pour the dip on top or serve with the shrimp.

Nutrition:
Calories 87
Total carbs 2g
Net carbs 2g
Protein 16g
Sodium 1241mg

410. Salmon Cakes

Preparation Time: 5 Minutes
Cooking Time: 25 Minutes
Servings: 4
Ingredients:

- 1 cup cooked salmon, flaked
- 1/2 red bell pepper, chopped
- Two eggs, beaten
- 1/4 cup mayonnaise
- 1/2 tablespoon dry sweet rub
- 1 1/2 cups breadcrumbs
- One tablespoon mustard
- Olive oil

Directions:

1. Combine all the fixings except the olive oil in a bowl.
2. Form patties from this mixture.
3. Let sit for 15 minutes.
4. Turn on your wood pellet grill.
5. Set it to 350 degrees F.
6. Add a baking pan to the grill.
7. Drizzle a little olive oil on top of the pan.
8. Add the salmon cakes to the pan.
9. Grill each side for 3 to 4 minutes.

Nutrition:
Calories 119
Total fat 10g
Saturated fat 2g
Sodium 720mg

Chapter 30. Vegetables

411. Sweet Potato Fries

Preparation Time: 30 Minutes
Cooking Time: 40 Minutes
Servings: 4
Ingredients:

- Three sweet potatoes, sliced into strips
- Four tablespoons olive oil
- Two tablespoons fresh rosemary, chopped
- Salt and pepper to taste

Directions:

1. Set the Traeger wood pellet grill to 450 degrees F.
2. Preheat it for 10 minutes.
3. Spread the sweet potato strips in the baking pan.
4. Toss in olive oil and sprinkle with rosemary, salt, and pepper.
5. Cook for 15 minutes.
6. Flip and cook for another 15 minutes.
7. Flip and cook for ten more minutes.

Nutrition:
Calories 118
Total fat 7.6g
Total carbs 10.8g
Protein 5.4g
Sugars 3.7g
Fiber 2.5g,
Sodium 3500mg
Potassium 536mg

412. Potato Fries with Chipotle Peppers

Preparation Time: 30 Minutes
Cooking Time: 30 Minutes
Servings: 4
Ingredients:

- Four potatoes, sliced into strips
- Three tablespoons olive oil
- Salt and pepper to taste
- 1 cup mayonnaise
- Two chipotle peppers in adobo sauce
- Two tablespoons lime juice

Directions:

1. Set the Traeger wood pellet grill to high.
2. Preheat it for 15 minutes while the lid is closed.
3. Coat the potato strips with oil.
4. Sprinkle with salt and pepper.
5. Put a baking pan on the grate.
6. Transfer potato strips to the pan.
7. Cook potatoes until crispy.
8. Mix the remaining ingredients.
9. Pulse in a food processor until pureed.
10. Serve potato fries with chipotle dip.

Nutrition:
Calories 118
Total fat 7.6g
Total carbs 10.8g
Protein 5.4g
Sugars 3.7g
Fiber 2.5g,
Sodium 3500mg
Potassium 536mg

413. Grilled Zucchini

Preparation Time: 30 Minutes
Cooking Time: 10 Minutes
Servings: 4

Ingredients:

- Four zucchinis, sliced into strips
- One tablespoon sherry vinegar
- Two tablespoons olive oil
- Salt and pepper to taste
- Two fresh thyme, chopped

Directions:

1. Place the zucchini strips in a bowl.
2. Mix the remaining fixings and pour them into the zucchini.
3. Coat evenly.
4. Set the Traeger wood pellet grill to 350 degrees F.
5. Preheat for 15 minutes while the lid is closed.
6. Place the zucchini on the grill.
7. Cook for 3 minutes per side.

Nutrition:
Calories 118
Total fat 7.6g
Total carbs 10.8g
Protein 5.4g
Sugars 3.7g
Fiber 2.5g,
Sodium 3500mg
Potassium 536mg

414. Smoked Potato Salad

Preparation Time: 1 Hour and 15 Minutes
Cooking Time: 40 Minutes
Servings: 4
Ingredients:

- 2 lb. potatoes
- Two tablespoons olive oil
- 2 cups mayonnaise

- One tablespoon white wine vinegar
- One tablespoon dry mustard
- 1/2 onion, chopped
- Two celery stalks, chopped
- Salt and pepper to taste

Directions:
1. Coat the potatoes with oil.
2. Smoke the potatoes in the Traeger wood pellet grill at 180 degrees F for 20 minutes.
3. Increase temperature to 450 degrees F and cook for 20 more minutes.
4. Transfer to a bowl and let cool.
5. Peel potatoes.
6. Slice into cubes.
7. Refrigerate for 30 minutes.
8. Stir in the rest of the ingredients.

Nutrition:
Calories 118
Total fat 7.6g
Total carbs 10.8g
Protein 5.4g
Sugars 3.7g
Fiber 2.5g,
Sodium 3500mg
Potassium 536mg

415. Baked Parmesan Mushrooms

Preparation Time: 15 Minutes
Cooking Time: 15 Minutes
Servings: 8
Ingredients:
- Eight mushroom caps

- 1/2 cup Parmesan cheese, grated
- 1/2 teaspoon garlic salt
- 1/4 cup mayonnaise
- Pinch paprika
- Hot sauce

Directions:
1. Place mushroom caps in a baking pan.
2. Mix the remaining ingredients in a bowl.
3. Scoop the mixture onto the mushroom.
4. Place the baking pan on the grill.
5. Cook in the Traeger wood pellet grill at 350 degrees F for 15 minutes while the lid is closed.

Nutrition:
Calories 118
Total fat 7.6g
Total carbs 10.8g
Protein 5.4g
Sugars 3.7g
Fiber 2.5g,
Sodium 3500mg
Potassium 536mg

416. Roasted Spicy Tomatoes

Preparation Time: 30 Minutes
Cooking Time: 1 Hour and 30 Minutes
Servings: 4
Ingredients:
- 2 lb. large tomatoes, sliced in half
- Olive oil
- Two tablespoons garlic, chopped
- Three tablespoons parsley, chopped
- Salt and pepper to taste
- Hot pepper sauce

Directions:
1. Set the temperature to 400 degrees F.
2. Preheat it for 15 minutes while the lid is closed.
3. Add tomatoes to a baking pan.
4. Drizzle with oil and sprinkle with garlic, parsley, salt, and pepper.
5. Roast for 1 hour and 30 minutes.
6. Drizzle with hot pepper sauce and serve.

Nutrition:
Calories 118
Total fat 7.6g
Total carbs 10.8g
Protein 5.4g
Sugars 3.7g
Fiber 2.5g,
Sodium 3500mg
Potassium 536mg

417. Grilled Corn with Honey and Butter

Preparation Time: 30 Minutes
Cooking Time: 10 Minutes
Servings: 4
Ingredients:
- Six pieces of corn
- Two tablespoons olive oil
- 1/2 cup butter
- 1/2 cup honey
- One tablespoon smoked salt
- Pepper to taste

Directions:
1. Preheat the wood pellet grill too high for 15 minutes while the lid is closed.

2. Brush the corn with oil and butter.
3. Grill the corn for 10 minutes, turning from time to time.
4. Mix honey and butter.
5. Brush corn with this mixture and sprinkle with smoked salt and pepper.

Nutrition:
Calories 118
Total fat 7.6g
Total carbs 10.8g
Protein 5.4g
Sugars 3.7g
Fiber 2.5g,
Sodium 3500mg
Potassium 536mg

418. Grilled Sweet Potato Planks

Preparation Time: 30 Minutes
Cooking Time: 30 Minutes
Servings: 8
Ingredients:
- Five sweet potatoes, sliced into planks
- One tablespoon olive oil
- One teaspoon onion powder
- Salt and pepper to taste

Directions:
1. Set the Traeger wood pellet grill to high.
2. Preheat it for 15 minutes while the lid is closed.
3. Coat the sweet potatoes with oil.
4. Sprinkle with onion powder, salt, and pepper.
5. Grill the sweet potatoes for 15 minutes.

Nutrition:
Calories 118
Total fat 7.6g
Total carbs 10.8g
Protein 5.4g
Sugars 3.7g
Fiber 2.5g,
Sodium 3500mg
Potassium 536mg

419. Roasted Veggies and Hummus

Preparation Time: 30 Minutes
Cooking Time: 20 Minutes
Servings: 4
Ingredients:
- One white onion, sliced into wedges
- 2 cups butternut squash
- 2 cups cauliflower, sliced into florets
- 1 cup mushroom buttons
- Olive oil
- Salt and pepper to taste
- Hummus

Directions:
1. Set the Traeger wood pellet grill to high.
2. Preheat it for 10 minutes while the lid is closed.
3. Add the veggies to a baking pan.
4. Roast for 20 minutes.
5. Serve roasted veggies with hummus.

Nutrition:
Calories 118
Total fat 7.6g
Total carbs 10.8g
Protein 5.4g
Sugars 3.7g
Fiber 2.5g,
Sodium 3500mg
Potassium 536mg

420. Traeger Smoked Mushrooms

Preparation Time: 15 Minutes
Cooking Time: 45 Minutes
Servings: 2
Ingredients:
- 4 cups whole baby portobello, cleaned
- 1 tbsp canola oil
- 1 tbsp onion powder
- 1 tbsp garlic, granulated
- 1 tbsp salt
- 1 tbsp pepper

Directions:
1. Place all the ingredients in a bowl, mix, and combine.
2. Set your Traeger to 180oF.
3. Place the mushrooms on the grill directly and smoke for about 30 minutes.
4. Increase heat to high and cook the mushroom for another 15 minutes.
5. Serve warm and enjoy!

Nutrition:
Calories 118
Total fat 7.6g
Total carbs 10.8g
Protein 5.4g
Sugars 3.7g
Fiber 2.5g,
Sodium 3500mg
Potassium 536mg

421. Grilled Zucchini Squash Spears

Preparation Time: 5 Minutes
Cooking Time: 10 Minutes
Servings: 4
Ingredients:

- Four zucchinis, medium
- 2 tbsp olive oil
- 1 tbsp sherry vinegar
- Two thyme leaves pulled
- Salt to taste
- Pepper to taste

Directions:
1. Clean zucchini, cut ends off, half each lengthwise, and cut each half into thirds.
2. Combine all the other ingredients in a zip lock bag, medium, then add spears.
3. Toss well and mix to coat the zucchini.
4. Preheat Traeger to 350oF with the lid closed for 15 minutes.
5. Remove spears from the zip lock bag and place them directly on your grill grate with the cut side down.
6. Cook for about 3-4 minutes until zucchini is tender and grill marks show.
7. Remove them from the grill and enjoy.

Nutrition:
Calories 93
Total fat 7.4g
Total carbs 7.1g
Protein 2.4g
Sugars 3.4g
Fiber 2.5g,
Sodium 3500mg
Potassium 536mg

422. Grilled Asparagus & Honey-Glazed Carrots

Preparation Time: 15 Minutes
Cooking Time: 35 Minutes
Servings: 4
Ingredients:
- One bunch asparagus, woody ends removed
- 2 tbsp olive oil
- 1 lb. peeled carrots
- 2 tbsp honey
- Sea salt to taste
- Lemon zest to taste

Directions:
1. Rinse the vegetables under cold water.
2. Splash the asparagus with oil and generously with a splash of salt.
3. Drizzle carrots generously with honey and splash lightly with salt.
4. Preheat your Traeger to 350oF with the lid closed for about 15 minutes.
5. Place the carrots first on the grill and cook for about 10-15 minutes.
6. Now place asparagus on the grill and cook both for about 15-20 minutes or until done to your liking.
7. Top with lemon zest and enjoy.

Nutrition:
Calories 184
Total fat 7.3g
Total carbs 28.6g
Protein 6g
Sugars 18.5g
Fiber 7.6g,
Sodium 142mg
Potassium 826mg

423. Traeger Grilled Vegetables

Preparation Time: 5 Minutes
Cooking Time: 15 Minutes
Servings: 12
Ingredients:
- One veggie tray
- 1/4 cup vegetable oil
- 1-2 tbsp Traeger veggie seasoning

Directions:
1. Preheat your Traeger to 375oF.
2. Meanwhile, toss the veggies in oil placed on a sheet pan, large, then splash with the seasoning.
3. Place on the Traeger and grill for about 10-15 minutes.
4. Remove, serve, and enjoy.

Nutrition:
Calories 44
Total fat 5g
Total carbs 10.8g
Protein 0g
Sugars 0g
Fiber 0g,
Sodium 36mg
Potassium 116mg

424. Smoked Acorn Squash

Preparation Time: 10 Minutes
Cooking Time: 2 Hours
Servings: 6
Ingredients:
Three acorn squash, seeded and halved
3 tbsp olive oil
1/4 cup butter, unsalted
1 tbsp cinnamon, ground

1 tbsp chili powder
1 tbsp nutmeg, ground
1/4 cup brown sugar
Directions:
1. Brush the cut sides of your squash with olive oil, then cover with foil poking holes for smoke and steam to get through.
2. Preheat your Traeger to 225oF.
3. Place the squash halves on the grill with the cut side down and smoke for about 1½- 2 hours. Remove from the Traeger.
4. Let it sit while you prepare spiced butter. Melt butter in a saucepan, then adds spices and sugar, stirring to combine.
5. Remove the foil from the squash halves.
6. Place 1 tbsp of the butter mixture onto each half.
7. Serve and enjoy!

Nutrition:
Calories 149
Total fat 10g
Total carbs 14g
Protein 2g
Sugars 2g
Fiber 2g,
Sodium 19mg
Potassium 101mg

425. Roasted Green Beans with Bacon

Preparation Time: 15 minutes
Cooking Time: 20 minutes
Servings: 6
Ingredients:

- 1-pound green beans
- 4 strips bacon, cut into small pieces
- 4 tablespoons extra virgin olive oil
- 2 cloves garlic, minced
- 1 teaspoon salt

Directions:
1 Fire the Traeger Grill to 4000F. Use desired wood pellets when cooking. Keep lid unopened and let it preheat for at most 15 minutes
2 Toss all ingredients on a sheet tray and spread out evenly.
3 Place the tray on the grill grate and roast for 20 minutes.

Nutrition:
Calories: 65 Cal
Fat: 5.3 g
Carbohydrates: 3 g
Protein: 1.3 g
Fiber: 0 g

426. Smoked Watermelon

Preparation Time: 15 minutes
Cooking Time: 45-90 minutes
Servings: 5
Ingredients:

- 1 small seedless watermelon
- Balsamic vinegar
- Wooden skewers

Directions:
1 Slice ends of small seedless watermelons
2 Slice the watermelon in 1-inch cubes. Put the cubes in a container and drizzle vinegar on the cubes of watermelon.
3 Preheat the smoker to 225°F. Add wood chips and water to the smoker before starting preheating.
4 Place the cubes on the skewers.
5 Place the skewers on the smoker rack for 50 minutes.
6 Cook
7 Remove the skewers.
8 Serve!

Nutrition:
Calories: 20 Cal
Fat: 0 g
Carbohydrates: 4 g
Protein: 1 g
Fiber: 0.2 g

427. Grilled Corn with Honey Butter

Preparation Time: 15 minutes
Cooking Time: 10 minutes
Servings: 6
Ingredients:

- 6 pieces corn, husked
- 2 tablespoons olive oil
- Salt and pepper to taste
- ½ cup butter, room temperature
- ½ cup honey

Directions:
1 Fire the Traeger Grill to 3500F. Use desired wood pellets when cooking. Keep lid unopened to preheat until 15 minutes
2 Coat corn with oil and add salt and pepper
3 Place the corn on the grill grate and cook for 10 minutes. Make sure to flip the corn halfway

through the cooking time for even cooking.

4 Meanwhile, mix the butter and honey on a small bowl. Set aside.

5 Remove corn from grill and coat with honey butter sauce

Nutrition:
Calories: 387 Cal
Fat: 21.6 g
Carbohydrates: 51.2 g
Protein: 5 g
Fiber: 0 g

428. Smoked Mushrooms

Preparation Time: 20 minutes
Cooking Time: 2 hours
Servings: 6
Ingredients:

- 6-12 large Portobello mushrooms
- Sea salt
- black pepper
- Extra virgin olive oil
- Herbs de Provence

Directions:
1 Preheat the smoker to 200°F while adding water and wood chips to the smoker bowl and tray, respectively.

2 Wash and dry mushrooms

3 Rub the mushrooms with olive oil, salt and pepper seasoning with herbs in a bowl.

4 Place the mushrooms with the cap side down on the smoker rack. Smoke the mushrooms for 2 hours while adding water and wood chips to the smoker after every 60 minutes.

5 Remove the mushrooms and serve

Nutrition:
Calories: 106 Cal
Fat: 6 g
Carbohydrates: 5 g
Protein: 8 g
Fiber: 0.9 g

429. Smoked Cherry Tomatoes

Preparation Time: 20 minutes
Cooking Time: 1 ½ hours
Servings: 8-10
Ingredients:

- 2 pints of tomatoes

Directions:
1 Preheat the electric smoker to 225°F while adding wood chips and water to the smoker.

2 Clean the tomatoes with clean water and dry them off properly.

3 Place the tomatoes on the pan and place the pan in the smoker.

4 Smoke for 90 minutes while adding water and wood chips to the smoker.

Nutrition:
Calories: 16 Cal
Fat: 0 g
Carbohydrates: 3 g
Protein: 1 g
Fiber: 1 g

430. Smoked and Smashed New Potatoes

Preparation Time: 5 minutes
Cooking Time: 8 hours
Servings: 4
Ingredients:

- 1-1/2 pounds small new red potatoes or fingerlings
- Extra virgin olive oil
- Sea salt and black pepper
- 2 tbsp softened butter

Directions:
1 Let the potatoes dry. Once dried, put in a pan and coat with salt, pepper, and extra virgin olive oil.

2 Place the potatoes on the topmost rack of the smoker.

3 Smoke for 60 minutes.

4 Once done, take them out and smash each one

5 Mix with butter and season

Nutrition:
Calories: 258 Cal
Fat: 2.0 g
Carbohydrates: 15.5 g
Protein: 4.1 g
Fiber: 1.5 g

431. Smoked Brussels Sprouts

Preparation Time: 15 minutes
Cooking Time: 45 minutes
Servings: 6
Ingredients:

- 1-1/2 pounds Brussels sprouts
- 2 cloves of garlic minced
- 2 tbsp extra virgin olive oil
- Sea salt and cracked black pepper

Directions:
1 Rinse sprouts

2 Remove the outer leaves and brown bottoms off the sprouts.
3 Place sprouts in a large bowl then coat with olive oil.
4 Add a coat of garlic, salt, and pepper and transfer them to the pan.
5 Add to the top rack of the smoker with water and woodchips.
6 Smoke for 45 minutes or until reaches 250°F temperature.
7 Serve

Nutrition:
Calories: 84 Cal
Fat: 4.9 g
Carbohydrates: 7.2 g
Protein: 2.6 g
Fiber: 2.9 g

432. Apple Veggie Burger

Preparation Time: 10 minutes
Cooking Time: 35 minutes
Servings: 6
Ingredients:
- 3 tbsp ground flax or ground chia
- 1/3 cup of warm water
- 1/2 cups rolled oats
- 1 cup chickpeas, drained and rinsed
- 1 tsp cumin
- 1/2 cup onion
- 1 tsp dried basil
- 2 granny smith apples
- 1/3 cup parsley or cilantro, chopped
- 2 tbsp soy sauce
- 2 tsp liquid smoke
- 2 cloves garlic, minced

- 1 tsp chili powder
- 1/4 tsp black pepper

Directions:
1 Preheat the smoker to 225°F while adding wood chips and water to it.
2 In a separate bowl, add chickpeas and mash. Mix together the remaining ingredients along with the dipped flax seeds.
3 Form patties from this mixture.
4 Put the patties on the rack of the smoker and smoke them for 20 minutes on each side.
5 When brown, take them out, and serve.

Nutrition:
Calories: 241 Cal
Fat: 5 g
Carbohydrates: 40 g
Protein: 9 g
Fiber: 10.3 g

433. Smoked Tofu

Preparation Time: 10 minutes
Cooking Time: 41 hour and 30 minutes
Servings: 4
Ingredients:
- 400g plain tofu
- Sesame oil

Directions:
1 Preheat the smoker to 225°F while adding wood chips and water to it.
2 Till that time, take the tofu out of the packet and let it rest

3 Slice the tofu in one-inch thick pieces and apply sesame oil
4 Place the tofu inside the smoker for 45 minutes while adding water and wood chips after one hour.
5 Once cooked, take them out and serve!

Nutrition:
Calories: 201 Cal
Fat: 13 g
Carbohydrates: 1 g
Protein: 20 g
Fiber: 0 g

434. Easy Smoked Vegetables

Preparation Time: 15 minutes
Cooking Time: 1 ½ hour
Servings: 6
Ingredients:
- 1 cup of pecan wood chips
- 1 ear fresh corn, silk strands removed, and husks, cut corn into 1-inch pieces
- 1 medium yellow squash, 1/2-inch slices
- 1 small red onion, thin wedges
- 1 small green bell pepper, 1-inch strips
- 1 small red bell pepper, 1-inch strips
- 1 small yellow bell pepper, 1-inch strips
- 1 cup mushrooms, halved
- 2 tbsp vegetable oil
- Vegetable seasonings

Directions:

202

1. Take a large bowl and toss all the vegetables together in it.
2. Sprinkle it with seasoning and coat all the vegetables well with it.
3. Place the wood chips and a bowl of water in the smoker.
4. Preheat the smoker at 100°F or ten minutes.
5. Put the vegetables in a pan and add to the middle rack of the electric smoker.
6. Smoke for thirty minutes until the vegetable becomes tender.
7. When done, serve, and enjoy.

Nutrition:
Calories: 97 Cal
Fat: 5 g
Carbohydrates: 11 g
Protein: 2 g
Fiber: 3 g

435.   Zucchini with Red Potatoes

Preparation Time: 15 minutes
Cooking Time: 4 hours
Servings: 4
Ingredients:
- 2 zucchinis, sliced in 3/4-inch-thick disks
- 1 red pepper, cut into strips
- 2 yellow squash, sliced in 3/4-inch-thick disks
- 1 medium red onion, cut into wedges
- 6 small red potatoes, cut into chunks
- Balsamic Vinaigrette:

- 1/3 cup extra virgin olive oil
- 1/4 teaspoon salt
- 1/4 cup balsamic vinegar
- 2 tsp Dijon mustard
- 1/8 teaspoon pepper

Directions:
1. For Vinaigrette: Take a medium-sized bowl and blend together olive oil, Dijon mustard, salt, pepper, and balsamic vinegar.
2. Place all the veggies into a large bowl and pour the vinaigrette mixture over it and evenly toss.
3. Put the vegetable in a pan and then smoke for 4 hours at a temperature of 225°F.
4. Serve and enjoy the food.

Nutrition:
Calories: 381 Cal
Fat: 17.6 g
Carbohydrates: 49 g
Protein: 6.7 g
Fiber: 6.5 g

436.   Shiitake Smoked Mushrooms

Preparation Time: 15 minutes
Cooking Time: 45 minutes
Servings: 4-6
Ingredients:
- 4 Cup Shiitake Mushrooms
- 1 tbsp canola oil
- 1 tsp onion powder
- 1 tsp granulated garlic
- 1 tsp salt
- 1 tsp pepper

Directions:
1. Combine all the ingredients together
2. Apply the mix over the mushrooms generously.
3. Preheat the smoker at 180°F. Add wood chips and half a bowl of water in the side tray.
4. Place it in the smoker and smoke for 45 minutes.
5. Serve warm and enjoy.

Nutrition:
Calories: 301 Cal
Fat: 9 g
Carbohydrates: 47.8 g
Protein: 7.1 g
Fiber: 4.8 g

437.   Coconut Bacon

Preparation Time: 10 minutes
Cooking Time: 30 minutes
Servings: 2
Ingredients:
- 3 1/2 cups flaked coconut
- 1 tbsp pure maple syrup
- 1 tbsp water
- 2 tbsp liquid smoke
- 1 tbsp soy sauce
- 1 tsp smoked paprika (optional)

Directions:
1. Preheat the smoker at 325°F.
2. Take a large mixing bowl and combine liquid smoke, maple syrup, soy sauce, and water.

3. Pour flaked coconut over the mixture. Add it to a cooking sheet.
4. Place in the middle rack of the smoker.
5. Smoke it for 30 minutes and every 7-8 minutes, keep flipping the sides.
6. Serve and enjoy.

Nutrition:
Calories: 1244 Cal
Fat: 100 g
Carbohydrates: 70 g
Protein: 16 g
Fiber: 2 g

438. Garlic and Herb Smoke Potato

Preparation Time: 5 minutes
Cooking Time: 2 hours
Servings: 6
Ingredients:

- 1.5 pounds bag of Gemstone Potatoes
- 1/4 cup Parmesan, fresh grated
- For the Marinade
- 2 tbsp olive oil
- 6 garlic cloves, freshly chopped
- 1/2 tsp dried oregano
- 1/2 tsp dried basil
- 1/2 tsp dried dill
- 1/2 tsp salt
- 1/2 tsp dried Italian seasoning
- 1/4 tsp ground pepper

Directions:
1. Preheat the smoker to 225°F.
2. Wash the potatoes thoroughly and add them to a sealable plastic bag.

3. Add garlic cloves, basil, salt, Italian seasoning, dill, oregano, and olive oil to the zip lock bag. Shake.
4. Place in the fridge for 2 hours to marinate.
5. Next, take an Aluminum foil and put 2 tbsp of water along with the coated potatoes. Fold the foil so that the potatoes are sealed in
6. Place in the preheated smoker.
7. Smoke for 2 hours
8. Remove the foil and pour the potatoes into a bowl.
9. Serve with grated Parmesan cheese.

Nutrition:
Calories: 146 Cal
Fat: 6 g
Carbohydrates: 19 g
Protein: 4 g
Fiber: 2.1 g

439. Smoked Baked Beans

Preparation Time: 15 minutes
Cooking Time: 3 hours
Servings: 12
Ingredients:

- 1 medium yellow onion diced
- 3 jalapenos
- 56 oz pork and beans
- 3/4 cup barbeque sauce
- 1/2 cup dark brown sugar
- 1/4 cup apple cider vinegar
- 2 tbsp Dijon mustard

- 2 tbsp molasses

Directions:
1. Preheat the smoker to 250°F.
2. Pour the beans along with all the liquid in a pan. Add brown sugar, barbeque sauce, Dijon mustard, apple cider vinegar, and molasses.
3. Stir
4. Place the pan on one of the racks.
5. Smoke for 3 hours until thickened
6. Remove after 3 hours
7. Serve

Nutrition:
Calories: 214 Cal
Fat: 2 g
Carbohydrates: 42 g
Protein: 7 g
Fiber: 7 g

440. Mushrooms Stuffed with Crab Meat

Preparation Time: 20 Minutes
Cooking Time: 45 Minutes
Servings: 6
Ingredients:

- Six medium-sized Portobello mushrooms
- Extra virgin olive oil
- 1/3 Grated parmesan cheese cup
- Club Beat Staffing:
- 8 ounces fresh crab meat or canned or imitation crab meat
- Two tablespoons extra virgin olive oil
- 1/3 Chopped celery
- Chopped red peppers

- ½ cup chopped green onion
- ½ cup Italian bread crumbs

Directions:

1. Clean up the mushroom cap with a damp paper towel. Cut off the stem and save it.
2. Remove the brown gills from the bottom of the mushroom cap with a spoon and discard.
3. Prepare crab meat stuffing. If you are a fan of using canned crab meat, drain, rinse, and remove shellfish.
4. Put the crab mixture in each mushroom cap and make a mound in the center.
5. Sprinkle extra virgin olive oil and sprinkle parmesan cheese on each stuffed mushroom cap. Put the mushrooms in a 10 x 15-inch baking dish.
6. Use the pellets to set the wood pellet smoker and grill to indirect heating and preheat to 375 ° F.
7. Bake for 30-45 minutes until the filling becomes hot (165 degrees Fahrenheit as measured by an instant-read digital thermometer), and the mushrooms begin to release juice.

Nutrition:
Calories: 160
Carbs: 14g
Fat: 8g
Protein: 10g

441. Bacon-Wrapped with Asparagus

Preparation Time: 15 Minutes
Cooking Time: 30 Minutes
Servings: 6
Ingredients:

- 1-pound fresh thick asparagus (15-20 spears)
- Extra virgin olive oil
- Five sliced bacon
- One teaspoon of Western Love or salted pepper

Directions:

1. Cut off each wooden ends of the asparagus and make them all the same length.
2. Divide the asparagus into a bundle of three spears and split with olive oil. Wrap each other's bundle with a piece of bacon, then dust with seasonings or salt pepper for seasoning.
3. Set the wood pellet smoker and grill for indirect cooking.
4. Place a Teflon coated fiberglass mat on the grate (to prevent asparagus from sticking to the grated grate). Preheat to 400 degrees Fahrenheit using all types of pellets. The grill can be preheated during asparagus preparation.
5. Bake the asparagus wrapped in bacon for 25-30 minutes until the asparagus is soft and the bacon is cooked and crispy

Nutrition:
Calories: 71
Carbs: 1g
Fat: 4g
Protein: 6g

442. Brisket Baked Beans

Preparation Time: 20 Minutes
Cooking Time: 2 Hours
Servings: 10
Ingredients:

- Two tablespoons extra virgin olive oil
- One large diced onion
- One diced green pepper
- One red pepper diced
- 2 to 6 jalapeno peppers diced
- Texas-style brisket flat chopped three pieces
- One baked bean, like Bush's country-style baked beans
- One pork and beans
- One red kidney bean, rinse, drain
- 1 cup barbecue sauce like Sweet Baby Ray's barbecue sauce
- ½ cup stuffed brown sugar
- Three garlic, chopped
- Two teaspoons of mustard
- ½ teaspoon kosher salt
- ½ teaspoon black pepper

Directions:
1. Heat the skillet with olive oil over medium heat and add the diced onion, peppers, and jalapeno. Sauté the food for about 8-10 minutes until the onion is translucent.
2. In a 4-quart casserole dish, mix chopped brisket, baked beans, pork beans, kidney beans, cooked onions, peppers, barbecue sauce, brown sugar, garlic, mustard, salt, and black pepper.
3. Using the selected pellets, configure a wood pellet smoking grill for indirect cooking and preheat to 325 ° F. Cook the beans baked in the brisket for 1.5 to 2 hours until they become raw beans. Rest for 15 minutes before eating.

Nutrition:
Calories: 199
Carbs: 35g
Fat: 2g
Protein: 9g

443. Apple Wood Smoked Cheese

Preparation Time: 1 Hour and 15 Minutes
Cooking Time: 2 Hours
Servings: 6
Ingredients:
- Gouda
- Sharp cheddar
- Very sharp 3-year cheddar
- Monterey Jack
- Pepper jack
- Swiss

Directions:
1. According to the cheese block's shape, cut the cheese block into an easy-to-handle size (approximately 4 x 4-inch block) to promote smoke penetration.
2. Leave the cheese on the counter for one hour to form a very thin skin or crust, which acts as a heat barrier but allows smoke to penetrate.
3. Configure the wood pellet smoking grill for indirect heating and install a cold smokebox to prepare for cold smoke. Ensure that the louvers on the smoking box are fully open to allow moisture to escape from the box.
4. Preheat the wood pellet smoker and grill to 180 ° F or use apple pellets and smoke settings, if any, to get a milder smoke flavor.
5. Place the cheese on a Teflon-coated fiberglass non-stick grill mat and let cool for 2 hours.
6. Remove the smoked cheese and cool for 1 hour on the counter using a cooling rack.
7. After labeling the smoked cheese with a vacuum seal, refrigerate for two weeks or more, then smoke will permeate, and the cheese flavor will become milder.

Nutrition:
Calories: 102
Carbs: 0g
Fat: 9
Protein: 6g

444. Atomic Buffalo Turds

Preparation Time: 45 Minutes
Cooking Time: 2 Hours
Servings: 6
Ingredients:
- 10 Medium Jalapeno Pepper
- 8 ounces regular cream cheese at room temperature
- ¾Cup Monterey Jack and Cheddar Cheese Blend Shred (optional)
- One teaspoon smoked paprika
- One teaspoon garlic powder
- ½ teaspoon cayenne pepper
- Teaspoon red pepper flakes (optional)
- 20 smoky sausages
- Ten sliced bacon, cut in half

Directions:
1. Wear food service gloves when using them. Jalapeno peppers are washed vertically and sliced. Carefully remove seeds and veins using a spoon or paring knife and discard. Place Jalapeno on a grilled

vegetable tray and set aside.

2. In a small bowl, mix cream cheese, shredded cheese, paprika, garlic powder, cayenne pepper is used, and red pepper flakes if used, until thoroughly mixed.
3. Mix cream cheese with half of the jalapeno pepper.
4. Place the Little Smokiness sausage on half of the filled jalapeno pepper.
5. Wrap half of the thin bacon around half of each jalapeno pepper.
6. Fix the bacon to the sausage with a toothpick so that the pepper does not pierce. Place the ABT on the grill tray or pan.
7. Set the wood pellet smoker and grill for indirect cooking and preheat to 250 degrees Fahrenheit using hickory pellets or blends.
8. Suck jalapeno peppers at 250 ° F for about 1.5 to 2 hours until the bacon is cooked and crisp.
9. Remove the ABT from the grill and let it rest for 5 minutes before hors d'oeuvres.

Nutrition:
Calories: 131
Carbs: 1g
Fat: 12g
Protein: 5g

445. Jalapeno Poppers
Preparation Time: 15 Minutes
Cooking Time: 60 Minutes
Servings: 4
Ingredients:
- 6 Bacon slices halved
- 12 Jalapenos, medium
- 1 cup grated Cheese
- 8 ounces softened Cream cheese
- Two tablespoons Poultry seasoning

Directions:
1. Preheat the grill to 180F with a closed lid.
2. Cut the jalapenos lengthwise. Clean them from the ribs and seeds.
3. Mix the poultry seasoning, grated cheese, and cream. Fill each jalapeno with the mixture and wrap with one-half bacon. Place a toothpick to secure it. Place them on a baking sheet and smoke and grill for 20 minutes.
4. Increase the temperature of the grill to 375F. Cook for 30 minutes more.

Nutrition:
Calories: 60
Protein: 4g
Carbs: 2g
Fat: 8g

446. Smoked Guacamole
Preparation Time: 15 Minutes
Cooking Time: 30 Minutes
Servings: 8
Ingredients:

- 1/4 cup chopped Cilantro
- 7 Avocados, peeled and seeded
- ¼ cup chopped Onion, red
- ¼ cup chopped tomato
- Three ears corn
- One teaspoon of Chile Powder
- One teaspoon of Cumin
- Two tablespoons of Lime juice
- One tablespoon minced Garlic
- 1 Chile, poblano
- Black pepper and salt to taste

Directions:
1. Preheat the grill to 180F with a closed lid.
2. Smoke the avocado for 10 min.
3. Set the avocados aside and increase the temperature of the girl to high.
4. Once heated, grill the corn and chili—roast for 20 minutes.
5. Cut the corn. Set aside. Place the chili in a bowl. Cover it with a wrapper and let it sit for about 10 minutes. Peel the chili and dice. Add it to the kernels.
6. In a bowl, mash the avocados, leave few chunks. Add the remaining ingredients and mix.

7. Serve right away because it is best eaten fresh. Enjoy!

Nutrition:

Calories: 51

Protein: 1g

Carbs: 3g

Fat: 4.5g

447. Bacon BBQ Bites

Preparation Time: 10 Minutes

Cooking Time: 25 Minutes

Servings: 4

Ingredients:

- One tablespoon Fennel, ground
- ½ cup of Brown Sugar
- 1 lb. Slab Bacon, cut into cubes (1 inch)
- One tablespoon Black pepper
- Salt

Directions:

1. Take an aluminum foil and then fold in half. Once you do that, then turn the edges so that a rim is made. With a fork, make small holes on the bottom. In this way, the excess fat will escape and will make the bites crispy.
2. Preheat the grill to 350F with a closed lid.
3. In a bowl, combine the black pepper, salt, fennel, and sugar. Stir.
4. Place the pork in the seasoning mixture. Toss to coat—transfer on the foil.
5. Place the foil on the grill. Bake the mixture for 25 minutes, or until crispy and bubbly.

6. Serve and enjoy.

Nutrition:

Calories: 300

Protein: 27g

Carbs: 4g

Fat: 36g

448. Smoked Jerky

Preparation Time: 20 Minutes

Cooking Time: 6 Hours

Servings: 6

Ingredients:

- 1 Flank Steak (3lb.)
- ½ cup of Brown Sugar
- 1 cup of Bourbon
- ¼ cup Jerky rub
- Two tablespoons of Worcestershire sauce
- One can of Chipolata
- ½ cup Cider Vinegar

Directions:

1. Slice the steak into ¼ inch slices.
2. Combine the remaining ingredients in a bowl. Stir well.
3. Put the steak in an empty bag and add the marinade sauce. Marinade it in the fridge overnight.
4. Preheat the grill to 180F with a closed lid.
5. Remove the flank from the marinade. Place directly on a rack and the grill.
6. Smoke for 6 hours.
7. Cover them lightly for 1 hour before serving—store leftovers in the fridge.

Nutrition:

Calories: 105

Protein: 14g

Carbs: 4g

Fat: 3g

Chapter 31. Party recipes

449. Special Occasion's Dinner Cornish Hen

Preparation Time: 15 Minutes
Cooking Time: 1 Hour
Servings: 4
Ingredients:

- 4 Cornish game hens
- Four fresh rosemary sprigs
- 4 tbsp. butter, melted
- 4 tsp. chicken rub

Directions:

1. Set the temperature of Traeger Grill to 375 degrees F and preheat with a closed lid for 15 mins.
2. With paper towels, pat dries the hens.
3. Tuck the wings behind the backs, and with kitchen strings, tie the legs together.
4. Coat the outside of each hen with melted butter and sprinkle with rub evenly.
5. Stuff the cavity of each hen with a rosemary sprig.
6. Place the hens onto the grill and cook for about 50-60 mins.
7. Remove the hens from the grill and place onto a platter for about 10 mins.
8. Cut each hen into desired-sized pieces and serve.

Nutrition:
Calories per serving: 430
Carbohydrates: 2.1g
Protein: 25.4g
Fat: 33g
Sodium: 331mg
Fiber: 0.7g

450. Crispy and Juicy Chicken

Preparation Time: 15 Minutes
Cooking Time: 5 Hours
Servings: 6
Ingredients:

- ¾ C. dark brown sugar
- ½ C. ground espresso beans
- 1 tbsp. ground cumin
- 1 tbsp. ground cinnamon
- 1 tbsp. garlic powder
- 1 tbsp. cayenne pepper
- Salt and freshly ground black pepper
- 1 (4-lb.) whole chicken, neck and giblets removed

Directions:

1. Set the temperature of Traeger Grill to 200-225 degrees F and preheat with a closed lid for 15 mins.
2. In a bowl, mix brown sugar, ground espresso, spices, salt, and black pepper.
3. Rub the chicken with spice mixture generously.
4. Put the chicken onto the grill and cook for about 3-5 hours.
5. Remove chicken from grill and place onto a cutting board for about 10 mins before carving.
6. With a sharp knife, cut the chicken into desired sized pieces and serve.

Nutrition:
Calories per serving: 540
Carbohydrates: 20.7g
Protein: 88.3g
Fat: 9.6g
Sugar: 18.1g
Sodium: 226mg
Fiber: 1.2g

451. Ultimate Tasty Chicken

Preparation Time: 15 Minutes
Cooking Time: 3 Hours
Servings: 5
Ingredients:
For Brine:

- 1 C. brown sugar
- ½ C. kosher salt
- 16 C. water

For Chicken:

- 1 (3-lb.) whole chicken
- 1 tbsp. garlic, crushed
- 1 tsp. onion powder
- Salt and freshly ground black pepper
- One medium yellow onion, quartered
- Three whole garlic cloves, peeled
- One lemon, quartered
- 4-5 fresh thyme sprigs

Directions:

1. For the brine: in a bucket, dissolve brown sugar and kosher salt in water.
2. Place the chicken in brine and refrigerate overnight.
3. Set the temperature of Traeger Grill to 225 degrees F.

4. Preheat with closed lid for 15 mins.
5. Remove the chicken from the brine, and with paper towels, pat it dry.
6. In a small bowl, mix crushed garlic, onion powder, salt, and black pepper.
7. Rub the chicken with garlic mixture evenly.
8. Stuff the cavity of the chicken with onion, garlic cloves, lemon, and thyme.
9. With kitchen strings, tie the legs together.
10. Place the chicken onto grill and cook, covered for about 2½-3 hours.
11. Remove chicken from pallet grill and transfer onto a cutting board for about 10 mins before carving.
12. Cut the chicken into desired sized pieces and serve.

Nutrition:
Calories per serving: 641
Carbohydrates: 31.7g
Protein: 79.2g
Fat: 20.2g
Sugar: 29.3g
Sodium: 11500mg
Fiber: 0.6g

452. South-East-Asian Chicken Drumsticks

Preparation Time: 15 Minutes
Cooking Time: 2 Hours
Servings: 6
Ingredients:
- 1 C. fresh orange juice
- ¼ C. honey
- 2 tbsp. sweet chili sauce
- 2 tbsp. hoisin sauce
- 2 tbsp. fresh ginger, grated finely
- 2 tbsp. garlic, minced
- 1 tsp. Sriracha
- ½ tsp. sesame oil
- Six chicken drumsticks

Directions:
1. Set the condition of Traeger Grill to 225 degrees F.
2. Preheat with closed lid for 15 mins.
3. In a bowl, place all fixings except for chicken drumsticks and mix until well combined.
4. Reserve half of the honey mixture in a small bowl.
5. In the bowl of the remaining sauce, add drumsticks and mix well.
6. Arrange the chicken drumsticks onto the grill and cook for about 3 hours, basting with remaining sauce occasionally.
7. Serve hot.

Nutrition:
Calories per serving: 385
Carbohydrates: 22.7g
Protein: 47.6g
Fat: 10.5g
Sugar: 18.6g
Sodium: 270mg
Fiber: 0.6g

453. Glazed Chicken Thighs

Preparation Time: 15 Minutes
Cooking Time: 30 Minutes
Servings: 4
Ingredients:
- Two garlic cloves, minced
- ¼ C. honey
- 2 tbsp soy sauce
- ¼ tsp. red pepper flakes, crushed
- 4 (5-oz.) skinless, boneless chicken thighs
- 2 tbsp. olive oil
- 2 tsp. Sweet rub
- ¼ tsp. red chili powder
- Freshly ground black pepper, to taste

Directions:
1. Set the temperature of Traeger Grill to 400 degrees F and preheat with a closed lid for 15 mins.
2. In a small bowl, add garlic, honey, soy sauce, and red pepper flakes, and with a wire whisk, beat until well combined.
3. Coat chicken thighs with oil and season with sweet rub, chili powder, and black pepper generously.
4. Arrange the chicken drumsticks onto the grill and cook for about 15 mins per side.
5. In the last 4-5 mins of cooking, coat the thighs with garlic mixture.
6. Serve immediately.

Nutrition:
Calories per serving: 309
Carbohydrates: 18.7g
Protein: 32.3g

Fat: 12.1g
Sugar: 17.6g
Sodium: 504mg
Fiber: 0.2g

454. Cajun Chicken Breasts

Preparation Time: 10 Minutes
Cooking Time: 6 Hours
Servings: 6
Ingredients:

- 2 lb. skinless, boneless chicken breasts
- 2 tbsp. Cajun seasoning
- 1 C. BBQ sauce

Directions:

1. Set the temperature of Traeger Grill to 225 degrees F and preheat with a closed lid for 15 mins.
2. Rub the chicken breasts with Cajun seasoning generously.
3. Put the chicken breasts onto the grill and cook for about 4-6 hours.
4. During the last hour of cooking, coat the breasts with BBQ sauce twice.
5. Serve hot.

Nutrition:
Calories per serving: 252
Carbohydrates: 15.1g
Protein: 33.8g
Fat: 5.5g
Sugar: 10.9g
Sodium: 570mg
Fiber: 0.3g

455. BBQ Sauce Smothered Chicken Breasts

Preparation Time: 15 Minutes
Cooking Time: 30 Minutes
Servings: 4

Ingredients:

- 1 tsp. garlic, crushed
- 2 tbsp. spicy BBQ sauce
- ¼ C. olive oil
- 1 tbsp. sweet mesquite seasoning
- 1 tbsp. Worcestershire sauce
- Four chicken breasts
- 2 tbsp. regular BBQ sauce
- 2 tbsp. honey bourbon BBQ sauce

Directions:

1. Set the temperature of Traeger Grill to 450 degrees F and preheat with a closed lid for 15 mins.
2. In a large bowl, mix garlic, oil, Worcestershire sauce, and mesquite seasoning.
3. Brush chicken breasts with seasoning mixture evenly.
4. Place the chicken breasts onto the grill and cook for about 20-30 mins.
5. In the meantime, in a bowl, mix all 3 BBQ sauces.
6. In the last 4-5 mins of cooking, coat the breast with BBQ sauce mixture.
7. Serve hot.

Nutrition:
Calories per serving: 421
Carbohydrates: 10.1g
Protein: 41.2g
Fat: 23.3g
Sugar: 6.9g

Sodium: 763mg
Fiber: 0.2g

456. Thanksgiving Dinner Turkey

Preparation Time: 15 Minutes
Cooking Time: 4 Hours
Servings: 16
Ingredients:

- ½ lb. butter, softened
- 2 tbsp. fresh thyme, chopped
- 2 tbsp. fresh rosemary, chopped
- Six garlic cloves, crushed
- 1 (20-lb.) whole turkey, neck, and giblets removed
- Salt and freshly ground black pepper

Directions:

1. Set the temperature of Traeger Grill to 300 degrees F and preheat with closed lid for 15 mins, using charcoal.
2. Place butter, fresh herbs, garlic, salt, and black pepper and mix well in a bowl.
3. With your fingers, separate the turkey skin from the breast to create a pocket.
4. Stuff the breast pocket with a ¼-inch thick layer of the butter mixture.
5. Season the turkey with salt and black pepper evenly.
6. Arrange the turkey onto the grill and cook for 3-4 hours.

7. Remove the turkey from the grill and place onto a cutting board for about 15-20 mins before carving.

8. With a sharp knife, cut the turkey into desired-sized pieces and serve.

Nutrition:
Calories per serving: 965
Carbohydrates: 0.6g
Protein: 106.5g
Fat: 52g
Sugar: 0g
Sodium: 1916mg
Fiber: 0.2g

457. Perfectly Smoked Turkey Legs

Preparation Time: 15 Minutes
Cooking Time: 4 Hours
Servings: 6
Ingredients:
For Turkey:
- 3 tbsp. Worcestershire sauce
- 1 tbsp. canola oil
- Six turkey legs

For Rub:
- ¼ C. chipotle seasoning
- 1 tbsp. brown sugar
- 1 tbsp. paprika

For Sauce:
- 1 C. white vinegar
- 1 tbsp. canola oil
- 1 tbsp. chipotle BBQ sauce

Directions:
1. For turkey in a bowl, add the Worcestershire sauce and canola oil and mix well.

2. With your fingers, loosen the skin of legs.

3. With your fingers, coat the legs under the skin with an oil mixture.

4. In another bowl, mix rub ingredients.

5. Rub the spice mixture under and the outer surface of turkey legs generously.

6. Transfer the legs into a large sealable bag and refrigerate for about 2-4 hours.

7. Remove the refrigerator's turkey legs and set aside at room temperature for at least 30 mins before cooking.

8. Set the temperature of Traeger Grill to 200-220 degrees F and preheat with a closed lid for 15 mins.

9. In a small pan, mix all sauce ingredients on low heat and cook until warmed thoroughly, stirring continuously.

10. Place the turkey legs onto the grill cook for about 3½-4 hours, coating with sauce after every 45 mins.

11. Serve hot.

Nutrition:
Calories per serving: 430
Carbohydrates: 4.9g
Protein: 51.2g
Fat: 19.5g
Sugar: 3.9g
Sodium: 1474mg
Fiber: 0.5g

458. Texas-Style Brisket Rub

Preparation Time: 5 Minutes
Cooking Time: 10 Minutes
Servings: 1
Ingredients:
- 2 tsp Sugar
- 2 Tbsp Kosher salt
- 2 tsp Chili powder
- 2 Tbsp Black pepper
- 2 Tbsp Cayenne pepper
- 2 Tbsp Powdered garlic
- 2 tsp Grounded cumin
- 2 Tbsp Powdered onion
- 1/4 cup paprika, smoked

Directions:
1. Mix all the ingredients in a small bowl until it is well blended.

2. Transfer to an airtight jar or container. Store in a cool place.

Nutrition:
Calories: 18kcal
Carbs: 2g
Fat: 1g
Protein: 0.6g

459. Pork Dry Rub

Preparation Time: 5 Minutes
Cooking Time: 10 Minutes
Servings: 1 Cup
Ingredients:
- 1 Tbsp Kosher salt
- 2 Tbsp Powered onions
- 1 Tbsp Cayenne pepper
- 1 tsp Dried mustard
- 1/4 cup brown sugar

- 1 Tbsp Powdered garlic
- 1 Tbsp Powdered chili pepper
- 1/4 cup smoked paprika
- 2 Tbsp Black pepper

Directions:

1. Combine all the ingredients in a small bowl.
2. Transfer to an airtight jar or container.
3. Keep stored in a cool, dry place.

Nutrition:
Calories: 16kcal
Carbs: 3g
Fat:0.9g
Protein: 0.8g

460.   Texas Barbeque Rub

Preparation Time: 5 Minutes
Cooking Time: 10 Minutes
Servings: ½ cup
Ingredients:

- 1 tsp Sugar
- 1 Tbsp Seasoned salt
- 1 Tbsp Black pepper
- 1 tsp Chili powder
- 1 Tbsp Powdered onions
- 1 Tbsp Smoked paprika
- 1 tsp Sugar
- 1 Tbsp Powdered garlic

Directions:

1. Pour all the ingredients into a small bowl and mix thoroughly.
2. Keep stored in an airtight jar or container.

Nutrition:
Calories: 22kcal

Carbs: 2g
Fat: 0.2g
Protein: 0.6g

461. Barbeque Sauce

Preparation Time: 5 Minutes
Cooking Time: 10 Minutes
Servings: 2 Cups
Ingredients:

- 1/4 cup of water
- 1/4 cup red wine vinegar
- 1 Tbsp Worcestershire sauce
- 1 tsp Paprika
- 1 tsp Salt
- Tbsp Dried mustard
- 1 tsp black pepper
- 1 cup ketchup
- 1 cup brown sugar

Directions:

1. Pour all the ingredients into a food processor, one after the other.
2. Process until they are evenly mixed.
3. Transfer sauce to a close lid jar. Store in the refrigerator.

Nutrition:
Calories: 43kcal
Carbs: 10g
Fat: 0.3g
Protein: 0.9g

462.   Steak Sauce

Preparation Time: 5 Minutes
Cooking Time: 20 Minutes
Servings: ½ Cup
Ingredients:

- 1 Tbsp Malt vinegar
- 1/2 tsp Salt
- 1/2 tsp black pepper
- 1 Tbsp Tomato sauce
- 2 Tbsp brown sugar
- 1 tsp hot pepper sauce

- 2 Tbsp Worcestershire sauce
- 2 Tbsp Raspberry jam.

Directions:

1. Preheat your grill for indirect cooking at 150°F
2. Place a saucepan over grates, add all your ingredients, and allow to boil.
3. Reduce the temperature to Smoke and allow the sauce to simmer for 10 minutes or until sauce is thick.

Nutrition:
Calories: 62.1kcal
Carbs: 15.9g
Fat: 0.3g
Protein:0.1g

463.   Bourbon Whiskey Sauce

Preparation Time: 20 Minutes
Cooking Time: 25 Minutes
Servings: 3 Cups
Ingredients:

- 2 cups ketchup
- 1/4 cup Worcestershire sauce
- 3/4 cup bourbon whiskey
- 1/3 cup apple cider vinegar
- 1/2 onions, minced
- 1/4 cup of tomato paste
- 2 cloves of garlic, minced
- 1/2 tsp Black pepper
- 1/2 cup brown sugar
- 1/2 Tbsp Salt
- Hot pepper sauce to taste

- 1 Tbsp Liquid smoke flavoring

Directions:

1. Preheat your grill for indirect cooking at 150°F
2. Place a saucepan over grates, then add the whiskey, garlic, and onions.
3. Simmer until the onion is translucent. Then add the other ingredients and adjust the temperature to Smoke. Simmer for 20 minutes. For a smooth sauce, sieve.

Nutrition:
Calories: 107kcal
Carbs:16.6g
Fat: 1.8g
Protein:0.8g

464. Chicken Marinade

Preparation Time: 5 Minutes
Cooking Time: 30 Minutes
Servings: 3 Cups
Ingredients:

- halved chicken breast (bone and skin removed)
- 1 Tbsp Spicy brown mustard
- 2/3 cup of soy sauce
- 1 tsp Powdered garlic
- 2 Tbsp Liquid smoke flavoring
- 2/3 cup extra virgin olive oil
- 2/3 cup lemon juice
- 2 tsp Black pepper

Directions:

1. Mix all the ingredients in a large bowl.

2. Pour the chicken into the bowl and allow it to marinate for about 3-4hours in the refrigerator. Remove the chicken, then smoke, grill, or roast the chicken.

Nutrition:
Calories: 507kcal
Carbs:46.6g
Fat: 41.8g
Protein: 28g

465. Carne Asada Marinade

Preparation Time: 30 Minutes
Cooking Time: 1 Hour and 30 Minutes
Servings: 5 Cups111
Ingredients:

- 2 cloves garlic, chopped
- 1 tsp Lemon juice
- 1/2 cup extra virgin olive oil
- 1/2 tsp Salt
- 1/2 tsp Pepper

Directions:

1. Mix all your ingredients in a bowl.
2. Pour the beef into the bowl and allow to marinate for 2-3hours before grilling.

Nutrition:
Calories: 465kcal
Carbs: 26g
Fat: 15g
Protein: 28g

466. Grapefruit Juice Marinade

Preparation Time: 25 Minutes
Cooking Time: 35 Minutes
Servings: 3 Cups
Ingredients:

- 1/2 reduced-sodium soy sauce
- 3 cups grapefruit juice, unsweetened
- 1-1/2 lb. Chicken, bone and skin removed
- 1/4 brown sugar

Directions:

1. Thoroughly mix all your ingredients in a large bowl.
2. Add the chicken and allow it to marinate for 2-3 hours before grilling.

Nutrition:
Calories: 489kcal
Carbs: 21.3g
Fat: 12g
Protein: 24g

467. Steak Marinade

Preparation Time: 5 Minutes
Cooking Time: 10 Minutes
Servings: 2 Cups
Ingredients:

- 1 Tbsp Worcestershire sauce
- 2 Tbsp Red wine vinegar
- 1/2 cup barbeque sauce
- 3 Tbsp soy sauce
- 1/4 cup steak sauce
- 1 clove garlic (minced)
- 1 tsp Mustard
- Pepper and salt to taste

Directions:

1. Pour all the ingredients in a bowl and mix thoroughly.
2. Use immediately or keep refrigerated.

Nutrition:
Calories: 303kcal

Carbs: 42g
Fat: 10g
Protein:2.4g

468.   Dry Rub for Ribs

Preparation Time: 10 Minutes
Cooking Time: 0 Minutes
Servings: 8
Ingredients:

- three tablespoons brown sugar
- One and a half tablespoons paprika
- One and a half tablespoons salt
- one teaspoon garlic powder
- One and a half tablespoons ground black pepper

Directions:

1. Combine black pepper, brown sugar, salt, paprika, and garlic powder. Now, rub into the pork ribs. Let ribs to marinate whole night and then grill as you want.

Nutrition:
Calories: 16kcal
Carbs: 3g
Fat:0.9g
Protein: 0.8g

469.   Special BBQ Sauce

Preparation Time: 10 Minutes
Cooking Time: 0 Minutes
Servings: 32
Ingredients:

- One and half cups brown sugar
- One and a half cups ketchup

- one tablespoon Worcestershire sauce
- Two and a half tablespoons dry mustard
- Two teaspoons paprika
- Two teaspoons salt
- Half cup red wine vinegar
- Half cup waters
- One and a half teaspoons black pepper
- Two dashes hot pepper sauce

Directions:

- Take a blender; merge Worcestershire sauce, vinegar, brown sugar, water, and ketchup. Now, season with hot pepper sauce, paprika, mustard, pepper, and salt. Mix until it gets smooth.

Nutrition:
Calories: 43kcal
Carbs: 10g
Fat: 0.3g
Protein: 0.9g

470.   Special Teriyaki Marinade

Preparation Time: 10 Minutes
Cooking Time: 0 Minutes
Servings: 24
Ingredients:

- one cup soy sauce
- one cup water
- ¾ cup white sugar
- ¼ cup Worcestershire sauce
- 0three tablespoons distilled white vinegar
- three tablespoons vegetable oil

- one teaspoon grated fresh ginger
- 1/3 cup dried onion flakes
- two teaspoons garlic powder

Directions:

1. Take an intermediate bowl and combine sugar, onions, ginger, water, Worcestershire sauce, soy sauce, garlic powder, vinegar, and oil. Now, stir well until sugar dissolves completely

Nutrition:
Calories: 465kcal
Carbs: 26g
Fat: 15g
Protein: 28g

471. Grilled Pineapple with Chocolate Sauce

Preparation Time: 10 Minutes
Cooking Time: 25 Minutes
Servings: 8
Ingredients:

- 1pineapple
- 8 oz bittersweet chocolate chips
- 1/2 cup spiced rum
- 1/2 cup whipping cream
- 2tbsp light brown sugar

Directions:

1. Preheat pellet grill to 400°F.
2. De-skin, the pineapple, then slice the pineapple into 1 in cubes.
3. In a saucepan, combine chocolate chips. When chips begin to melt, add rum to the

saucepan. Continue to stir until combined, then add a splash of the pineapple's juice.

4. Add in whipping cream and continue to stir the mixture. Once the sauce is smooth and thickening, lower heat to simmer to keep warm.

5. Thread pineapple cubes onto skewers. Sprinkle skewers with brown sugar.

6. Place skewers on the grill grate. Grill for about 5 minutes per side, or until grill marks begin to develop.

7. Remove skewers from grill and allow to rest on a plate for about 5 minutes. Serve alongside warm chocolate sauce for dipping.

Nutrition:
Calories: 112.6
Fat: 0.5 g
Cholesterol: 0
Carbohydrate: 28.8 g
Fiber: 1.6 g
Sugar: 0.1 g
Protein: 0.4 g

472. Nectarine and Nutella Sundae

Preparation Time: 10 Minutes
Cooking Time: 25 Minutes
Servings: 4
Ingredients:

- 2nectarines halved and pitted
- 2tsp honey
- 4tbsp Nutella

- 4scoops vanilla ice cream
- 1/4 cup pecans, chopped
- Whipped cream, to top
- 4cherries, to top

Directions:
1. Preheat pellet grill to 400°F.
2. Slice nectarines in half and remove the pits.
3. Brush the inside (cut side) of each nectarine half with honey.
4. Place nectarines directly on the grill grate, cut side down— Cook for 5-6 minutes, or until grill marks develop.
5. Flip nectarines and cook on the other side for about 2 minutes.
6. Remove nectarines from the grill and allow it to cool.
7. Fill the pit cavity on each nectarine half with 1 tbsp Nutella.
8. Place one scoop of ice cream on top of Nutella. Top with whipped cream, cherries, and sprinkle chopped pecans. Serve and enjoy!

Nutrition:
Calories: 90
Fat: 3 g
Carbohydrate: 15g
Sugar: 13 g
Protein: 2 g

473. Cinnamon Sugar Donut Holes

Preparation Time: 10 Minutes
Cooking Time: 35 Minutes
Servings: 4
Ingredients:

- 1/2 cup flour
- 1tbsp cornstarch
- 1/2 tsp baking powder
- 1/8 tsp baking soda
- 1/8 tsp ground cinnamon
- 1/2 tsp kosher salt
- 1/4 cup buttermilk
- 1/4 cup sugar
- 11/2 tbsp butter, melted
- 1egg
- 1/2 tsp vanilla
- Topping
- 2tbsp sugar
- 1tbsp sugar
- 1tsp ground cinnamon

Directions:
1. Preheat pellet grill to 350°F.
2. In a medium bowl, combine flour, cornstarch, baking powder, baking soda, ground cinnamon, and kosher salt. Whisk to combine.
3. In a separate bowl, combine buttermilk, sugar, melted butter, egg, and vanilla. Whisk until the egg is thoroughly combined.
4. Pour wet mixture into the flour mixture and stir. Stir just until combined, careful not to overwork the mixture.

5. Spray mini muffin tin with cooking spray.
6. Spoon 1 tbsp of donut mixture into each mini muffin hole.
7. Place the tin on the pellet grill grate and bake for about 18 minutes, or until a toothpick can come out clean.
8. Remove muffin tin from the grill and let rest for about 5 minutes.
9. In a small bowl, combine 1 tbsp sugar and 1 tsp ground cinnamon.
10. Melt 2 tbsp of butter in a glass dish. Dip each donut hole in the melted butter, then mix and toss with cinnamon sugar. Place completed donut holes on a plate to serve.

Nutrition:
Calories: 190
Fat: 17 g
Carbohydrate: 21 g
Fiber: 1 g
Sugar: 8 g
Protein: 3 g

474. Pellet Grill Chocolate Chip Cookies

Preparation Time: 20 Minutes
Cooking Time: 45 Minutes
Servings: 12
Ingredients:
- 1cup salted butter softened
- 1cup of sugar
- 1cup light brown sugar
- 2tsp vanilla extract
- 2large eggs
- 3cups all-purpose flour
- 1tsp baking soda
- 1/2 tsp baking powder
- 1tsp natural sea salt
- 2cups semi-sweet chocolate chips or chunks

Directions:
1. Preheat pellet grill to 375°F.
2. Line a large baking sheet with parchment paper and set aside.
3. In a medium bowl, mix flour, baking soda, salt, and baking powder. Once combined, set aside.
4. In stand mixer bowl, combine butter, white sugar, and brown sugar until combined. Beat in eggs and vanilla. Beat until fluffy.
5. Mix in dry ingredients, continue to stir until combined.
6. Add chocolate chips and mix thoroughly.
7. Roll 3 tbsp of dough at a time into balls and place them on your cookie sheet. Evenly space them apart, with about 2-3 inches in between each ball.
8. Place cookie sheet directly on the grill grate and bake for 20-25 minutes until the cookies' outside is slightly browned.
9. Remove from grill and allow to rest for 10 minutes. Serve and enjoy!

Nutrition:
Calories: 120
Fat: 4
Cholesterol: 7.8 mg
Carbohydrate: 22.8 g
Fiber: 0.3 g
Sugar: 14.4 g
Protein: 1.4 g

475. Delicious Donuts on a Grill

Preparation Time: 5 Minutes
Cooking Time: 10 Minutes
Servings: 6
Ingredients:
- 1-1/2 cups sugar, powdered
- 1/3 cup whole milk
- 1/2 teaspoon vanilla extract
- 16 ounces of biscuit dough, prepared
- Oil spray, for greasing
- 1cup chocolate sprinkles, for sprinkling

Directions:
1. Take a medium bowl and mix sugar, milk, and vanilla extract.
2. Combine well to create a glaze.
3. Set the glaze aside for further use.
4. Place the dough onto the flat, clean surface.
5. Flat the dough with a rolling pin.
6. Use a ring mold, about an inch, and cut the hole in each round dough's center.

7. Place the dough on a plate and refrigerate for 10 minutes.
8. Open the grill and install the grill grate inside it.
9. Close the hood.
10. Now, select the grill from the menu, and set the temperature to medium.
11. Set the time to 6 minutes.
12. Select start and begin preheating.
13. Remove the dough from the refrigerator and coat it with cooking spray from both sides.
14. When the unit beeps, the grill is preheated; place the adjustable amount of dough on the grill grate.
15. Close the hood, and cook for 3 minutes.
16. After 3 minutes, remove donuts and place the remaining dough inside.
17. Cook for 3 minutes.
18. Once all the donuts are ready, sprinkle chocolate sprinkles on top.
19. Enjoy.

Nutrition:
Calories: 400
Total Fat: 11g
Cholesterol: 1mg
Sodium: 787mg
Total Carbohydrate: 71.3g
Dietary Fiber 0.9g
Total Sugars: 45.3g
Protein: 5.7g

476. Smoked Pumpkin Pie

Preparation Time: 10 Minutes
Cooking Time: 50 Minutes
Servings: 8
Ingredients:

- 1tbsp cinnamon
- 1-1/2 tbsp pumpkin pie spice
- 15oz can pumpkin
- 14oz can sweetened condensed milk
- 2beaten eggs
- 1unbaked pie shell
- Topping: whipped cream

Directions:
1. Preheat your smoker to 325oF.
2. Place a baking sheet, rimmed, on the smoker upside down, or use a cake pan.
3. Combine all your ingredients in a bowl, large, except the pie shell, then pour the mixture into a pie crust.
4. Place the pie on the baking sheet and smoke for about 50-60 minutes until a knife comes out clean when inserted. Make sure the center is set.
5. Remove and cool for about 2 hours or refrigerate overnight.
6. Serve with a whipped cream dollop and enjoy it!

Nutrition:
Calories: 292
Total Fat: 11g
Total Carbs: 42g
Protein: 7g

Sugars: 29g
Fiber: 5g
Sodium: 168mg

477. Wood Pellet Smoked Nut Mix

Preparation Time: 15 Minutes
Cooking Time: 20 Minutes
Servings: 12
Ingredients:

- 3cups mixed nuts (pecans, peanuts, almonds, etc.)
- 1/2 tbsp brown sugar
- 1tbsp thyme, dried
- 1/4 tbsp mustard powder
- 1tbsp olive oil, extra-virgin

Directions:
1. Preheat your pellet grill to 250oF with the lid closed for about 15 minutes.
2. Combine all ingredients in a bowl, large, then transfer into a cookie sheet lined with parchment paper.
3. Place the cookie sheet on a grill and grill for about 20 minutes.
4. Remove the nuts from the grill and let cool.
5. Serve and enjoy.

Nutrition:
Calories: 249
Total Fat: 21.5g
Saturated Fat: 3.5g
Total Carbs: 12.3g
Net Carbs: 10.1g
Protein: 5.7g
Sugars: 5.6g
Fiber: 2.1g
Sodium: 111mg

478. Grilled Peaches and Cream

Preparation Time: 15 Minutes
Cooking Time: 8 Minutes
Servings: 8
Ingredients:

- 4halved and pitted peaches
- 1tbsp vegetable oil
- 2tbsp clover honey
- 1cup cream cheese, soft with honey and nuts

Directions:

1. Preheat your pellet grill to medium-high heat.
2. Coat the peaches lightly with oil and place on the grill pit side down.
3. Grill for about 5 minutes until nice grill marks on the surfaces.
4. Turn over the peaches, then drizzle with honey.
5. Spread and cream cheese dollop where the pit was and grill for additional 2-3 minutes until the filling becomes warm.
6. Serve immediately.

Nutrition:
Calories: 139
Total Fat: 10.2g
Total Carbs: 11.6g
Protein: 1.1g
Sugars: 12g
Sodium: 135mg

479. Berry Cobbler on a Pellet Grill

Preparation Time: 15 Minutes
Cooking Time: 35 Minutes
Servings: 8
Ingredients:
For fruit filling

- 3cups frozen mixed berries
- 1lemon juice
- 1cup brown sugar
- 1tbsp vanilla extract
- 1bsp lemon zest, finely grated
- A pinch of salt

For cobbler topping

- 1-1/2 cups all-purpose flour
- 1-1/2 tbsp baking powder
- 3tbsp sugar, granulated
- 1/2 tbsp salt
- 8tbsp cold butter
- 1/2 cup sour cream
- 2tbsp raw sugar

Directions:

1. Set your pellet grill on "smoke" for about 4-5 minutes with the lid open until fire establishes, and your grill starts smoking.
2. Preheat your grill to 350 for about 10-15 minutes with the grill lid closed.
3. Meanwhile, combine frozen mixed berries, Lemon juice, brown sugar, vanilla, lemon zest, and salt pinch. Transfer into a skillet and let the fruit sit and thaw.
4. Mix flour, baking powder, sugar, and salt in a bowl, medium. Cut cold butter into peas sizes using a pastry blender, then add to the mixture. Stir to mix everything.
5. Stir in sour cream until dough starts coming together.
6. Pinch small pieces of dough and place over the fruit until fully covered. Splash the top with raw sugar.
7. Now place the skillet directly on the grill grate, close the lid, cook for about 35 minutes until juices bubble, and a golden-brown dough topping.
8. Remove the skillet from the pellet grill and cool for several minutes.
9. Scoop and serve warm.

Nutrition:
Calories: 371
Total Fat: 13g
Total Carbs: 60g
Protein: 3g
Sugars: 39g
Fiber: 2g
Sodium: 269mg

480. Pellet Grill Apple Crisp

Preparation Time: 20 Minutes
Cooking Time: 60 Minutes
Servings: 15
Ingredients:

- Apples
- Ten large apples
- 1/2 cup flour
- 1cup sugar, dark brown
- 1/2 tbsp cinnamon
- 1/2 cup butter slices
- Crisp
- 3cups oatmeal, old-fashioned

- 1-1/2 cups softened butter, salted
- 1-1/2 tbsp cinnamon
- 2cups brown sugar

Directions:

1. Preheat your grill to 350.
2. Wash, peel, core, and dice the apples into cubes, medium-size
3. Mix flour, dark brown sugar, and cinnamon, then toss with your apple cubes.
4. Spray a baking pan, 10x13", with cooking spray, then place apples inside. Top with butter slices.
5. Mix all crisp ingredients in a medium bowl until well combined. Place the mixture over the apples.
6. Place on the grill and cook for about 1-hour checking after every 15-20 minutes to ensure cooking is even. Do not place it on the hottest grill part.
7. Remove and let sit for about 20-25 minutes
8. It's very warm.

Nutrition:
Calories: 528
Total Fat: 26g
Total Carbs: 75g
Protein: 4g
Sugars: 51g
Fiber: 5g
Sodium: 209mg

481. Fromage Macaroni and Cheese

Preparation Time: 30 Minutes
Cooking Time: 1 Hour
Servings: 8
Ingredients:

- ¼ c. all-purpose flour
- ½ stick butter
- Butter, for greasing
- One-pound cooked elbow macaroni
- One c. grated Parmesan
- 8 ounces cream cheese
- Two c. shredded Monterey Jack
- 3 t. garlic powder
- Two t. salt
- One t. pepper
- Two c. shredded Cheddar, divided
- Three c. milk

Directions:

1. Add the butter to a pot and melt. Mix in the flour. Stir constantly for a minute. Mix in the pepper, salt, garlic powder, and milk. Let it boil.
2. After lowering the heat, let it simmer for about 5 mins, or until it has thickened. Remove from the heat.
3. Mix in the cream cheese, parmesan, Monterey Jack, and 1 ½ c. of cheddar. Stir everything until melted. Fold in the pasta.
4. Add wood pellets to your smoker and keep your cooker's startup procedure. Preheat your smoker, with your lid closed, until it reaches 225.
5. Butter a 9" x 13" baking pan. Pour the macaroni mixture into the pan and lay on the grill. Cover and allow it to smoke for an hour, or until it has become bubbly. Top the macaroni with the rest of the cheddar during the last
6. Serve.

Nutrition:
Calories: 180
Carbs: 19g
Fat: 8g
Protein: 8g

482. Spicy Barbecue Pecans

Preparation Time: 15 Minutes
Cooking Time: 1 Hour
Servings: 2
Ingredients:

- 2 ½ t. garlic powder
- 16 ounces raw pecan halves
- One t. onion powder
- One t. pepper
- Two t. salt
- One t. dried thyme
- Butter, for greasing
- 3 T. melted butter

Directions:

1. Add wood pellets to your smoker and follow your cooker's startup method.
2. Preheat your smoker, with your lid closed, until it reaches 225.

3. Cover and smoke for an hour, flipping the nuts one. Make sure the nuts are toasted and heated. They should be removed from the grill.
4. Set aside to cool and dry.

Nutrition:
Calories: 150
Carbs: 16g
Fat: 9g
Protein: 1g

483. Blackberry Pie

Preparation Time: 10 Minutes
Cooking Time: 40 Minutes
Servings: 8
Ingredients:

- Butter, for greasing
- ½ c. all-purpose flour
- ½ c. milk
- Two pints blackberries
- Two c. sugar, divided
- One box of refrigerated piecrusts
- One stick melted butter
- One stick of butter
- Vanilla ice cream

Directions:

1. Add wood pellets to your smoker and follow your cooker's startup method.
2. Preheat your smoker, with your lid closed, until it reaches 375.
3. Unroll the second pie crust and lay it over the skillet.
4. Lower the lid, then smoke for 15 to 20 minutes or until it is browned and bubbly.

5. Serve the hot pie with some vanilla ice cream.

Nutrition:
Calories: 100
Carbs: 10g
Fat: 0g
Protein: 15g

484. S'mores Dip

Preparation Time: 0 Minutes
Cooking Time: 15 Minutes
Servings: 6-8
Ingredients:

- 12 ounces semisweet chocolate chips
- ¼ c. milk
- Two T. melted salted butter
- 16 ounces marshmallows
- Apple wedges
- Graham crackers

Directions:

1. Add wood pellets to your smoker and get your cooker's startup procedure. Preheat your smoker, with your lid closed, until it reaches 450.
2. Put a cast-iron skillet on your grill and add in the milk and melted butter. Stir together for a minute.
3. Cover, and let it smoke for five to seven minutes. The marshmallows should be toasted lightly.
4. Take the skillet off the heat and serve with apple wedges and graham crackers.

Nutrition:
Calories: 90

Carbs: 15g
Fat: 3g
Protein: 1g

485. Bacon Chocolate Chip Cookies

Preparation Time: 10 Minutes
Cooking Time: 30 Minutes
Servings: 24
Ingredients:

- Eight slices of cooked and crumbled bacon
- 2 ½ t. apple cider vinegar
- One t. vanilla
- Two c. semisweet chocolate chips
- Two-room temp eggs
- 1 ½ t. baking soda
- One c. granulated sugar
- ½ t. salt
- Two ¾ c. all-purpose flour
- One c. light brown sugar
- 1 ½ stick softened butter

Directions:

1. Mix the flour, baking soda, and salt.
2. Cream the sugar and the butter together. Then lower the speed. Add in the eggs, vinegar, and vanilla.
3. Still on low, slowly add in the flour mixture, bacon pieces, and chocolate chips.
4. Add wood pellets to your smoker and follow your cooker's startup method.

5. Preheat your smoker, with your lid closed, until it reaches 375.
6. Place some parchment on a baking sheet and drop a teaspoonful of cookie batter on the baking sheet. Let them cook on the grill,
7. covered, for approximately 12 minutes or until they are browned. Enjoy.

Nutrition:
Calories: 167
Carbs: 21g
Fat: 9g
Protein: 2g

486. Cinnamon Sugar Pumpkin Seeds

Preparation Time: 12 Minutes
Cooking Time: 30 Minutes
Servings: 8-12
Ingredients:
- Two T. sugar
- seeds from a pumpkin
- One t. cinnamon
- Two T. melted butter

Directions:
1. Add wood pellets to your smoker and follow your cooker's startup operation. Preheat your smoker, with your lid closed, until it reaches 350.
2. Clean the seeds and toss them in the melted butter. Add them to the sugar and cinnamon. Spread them out on a baking sheet, place on the grill, and smoke for 25 minutes.
3. Serve.

Nutrition:
Calories: 160
Carbs: 5g
Fat: 12g
Protein: 7g

487. Feta Cheese Stuffed Meatballs

Preparation Time: 12 Minutes
Cooking Time: 35 Minutes
Servings: 6
Ingredients:
- Pepper
- Salt
- ¾ c. Feta cheese
- ½ t. thyme
- Two t. chopped oregano
- Zest of one lemon
- One-pound ground pork
- One-pound ground beef
- One T. olive oil

Directions:
1. Place the pepper, salt, thyme, oregano, olive oil, lemon zest, and ground meats into a large bowl.
2. Combine the ingredients thoroughly using your hands.
3. Cut the Feta into little cubes and begin making the meatballs. Take a half tablespoon of the meat mixture and roll it around a piece of cheese. Continue until all meat has been used.
4. Add wood pellets to your smoker and follow your cooker's startup procedure.

5. Preheat your smoker, with your lid closed, until it reaches 350.
6. Brush the meatballs with more olive oil and put onto the grill. Grill for ten minutes until browned.

Nutrition:
Calories: 390
Carbs: 8g
Fat: 31g
Protein: 20g

488. Butternut Squash

Preparation Time: 30 Minutes
Cooking Time: 2 Hours
Servings: 4-6
Ingredients:
- Brown sugar
- Maple syrup
- 6 T. butter
- Butternut squash

Directions:
1. Add wood pellets to your smoker and follow your cooker's startup procedure. Preheat your smoke, with your lid closed, until it reaches 300.
2. Place each half of the squash onto aluminum foil.
3. Increase temperature to 400 and place onto the grill for another 35 minutes.
4. Carefully unwrap each half, making sure to reserve juices in the bottom. Place onto serving platter and drizzle juices over each half. Use a spoon to scoop out and enjoy.

Nutrition:
Calories: 82
Carbs: 22g
Fat: 0g
Protein: 2g

489. Apple Cobbler

Preparation Time: 20 Minutes
Cooking Time: 1 Hour and 30 Minutes
Servings: 8
Ingredients:

- 8 Granny Smith apples
- One c. sugar
- Two eggs
- Two t. baking powder
- Two c. plain flour
- 1 ½ c. sugar

Directions:

1. Peel and quarter apples, place into a bowl. Add in the cinnamon and one c. sugar. Stir well to coat and let it sit for one hour.
2. Add wood pellets to your smoker and follow your cooker's startup form. Preheat your smoker, with your lid closed, until it reaches 350.
3. Place apples into a Dutch oven. Add the crumble mixture on top and drizzle with melted butter.
4. Place on the grill and cook for 50 minutes.

Nutrition:
Calories: 152
Carbs: 26g
Fat: 5g
Protein: 1g

490. Pineapple Cake

Preparation Time: 20 Minutes
Cooking Time: 60 Minutes
Servings: 8
Ingredients:

- One c. sugar
- One T. baking powder
- One c. buttermilk
- Two eggs
- ½ t. salt
- One jar maraschino cherry
- One stick butter, divided
- ¾ c. brown sugar
- One can pineapple slice
- 1 ½ c. flour

Directions:

1. Add wood pellets to your smoker and observe your cooker's startup procedure. Preheat your smoker, with your lid closed, until it reaches 350.
2. Take a medium-sized cast-iron skillet and melt one half stick butter. Be sure to coat the entire skillet. Sprinkle brown sugar into a cast-iron skillet.
3. Lay the sliced pineapple on top of the brown sugar. Place a cherry into the middle of each pineapple ring.
4. Mix the salt, baking powder, flour, and sugar. Add in the eggs; one-half stick melted butter and buttermilk. Whisk to combine.
5. Put the cake on the grill and cook for an hour.
6. Take off from the grill and let it sit for ten minutes. Flip onto a serving platter.

Nutrition:
Calories: 165
Carbs: 40g
Fat: 0g
Protein: 1g

491. Ice Cream Bread

Preparation Time: 10 Minutes
Cooking Time: 1 Hour
Servings: 12-16
Ingredients:

- 1 ½ quart full-fat butter pecan ice cream, softened
- One t. salt
- Two c. semisweet chocolate chips
- One c. sugar
- One stick melted butter
- Butter, for greasing
- 4 c. self-rising flour

Directions:

1. Add wood pellets to your smoker and follow your cooker's startup program. Preheat your smoker, with your lid closed, until it reaches 350.
2. Set the cake on the grill, cover, and smoke for 50 minutes to an hour. A toothpick should come out clean.
3. Take the pan off of the grill. For 10 mins., cool the bread.

Nutrition:
Calories: 135

Carbs: 0g

Fat: 0g

Protein: 0g

492. Mediterranean Meatballs

Preparation Time: 15 Minutes

Cooking Time: 35 Minutes

Servings: 8

Ingredients:

- Pepper
- Salt
- One t. vinegar
- Two T. olive oil
- Two eggs
- One chopped onion
- One soaked slice of bread
- ½ t. cumin
- One T. chopped basil
- 1 ½ T. chopped parsley
- 2 ½ pounds ground beef

Directions:

1. Use your hands to combine everything until thoroughly combined. If needed, when forming meatballs, dip your hands into some water. Shape into 12 meatballs.
2. Add wood pellets to your smoker.
3. Preheat your smoker, with your lid closed, until it reaches 380.
4. Place the meatballs onto the grill and cook on all sides for eight minutes. Take off the grill and let sit for five minutes.
5. Serve with favorite condiments or a salad.

Nutrition:

Calories: 33

Carbs: 6g

Fat: 0g

Protein: 1g

493. Greek Meatballs

Preparation Time: 10 Minutes

Cooking Time: 40 Minutes

Servings: 6

Ingredients:

- Pepper
- Salt
- Two chopped green onions
- One T. almond flour
- Two eggs
- ½ pound ground pork
- 2 ½ pound ground beef

Directions:

1. Mix all the ingredients using your hands until everything is incorporated evenly. Form mixture into meatballs until all meat is used.
2. Add wood pellets to your smoker and follow your cooker's startup procedure. Preheat your smoker, with your lid closed, until it reaches 380.
3. Brush the meatballs with olive oil and place onto the grill—Cook for ten minutes on all sides.

Nutrition:

Calories: 161

Carbs: 10g

Fat: 6g

Protein: 17g

Chapter 32. Light recipes (without heavy ingredients)

494. Simple Wood Pellet Smoked Pork Ribs

Preparation Time: 15 Minutes
Cooking Time: 5 Hours
Servings: 7
Ingredients:
- Three rack baby back ribs
- 3/4 cup pork and poultry rub
- 3/4 cup Que BBQ Sauce

Directions:
1. Peel the membrane from the backside of the ribs and trim any fat.
2. Season the pork generously with the rub.
3. Set the wood pellet grill to 180°F and preheat for 15 minutes with the lid closed.
4. Place the pork ribs on the grill and smoke them for 5 hours.
5. Remove it from the grill and wrap them in a foil with the BBQ sauce.
6. Place back the pork and increase the temperature to 350°F—Cook for 45 more minutes.
7. Remove the pork from the grill and let it rest for 20 minutes before serving. Enjoy.

Nutrition:
Calories 762
Total Fat 57g
Saturated Fat 17g
Total Carbs 23g
Net Carbs 22.7g
Protein 39g
Sugar 18g
Fiber 0.5g
Sodium: 737mg
Potassium 618mg

495. Wood Pellet Grilled Bacon

Preparation Time: 30 Minutes
Cooking Time: 25 Minutes
Servings: 6
Ingredients:
- 1 lb. bacon, thickly cut

Directions:
1. Preheat your wood pellet grill to 375°F.
2. Line a baking sheet with parchment paper, then place the bacon on it in a single layer.
3. Close the lid and bake for 20 minutes. Flip over, close the top, and bake for an additional 5 minutes.
4. Serve with the favorite side and enjoy it.

Nutrition:
Calories 315
Total fat 14g
Saturated fat 10g
Protein 9g
Sodium: 500mg

496. Wood Pellet Grilled Pork Chops

Preparation Time: 20 Minutes
Cooking Time: 10 Minutes
Servings: 6
Ingredients:
- Six pork chops, thickly cut
- BBQ rub

Directions:
1. Preheat the wood pellet to 450°F.
2. Season the pork chops generously with the BBQ rub. Place the pork chops on the grill and cook for 6 minutes or until the internal temperature reaches 145°F.
3. Remove from the grill and let sit for 10 minutes before serving.
4. Enjoy.

Nutrition:
Calories 264
Total fat 13g
Saturated fat 6g
Total Carbs 4g
Net Carbs 1g
Protein 33g
Fiber 3g
Sodium: 66mg

497. Wood Pellet Blackened Pork Chops

Preparation Time: 5 Minutes
Cooking Time: 20 Minutes
Servings: 6
Ingredients:
- Six pork chops
- 1/4 cup blackening seasoning
- Salt and pepper to taste

Directions:
1. Preheat your grill to 375°F.
2. Meanwhile, generously season the pork chops with the blackening seasoning, salt, and pepper.

3. Place the pork chops on the grill and close the lid.

4. Let grill for 8 minutes, then flip the chops. Cook until the internal temperature reaches 142°F.

5. Remove the chops from the grill and let rest for 10 minutes before slicing.

6. Serve and enjoy.

Nutrition:
Calories 333
Total fat 18g
Saturated fat 6g
Total Carbs 1g
Protein 40g,
Fiber 1g
Sodium: 3175mg

498. Wood Pellet Togarashi Pork Tenderloin

Preparation Time: 5 Minutes
Cooking Time: 25 Minutes
Servings: 6
Ingredients:

- 1 Pork tenderloin
- 1/2tbsp kosher salt
- 1/4 cup Togarashi seasoning

Directions:

1. Cut any excess silver skin from the pork and sprinkle with salt to taste. Rub generously with the togarashi seasoning

2. Place in a preheated oven at 400°F for 25 minutes or until the internal temperature reaches 145°F.

3. Remove from the grill and let rest for 10

minutes before slicing and serving.

4. Enjoy.

Nutrition:
Calories 390
Total fat 13g
Saturated fat 6g
Total Carbs 4g
Net Carbs 1g
Protein 33g
Sugar 0g
Fiber 3g
Sodium: 66mg

499. Wood Pellet Pulled Pork

Preparation Time: 15 Minutes
Cooking Time: 12 Hours
Servings: 12
Ingredients:

- 8 lb. pork shoulder roast, bone-in
- BBQ rub
- 3 cups apple cider, dry hard

Directions:

1. Fire up the wood pellet grill and set it to smoke.

2. Meanwhile, rub the pork with BBQ rub on all sides, then place it on the grill grates. Cook for 5 hours, flipping it every 1 hour.

3. Increase the heat to 225°F and continue cooking for 3 hours directly on the grate.

4. Transfer the pork to a foil pan and place the apple cider at the bottom of the pan.

5. Cook until the internal temperature reaches 200°F then remove it from the grill. Wrap the pork loosely with foil,

then let it rest for 1 hour.

6. Remove the fat layer and use forks to shred it.

7. Serve and enjoy.

Nutrition:
Calories 912
Total fat 65g
Saturated fat 24g
Total Carbs 7g
Net Carbs 7g
Protein 70g
Sugar 6g
Fiber 0g
Sodium: 208mg

500. Quick Rosemary Garlic Rub

Preparation Time: 5 Minutes
Cooking Time: 0 Minutes
Servings: 4
Ingredients:

- one tablespoon ground black pepper
- one tablespoon dried rosemary
- eight cloves garlic
- 1/3 cup olive oil
- one tablespoon kosher salt
- three tablespoons chopped fresh rosemary

Directions:

1. Take a little bowl and merge fresh rosemary, kosher salt, black pepper, garlic, and dried rosemary. Just slowly stir in olive oil to make a thick paste. Now, rub into meat before grilling.

Nutrition:
Calories: 489kcal
Carbs: 21.3g
Fat: 12g
Protein: 24g

501. Easy Jerk Seasoning

Preparation Time: 10 Minutes
Cooking Time: 0 Minutes
Servings: 1
Ingredients:

- Two tablespoons dried minced onion
- Two and a half teaspoons dried thyme
- two teaspoons ground allspice
- Half teaspoon cayenne pepper
- Half teaspoon salts
- Two tablespoons vegetable oil
- two teaspoons ground black pepper
- half teaspoon ground cinnamon

Directions:
1. Take a little bowl and stir thyme, ground black pepper, salt, dried onion, allspice, cayenne pepper, and cinnamon. Now, coat meat lightly with oil and then rub seasoning onto meat.

Nutrition:
Calories: 43kcal
Carbs: 10g
Fat: 0.3g
Protein: 0.9g

502. Grilled Sausage Ala Carte

Preparation Time: 5 minutes
Cooking Time: 30-45 minutes

Servings: 1
Ingredients:

- lbs. hot Italian sausage
- 2 bottles (18 oz. each) barbecue sauce
- cups packed brown sugar

Directions:
1. Divide the sausages between 2 ungreased 13" x 9" baking dishes.
2. Combine the barbecue sauce and brown sugar.
3. Pour over the sausages, and make sure to coat thoroughly.
4. Bake uncovered at 350 degrees for 35 to 40 minutes or until the sauce has thickened.
5. Stir gently for 1 minute and then let it rest.

Nutrition:
Calories: 439 Cal
Fat: 31 g
Carbohydrates: 23 g
Protein: 16 g
Fiber: 0 g

503. Pigs in a Blanket

Preparation Time: 10 minutes
Cooking Time: 15 minutes
Servings: 8
Ingredients:

- Hot dogs, 8
- slices good-quality cheddar cheese, each cut into 6 strips
- 1 can (8 oz) refrigerated crescent dinner rolls (or better yet, make your own pastry)

Directions:

1. Heat the oven to 375°F. Slit the ends of hot dogs, 1/2 inch in width. Insert 3 strips of cheese into each slit.
2. Separate the dough into triangles. Wrap the dough triangle around each hot dog. Place on an ungreased cookie sheet, cheese side up.
3. Bake at 375°F for 12 to 15 minutes or until golden brown.

Nutrition:
Calories: 439 Cal
Fat: 31 g
Carbohydrates: 23 g
Protein: 16 g
Fiber: 0 g

Chapter 33.   Conclusion

So now that we have reached the end of the book, I am very optimistic that you are well acquainted with some of the finest smoker grill recipes which will make you a pro at grilling, BBQ, and cooking in general.

Sometimes seeing so many recipes briefly can be very overwhelming. So, go through the book as and when needed and make sure to follow the instructions in the recipe thoroughly.

You have obtained every secret to cooking with a Wood Pellet Smoker-Grill, and you have tons of great recipes to try again and again. All you need to do is follow the ingredients and instructions accurately. You have many kinds of recipes, so you can try a new dish every day and test your cooking skills. Practicing will improve your ability to obtain great flavors from this smoker-grill.

When you put a smoker to right use and use the best kind of pellets, the flavor induced is so good that not only you but every guest who ends up eating the food is sure to be amazed at the exceptional culinary skills which you possess. I have put in a lot of love, effort, and time in this book to make sure that every recipe is as good as I wanted it to be. Of course, like always, most recipes allow you to do a little makeshift if suppose you are missing out on some ingredients. However, to get the best results, we want you to stick to the details as closely as it is possible for you.

To start cooking, go through the process of using your Wood Pellet Smoker-Grill and understanding the benefits, so you can leverage the equipment to its fullest ability when cooking.

That way, you will be trying different methods of cooking, such as smoking, grilling, searing, and more. The instructions are simple, so you just need to follow them as they are presented.

The Wood Pellet Smoker-Grill is much easier than your traditional grills and smokers, so you do not have to feel concerned at all. Just give yourself the required initial practice to obtain a complete understanding of the functionality of this appliance. With regular practice, you will grow more confident and comfortable using the smoker-grill to cook a variety of dishes.

So, make the most of this amazing cookbook and try these recipes so that you could take your food buds for a real ride.

I hope you enjoy cooking these recipes as much as I enjoyed jotting it down for you. I'm telling this from personal experience that once you get hooked to the BBQ style of cooking; there is no way you're going to stay away from it.

Last but not the least, as we had mentioned at the very start of the book, you have to make sure that you end up buying the best kind of smokers and use the perfect pellets, or else you will lose out on getting the real authentic flavor for these perfect recipes. Tweak them a little if you so desire, but I believe they are as perfect as you would want them to be.

So, be all set to enjoy the good cooking times.

Made in the USA
Las Vegas, NV
25 November 2021